Lawyer Negotiation

ASPEN CASEBOOK SERIES

Lawyer Negotiation
Theory, Practice, and Law

Third Edition

Jay Folberg

Professor and Dean Emeritus
University of San Francisco School of Law

Dwight Golann

Professor and Director, Center for Representation in
Dispute Resolution
Suffolk University Law School

To contact Customer Service, e-mail customer.service@wolterskluwer.com, call 1-800-234-1660, fax 1-800-901-9075, or mail correspondence to:

> Wolters Kluwer
> Attn: Order Department
> PO Box 990
> Frederick, MD 21705

Printed in the United States of America.

4 5 6 7 8 9 0

ISBN 978-1-4548-5206-3

Library of Congress Cataloging-in-Publication Data

Names: Folberg, Jay, 1941- author. | Golann, Dwight, author.
Title: Lawyer negotiation : theory, practice, and law / Jay Folberg, Dwight Golann.
Description: Third edition. | New York : Wolters Kluwer, [2016] | Includes index.
Identifiers: LCCN 2015044567 | ISBN 9781454852063
Subjects: LCSH: Negotiation — United States. | Dispute resolution (Law) — United States.
Classification: LCC KF9084 .F65 2016 | DDC 347.73/9--dc23
LC record available at http://lccn.loc.gov/2015044567

About Wolters Kluwer Legal & Regulatory US

Wolters Kluwer Legal & Regulatory US delivers expert content and solutions in the areas of law, corporate compliance, health compliance, reimbursement, and legal education. Its practical solutions help customers successfully navigate the demands of a changing environment to drive their daily activities, enhance decision quality and inspire confident outcomes.

Serving customers worldwide, its legal and regulatory portfolio includes products under the Aspen Publishers, CCH Incorporated, Kluwer Law International, ftwilliam.com and MediRegs names. They are regarded as exceptional and trusted resources for general legal and practice-specific knowledge, compliance and risk management, dynamic workflow solutions, and expert commentary.

To my father, Lew Folberg, the pawn broker who taught me the art of negotiation

—J.F.

To my father, Herbert Goldberg, whose inventiveness in other fields has inspired my work

—D.G.

SUMMARY OF CONTENTS

CONTENTS

CHAPTER 10
NEGOTIATION ETHICS

CHAPTER 11
THE LAW OF NEGOTIATION

CHAPTER 12
OBSTACLES TO AGREEMENT AND MEDIATION ASSISTANCE

PREFACE

This book is based on three key assumptions: First, to represent clients effectively, lawyers must be skilled negotiators. Second, lawyer negotiation differs from direct negotiation between parties because lawyers are professional agents representing clients and therefore have unique responsibilities and potential conflicts. Finally, a negotiation textbook should be interesting to read; bring together the latest, best, and most provocative writing on negotiation; and lend itself to interactive teaching.

Our book, therefore, has a different perspective from most other texts on negotiation. It focuses on legal negotiation — the settling of substantial legal claims in which the disputants are represented by attorneys. Although the emphasis is on negotiating settlements of disputes, negotiation of deals and transactions is also covered. This book includes a chapter on obstacles to reaching agreements and assisted negotiation. Another chapter covers how to negotiate in a mediation. The reality is that lawyers now regularly use mediation to conclude difficult negotiations of litigated disputes and need to understand how mediation works and how to use it as an advantageous negotiation tool to best meet their clients' needs. Most students enrolling in a negotiation course will not take a separate mediation course, and if they do it may focus on how to be a mediator rather than an advocate in the process, as emphasized here. This book concludes with a chapter that asks if there are situations in which you should not negotiate and examines settlement policy.

The text is practical while grounded in theory, and lawyer-focused but also enriched by interdisciplinary material. This book asks many questions and poses problems designed to provoke critical thinking about the readings and stimulate class discussion. Accompanying role-plays and exercises provided in the Teacher's Manual allow students to apply the readings and bring the text material to life. These role-plays center on the types of disputes in which students are likely to find themselves as practicing lawyers — cases with legal claims or issues, rather than purely personal conflicts or neighborhood quarrels.

This third edition of *Lawyer Negotiation* follows the same organization that proved popular in prior editions and contains the same core elements. We have updated some of our narrative and included excerpts from the most recent writings on negotiation. Readings have been carefully edited to keep the material interesting and lively. Additional notes and examples extend the topic coverage, including game theory, heuristics, psychological traps, the role of emotions, decision analysis, neuroscience, computer software and apps, apologies, collaborative law and mindfulness. We also take advantage of technology, and of students' increasing preference for electronic and video formats. Items that have traditionally gone into a paper appendix now appear on the book's Web site. This makes this book easier to carry without sacrificing depth, allows readers to download specific codes or standards for discussion. The Web site also provides streaming videos of negotiations and mediations to illustrate some of the points and techniques presented in the readings.

The book's fourteen chapters are designed for a semester course with readings assigned before class so that class time can be devoted to exercises, role-plays, and discussion. The first chapter explores the nature of conflict and the second the role of perceptions and settlement psychology. We then analyze in chapter 3 both competitive and cooperative negotiation, and in chapter 4 provide help in combining the approaches and choosing a comfortable style. After setting out an analytic structure to help students make sense of negotiation and understand styles, we offer in chapters 5 through 7 a step-by-step explanation and comparison. The negotiation process and outcome-enhancing skills are covered in these three chapters, which provide instruction from preparation through writing the agreement. Following a chapter on telephone and cyber negotiation, students are guided in chapter 9 to explore issues of gender, culture, and race. Chapters 10 and 11 then examine negotiation ethics and the law of negotiation. Obstacles to negotiation and the role of mediation are reviewed in chapter 12, and how to most effectively negotiate in mediation is then presented in chapter 13. Finally, in chapter 14, there is an exploration of negotiation limits and policy.

A note about form: To focus discussion and conserve space, we have substantially edited the readings and have deleted most footnotes, references, and case citations. Deletions of material are shown by three dots or ellipses, but omitted footnotes and other references are not indicated. Cited authority in the text usually appears only by author's last name and year of publication, with a full citation found in the list of references.

This book is the culmination of our combined decades of teaching and training negotiation in legal contexts. Although our acknowledgments follow, we are especially grateful to the many students and lawyers whom we have had the pleasure of teaching negotiation and from whom we have learned much about what works in a negotiation class. We are also thankful to the professors who have suggested corrections and improvements for this new edition.

January 2016

                                                                                    J.F.
                                                                                    D.G.

ACKNOWLEDGMENTS

This negotiation book has evolved from our comprehensive ADR course book, Resolving Disputes: Theory, Practice, and Law, which we wrote with Thomas Stipanowich and Lisa Kloppenberg. Although this book has grown to become a text of its own with multiple editions, it would not exist without Tom's and Lisa's encouragement. We are grateful for their continuing collaboration.

We are thankful for the resources and assistance we have each received from the staffs and librarians of the law schools at the University of San Francisco and Suffolk University. The assistance of USF law student Minh Le and Berkeley law student Justine Kentla has been particularly helpful. Special thanks also go to the professors who suggested corrections and improvements for this third edition.

We are most grateful to all the students and lawyers whom we have trained and worked with in negotiation and mediation. They have inspired us and guided what we have selected here to present to the next generation of lawyers.

Finally, we are indebted to the many authors and publishers who have granted their permission for us to edit and include parts of their publications. More specifically, we thank the following sources for permission to publish excerpts of their work:

Finally, we are indebted to the many authors and publishers who have granted their permission for us to edit and include parts of their publications. More specifically, we thank the following sources for permission to publish excerpts of their work:

Adair, Wendy, L. and Jeanne M. Brett, "Culture and Negotiation Process" in The Handbook of Negotiation and Culture by M. Gelfand and J. Brett, eds. Copyright © 2004 M. Gelfand and J. Brett. Reprinted by permission.

Adler, Robert S., and Elliot M. Silverstein, "When David Meets Goliath: Dealing with Power Differentials in Negotiations," 5 Harvard Negotiation Law Review. Copyright © 2000 Harvard Negotiation Law Review. Reprinted by permission.

Arnold, Tom, "20 Common Errors in Mediation Advocacy," 13 Alternatives 69 (1995). Copyright © 1995 John Wiley & Sons, Inc. Reprinted by permission.

Birke, Richard, Decision Trees Made Easy. Copyright © 2004 Richard Birke. Reprinted by permission.

Bryan, Kathy, A., "Why Should Businesses Hire Settlement Counsel," 195 Journal of Dispute Resolution. Copyright © 2008 Journal of Dispute Resolution. Reprinted by permission.

Cohen, Amy, "Gender: An (Un)Useful Category of Prescriptive Negotiation Analysis," 13 Texas Journal of Women and Law. Copyright © 2003 Texas Journal of Women and Law. Reprinted by permission.

Craver, Charles B., "Effective Legal Negotiation and Settlement," in Effective Legal Negotiation and Settlement. Copyright © 2001 Matthew Bender & Company, Inc., a member of the LexisNexis Group. Reprinted by permission.

Craver, Charles B., "The Impact of Gender on Negotiation Performance," 14 Cardozo Journal of Conflict Resolution. Copyright © 2013 Cardozo Journal of Conflict Resolution. Reprinted by permission.

Craver, Charles B., "The Inherent Tension Between Value Creation and Value Claiming During Bargaining Interactions," 101 Cardozo Journal of Conflict Resolution. Copyright © 2010 Cardozo Journal of Conflict Resolution. Reprinted by permission.

Ebner, Noam, "Negotiation Via (The New) Email," in Negotiation Excellence: Successful Deal Making, Second Edition, by M. Benoliel, ed. Copyright © 2014 World Scientific Publishing, Singapore. Reprinted by permission.

Epstein, Lynn A., "Post-Settlement Malpractice: Undoing the Done Deal," 46 Catholic University Law Review. Copyright © 1997 Catholic University Law Review. Reprinted by permission.

Fisher, Roger, "Negotiating Powers: Getting and Using Influence," in J. William Breslin and Jeffrey Rubin, eds., 27 Negotiation American Behavioral Scientist. Copyright © 1983 Sage Publications. Reprinted by permission.

Fiss, Owen M., "Against Settlement." 93 Yale Law Journal. Copyright © 1983 the Yale Law Journal Company, Inc. Reprinted by permission.

Goodpaster, Gary, "A Primer on Competitive Bargaining," 325 Journal of Dispute Resolution. Copyright © 1996 Journal of Dispute Resolution. Reprinted by permission.

Heen, Sheila, and John Richardson, "I See a Pattern Here and the Pattern is You," in The Handbook of Dispute Resolution by M. I. Moffitt and Robert C. Bordone, eds. Copyright © 2005 John Wiley & Sons, Inc. Reprinted by permission.

Hetherington, H., Lee, "The Wizard and Dorothy, Patton and Rommel: Negotiation Parables in Fiction and Fact," 289 Pepperdine Law Review. Copyright © 2001 Pepperdine Law Review. Reprinted by permission.

Hinshaw, Art, and Jess K. Alberts, "Doing the Right Thing: An Empirical Study of Attorney Negotiation Ethics," 16 Harvard Negotiation Law Review. Copyright © 2011 Harvard Negotiation Law Review. Reprinted by permission.

Kichaven, Jeffrey, G. "How Advocacy Fits in Effective Mediation," 16 Alternatives. Copyright © 1999 John Wiley & Sons, Inc. Reprinted by permission.

Kiser, Randall, "The Emotionally Attentive Lawyer: Balancing the Rule of Law with the Realities of Human Behavior," 15 Nevada Law Journal. Copyright © 2015 Nevada Law Journal. Reprinted by permission.

Korobkin, Russell, "A Positive Theory of Legal Negotiation," 88 Georgetown Law Journal. Copyright © 2000 Georgetown Law Journal. Reprinted by permission.

Korobkin, Russell, Michael Moffit, and Nancy Welsh, "The Law of Bargaining," 87 Marquette Law Review. Copyright © 2004 Marquette Law Review. Reprinted by permission.

Longan, Patrick, "Ethics in Settlement Negotiations: Foreword," 52 Mercer Law Review. Copyright © 2001 Mercer Law Review. Reprinted by permission.

Menkel-Meadow, Carrie, "Toward Another View of Legal Negotiation: The Structure of Problem Solving" 31 UCLA Law Review. Copyright © 1984 Carrie Menkel-Meadow. Reprinted by permission.

Miller, Lee E., and Jessica Miller, "A Woman's Guide to Successful Negotiating." Copyright © 2002 the McGrawHill Companies. Reprinted by permission.

Mnookin, Robert H., Bargaining with the Devil: When to Negotiate, When to Fight. Copyright © 2010 Simon & Schuster. Reprinted by permission.

Mnookin, Robert H, "Why Negotiations Fail: An Exploration of Barriers to the Resolution of Conflict," 8 Ohio State Journal of Dispute and Resolution. Copyright © 1993 Robert H Mnookin. Reprinted by permission.

Mnookin, Robert H., Scott R. Peppet, and Andrew S. Tulumello. Beyond Winning: Negotiation to Create Value in Deals and Disputes, pp. 37-42, 282-286. Cambridge, MA: The Belknap Press of Harvard University Press. Copyright © 2000 the President and Fellows of Harvard College. Reprinted by permission.

Moffitt, Michael, "Contingent Agreements: Agreeing to Disagree About the Future," 87 Marquette Law Review. Copyright © 2004 Marquette Law Review. Reprinted by permission.

Moffitt, Michael, "Three Things to Be Against (Settlement, Not Included)," 78 Fordham Law Review. Copyright © 2009 Fordham Law Review. Reprinted by permission.

Nadler, Janice, "Rapport in Legal Negotiation: How Small Talk Can Facilitate E-Mail Deal Making," 223 Harvard Negotiation Law Review. Copyright © 2004 Harvard Negotiation Law Review. Reprinted by permission.

Nelken, Melissa, Understanding Negotiation. Copyright © 2007 Matthew Bender & Company, Inc., a member of the LexisNexis Group. Reprinted by permission.

Peppet, Scott R., "Contract Formation in Imperfect Markets: Should We Use Mediators in Deals?" 38 Ohio State Journal on Dispute Resolutions. Copyright © 2004 Ohio State Journal on Dispute Resolutions. Reprinted by permission.

Peppet, Scott R., "Mindfulness in the Law and ADR: Can Saints Negotiate?" 7 Harvard Negotiation Law Review. Copyright © 2002 Harvard Negotiation Law Review. Reprinted by permission.

Poswall, John M., The Lawyers: Class of '69. Copyright © 2003 John M. Poswall. Reprinted by permission.

Robbennolt, Jennifer, K., "Apologies and Legal Settlement: An Empirical Examination," 102 Michigan Law Review. Copyright © 2003. Reprinted by permission.

Rosenberg, Joshua D., "Interpersonal Dynamics Helping Lawyers Learn the Skills, and the Importance of Human Relationships in the Practice of Law," 55 University of Miami Law Review. Copyright © 2004 the University of Miami Law Review. Reprinted by permission.

Ross, David, S., "Strategic Considerations in Choosing a Mediator: A Mediator's Perspective," 2 Journal of Alternative Dispute Resolutions in Employment. Copyright © 2000 Journal of Alternative Dispute Resolutions in Employment. Reprinted by permission.

Rummel, R.J. "The Subjectivity Principle," in The Conflict Helix. Copyright © 1991 Transaction Publishers. Reprinted by permission.

Saperstein, Guy T., Civil Warrior: Memoirs of a Civil Rights Attorney. Copyright © 2003 by Guy T. Saperstein. Reprinted by permission.

Sebenius, James K., "Caveats for Cross-Border Negotiations," 18 Negotiation Journal. Copyright © 2002 Blackwell Publishers Ltd. Reprinted by permission.

Shell, G. Richard, "The Second Foundation: Your Goals and Expectations," and "Step Four: Closing and Gaining Commitment," in Bargaining for Advantage by G. Richard Shell, Copyright © 1999, 2006 Viking Penguin, a division of Penguin Group (USA), Inc. Reprinted by permission.

Welsh, Nancy A., "Perceptions of Fairness in Negotiation," 87 Marquette Law Review. Copyright © 2004 Marquette Law Review. Reprinted by permission.

Wetlaufer, Gerald, "The Limits of Integrative Bargaining," 85 Georgetown Law Journal. Copyright © 1996 Georgetown Law Journal. Reprinted by permission.

White, James J., "Pros and Cons of 'Getting to YES'; Roger Fisher, Comments on White's Review," 34 Journal of Legal Education. Copyright © 1984 Journal of Legal Education. Reprinted by permission.

Williams, Gerald R., "Negotiation as a Healing Process," 1 Journal of Dispute Resolution. Copyright © 1996 Journal of Dispute Resolution. Reprinted by permission.

Williams, Gerald R., and Charles Craver, 79 Legal Negotiatio, Copyright © 2007 West Publishing. Reprinted by permission.

Wood, Robert, W., "Taxing Matters in Settling Cases," 41 California Lawyer. Copyright © 2007 California Lawyer. Reprinted by permission.

Zitrin, Richard A., and Carol M. Langford, "The Moral Compass of the American Lawyer," in The Moral Compass of the American Lawyer. Copyright © 1999 Richard Zitrin and Carol M. Langford. Reprinted by permission of Ballantine Books, a division of Random House, Inc.

Lawyer Negotiation

CHAPTER
1

Negotiation and Conflict

A. Introduction to Negotiation

Negotiation is the process of communication used to get something we want when another person has control over whether or how we can get it. If we could have everything we wanted, materially and emotionally, without the concurrence of anyone else, there would be no need to negotiate. Because of our interdependence, the need to negotiate is pervasive.

Everyone negotiates as part of modern life. However, because lawyers are paid to negotiate for others, we are considered professionals. A law student reading only casebooks might not know that the vast majority of disputes in which lawyers are involved are negotiated to a settlement without trial. Many major transactions are also the result of lawyer-negotiated agreements. Negotiation is at the core of what lawyers do in representing clients.

Most lawyers think they are skilled negotiators because they negotiate frequently. However, negotiating frequently does not necessarily result in negotiating effectively. Unlike trial practice, negotiation is usually done in private without the opportunity to compare results or benefit from a critique. Those with whom you negotiate rarely give you an honest assessment of how you did, and it is most often in their interest for you to believe you did well. Regardless of our intuitive ability, negotiation skills and results can be improved with analysis and understanding, as well as practice.

Lawyer negotiation takes place within the dynamics of settling a dispute or shaping a deal. It is not always a tidy process that tracks a textbook diagram. In this book we use a seven-stage model of negotiation, recognizing that all negotiations do not follow the same lineal staging and each stage will not necessarily be completed. The negotiation dance can be improvised to fit the situation. For example, we list initial interactions and offers as part of Stage 2 before exchanging information; however, the initial offer or demand may often follow an exchange of information. The seven stages are:

1. Preparation and Setting Goals
2. Initial Interaction and Offers
3. Exchanging and Refining Information
4. Bargaining
5. Moving Toward Closure
6. Reaching Impasse or Agreement
7. Finalizing the Agreement

Negotiation occurs because there are conflicts between what parties want or how they perceive a situation. As a professional negotiator you have an edge if you understand the nature of the conflict to be resolved, the psychology of negotiation, and contrasting styles of bargaining. So, we begin with the nature of conflict and the role of perceptions, as well as emotional dimensions and psychological traps. Next we look at the advantages and disadvantages of using a more competitive or cooperative bargaining style. We then examine the stages of negotiation and the activities associated with each step. Subsequent chapters look at cyber negotiation, gender and culture, ethics, the role of law, negotiation assistance, and policy issues.

B. Conflict

Although conflict can cause distress and is usually viewed negatively, it can function in positive ways. Conflict may motivate you to take action and change your situation in ways that improve your life and better fulfill your self-interests. Conflict can, however, also create a crisis mentality that becomes destructive. Lawyers can help create more constructive outcomes from conflicts or they can make a difficult situation worse. The ability to help clients better understand the conflict, reframe the issues, and realistically analyze their interests and how those interests can be advantageously negotiated is an important lawyering skill.

Conflict is divided into two categories: interpersonal (differences that arise between individuals or groups) and intrapersonal (conflicts within ourselves). Interpersonal conflict is a situation in which the parties each want something that they perceive as incompatible with what the other wants. Because the parties in an interpersonal conflict cannot both have all that they want, their interests or goals are divergent. Lawyers are retained to help resolve interpersonal conflicts between our clients and others. A client may also be conflicted internally about what it is they really want and how they prioritize their interests. For example, does your client really want to return to the job from which she was fired, or does she want only to restore her self-respect and get compensation? Does the father you represent in a divorce really want custody of the children, or is he internally conflicted about the decision to divorce and trying to hold onto the marital relationship? Recognizing these two different types of conflict can be critical in achieving client goals.

Another distinction that can be useful in negotiation and mediation is between the manifest conflict, which is overt or expressed, and the underlying conflict, which is hidden or not recognized. Lawyers most often deal with manifest conflicts, which we refer to as disputes. A conflict may not become a dispute if it is not communicated in the form of a complaint or claim. However, what is communicated may be only a part of or symbol of the underlying conflict. The dispute between brothers over control of a family business seems safer to contest than the underlying conflict of who was the favored son or a better child. A patent or copyright dispute may focus on lost revenue, while the fundamental conflict is over public recognition of creative accomplishment and originality. Residential development disputes may focus in court on specific environmental regulations or traffic issues, but the underlying conflict is about the changing character of the community. This dichotomy between the overt dispute and the hidden conflict can be viewed for purposes of negotiation as the presenting problem and the hidden agenda.

If the agreements reached in negotiation resolve only the presenting problems, they are less likely to last unless legally enforced. Surfacing the underlying conflict can clarify issues, focus objectives, generate new possibilities for settlement, and ultimately improve relationships. Dealing with the underlying conflicts, however, may be emotionally difficult for clients and can stimulate internal conflict. Many lawyers are not comfortable with opening emotional issues and may not have the capacity to address them. We will look more into the emotional aspects of conflict and psychological issues shortly.

First, it is helpful to note that lawyers generally negotiate to reach a settlement, not necessarily to resolve the underlying conflict. The resulting negotiated settlement usually involves the payment of money, now or in the future; an agreement to provide goods or services, or to change behavior; or some combination of these. Conflicts over fundamental beliefs, religion, and love are not negotiated by lawyers, even if changes in behavior or payments of money for past behavior based on religion or belief may be within the realm of lawyer negotiation. Although we don't negotiate to change feelings or beliefs, our clients may come to change how they feel about their dispute through discussion, sharing information, and exchanging views.

As lawyers dealing with other people's conflicts, we tend to view our approach to negotiating in their behalf as a choice of different styles reflecting our own understanding about conflict and our own values. These choices may seem like polar opposites that go to the core of how we approach conflict and who we are. This seeming paradox of negotiating approaches can be very challenging for law students and for attorneys. In a recent book, *The Conflict Paradox* (2015), Bernard Mayer lists seven dilemmas in dealing with conflict:

- Competition or cooperation
- Optimism or realism
- Avoidance or engagement
- Principle or compromise
- Emotion or logic
- Neutrality or advocacy
- Autonomy or community

Mayer writes that these polarities are not true choices but are part of the dynamics of human interaction and the nature of conflict. He urges a more sophisticated, nuanced, and complex approach that recognizes in most incidents both sides of these polarities must be embraced. We have to get past understanding them as contradictions forcing either-or choices and accept the complementary unity of both elements. In other words, you need not choose a thoroughly cooperative or competitive stance. You need not be guided by only emotions or logic—one does not foreclose the other. We will look at competitive or cooperative negotiation in detail, the dual roles of emotion and logic, as well as other dilemmas in settling conflicts. For now, there is one other preliminary aspect of conflict that must be considered before negotiation can begin.

C. Ripeness

Before you can negotiate, the conflict must be "ripe" for negotiation. Professor Jeffrey Rubin describes the role of ripeness in his classic article, *Some Wise and Mistaken Assumptions About Conflict and Negotiation* (1991). He explains that just as it takes two hands to clap, it takes two participants to negotiate. Even if you are ready to start serious discussion toward settlement, there must be a counterpart at the table, on the phone, or at the other end of your email. Unless there is someone ready to communicate on the other side, there can be no negotiation.

Even if all parties agree to negotiate, there can be no settlement without mutual motivation to take the conflict seriously. A non-motivated disputant will put off reaching an agreement until the situation changes. People typically do not sit down to negotiate until they realize it is in their interest to do so or they have reached a point where they fear the consequences of not pursuing an agreement. Each side, according to Rubin, must no longer believe "it possible to obtain what he or she wants through efforts at domination or coercion. It is only at this point, when the two sides grudgingly acknowledge the need for joint work if any agreement is to be reached, that negotiation can take place."

Rubin defines "ripeness" as "a stage of conflict in which all parties are ready to take their conflict seriously, and are willing to do whatever may be necessary to bring the conflict to a close. To pluck fruit from a tree before it is ripe is as problematic as waiting too long. There is a right time to negotiate, and the wise negotiator will attempt to seek out this point." He notes that it is possible to create ripeness through the use of threat and coercion so that the opposing side can see the consequences of failing to reach agreement. However, he cautions against coercion and threats as a means to ripen the conflict because it encourages conflict escalation and invites a game of "chicken," in which each side hopes that the other be the first to succumb to coercion.

A better way to create a situation that is ripe for negotiation and settlement is through the introduction of new opportunities for joint gain. If all sides can be persuaded that there is more to gain than to lose through negotiation, rewards can be harvested that can advance each side's agenda and form a basis for agreement.

Notes and Questions

1. Morton Deutsch, who pioneered the modern study of conflict resolution, distinguished manifest conflict from underlying conflict, as summarized in our introductory comments. (See Deutsch 1973.) Rubin, a former student of Deutsch, separates settlement of the manifest conflict behaviors from the attitude changes necessary to bring an end to the underlying base of conflict. We noted a similar distinction between the presenting problem and the hidden agenda. Do you agree that settlement only of the manifest problem is unlikely to last? Why or why not? Is litigation limited only to the manifest or presenting issues? Is Rubin correct in indicating that negotiation is only a method of settling conflict rather than resolving it?

2. Just as it takes two or more people to have a conflict, so it takes two or more people to reach agreement. Ripeness of the conflict is critical for those involved to begin serious negotiation toward resolution. What do you think Rubin means when he suggests that new opportunities for joint gain create ripeness? How might this concept help lawyers get disputes resolved?
3. How do lawyers most often create "ripeness" to seriously negotiate and settle disputes?

D. The Triangle of Conflict and Negotiation

You are now aware that the issue initially presented by your client, which may focus on monetary claims and legal rights, is not necessarily the entirety of the conflict or even the main element. You also know that logic is not the singular path to negotiating settlement of a conflict. There is increasing recognition that to negotiate a satisfactory resolution of a conflict there must be an understanding of and attention to the emotional and relationship components, which may be the underlying bases of the conflict. Even though the dominant focus in most lawyer negotiations is on the trade-offs involving legal claims or economic considerations measured in money damages, neglecting the non-monetary components resulting from conflicts can lead to an impasse or a settlement that does not hold.

There are three sets of factors, or interests, at work in most conflicts. These interests can be thought of as the three "Es": economic, emotional, and extrinsic. They form the three sides of the negotiation triangle, which represent the three sets of interests that must be addressed to reach a satisfactory settlement of a dispute.

NEGOTIATION TRIANGLE

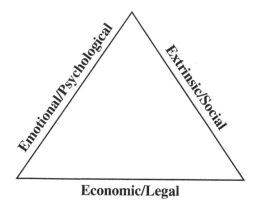

Legal issues and rights are what often bring lawyers to the negotiation table to bargain over economic damages. Once there, the other two sides of the triangle that impact clients enclose and influence the negotiation process and outcome. The emotional component refers to the internal pushes and pulls on parties created by the conflict that affect how they feel about themselves. The extrinsic elements are the setting and social considerations, including how others will view what is going on and how the resolution will appear to third parties. "Face saving" is frequently referred to in the negotiation literature; it is an extrinsic social factor that also has an emotional impact. The three sides of the triangle are interrelated and have an impact on one another. The mix of what matters for purposes of resolving a conflict will vary depending on the subject and the sensitivities and history between the parties, as well as their attorneys. A purely commercial case will most heavily involve economic considerations. However, all three elements are involved to some extent in every type of dispute. A business person sued for breach of contract has feelings about accusations from a longtime supplier and concerns about his reputation in the business community. A divorce or employment dispute, although focused on legal rights and money, will invoke more emotional and extrinsic factors. For example, in a divorce, what will children, grandparents, and neighbors think about new parenting arrangements? In a wrongful termination case, how will acceptance of the economic offer appear to co-workers who remain friends with the terminated worker? Attention to the non-economic factors can help prevent or end a negotiation impasse and move the matter to resolution.

It can be difficult to quantify the emotional and extrinsic factors, but there might be ways to satisfy the internal-emotional and external-social factors in a manner that both settles the case and helps resolve the conflict. As you read the following real-life fact situation and resulting lawsuit, settled a year and a half after the incident, consider what roles both emotional and social factors might have played in negotiating a settlement agreement.

Problem — Tiger Attack

Tatiana, a 250-pound Siberian tiger in the San Francisco Zoo, leapt out of her enclosure, killed 17-year-old Carlos Sousa, Jr., and injured two of his friends, brothers Amritpal Dhaliwal, then 19, and Kulbir Dhaliwal, then 23. The tiger was shot dead by police. The media coverage was extensive. Zoo spokesman Sam Singer, hired by the zoo for damage control, seemed to blame the brothers for the incident, suggesting that they taunted the tiger. Animal rights advocates protested the shooting of the tiger. Zoo attendance and donations dropped.

A claim for the death of Carlos Sousa, Jr. was settled. The Dhaliwal brothers sued the San Francisco Zoological Society, the City of San Francisco, and Sam Singer. Their federal lawsuit alleged that the zoo was negligent in maintaining a tiger enclosure several feet below recommended standards, claimed their civil rights were violated because their car was improperly seized, and accused Singer of libel and slander for comments he made to media implying that they might have been taunting the tiger. They also alleged that police officials had ordered officers to issue warrants for their arrest, accusing them of manslaughter in the death of their deceased friend, Carlos Sousa, Jr., even though an investigation could not substantiate any basis for bringing charges against them. Substantial damages were sought by the brothers, well beyond the relatively modest amounts for physical injuries and medical expenses.

1. If you were advising the zoo, would you recommend that it negotiate a settlement? Is there any downside for the zoo in negotiating? Would your answers be different if you were representing the Dhaliwal brothers?
2. What are the non-economic factors in this conflict, and how might they be addressed in negotiation?
3. What might the Dhaliwal brothers obtain in a negotiated settlement that they could not win at trial?

The emotional side of the triangle of conflict might be the most difficult for you to deal with if you are not trained in psychology. You might negotiate what you think is a great resolution of a dispute, only to have it rejected by your client, who must agree before a settlement or deal is finalized. Understanding the emotional stages experienced by a client in a conflict can help you better represent your client in negotiations. Professor Gerald Williams identifies the emotional stages a client might follow to move out of a conflict and get on with life or business. The last phase of renewal or transformation listed by Williams may be more an inspirational hope than a realized reality.

❖ Gerald R. Williams, *NEGOTIATION AS A HEALING PROCESS*

J. Disp. Resol. 1 (1996)

The Five Steps for Recovering from Conflict

. . . Just as researchers have found that getting *into* a conflict is a multi-step process that typically involves naming, blaming, claiming, rejection, and a decision to go public, even so, the task of getting *out of* a conflict requires the disputants to work their way through a multistage process.

A. Denial

As a preliminary model of the process of recovering from conflict, the first stage is typically a condition of *denial.* As James Hall explains, there is in each of us "a deep-seated human desire *not* to be the one at fault, *not* to be the one who must change." This resistance to being the one at fault, to being the one who must change, is part of what makes conflict so painful and its resolution so difficult. Most conflicts are a story of two parties, both of whom contributed to the problem, and neither of whom wants to admit his or her role in it. In the literature on grieving we gain a broader sense of what is meant by the term *denial* and some of the risks it poses to the parties and others: "The person will strongly deny the reality of what has happened, or search for reasons why it has happened, and take revenge on themselves and others." . . . From this perspective, we might even say that, in most instances, conflicts are meaningful; they have a purpose. Their purpose is to hold up a mirror so disputants may see themselves in a new light, an experience as painful as it is valuable. . . .

Properly understood, then, conflicts serve as such a mirror. They expose the disputants' weaknesses; the areas in which they have been too much the victim, or too much the exploiter; their complexes, their unresolved angers, and their feelings of specialness and entitlement. Because it is so painful for disputants to see these parts of themselves exposed by their own involvement in the conflict, they need the protection and reinforcement, the containment and channeling, that the lawyer-client relationship provides, and they need the benefit of the full play of the negotiation process to help them gradually face what they see in the mirror and to come to terms with it. . . .

B. Acceptance

The next step is *acceptance*. It may take time, but at some point the parties need to move beyond denial and to *accept the possibility that they themselves are part of the problem*. They do not yet need to *do* anything about it, just to accept the possibility that the problem does not begin and end with the other side, that they themselves may have some complicity in the problem. In some cases, however, it may be that one side actually is wholly innocent and the other wholly to blame for the problem. But even when parties are wholly innocent, they still need to accept the possibility there is *something they could do now to move the situation in the direction of an appropriate resolution*. Again, they don't need to actually take action, they simply need to register a change in attitude that opens them to the possibility of movement in the direction of an appropriate solution.

C. Sacrifice

Assuming the parties have accepted the possibility they are part of the problem, or the possibility there is something they could do now to move in the direction of a resolution, the next step is to consider what they might be willing to do about it. In its starkest form, the principle is that, for the conflict to be resolved, the parties must be willing to make a sacrifice. From a judge's point of view, the minimum sacrifice required for a valid settlement agreement is a *compromise* by each side, meaning that both parties must make some concession, must move from their original position. But as a general matter, mere concessions or compromises do not require a change of heart. It has been observed that people usually are not willing to make a sacrifice until they have been brought to a more humble attitude. . . . Assuming that sacrifices need to be made, what should they be? This is an extremely delicate question. We know, for example, that some people have a history of being *too compliant*, of giving away too much, whether motivated by a need for affection and approval, by fear of reprisals, or for some other reason. For those who are too compliant, the sacrifice called for would probably *not* be to make more concessions to their antagonist, but rather to forebear from giving, to reverse themselves, to give up the part of themselves that always wants to please others. For other people, the problem may be just the opposite. They may be exploiters who are too good at looking out for themselves at others' expense. For them, the sacrifice may be to recognize their exploitive patterns and become more conscious of the interests and needs of other people. There are many other possibilities. The answer will depend on the personalities involved and the particularities of their situations. In some situations, parties may need to sacrifice—to let go of—such things as a desire for a total victory, or an impulse for revenge, a mistaken belief that they themselves are faultless and the other side totally to blame, their pride, their unwillingness to acknowledge or appreciate another's point of view, or their unwillingness to forgive another for his or her mistake. In other situations, parties may need to give up the belief that they can get away with exploiting others, their belief that they are better or more deserving than others, or their excessive opinions of their own abilities, worth, privileged status, etc. There may be situations in which parties need to give up their hope of obtaining a windfall or other unearned benefit, or give up their envy or spite or jealousy with respect to possessions, luck, and social position.

Before proceeding to the fourth step, there is one final consideration. Is it mandatory that parties make a sacrifice? The answer is a firm "no." There can be no *requirement* that the client have a change of heart. It is fundamental that, as lawyers, we implicitly and explicitly declare to our clients that they can stay just the way they are, and so long as they do not expect us to do that which is illegal or unethical, we will stand by them. Our willingness to represent our clients should not depend upon their willingness to change, much less to move in directions *we* think right. As Shaffer and Elkins remind us, "the client has to be free to be wrong." The negotiation process, then, is not intended for lawyers to impose our values upon our clients, but for us to help contain and channel our clients' energies in appropriate ways until they have had enough time to see their own situations more clearly and to discover for themselves what steps they may be willing to make.

D. Leap of Faith

The fourth stage refers to action or movement, what might be called the *leap of faith*. It is a leap of faith, for example, to admit to the other side that you might be *willing* to make a sacrifice to resolve the case. Practicing lawyers recognize it as the moment when their client looks them in the eye and asks, "If I do this, can you guarantee it will work?" And the lawyer has to reply, "No, I can't guarantee that, because I don't know that. But the trial is coming up really soon, and we haven't thought of anything better to do, but you decide." And the client must decide. . . .

E. Renewal or Healing from Conflict

If the process works well enough, and both parties are willing to move by incremental leaps of faith in the direction of agreement, and if they seek in the process to fathom the underlying problems and address them along the way, the effect can be two-fold: they may reach a mutually acceptable solution and, in the best of circumstances, they may also experience a change of heart, be reconciled to one another and healed and feel renewed as human beings. This is the transformation objective; it is the goal or purpose of all ritual processes, whether it be theater or court trial or graduation exercise or religious rite or negotiated settlement. Rituals are to help prepare the participants, those on whose behalf the ceremony is enacted, to move forward in a new condition, to a new phase of life. *Renewal* or transformation in this context means not simply they are as good as they were before the conflict, but they are better—they are more whole, or more compassionate, or less greedy, or otherwise changed in an important way from their attitude or condition before the crisis began. Certainly, when people experience such a fundamental change through the process of conflict resolution, they will be far less likely to find themselves in a similar conflict again. On the other hand, if they fail at this process, then to the extent the conflict was a product of their own developmental shortcomings, it is likely they will find themselves in similar conflicts in the future, returning again and again until the party acknowledges and addresses the underlying developmental need. . . .

Notes and Questions

4. Elizabeth Kubler-Ross, in her 1969 book *On Death and Dying*, introduced a model known as the five stages of grief, by which people deal with grief and tragedy, specifically when diagnosed with a terminal illness. Kubler-Ross's five stages are denial, anger, bargaining, depression, and acceptance. This five-stage model, or some variation, has since been applied by authors to every type of personal loss, including divorce and bankruptcy. How does Professor Williams's five-stage model differ from Kubler-Ross's five stages of dealing with death? Do you agree with Williams's five-stage analysis as applied to conflict?

5. Many people have a negative view of conflict and try to avoid it. Do you? Was conflict viewed as negative in your family? During your childhood, how did your family deal with conflict? Will you try to model the same conflict process for your children?

6. As a lawyer, will you welcome representing clients who seek your help to resolve their conflicts with others? Why or why not?

CHAPTER
2

Perception, Fairness, Psychological Traps, and Emotions

A. The Role of Perceptions

"We do not see things as they are. We see things as we are."

— *The Talmud*

The key to understanding and mastering negotiation is to be aware that those in conflict and who want something from one another see the situation differently. It is these differences that give root to conflict and to the need to negotiate, as well as to the possibility of agreement. We assess conflict and evaluate a case or the worth of an item differently because of differing perceptions. Our individual perceptions determine how we view ourselves, others, and the world. No two views are exactly the same. For example, we may selectively perceive or differ in our perceptions of the following:

- facts
- people
- interests
- history
- fairness
- priorities
- relative power
- abilities
- available resources
- scarcity
- timing
- costs
- applicable law or rules
- likely outcomes

Our view of each of these elements, as well as our perceptions of other variables, shape how we see the world and how we form differences. It is because of such differences in perceptions that people bet on horse races, wage war, and pursue lawsuits.

Rashomon Effect

The *Rashomon effect* is the name given to contradictory perceptions of the same event by different people. The phrase derives from a classic Japanese story, on which the film *Rashomon* is based, illustrating the subjectivity of perceptions and how the truth through one person's eyes may be very different from another's, as seen through the prism of the individuals' own perceptions. The story and the film explore how perceptions distort or enhance different people's memories of a single event, in this case, the death of a Samurai warrior. Each tells the "truth" but perceives it very differently. The film, like the story, is unsettling because, as in much of life, no single truth emerges.

Similarly the parable of blind men, each touching a different part of an elephant and from that experience describing what an elephant is, has been used to illustrate that there is a range of "truths" based on where you are in relation to what you are experiencing and differing perceptions. The parable implies that one's subjective experience can be true, but that such experience is inherently limited by its failure to account for other truths or a totality of a single truth.

And so these men of Hindustan
Disputed loud and long,
Each in his own opinion
Exceeding stiff and strong,
Though each was partly in the right
And all were in the wrong.
"The Blind Men and the Elephant" by John Godfrey Saxe (1816–1887)

The Rashomon effect is more recently illustrated in *The Girl on the Train*, a best-selling novel by Paula Hawkins (2015). The story is told from three character's perspectives. Each person's account is very compelling, but each person perceives the same events through a different prism of their own reality, creating a suspenseful tale where the "true" picture only emerges at the end after the three separate versions are contrasted.

As a new lawyer negotiating a dispute, it may seem puzzling when those on the other side of the conflict insist that your earnest client is misstating the facts and is wrong. Lawyers are often presented only their client's factual account, which may be very different than what is told to opposing counsel by their client. Each client may well be stating the situation truthfully as they perceive it. The following reading further develops the theme that conflict is subjective and flows from different perceptions in people's minds. Rummel's "subjectivity principle" may help to explain many conflicts that would otherwise defy understanding and resolution.

R.J. Rummel, *The Conflict Helix*

13 (Transaction Publishers, 1991)

The Subjectivity Principle

Perceived reality is your painting. You are the artist. You mix the colors, draw the lines, fix the focus, achieve the artistic balance. Reality disciplines your painting; it is your starting point. As the artist, you add here, leave out there; substitute color, simplify; and provide this reality with a point, a theme, a center of interest. You produce a thousand such paintings every moment. With unconscious artistry. Each a personal statement. Individualistic.

Now, most people realize that their perception of things can be wrong, that they may be mistaken. No doubt you have had disagreements with others on what you all saw or heard. And probably you have heard of eyewitnesses who widely disagree over the facts of a crime or accident. Some teachers who wish to dramatically illustrate such disagreement have staged mock fights or holdups in a classroom. A masked man rushes in, pointing some weapon at the teacher; demands his wallet; and with it hastily exits, leaving the class stunned. Then each member of the class is asked to write down what he saw and heard. Their versions usually differ widely.

But, of course, such are rapidly changing situations in which careful observation is difficult. Surely, you might think, if there were time to study a situation or event you would perceive it as others do. This is easy enough to test. Ask two people to describe in writing a furnished room, say your living room, or a car you may own. Then compare. You will find many similarities, but you should also find some important and interesting differences. Sometimes such differences result from error, inattentiveness. However, there is something more fundamental. Even attentive observers often will see things differently. And each can be correct.

There are a number of reasons for this. First, people may have different vantage points and their visual perspectives thus will differ. A round, flat object viewed from above will appear round, from an angle it will appear an ellipse, from the side a rectangle. This problem of perspective is acute in active, contact sports such as football or basketball. From the referee's line of sight there is no foul, but many spectators (especially the television audiences who see multiple angles and instant replays) know they saw an obvious violation.

But people can compare or change perspectives. Were this all, perception would not be a basic problem. The second reason for different perceptions is more fundamental. You endow what you sense with meaning. The outside world is an amorphous blend of a multitude of interwoven colors, lights, sounds, smells, tastes and material. You make sense of this complex by carving it into different concepts, such as table, chair, or boy. Learning a language is part of learning to perceive the world.

You also endow this reality with value. Thus what you perceive becomes good or bad, repulsive or attractive, dangerous or safe. You see a man running toward you with a knife as dangerous; a calm lake as peaceful; a child murderer as bad; a contribution to charity as good. And so on.

Cultures are systems of meanings laid onto reality; to become acculturated is to learn the language through which a culture gives the world unique shape and evaluation. A clear example of this is a cross, which to a Christian signifies the death of Jesus for mankind as well as the whole complex of values and beliefs bound up in the religion. Yet, to non-Christian cultures a cross may be meaningless: simply two pieces of wood connected at right angles. . . .

Besides varying perspectives and meanings, a third reason for different perceptions is that people have unique experiences and learning capacities, even when they share the same culture. Each person has his own background. No two people learn alike. Moreover, people have different occupations, and each occupation emphasizes and ignores different aspects of reality. Simply by virtue of their separate occupational interests, the world will be perceived dissimilarly by a philosopher, priest, engineer, union worker, or lawyer.

Two people may perceive the same thing from the same perspective, therefore, but each through their diverse languages, evaluations, experience, and occupations, may perceive it differently and endow it with personal meaning. Dissimilar perspective, meaning, and experience together explain why your perception will often differ radically from others.

There is yet an even more basic reason: what you sense is unconsciously transformed within your mental field in order to maintain a psychological balance. This mental process is familiar to you. People often perceive what they want to perceive, what they ardently hope to see. Their minds go to great pains to extract from the world that which they put there. People tend to see things consistent with their beliefs. If you believe businesspeople, politicians, or bureaucrats are bad, you will tend to see their failings. If you like a person, you tend to see the good; hate him and you tend to see the worst. Some people are optimists, usually seeing a bottle half full; others are pessimists, seeing the same bottle half empty.

Your perception is thus the result of a complex transformation of amorphous sensory stimuli. At various stages your personal experience, beliefs, and character affect what you perceive. . . . Independent of the outside world's powers to force your perception, you have power to impose a perception on reality. You can hallucinate. You can magnify some things to fill your perception in spite of what else is happening. . . .

No wonder, then, that you are likely to perceive things differently from others. Your perception is subjective and personal. Reality does not draw its picture on a clean slate—your mind. Nor is your mind a passive movie screen on which sensory stimuli impact, to create a moving picture of the world. Rather, your mind is an active agent of perception, creating and transforming reality, while at the same time being disciplined and sometimes dominated by it. . . .

Notes and Questions

Rummel's subjectivity principle explains how we process the information and stimuli around us through the filters of our experience, needs, culture, and biases. The complexity of our environment and our minds prevents us from taking it all in whole, so we focus selectively on some stimuli and ignore others. We develop shortcuts in our perceptual systems that allow us to function and process information more quickly and make timely decisions. These shortcuts, known as *heuristics*, can serve us well. However, mental shortcuts create the risk that our selectivity will distort reality as seen by others. The different ways we process information can lead to conflict based on our different realities.

A key concept in understanding the cause of disputes is *selective perception* or what is known as the *confirmation bias*. We tend to unconsciously notice information that confirms our already existing views and disregard conflicting information that doesn't support what we think. The offspring of selective perceptions is *self-fulfilling prophecies*, which occur when our behavior is influenced by our selective perceptions, which causes others to behave toward us in a way that further confirms the "truth" of our thinking.

> In an escalating conflict, we tend to see what we want to see and to distort information to support our expectations. One way we do this is by selectively testing hypotheses. We form a hypothesis about the adversary such as, this person is nasty. Then we gather information to confirm our hypothesis and ignore information that does not support it. In selective perception we have only dealt with perceptions. When behavior is introduced, we have a self-fulfilling prophecy, which connects attitudes and behaviors. I have an expectation of you that leads me to behave in a way that produces a response in you that confirms my expectation. My prophecy about the kind of person that you are is fulfilled. (Rubin 1993)

1. Can you recall a conflict you have experienced that might be better understood in light of the subjectivity principle or selective perceptions?
2. John Milton, in *Paradise Lost*, poetically stated: "The mind is its own place, and in itself can make a heaven of Hell, a hell of Heaven" (Milton 1909). In explaining his subjectivity principle, is Rummel just restating Milton?
3. If a conflict between people is the result of different perceptions, what might be of help in resolving the conflict?
4. Is there a connection between Rummel's subjectivity principle and the distinction made in Chapter 1 between the manifest conflict and the underlying conflict? Can you articulate an explanation of manifest conflict or underlying conflict based on Rummel's subjectivity principle?

B. Heuristics—Thinking Fast and Slow

There are two methods by which we make decisions. One is fast and the other is slower. Intuition based on experience and the functioning of the reptilian part of our brain allows us to make quick "gut" decisions using instinctual shortcuts that can be convenient, if not life-saving. The more deliberate, rational process of decision making is what we are trained in law school to utilize, commonly referred to as "thinking like a lawyer." This method takes in and processes more information and slows down decision making through the use of our cerebral cortex. The two decision systems modulate one another and can be in conflict, with the instinctive approach initially predominating because of its speed and utility.

Malcolm Gladwell popularized the benefit of nurturing quick, experience-based decisions not encumbered by deliberation in his best-selling book *Blink* (2007). Nobel prize winning psychologist Daniel Kahneman utilizes decades of research in explaining and labeling decision-making shortcuts, or cognitive heuristics, and the errors we can make when depending on intuitive judgment and how they can interfere with more rational, information-based decision making. (*Thinking Fast and Thinking Slow*, 2011) Kahneman, however acknowledges that our thoughts and actions are routinely guided by intuitive decisions that are generally on the mark and that we cannot live without them. Instinctive, fast judgments generally produce adequate solutions, but also create biases and flawed decisions if not monitored by rationality and more information.

> **Problem**
>
> Students at your school, who had expected to attend a required lecture without charge, are told after they arrive that they will each have to pay $20 to cover unexpected expenses. They can, however, spin a roulette wheel with four chances in five of paying nothing and one chance of having to pay $100. Which will most choose and why? (Hint: The answer is within the list below.)

Top Ten Psychological Traps

The following is an alphabetical list of the top ten common mental traps that can create disputes or make them more difficult to resolve. Some are interrelated; some have multiple labels. We return to these cognitive shortcuts and expand the list later when we examine why negotiations fail. They also come into play in a later chapter on how mediators can move negotiations through an impasse to settlement.

- *Anchoring*: A dispute over the value of an item often arises because we form an estimate of an unsure value by comparing it to something we know or to a number to which we are exposed that is then planted in our brain. The number you are exposed to as a value anchors your calculation and influences your thinking. When a client is burnt by hot soup at a restaurant, she may think the restaurant is to blame and her claim is worth millions because she read about a multimillion-dollar verdict against McDonald's for coffee that was served too hot. You, as a sophisticated lawyer, understand that this case is distinguishable from the McDonald's case, which was reduced on appeal as excessive, and that this client's case is much weaker and worth less than that one, so you adjust from the McDonald's verdict downward. The question is whether you adjust far enough. Research suggests that you will not adjust sufficiently because of the anchoring effect of the headline verdict, which distorts your analysis and expectation.

- *Confirmation bias:* We tend to give credit to information that is consistent with our preexisting beliefs and wishes rather than information that challenges or contradicts them. This can dig us deeper into conflict when dealing with those who have different beliefs or values. We read and believe articles that confirm dark chocolate and red wine are good for us, and skim past articles that question the studies.
- *Consensus error (projection):* We tend to falsely believe that others think the way we do or have values similar to ours. We also believe that others like what we like and want what we want. Those who enjoy loud music assume that everyone will enjoy their amplified radio selections. Conflict can be created when we find out we were wrong.
- *Framing:* Our thinking about an issue and our answer to a question are affected by how the question is presented. For instance, asking a priest if you can smoke while you pray is likely to result in a different answer than asking if you can pray while you smoke.
- *Loss aversion (status quo bias):* Losses tend to be felt more than equivalent gains are relished, so that the pain from the loss of a dollar is felt greater than the joy of a dollar gain. We tend to overvalue what we have to give up relative to what we might get. Most will not give up a "bird in the hand for two in the bush." In other words, we are willing to take more risk to avoid a loss than to obtain a gain. As a corollary, negotiating parties are more likely to view their own concessions (losses) as more valuable than equivalent concessions they get from the other side (gains).
- *Naive realism:* We tend to think that the way we see the world is the way it really is and anyone seeing it differently is naive. We each see the world through the lens of our own experience and culture, believing what we see is reality. This bias is in play when your idea or offer is rejected with the preface that in the "real world" things are different.
- *Overconfidence (egocentric bias):* We tend to rate our abilities, chance of being right, and good luck more highly than is warranted. Why else would people buy lottery tickets? We are also overconfident about our ability to assess uncertain data and tend to give more weight to what we know than what we don't know. As a matter of fact, we are overconfident about ourselves in general. As examples, surveys have found that 70 percent of all drivers believe that they are more competent than the average driver, and 80 percent of lawyers think that they are more ethical than the average attorney (Fox and Birke 2000). In negotiation, overconfidence can be compounded by positive illusions we have about the relative righteousness of our case or cause and how much we deserve.
- *Reactive devaluation:* Whatever proposal comes from the other side cannot be good for us. Anything done or suggested by them is suspect. For example, if Democrats propose legislation, Republicans are likely to reject it, and vice versa. Also, any information or offer received is perceived as less valuable than what might be withheld. This tends to escalate conflict.
- *Selective perception:* Whenever we encounter a new situation, we must interpret a universe of unfamiliar, often conflicting data that is more than we can process. We respond by instinctively forming a hypothesis about the situation,

then organizing what we see and hear with the help of that premise. Our hypothesis also operates as a filter, by automatically screening out anything that doesn't support it—which in turn reinforces the belief that our initial view was correct. Henry David Thoreau was probably thinking about this when he said, "We see only the world we look for." Selective perception is also the basis of self-fulfilling prophesies and stereotyping. For example, if you are negotiating with a lawyer you believe is hostile and not to be trusted, you may dismiss his initial friendly greeting as manipulative and selectively see him scrutinizing you with suspicion. Your stilted behavior toward him will likely result in him seeing you as antagonistic. Mutually reinforced surly behavior will be selectively observed and remembered to the exclusion of overtures of civility. You will feel that your own insight and keen ability to "read" others is confirmed, and your self-fulfilling prophecy will be realized.

- *Self-serving bias (attribution error)*: We are our own best friend in justifying our actions while seeing the same behavior in someone else as a shortcoming. For instance, we know that we are personally responsible for our successes, but our failures are the result of bad luck or circumstances beyond our control. When we are late it is for good reason; others keep us waiting because of their bad planning and insensitivity. Our miscalculation or misstatement is a simple mistake, but our opponent's similar error is attributed to deception. We also tend to take more credit for favorable results than others attribute to us.

Some of the psychological factors and biases described above may work against one another when making tactical decisions driving a negotiation. For example, as will be discussed later, there are differing views about the advantages and disadvantages of making the first offer in a negotiation. Making the first offer, particularly if the values involved are uncertain or without ready comparisons, could take advantage of the anchoring bias set by your offer. However, reactive devaluation, which may be at a peak near the beginning of negotiations, could cause the other side to radically discount your first offer because of their suspicion. (For a more extensive catalogue of psychological principles impacting negotiation and decision making, see Birke, "Neuroscience and Settlement: An Examination of Scientific Innovations and Practical Applications," 25 Ohio St. J. on Disp. Resol. 477 (2010).)

The Myth of Professional Objectivity

Studying the perceptions and psychological traps that immerse people in conflict helps us better understand clients' disputes. Although lawyers advocate and negotiate on behalf of clients, we are less subject to the selective perspectives that can skew our client's perceptions. As lawyers, without a direct stake in the outcomes of our client's disputes, we tend to believe we can think more clearly and rationally. After all, we have been educated to think like lawyers, right? This is the common wisdom, but is it true?

We can often recognize our clients' partisan perceptions, but we are easily fooled by our own ingrained biases and distortions. By definition, what we believe is our reality. The longer we work with a client on a case or a deal, the more we share the same reality—distorted or not. We might be no more able than our clients to objectively analyze the weaknesses of their case or the strengths of the other side's arguments. It can be very helpful for you to recognize that the psychological factors likely to affect your client's thinking and decision errors can also affect your own assessment of case value and the attractiveness of offers to settle. (See Randall Kiser, *Beyond Right and Wrong: The Power of Effective Decision Making for Attorneys and Clients* (2010).)

Questions

5. Does knowing about the potential of these perceptual biases and cognitive errors result in not being affected by them? How can you best guard against them or overcome your own cognitive errors?
6. What is your role if you are aware of your client's perception biases and cognitive distortions? Must you agree to a desired goal or an outcome acceptable to your client if you are aware that the goal or acceptance is the result of a misperception or cognitive error?
7. How might you counter cognitive error and perceptual distortion that may result in your negotiating counterpart rejecting a settlement that is otherwise acceptable? For example, how would you handle the anchoring problem, where your opponent is fixed on what you regard as an unrealistic outcome in another case, or the tendency of your opponent to reject your truly generous offer because of suspicion of any offer coming from you?

C. The Impact of Fairness

Our list of selective perceptions at the beginning of this chapter included "fairness." Differing views of fairness are at the heart of many litigated conflicts and failed negotiations. Fairness, like other perceptions, is in the mind of the beholder. A client may hire you to negotiate on her behalf because she feels she has been treated unfairly and that you, as a lawyer, can help her obtain what is fair. Fairness, as perceived by clients, can also become central in assessing whether to accept or reject a negotiated settlement or deal.

An outcome that appears to be fair can be more important than winning or losing. Fairness may define for some whether they have won or lost. Offers may be rejected even though they are economically advantageous because in the client's mind the result is not fair.

Classroom experiments with "ultimatum games" illustrate the importance of perceived fairness in negotiation. In these games, Player 1 is given a fixed sum of money or chips (e.g., $100) as a windfall that she might have found on the street and is asked to propose a division of that sum with Player 2 (e.g., $75 to Player 1 and $25 to Player 2). Player 1 has complete discretion to divide the money as she wishes; Player 2 can choose only whether to accept or reject Player 1's proposal. If Player 2 accepts the offer, both players will keep the money as allocated. If Player 2 rejects the offer, neither player will receive anything.

Economic theory dictates that Player 1 should offer only a little more than zero to Player 2, and that Player 2 should accept this amount as better than nothing. In fact, in classroom experiments Player 1 generally offers 30 to 50 percent of the sum to Player 2, and when less than 50 percent is offered, many Player 2 recipients will reject the offer, preferring to walk away with nothing rather than accept what they perceive to be an unfair result. The results of this game reflect the importance of our innate value of being treated fairly.

Perceptions of fairness consist of two components. Distributional fairness is a quantitative notion of material outcome—what you get as the result of a negotiation. Procedural fairness relates to the process used to reach the outcome—how you were treated during the negotiation. Both of these components shape people's willingness to accept settlements and their feelings of how well attorneys represented them in the negotiation process. (See Robbenholt and Sternlight, *Psychology for Lawyers* (2012).)

Problem—The Home-Run Ball Catch

More than 40,000 fans were at the ballpark to see the San Francisco Giants' last game of the season. Most had come to see Barry Bonds add another home run to his already record-breaking total of 72. Alex Popov and Patrick Hayashi, who did not know one another, were two fans in the right-field arcade standing-room section, hoping to catch a Bonds home-run ball. Sure enough, Bonds's 73rd home-run ball came sailing over the right-field bleachers into Popov's outstretched glove. Within seconds, Popov fell to the ground as a rush of people converged on him and the ball. Madness followed before security officers arrived. When Popov was pulled from the pile of fans, the ball was no longer in his glove. Patrick Hayashi emerged with the ball in hand.

Both men claimed ownership of the valuable home-run ball, temporarily in Hayashi's possession. Both thought the ball was worth more than $1 million, based on the sale of Mark McGwire's 70th home-run ball a couple of years earlier for more than $3 million. Each man offered the other less than $100,000 to relinquish any claim on the ball. Each expressed strong public views that he was entitled to complete ownership and was making a generous offer to the other. Both Popov and Hayashi cited principles of fairness and baseball fan culture entitling them to the ball. Popov argued that first possession controls, and Hayashi believed the fan who ended up in possession owned the ball. They insulted one another as liars and thieves. They both hired lawyers and filed suit in the California Superior Court.

Newspaper editorials, letters, talk show hosts, Barry Bonds, and several mediators all suggested that the ball be sold and the proceeds be split by the men or that the money be given to charity. Neither Popov nor Hayashi thought that evenly splitting what they were individually entitled to was fair, nor did they feel that they could concede anything in light of the insults cast on them by the other. Following 18 months of public bickering and litigation about what was fair, the judge ordered that the ball be sold and the proceeds evenly split. Twenty months after it was hit into the bleachers, the ball, resting on black velvet and encased in glass, was sold at auction to a comic book impresario for a final bid of $450,000. Popov and Hayashi each received $225,000, minus auction expenses, and each incurred attorneys' fees exceeding that amount. Popov was sued by his attorney for fees and expenses of $473,530, and also for $19,000 by a law professor who served as an expert witness. (The whole sorry story and background is captured in the 2004 film *Up for Grabs*.)

1. Did the fact that the entire home-run ball melee was televised and that both men made boastful and insulting public statements influence the negotiation? How might you explain this in terms of the conflict/negotiation triangle presented in Chapter 1?

2. Neither Popov nor Hayashi appeared to be guided by rational self-interest in making decisions about how to maximize their ultimate economic outcome. What do you think got in the way? Might the negotiation result have been different if they had been friends or at least had not publicly insulted one another?

3. Do any of the psychological traps listed above help explain why both men were not happy to evenly divide the economic windfall?

4. Did both men suffer from the litigation curse of being in a lawsuit in which they were absolutely convinced fairness was on their side?

5. If you were representing Popov, how might you have approached the negotiation in terms of the fairness issues? What fairness criteria might you have suggested?

Fairness perceptions are significant in understanding clients' expectations and the negotiation behaviors of participants in negotiating deals and litigation settlements, as illustrated by the above example of the home-run ball. The following reading examines the criteria that people use to judge fairness and the variables that determine perceptions of fairness.

Nancy A. Welsh, *PERCEPTIONS OF FAIRNESS IN NEGOTIATION*

87 Marq. L. Rev. 753 (2004)

Distributive Fairness Perceptions

As is obvious from reading judicial opinions in appellate cases, even impartial and educated people can review the identical record and reach widely disparate yet equally principled conclusions regarding what constitutes a fair outcome. The definition of distributive fairness is, therefore, inevitably subjective. This realization leads to the following questions: What criteria do people—including negotiators—use to guide their judgments regarding distributive fairness? What variables influence people's selection among different criteria, and why do people find it difficult to reach agreement even when they share a commitment to achieving an equitable outcome?

A. Competing Criteria for Judging Distributive Fairness

The various criteria for judging outcomes' fairness can be distilled into four basic, competing principles or rules—equality, need, generosity, and equity. The equality principle provides that everyone in a group should share its benefits equally. According to the need principle, "those who need more of a benefit should get more than those who need it less." The generosity principle decrees that one person's outcome should not exceed the outcomes achieved by others. Finally, the equity principle ties the distribution of benefits to people's relative contribution. Those who have—contributed more should receive more than those who have contributed less. The closer that the actual outcome of a negotiation is to the outcome a negotiator anticipated based on the application of one of these principles, the greater the likelihood that the negotiator will perceive the outcome as fair.

Imagine the application of the four principles described supra to a negotiation between two individuals who are establishing a joint venture and negotiating the distribution of income. The first negotiator, who has little capital, is contributing the idea and the time and energy to implement the idea. The other negotiator is supplying the needed funds for the development and marketing of the idea. If these individuals are guided by the equality principle, they will distribute the income from the joint venture equally. If they use the need principle, the poorer negotiator who is contributing "sweat equity" will receive a greater share of the income. Under the generosity principle, neither negotiator would want his income to exceed the income of the other. Last, and perhaps most difficult, is the application of the equity principle. Both contributions are needed. Whose is more valuable? . . .

B. Variables Affecting Negotiators' Selection Among Competing Fair Allocation Principles

Research has shown that several variables influence negotiators' selections among the various fair allocation principles that could apply to a particular negotiation. These variables include self-interest, social relationships, and the interaction between cultural norms and situational needs.

1. The Influence of Self-Interest and Relationships Between Negotiators

If no relationship exists between negotiators, self-interest will guide their choice of the appropriate allocation principle to use in negotiation. A negotiator who does not expect future interactions with the other person will use whatever principle—need, generosity, equality, or equity—produces the better result for her. When a negotiator has a negative relationship with the other person, she will aim to gain more than the other negotiator, even if this requires undertaking a risky strategy. She certainly will not worry about achieving an outcome that is fair for that other, despised negotiator. Thus, "[n]egative affect within the context of potential relationships can remove fairness barriers."

On the other hand, the existence of a positive relationship with another negotiator makes the attainment of a fair outcome relevant. Further, positive social relationships influence negotiators' selection of the particular fair allocation principle that will anchor their negotiations. If a negotiator is divid-ing a resource with someone else and expects future, positive interactions with that person, the negotiator tends to use the equality principle to define distrib-utive fairness. . . . Relationships obviously matter in negotiators' definitions of fair outcomes. . . .

2. The Influence of Situational Needs and Cultural Norms

As commerce has become increasingly global, cross-cultural negotiation has also become more commonplace. Some cultures are known for placing greater emphasis upon maintaining social relationships than attaining individual objectives. Many believe, therefore, that the cultural dimension of collectivism-individualism should have great salience in the negotiation context. Simply, "individualism refers to a tendency to put a stronger emphasis on one's personal interest and goals, whereas collectivism refers to a stronger emphasis on the interests and goals of one's in-group members." Collectivist negotiators ought to be more likely than individualists to choose harmony-enhancing principles for the distribution of benefits (e.g., equality, need, or generosity principles).

Research indicates, however, that negotiators' choices among the various allocation principles are not so predictable. First, and consistent with the impor-tance of relationships noted above, it is only when collectivists are negotiating with other in-group members that they are more likely to use a harmony-enhanc-ing principle. If they are not closely related to the other negotiators, collectivists behave like individualists and tie fair allocation to contribution, thus leading to their use of the equitable principle. . . . . . .

Procedural Fairness Perceptions

Procedural fairness is concerned with people's perceptions of the fairness of the procedures or processes used to arrive at outcomes. Researchers have found that people's perceptions of procedural justice have profound effects. First, people who believe that they have been treated in a procedurally fair man-ner are more likely to conclude that the resulting outcome is substantively fair. In effect, a person's perception of procedural fairness anchors general fairness impressions or serves as a fairness heuristic. Second, people who believe that they were treated fairly in a dispute resolution or decision-making procedure are more likely to comply with the outcome of the procedure. This effect will occur even if the outcomes are not favorable or produce unhappiness. . . .

Conclusion

Lawyers and clients rely upon their assessments of fairness to make all sorts of decisions during negotiation: What offer shall we make? How should we respond to the other side's demand? Should we settle or make a counteroffer? Is the other side being so ridiculous that it is time to call an impasse?

Each one of these questions requires consideration of fairness, and it should now be quite clear that fairness is largely a matter of perception. Perhaps what is most interesting about the research that has been done regarding fairness per-ceptions is the extent to which it undermines the iconic image of two rational negotiators locked in a battle of logic, economics, and will. Rather, the research reveals that negotiators' aspirations and moves will be significantly influenced by the culture and context within which they are negotiating, their own self-interest, and most intriguing of all, their sense of connection to each other. Ironically, as negotiations become increasingly global and virtual, it is the development of those old-fashioned relationships that may matter most.

D. The Role of Emotions, Emotional Intelligence, and Neuroscience

Many of us are attracted to the study of law because we value a rational approach to issues rather than emotional responses that seem to get in the way of logic and problem solving. The conventional wisdom is that lawyers should leave their emotions behind in their professional roles, including negotiating. This is easier said than done, and might not always be wise.

None of us are automatons, even though we may try to appear so. Nor are those with whom we negotiate without emotional content that helps shape their conduct. We all have emotional needs and reactions that contribute to the creation of conflicts and are part of how we interact and deal with others. Recognizing and mastering these emotions is usually more helpful than denying and ignoring them.

More important, our clients have emotional needs that they might not readily express to us. As you learned from the readings in Chapter 1, emotional concerns, as well as substantive needs, may be critical factors that have to be satisfied to reach a settlement. Learning to recognize emotions and understanding their role in creating conflict and resolving it can be an important key to negotiation success.

Negotiation effectiveness depends, in part, on interpersonal competency and a type of emotional intelligence. Emotional intelligence is the capacity to monitor our feelings and read the feelings of those whom we encounter. This then serves as a guide to our actions and responses. (See Mayer 2001.) The theme of emotional intelligence and its role in success, although not new, was brought to public attention by Daniel Goleman in his popular book *Emotional Intelligence: Why It Can Matter More Than IQ* (1995). An emotionally intelligent negotiator has an advantage in controlling her own emotions and understanding the emotions of an opponent to better control the negotiating process. Emotional intelligence has been found to contribute to successful negotiator behavior. (See Barry et al. 2004.) However, the ability to read the emotions of others may be on the decline. A meta-analysis study found that today's college students score 40 percent lower than their predecessors in the 1970s in their ability to understand what another person is feeling. (See Konrath 2011.)

Randall Kiser, an attorney who has empirically studied how lawyers make decisions regarding settlement of lawsuits and measured the frequency and cost of not settling, has identified and interviewed many of the most successful lawyer negotiators in California and New York. One of the qualities that appeared to distinguish these lawyers from others was emotional intelligence. Kiser summarizes some of his findings and quotes from the interviews in the article that follows.

❖ **Randall Kiser,** *THE EMOTIONALLY ATTENTIVE LAWYER: BALANCING THE RULE OF LAW WITH THE REALITIES OF HUMAN BEHAVIOR*

15 Nev. L.J., 2015

Although the law may denigrate the role of emotions, the successful practice of law requires a high level of emotional intelligence. The traits that comprise emotional intelligence (self-awareness, self-management, social awareness, and relationship management skills) are essential to superior attorney performance. These traits also are essential to developing the sense of personal meaning, responsibility, and fulfillment that distinguish expert performers. . . .

At the most elemental level of law practice, emotional intelligence appears to be necessary for attorneys to avoid malpractice liability. Malpractice claims data show a significant and persistent conflict between client expectations and attorney performances in "soft" skills requiring judgment, discernment, awareness, and perspective: case evaluation, risk assessment, strategy development, client communication, and settlement negotiations. According to the American Bar Association's "Profile of Legal Malpractice Claims," . . . more than one-third of all malpractice claims allege errors relating to professional skills required in pre-trial evaluations, discovery, procedures, counseling, negotiations, and settlements. These skills necessarily entail an integration of substantive legal knowledge with a broader range of competencies embraced by emotional intelligence — listening, understanding, communicating, conceptualizing, anticipating, simulating, and perspective-taking. . . .

Attorney Views of the Role of Emotions in Law Practice

Seventy-eight leading litigation attorneys were interviewed for the book *How Leading Lawyers Think: Expert Insights into Judgment and Advocacy, Kiser* (2011). These attorneys were selected from a dataset of 8,114 attorneys in New York and California based on superior performances in predicting case outcomes. Among the topics addressed in the attorney interviews was the role of emotions and the relative importance of technical legal competence and "soft" skills like empathy, maturity, judgment, and self-awareness.

When asked whether other attorneys' errors in case evaluation are attributable to errors about the law or intangible factors like witness appeal and credibility, the attorneys generally point to subjective judgments as being the culprit:

- [O]f course you have to know the law. But when lawyers fail, it's the subjective that they do not take into account. The law is not as critical as the guts that go into the [case evaluation].
- The emotional component that a good plaintiff's case has is something that is not considered by [medical malpractice] defendants because they get more attuned to the medicine. There is an emotional component that some defendants lose sight of as it relates to a juror's sympathy. . . .

- They don't understand how these personal factors, the intangible factors, will evolve through the process, how the facts will unfold. It comes full circle.
- We never know the truth; we know the perception. The law is the simplest part of it. . . .

Risks of Emotional Involvement

When asked whether emotions interfere with case evaluation and, specifically, whether emotions promote or hinder sound judgment and effective trial advocacy, the attorneys made some critical distinctions and highlighted the ongoing tension between emotional commitment and professional objectivity. Referring to the role of emotions in case evaluation, some attorneys remarked:

- A lot of attorneys can't take the emotion out of it. That can be a good thing but you have to be able to stand back. . . .
- There are times when you need to be emotional. There are times when you have to use some emotions to decide what to do. I'm probably more emotional than my male partners, but I think that's to my advantage.
- There are cases that benefit from a more passionate approach, some from a dispassionate approach. Whatever approach you take, you still have to be very professional.
- There has to be a fire in the guts for the attorney and the client. . . .

Another attorney who had changed his career from a defense practice to a plaintiffs' practice noted that an attorney has to understand his own emotions very well. "You should know where your emotions are and how to stop that emotional train," he commented. Asked whether he was emotionally more mature now than when he started practicing law, he responded immediately, "Undoubtedly. I know myself better. You learn things about yourself, if you're paying attention."

Effect of Emotions on Clients, Adversaries, Jurors and Insurers

Apart from knowing how emotions could affect their own judgment and advocacy, the [most successful] attorneys repeatedly pointed to the importance of understanding how emotions affect clients and adversaries, especially in settlement negotiations:

- When I started representing plaintiffs, my first case settled for $900,000. That's a case I would have paid $75,000 for if we represented the defendant. Everybody is afraid—plaintiffs and defendants laying out all of this money. You have to manipulate the other side's fear and have none yourself. Fear equals the perception of risk—not even risk, but the perception of risk . . . .
- People do not realize the emotional effect litigation has on clients. Young attorneys do not realize the damage that is done by having to relive the trauma of an emotionally devastating event like wrongful death. Humans have a capacity to mend, to recover over time, and litigation reopens memories that people are trying to recover from. They do not realize the damage they will do to their own clients even if they win. They [clients] have to relive

all the painful events they are trying to put behind them. Most attorneys do not realize that winning is resolving a case earlier rather than winning at trial.

Joshua Rosenberg, a law professor and psychologist, weaves together our previous readings on perception and self-fulfilling prophecies with emotional intelligence and their impact on negotiating.

❖ **Joshua D. Rosenberg,** *Interpersonal Dynamics: Helping Lawyers Learn the Skills, and the Importance, of Human Relationships in the Practice of Law*

55 U. of Miami L. Rev. 1225 (2004)

Basically, most lawyers and academics vastly overestimate the importance of reason and logic. We tend to view them as both the primary motivator of our own behavior and the primary tool to change the thinking and behavior of others. Although they are important, they are only one part of the puzzle. There are important differences between the kind of dispassionate reasoning and analysis in which lawyers and law students engage while sitting at desks at home, in the office, or in the library, and the kind of activities in which we engage when we are dealing in real time with real people. Real time, real life interactions implicate emotions, learned patterns of behavior, habituated perspectives and frames of reference, and other human, but not reasoned, responses.

The reactions to emotions occur whether or not the person is aware of either the reaction or the emotion, and they significantly impact the outcome of most negotiations and most other interpersonal interactions. People who become anxious may tend to over-accommodate the other by inappropriately giving in on the substance of the discussion, or may tend to talk too much (or too little) in an unconscious effort to forestall that anxiety. People who become irritated may tend to become slightly belligerent or withdrawn in ways that can harm their interactions. Any feelings are likely to trigger unconscious patterns of thought and behavior that will inevitably influence an interaction. . . .

It is not just how we think about what we perceive that is tainted by our feelings. Our very perceptions themselves are determined, in part, by our feelings (and thoughts). As an initial matter, emotions precipitate changes in the autonomic nervous system. These changes include increasing the heart rate, changing breathing patterns, skin changes such as perspiration or blushing, and redirecting blood flow (anger has been found to direct blood to the hands, presumably for combat; fear has been shown to redirect blood to the legs, presumably for running). At a micro level, these changes in the autonomic nervous system change not only our ability to think, but also our ability to act and perceive. Along with our thoughts, our blood flow, and our energy, the focus of our attention and our ability to take in data are significantly changed by our emotional state. Not only our behavior, but also our perceptions become both differently focused and less accurate. . . .

The Result: Interacting Systems and Self-Fulfilling Prophecies

Basically, our thoughts, feelings, behaviors and perceptions influence each other. We react to our perceptions of the world around us while our own behavior impacts on the world. Of course, the patterns of our behavior, thoughts, perceptions and feelings are far from random. We tend to learn patterns of thought, feeling, and behavioral reactions in childhood. In adult-hood we tend to engage in those patterns we learned as children, often resulting in "self-fulfilling prophecies" that tend to reinforce those same old patterns. Basically, because of our particular frame of reference (thoughts, feelings, etc.), we expect people to act in certain ways, and we act toward them in ways that tend to precipitate the behaviors we expect. When people do act in the ways we expected, we interpret that behavior in line with our expectations, and we react in certain predictable ways (which tend to confirm to us the validity of our earlier expectations).

Negotiation experts are aware of the significant impact of self-fulfilling prophecies on negotiations, but the actual impact of these patterns extends well beyond "negotiations," to encompass most of our interactions in life. . . . [S]elf-fulfilling prophecies and other generally unconscious learned responses significantly impact the outcome of most negotiations and most other interpersonal interactions.

Human Communication: Colliding Systems

As all of the above suggests, despite our typical estimation to the contrary, we are often unaware of the actual causes (and unintentional consequences) of our own behavior, thinking, emotions, and perceptions. We are not sufficiently self-aware to realize how many of our patterns of acting and thinking are ingrained, unconscious or triggered by our autonomic nervous system rather than by reason. Communication, of course, is a two-way street, and much of the time we are even more misguided about what is headed toward us than we are about where we ourselves are going. Just as we incorrectly believe that we understand our own behavior better than we do, we also (and to a much greater degree) wrongly believe that we understand others much better than we actually do. . . .

As an initial matter, researchers have concluded that the single greatest weakness of most negotiators is that they too often fail to even consider the thinking and emotions of others. Perhaps even more significantly, when we do attempt to consider the thinking and feelings of others, we usually get it wrong. We often attribute to them moods, goals or motivations that simply are not there, or we exaggerate the significance of one of many reactions they may be having and forget that, like our own, their reactions might be both dynamic and complex.

While we tend to be accepting of situational factors that impact our own behavior, we tend to be unaware of, and inattentive to, the impact of such situational factors on others. As a result, we tend to think of ourselves as more sympathetic, as having a better case, or as being a better person than the one with whom we are dealing. In turn, this often leads us to devalue the other's case and proposals, and to fail to reach agreements that are available and would have been in our client's (or our own, as the case may be) best interest.

Questions

8. Do you agree that we vastly overestimate the importance of reason and logic?
9. How would you describe the connection between emotional intelligence and successful negotiation?
10. Can emotional intelligence be taught?
11. Thinking back to the most important decisions you have made, can you honestly say that emotions played no part?

Neuroscience and Negotiation

The Rosenberg article you just read explains how emotions precipitate changes in the autonomic nervous system, which result in physiological reactions like sweating and blushing. Our emotions are also manifested by increased oxygen to specific parts of our brains that effect how we respond to stimuli and make decisions. Neuroscientists have recently been able to use brain imaging (functional magnetic resonance imagery, or fMRI) to map areas of the brain that show increased oxygen supply during decision making and other brain functions. These brain maps give clues to the effect of emotions in various types of decisions. Through brain imaging or brain mapping, it can be understood how anxiety, disgust, fear, and joy can influence decision making. We think that our decisions are logical, based on our perceptions and our conclusions about what is. What we think is logical may not seem logical to others who perceive, interpret, and react to the same information. Brain mapping demonstrates that it is not just about how things are, but also about how they feel. In short, don't underestimate the role of emotions in the decisions made by our clients, lawyers on the other side, and by us in our representational roles. The more you understand how the brain works and about the role of emotions in decision making, the better you can apply it to your mastery of negotiation. (See Richard Birke, "Neuroscience and Negotiation: What the New Science of Mind May Offer the Practicing Attorney," 17 Disp. Resol. Mag. 4 (2011).)

CHAPTER
3

Competitive and Cooperative Negotiation

We each have our own approach of how to get what we want. So it is with negotiation. Many terms are used to describe different negotiating styles in a range from "hard" to "soft." For purposes of introducing the approaches and distinguishing them, we use here two basic categories: competitive and cooperative. Following the problem situation presented below, we will contrast the characteristics and use of competitive negotiation with the cooperative approach. We will also look at adversarial bargaining, the more aggressive form of the competitive approach, and problem-solving negotiation, a close cousin of the cooperative approach. The distinctions between competitive and adversarial styles (often used interchangeably), on the one hand, and cooperative and problem-solving styles (also used interchangeably), on the other hand, are not always clear. We will also discuss the "negotiator's dilemma" occurring when it comes time to divide the enhanced value created through cooperative moves.

Problem — Microsoft v. Stac

Bill Gates became the richest man in the world by being smart, diligent, and keenly competitive. As a negotiator, he is known for being aggressive and competitive, although there are accounts of him using his considerable creative skills to negotiate value-added cooperative outcomes. In the following example, Gates used two different approaches to an intellectual property claim at different stages in the dispute.

Stac Electronics was a computer engineering company founded by seven friends at Caltech. The company developed its "Stacker" disc compression software to substantially expand the data storage capacity of computer disks. Bill Gates, then CEO of Microsoft, wanted Stac's data compression technology and met personally with Stac's president, Gary Clow, to discuss licensing of Stac's software. The negotiations were turned over to other Microsoft executives and lawyers to negotiate. Although willing to pay Stac a modest gross license fee, Microsoft refused to pay Stac any per-user royalty for its patented compression technology. Microsoft took a hard line, saying that it could have other sources develop reliable data compression technology that could be incorporated into the MS-DOS operating system, which would have an immediate and adverse effect on the viability of Stacker and threaten Stac's continued economic viability. Microsoft had a reputation of using its huge market share and resources to negotiate in a hard fashion and favorably license software that it incorporated into its products. Negotiations broke off and Microsoft released a new system, which included a disk compression program called Double Space that provided disk capacity similar to that of Stac's data compression technology. Stac was outraged, as Microsoft had previously examined the Stacker code as part of the due diligence process in their earlier negotiations and Stac believed that Microsoft infringed its patent.

Microsoft would not budge on Stac's claim, and Stac filed a patent infringement suit against Microsoft. Microsoft counterclaimed that Stac had misappropriated the Microsoft trade secret of a preloading feature that was included in Stacker. A federal court jury in California awarded Stac $120 million in compensatory damages, coming to about $5.50 per copy for every one of the new Microsoft program sold. The jury also concluded that Stac misappropriated Microsoft's trade secret and simultaneously awarded Microsoft $13.6 million on the counterclaim. Feelings on both sides were negative and intense. Both Clow and Gates made public statements the demeaning the others negotiation style and integrity.

A new round of negotiations commenced in the changed circumstances of the jury verdict. Both sides had the option of legal appeals over the jury verdicts. Instead, their lawyers negotiated in a more cooperative manner and created a deal that caught Wall Street off guard, favorably affecting the share price of both companies. Each side agreed to drop its claims in exchange for cross-licensing all of their existing patents, as well as future ones over the next five years. The pact called for Microsoft to pay Stac license royalties totaling $43 million over 43 months, while also investing $39.9 million for a 15-percent equity stake in Stac. The total $82.9 million outlay represented a gain for Microsoft, which had already charged off $120 million for the jury award in its fiscal third quarter and now was able to credit much of the difference in the current period. Stac also came out ahead, by getting a significant cash infusion without a long appeals process to collect money from Microsoft. Mr. Clow said that $82.9 million being turned over by Microsoft represented more than Stac would have gotten had the $120 million been paid, because income taxes and Stac's own $13.6-million penalty would have whittled the final amount to about $64 million. In addition, Stac formed an alliance with the most powerful player in the software industry. Mr. Clow stated that, "this is not personal. This makes good business sense going forward. . . . This demonstrates it is possible to do win-win deals." Microsoft's executives concurred. "This is a lot more fun than disagreeing," said Michael Brown, Microsoft's vice president of finance, referring to the more cooperative final round of negotiation.

1. Why might Gates have played hardball when he first negotiated with Stac's Clow?
2. Why did Gates then change his approach and have his lawyers negotiate a more cooperative deal going forward?
3. What are the advantages and disadvantages of each approach to negotiation?
4. How do you decide when to use a competitive or cooperative negotiation style?

A. Competitive/Adversarial Approach

1. Competitive Approach

We begin with the competitive model because it is frequently encountered in everyday bargaining as well as in many lawyer encounters. It was considered the negotiation norm prior to the popularization of cooperative negotiation spurred by the publication in 1981 of *Getting to Yes* (now in its third edition, Fisher, Ury, and Patton 2011). Understanding competitive/adversarial negotiating will provide a base to contrast cooperative/problem-solving negotiation. The *competitive* approach assumes that the purpose of bargaining is to obtain the best possible economic result for your client, usually at the expense of the other side. A competitive bargainer is likely to think that negotiation involves a limited resource or fund that must be distributed between competing parties — in effect, a fixed economic "pie." In a competitive approach, the parties' relationships and other intangibles are not of primary importance. The competitive bargainer's goal is to pay as little as possible (if a buyer or defendant) or obtain as much as possible (if a seller or plaintiff), as a dollar more for your opponent is necessarily a dollar less for you. A competitive bargainer, in other words, sees negotiation much as a litigator sees a trial: Someone must win and someone must lose, and her central mission is to win. This approach is also known as "distributive" or "zero-sum" bargaining, because the negotiators see their task as distributing a fixed, limited resource between them.

Competitive negotiating covers a continuum of behaviors from the simplest, unreflective actions to improve your position and achieve a better outcome to highly conscious, planned moves. So, competitive bargaining may consist of natural responses in some situations and advantageous scripted strategies in others.

A competitive negotiator often begins a negotiation as a contest of hiding the ball. The object is to get as much information from the other side as possible while disclosing as little information as possible. The information sought goes to the other party's unrevealed, real bottom line. What's the least he will take or the most he will give to reach agreement? While the competitive negotiator wants to convince the other side that the negotiator's own asserted bottom line is firm. He may try to persuade his opponent that he will stick to his asserted no-deal point or walk, when he has no intention of doing so.

Competitive approaches may be used in complex negotiations involving multiple issues and parties. The competitive negotiation may occur in stages where it is hard to determine at the outset if the process will take on a more competitive or cooperative or mixed approach. A skilled competitive negotiator may cloak competitive moves with a benign cover or a cooperative demeanor. Competitive bargaining, however, is most transparently used in non-complex situations that involve the simple payment of money or exchange of goods.

An example a of where competitive negotiating is likely to occur is when a lawyer negotiates with an insurance adjuster in a distant city to settle a client's claim for property damage to a car caused by a falling tree limb. The client, we will assume, has since changed insurance companies, and the lawyer does not expect to do business with this adjuster again, so neither sees any interest in

nurturing a relationship. In this situation both sides have a joint interest in conducting the bargaining process efficiently and quickly. Both the lawyer and the
adjuster are likely to see their sole goal as agreeing on a dollar amount that the
company will pay the insured to give up his claim, and to assume that a better
settlement for one will necessarily be worse for the other.

In this negotiation, each side may posture about the dimensions of the issue
or conflict, initiate a demand or offer (a specific proposal for resolving the dispute), and bargain over that proposal or present a counterproposal. A competitive negotiator will attempt to change the other side's perception to persuade
them that their case is weaker and worth less than they thought and that her
case is stronger and more valuable than her opponent previously recognized.
Incremental concessions are usually made that narrow the bargaining range.
Finally, a compromise settlement may be agreed upon. This type of competitive
negotiation, with predetermined positions and the trading of dollar numbers
that simply chop from a high demand or add to a low offer, is akin to marketplace bargaining or haggling. The parties' progressively closer dollar figures
are not connected to any reason or rationale, other than a desire to close the
remaining gap between the previously stated numbers. Basically, both buyer
and seller, or claimant and defendant, are seeking to maximize their gain by
seeing how far the other party can be pushed.

This "naked-number" competitive bargaining often occurs in the ending
stage of a negotiation that may have started with information-based discussions
and rationalized demands and offers. Having narrowed the gap between the
initial offer and demand, and having exhausted persuasion pinned to facts and
merits, "final" offers and counteroffers are thrown back and forth, each testing
the other's resolve to stick close to their side of the gap or walk away. The negotiators move toward a compromise point where both are willing to get the deal
done rather than leave empty-handed, or not. This is the typical style of bargaining in flea markets and garage sales. It often becomes little more than a contest
of wills, much like a game of chicken.

Questions

1. Have you experienced competitive negotiation? What were the
   circumstances?
2. Why do some people negotiate competitively?

❖ **Gary Goodpaster, *A Primer on Competitive Bargaining***

J. Disp. Resol. 325 (1996)

Some people bargain competitively without giving much conscious attention to
the matter. Others compete in response to the other party's competitive behavior. In this response, they follow the common pattern that a particular kind of
behavior elicits a similar behavior in response. In other words, one party frames
the negotiation as a contest, and the other party picks up the competitive cues
and behaves accordingly. Further, people naturally incline to competitive

bargaining when they are non-trusting. In such situations, in order to avoid putting themselves at risk, non-trusting people act guardedly and adopt elements of the competitive strategy, for example, withholding information or misrepresenting a position. Finally, one can readily imagine ambiguous bargaining situations, in which at least one party is non-trusting, quickly devolving into a competitive negotiation between both parties. The non-trusting party acts defensively, and the other party senses this as competitive behavior and, therefore, acts in a similar fashion.

Negotiators, however, can also consciously adopt a competitive strategy. Negotiators are most likely to compete purposefully when:

- the parties have an adversarial relationship;
- a negotiator has a bargaining power advantage and can dominate the situation;
- a negotiator perceives an opportunity for gain at the expense of the other party;
- the other party appears susceptible to competitive tactics;
- the negotiator is defending against competitive moves; or
- there is no concern for the future relationship between the parties.

This list suggests that competitive bargaining most likely occurs in situations such as labor and lawsuit negotiations, insurance and similar claims type settlements, and in one-time transactions between a relatively experienced party and a relatively inexperienced party. One would, for example, expect to see it in sales transactions where the parties will probably not see each other again.

Representative bargaining or bargaining for a constituency may also prompt competitive bargaining even when there will be future negotiations between equally sophisticated parties. The negotiator's accountability may override relationship concerns and reasons for cooperation. The concerned audience, consisting of a client, constituency, coalition partner, or other phantom party at the table, is, in effect, looking over the negotiator's shoulder. The negotiator, therefore, takes positions and makes moves she believes her client either expects or would approve. International negotiations between countries, union-management, lawsuit negotiations, and negotiations between different parties in interest-group coalition negotiations sometimes evidence this pattern.

Aside from circumstantial or situational pressures, there are some parties who bargain competitively because they believe that is the way to conduct business. There are also parties who are simply predisposed to bargain competitively and will incline to do so opportunistically in any bargaining situation if possible.

Finally, it is important to note that one can bargain competitively in a negotiation on some issues and cooperatively on others. In other words, a negotiator can selectively use competitive strategy or tactics on particular issues, while using a cooperative or problem-solving strategy on other issues. In such a case, extracting gain competitively may not greatly endanger future relationships. . . .

Obviously, competitive bargaining covers a continuum of behaviors from the simplest, unreflective adversarial actions to highly conscious and virtually scripted contests. As such, competitive bargaining moves are natural responses in some negotiation situations and advantageous or profitable actions in others. . . .

2. Adversarial Approach

A negotiator may push the boundaries of the competitive approach and bleed into a style of negotiating which is a more aggressive or extreme version. These more aggressive negotiators, which we label adversarial bargainers, view negotiation as a kind of war and believe that all is fair in winning it. The boundaries and the labels are fussy and not always distinguishable. An adversarial negotiator may provide the other party with misleading clues, bluffs, and distorted facts that cannot easily be checked or challenged, for the purpose of creating incorrect conclusions that are beneficial to the competitor. Extreme adversarial bargainers may be willing to renege on tentative agreements, misrepresent the limits of their authority, make threats, and may also use tactics aimed at pressuring, or unbalancing the other party to secure a better outcome. Although these adversarial moves may provide an advantage for the negotiator, they increase the risk of ending the negotiation with no agreement, jeopardize any continuing relationship, and be long remembered.

There is no shortage of advice about how to be a tough, adversarial bargainer and how to get what you want in a negotiation. Check the self-help and business-advice sections of large booksellers for an array of titles on this subject. Many of these guides appear to assume that the opposing side is ignorant or gullible and will have no future opportunity to retaliate. Other books and articles bemoan "hardball" tactics, but catalog them to warn you of what you might encounter. These writings are premised on the theory that to be "forewarned is forearmed." Roger Dawson, the author of *Secrets of Power Negotiating* (2001), challenges the myth of cooperative "win-win" negotiation before sharing his adversarial secrets and what you need to watch out for so you do not become the victim of others' hardball tactics. His list of power negotiating gambits includes the following:

- *Ask for more than you expect to get*: You can get away with an outrageous opening position if you imply some flexibility.
- *Never say yes to the first offer*: Saying yes triggers two thoughts in the other person's mind: "I could have done better," and "something must be wrong."
- *Flinch at proposals*: The other side may not expect to get what is asked for; however, if you do not show surprise, then you're communicating that it is a possibility.
- *Always play the reluctant seller*: This is a great way to squeeze the other side's negotiating range before the negotiation even starts.
- *Use the vise technique*: "You'll have to do better than that."
- *Don't let the other side know you have the authority to make a decision*: Don't let the other person trick you into admitting that you have authority.
- *Don't fall into the trap of thinking that splitting the difference is the fair thing to do*: Splitting the difference doesn't mean down the middle, because you can do it more than once.
- *Always ask for a trade-off*: Any time the other side asks you for a concession, ask for something in return.
- *Good guy/bad guy*: It's an effective way of putting more pressure on the other person without creating confrontation.
- *Nibbling*: Using the nibbling gambit, you can get a little bit more even after you have agreed on everything.

- *Taper concessions:* Taper concessions to communicate that the other side is getting the best possible deal.
- *Withdrawing an offer:* You can do it by backing off your last price concession or by withdrawing an offer, for instance, to include freight, installation, and so on.
- *The decoy:* Use a decoy to take attention away from the real issue in the negotiation.
- *Red herring:* This is a phony demand that can be withdrawn, but only in exchange for a concession.
- *Cherry picking:* Ask for alternatives and then pick the best parts from multiple choices.
- *Escalation:* Raising demands after both sides reach an agreement.
- *Time pressure:* The rule in negotiating is that 80 percent of the concessions occur in the last 20 percent of time available.
- *Be prepared to walk away:* Project to the other side that you will walk away from the negotiations if you can't get what you want.
- *The fait accompli:* This occurs when one negotiator simply assumes the other will accept an assumed settlement rather than go to the trouble of reopening the negotiations.
- *Ultimatums:* Ultimatums are very high-profile statements that tend to strike fear into inexperienced negotiators.

Questions

3. Do any of these tactics seem unethical? Negotiation presents a fertile area for ethical transgressions, with relatively little guidance as to ethical limits. The ethics of negotiation are addressed in Chapter 10.
4. Is there a difference between hard, competitive negotiation and "dirty" bargaining tricks? If so, how would you distinguish them?
5. Are there any gambits or techniques that you could add to Dawson's list?
6. If the tactics listed by Dawson were used against you, what would you do?
7. If any of these behaviors did produce an adverse result for your client, what would be your approach the next time you found yourself matched against this opponent?

Note: Responses to Competitive Hardball and Difficult People

Some of the books and articles cataloging competitive negotiation tactics also prescribe competitive antidotes that could be used in response. Most of these reactive "hardball" tactics are either responses in kind or intended to notch up the positioning in a dance of "one-upmanship." The most effective countermove or response to sharp competitive tactics will depend on the context of the negotiation, your relationship with the other negotiators, your alternatives to continued negotiations, the strength of your own position, your goals in the negotiation, and the information available to you. The key to any effective response is being able to recognize aggressive and deceptive tactics and understanding their potential effect in distorting your perspective and masking the opposition's weaknesses.

There are alternatives to responding in kind to hardball tactics or ending the negotiation. The behavior can be recognized and labeled for what it is and then dismissed by making light of it, or you can just ignore it. You can be direct by making it clear that the tactic is not working and is interfering with either of you getting what you want out of a possible deal or settlement, and that it will not be tolerated. In effect, you can discuss and set ground rules for further negotiations. Hardball tactics are most commonly used in the absence of an ongoing relationship or friendship. Taking time to become friendlier before the bargaining begins or emphasizing the likely continuing contact or repeat plays following this negotiation might discourage hardball tactics—or it might not.

The subject of responding to aggressive moves is related more generally to how we can best negotiate with people we consider difficult. Seminars and training programs are frequently offered to help us deal with "difficult people." The proliferation of these programs, including ones offered for attorneys, reflects the commonly experienced frustration most of us have had in trying to work or negotiate with others whom we perceive as being insensitive, obstinate, selfish, overly competitive, or generally unreasonable. It is an interesting paradox that experience with difficult people should be so common when few, if any, of us view ourselves as being difficult. Do you think the people you consider difficult believe themselves to be so? Studies show that opponents usually see us as more demanding and less reasonable than we view ourselves (Thomas and Pondy 1977).

Negotiating with difficult people can be—well, difficult, Here are a few techniques you can use:

- Become an observer to an opponent's bad behavior rather than getting sucked into the game. This means controlling your own behavior and distancing yourself from your reactive impulses and emotions.
- Ask questions to figure out what motivates the difficult behavior and then defuse the anger, fear, or other causes of the bad behavior.
- Reshape the negotiation to address the issue you want to resolve and to move the negotiation in the direction you want it to move.
- Make your preferred outcome the opponent's idea by involving him in the solution, and helping him "save face" and look good.
- Act more like a mediator than an adversary by making it clear that what you are offering is better than the realistic alternatives. (See William Ury, *Getting Past No: Negotiating with Difficult People* (1991).)

Questions

8. How have you dealt or negotiated with difficult people?
9. If you had to choose, would you categorize your negotiation style as more competitive or more cooperative?

B. Cooperative/Problem-Solving Approach

1. Cooperative Approach

A cooperative negotiator does not view negotiation "pies" as fixed. Cooperative bargainers work to identify interests and examine differences in how the parties value items. They then search jointly with the other negotiator—viewed more as a partner rather than an opponent—for options and a solution that will best satisfy both parties' interests. Cooperative negotiation is marked by an effort to understand one another's perceptions and reexamine them together to arrive at a shared picture or a mutually acceptable valuation. This cooperative approach is frequently called "integrative" bargaining, because it emphasizes integrating the parties' needs to find the best joint solution. It is also referred to as "interest-based" negotiation because it sees the goal of bargaining as satisfying people's underlying interests.

Rather than moving from positions to counter-positions to a compromise settlement, cooperative negotiators search for a variety of alternatives that optimize the interests that they have prioritized. The parties can then create an outcome from a combination of generated options so that a joint decision, with more benefits to all, can be achieved. This more collaborative approach does not necessarily produce a simple compromise between competing positions. It seeks a creative settlement not bound by predetermined positions.

A classic situation that calls for cooperative bargaining is an effort by two businesses to form a joint venture. Cooperative bargainers would first ask what special resources and capabilities each partner could bring to the deal. (For example, does Partner A have special expertise in marketing, whereas Partner B has more strength in design? Does one have good access to financing, whereas the other has available office space?) The negotiators would also ask whether either partner had particular needs; for example, one for an assured stream of income and the other for cutting-edge technology. Cooperative bargainers would focus on finding terms that best exploit each partner's abilities and minimize weaknesses, creating the strongest possible future partnership.

Cooperative and competitive bargaining are not mutually exclusive. Working to create the biggest possible pie does not, in itself, say anything about how the final pie will be divided. Savvy competitive negotiators, for example, will look earnestly for ways to "expand the pie." Competitors, however, are likely to see expanding the pie as less important than getting the largest possible piece for their clients. Cooperative bargainers must also face the pie-dividing problem, but tend to give it less significance than competitors. In the joint venture example described above, cooperators would emphasize creating the best possible deal. They would then look for a principle for dividing the benefits (the "pie") that both partners saw as fair, rather than trying to outfox their partner to get the lion's share.

In practice, cooperative and competitive approaches may be mixed or sequenced, depending on the setting, subject matter, and personalities of the negotiators. However, descriptions of cooperative and competitive styles, as well as distinctions between these two approaches, provide a framework for understanding the dynamics of negotiation.

Cooperative negotiation involves parties in an effort to jointly meet each other's needs and satisfy interests. In their best-selling book *Getting to Yes* (2011), Roger Fisher, William Ury, and Bruce Patton suggest that "you can change the game" so that negotiation need not be positional or competitive. They prescribe an interest-based approach with suggested tactics and the use of objective criteria for joint decisions, which they refer to as "principled" negotiation or "negotiation on the merits." *Getting to Yes* is recommended reading in many courses and training classes, so you may be familiar with it. The five basic elements of principled negotiation as listed by Fisher, Ury, and Patton are:

1. *Separate the people from the problem.* The negotiators should focus on attacking the problem posed by the negotiations, not each other.
2. *Focus on interests, not positions.* Distinguish positions, which are what you want, from interests, which are why you want them. Look for mutual or complementary interests that will make agreement possible.
3. *Invent options for mutual gain.* Even if the parties' interests differ, there might be bargaining outcomes that will advance the interests of both. There is a story of two sisters who are trying to decide which of them should get the only orange in the house. Once they realize that one sister wants to squeeze the orange for its juice, and the other wants to grate the rind to flavor a cake. A "win-win" agreement that furthers the interests of each becomes apparent.
4. *Insist on objective criteria.* Not all disputes and negotiations lend themselves to a "win-win" outcome. An insurance claim for damage to a car may create such a dispute, as each dollar paid by the insurance company to the claimant is one less dollar that it has. (Bargaining about issues of this nature is generally referred to as "zero-sum" bargaining.) Fisher, Ury, and Patton suggest that the parties first attempt to agree on objective criteria to determine the outcome. Thus, instead of negotiating over the value of a destroyed car, both parties might agree that the standard "blue book" price will determine the settlement amount. "Commit yourself to reaching a solution based on principle, not pressure."
5. *Know your Best Alternative to a Negotiated Agreement (BATNA).* The reason you negotiate with someone is to produce better results than you could obtain without negotiating. If you do not know the best result you are likely to obtain without negotiating, you might accept an offer that you should reject or you might reject an offer that is better than you can otherwise get. Your BATNA is the measure to decide if you are better off agreeing to a negotiated outcome or pursuing alternatives, whether it be a trial or a deal with someone else. Your BATNA is the basis of comparison to protect you from bad negotiating decisions and permits the exploration of imaginative solutions to satisfy your interests.

Note: Positions vs. Interests

The central theme of cooperative negotiation is that the negotiators focus on the parties' underlying interests rather than on the positions they take. Interest-based bargainers begin with the assumption that a party's position is simply one way (and often not the most efficient or effective one) to satisfy a need or interest. In most disputes parties have multiple interests of varying intensities. In Chapter 1 we looked at the triangle of conflict and presented the three components of satisfactory settlements as the three "Es": economic, emotional, and extrinsic. These relate to the interests that cooperative negotiators attempt to meet in working toward an integrative resolution. Similarly, *Getting to Yes* explains interests in terms of "basic human needs," including security, economic well-being, a sense of belonging, recognition, and control over one's life. These needs or interests can be further explained as follows:

- *Process interests.* People have a "process" interest in having disagreements resolved in a manner or process they consider fair. This usually includes the opportunity to tell their story and have the feeling that they have been understood. A cooperative negotiator will sometimes address an opponent's process interest by listening quietly while he vents angry emotions or accusations, then demonstrating, for example, by summarizing what has been said, that while the listener does not agree with what the speaker has said, he has heard and made an effort to understand it—so-called active listening ("So if I understand you correctly, you believe that . . ."). Participants may also have an interest in having a negotiation proceed in an orderly and predictable way.

- *Personal interests.* Most people have a personal interest in feeling respected in their work and as unique human beings, and in being seen as acting consistently with what they have said in the past and in accordance with their moral standards. Negotiators might address these personal interests by treating everyone courteously and attending to "face saving" needs.

- *Relational interests.* The parties might also have an interest in preserving or creating an ongoing relationship. This is particularly true in contractual disputes, because the very existence of a contract indicates that the parties once saw a benefit in working together, but it can also be true in disputes that arise from less formal connections. Examples of situations with relational interests include divorce and child custody disputes, land use controversies between neighbors, workplace disputes, and disagreements between companies and longtime customers.

- *Economic interests.* Disputants usually have economic or substantive interests. This is where most negotiations begin and where many end unsuccessfully because other interests are not addressed. Economic interests are most easy to state in the form of demands and offers, which are statements of positions. These positions may be misleading when viewed only in terms of dollars. People need money to satisfy other needs, whether material, social, or emotional. Finding out how the money will be used or what needs it will satisfy is essential to fashioning an interest-based agreement or integrative outcome.

Fisher, Ury, and Patton recognize that it is not always easy in negotiations to identify interests, as distinguished from positions. The technique they recommend is to ask "Why?" Why do you want a particular outcome, and why does the other side take the position it does? Do not ask the person with whom you are negotiating "Why?" to seek justification of his position or challenge it, "but for an understanding of the needs, hopes, fears, or desires that it serves." If you understand why the person wants what he is insisting upon, you can better explore how his interests can be met so you can get from him what you need.

---

2. Problem-Solving Approach

A variation of the cooperative approach, or perhaps another label for it, is *problem solving*. Problem-solving negotiators employ intensely cooperative, interest-based tactics. Problem solvers focus almost exclusively on finding solutions that will maximize the value of the deal for both parties. Problem solvers do not want to obtain a better outcome for their client at the expense of their counterpart and insist on using genuinely neutral principles to accomplish the task of allocating benefits. Negotiation is viewed as a collaboration to solve the challenge of finding opportunities for creating additional value through complementary interests. An early voice for the problem-solving approach to negotiation, Professor Carrie Menkel-Meadow, explains the process, beginning with interviewing your client to ascertain her interests and objectives.

❖ **Carrie Menkel-Meadow,** *Toward Another View of Legal Negotiation: The Structure of Problem Solving*

31 UCLA L. Rev. 754 (1984)

The Structure of Problem Solving

1. Identifying the Parties' Underlying Needs and Objectives

Unlike the adversarial model which makes assumptions about the parties' desires to maximize individual gain, problem solving begins by attempting to determine the actual needs of particular clients. The problem-solving model seeks to avoid a lawyer who acts for a hypothetical, rather than a real, client by creating a "standardized person to whom he attributes standardized ends."

Ascertaining the client's needs will, of course, begin with the initial interview. This is not the place to review the extensive interview literature, but in thinking ahead to the negotiation which might occur, a lawyer might begin by asking the client such general questions as "how would you like to see this all turn out?" or "what would you like to accomplish here?" before channeling the client's objectives in directions the lawyer knows are legally possible. The client may be the best source of ideas that go beyond what the court or the legal system might commonly permit. Once the client's ideas are brought to the surface, the lawyer can explore the needs they are meant to satisfy, and the legal and nonlegal consequences of these and other solutions.

Since so many legal problems are reduced to monetary solutions, consideration of the economic needs and objectives of the client faced with a dispute or transaction is a good place to begin. What are the monetary requirements now—compensation, return on investment, liquidity for payment? What might be the future monetary needs? What is the money needed for? Are any cheaper means available? Are there cash substitutes that are available and acceptable? What are the tax consequences of payment/receipt now? Later? What payment structure is desirable—lump sum, installments? Why? What are the transaction costs or solution costs of negotiation as opposed to litigation?

Next the lawyer might consider that with which is most familiar—the legal issues. What legal regulations govern the parties' situation? Must there be an admission of liability? Is a legal judgment necessary? Why? Is a formal document evidencing agreement desirable or required? What are the likely future legal consequences of actions taken? What are the parties likely to do if one of them breaches an agreement? What assets will be available in the future for legal action, if necessary?

The negotiator might consider how any solution affects the client's relationship to others. What are the social needs of the parties? How do others feel about this dispute or transaction? Will family members, friends, business associates, employers, employees be affected by actions taken by the parties? If not affected now, how will any of these people feel if things change in the future?

The negotiator might also ask the client to consider the personal feelings generated by the dispute or transaction. What are the psychological needs of the parties? Does one desire vindication, retribution, power? Why? What will be the long-term psychological consequences of satisfying or not satisfying these needs? How risk averse are the parties? What are their motivations for pursuing their aims in the negotiation? How might some of these feelings change if they forego litigation now or if they insist on obtaining some advantage?

Finally, the negotiator might also consider the ethical concerns of the parties. How fair do they desire to be with each other? What are the consequences of acting altruistically or dishonestly now? In the future? Will there be feelings of guilt later for "taking advantage" or the other side?

For each of these basic categories of needs the negotiator should also consider how the needs may change over the long run. There may be additional needs which the client has not articulated and which have as yet unrealized consequences. Frequently, some of the latent needs or concerns can be ascertained by simply following up a client's statement of need with an inquiry as to why that item or thing is desired. For each stated need, the lawyer should engage in a systematic inquiry into long and short run consequences and the latent concerns behind those which are manifest.

Ideally, this framework for determining the parties' needs must be considered from both parties' perspectives. At the very least, it should encourage lawyers and clients to consider whether all the potential needs presented by a negotiation have been canvassed. . . .

In negotiation, as in counseling, the lawyer should be certain that she acts with full knowledge of the client's desires. Within the suggested framework, the lawyer ranks the client's preferences in terms of what is important to the client rather than what the lawyer assumes about the "typical" client.

In order to engage in problem-solving negotiation the lawyer must first ascertain her clients' underlying needs or objectives. In addition, the lawyer may want to explore whether there are unstated objectives, pursue those which she thinks appropriate to the situation, or probe the legitimacy and propriety of particular goals. It should be noted, however, that the lawyer's role in exploring latent concerns or discussing the propriety of objectives can come dangerously close to the role of the lawyer in the adversarial model who imposes his own values or makes assumptions about what the client wants to accomplish. Finally, in order to pursue solutions that will be advantageous for both parties, the lawyer must ascertain the likely underlying needs and objectives of the other party. The client is a primary source for this information, but the lawyer should pursue other sources throughout the negotiation process.

2. Creating solutions

a. Meeting the Parties' Needs

Having identified the parties' needs one can begin the search for solutions with those that are suggested by the parties or that otherwise directly meet the parties' needs.

For example, in a personal injury case the injured plaintiff may have economic needs for compensation and rehabilitation costs that extend into the future. In such cases, structured settlements, paid over time, and according to a variety of formulas, may more closely meet the needs of the parties than a single lump sum payment. . . .

Regardless of how limited the possible solutions may appear to be, they are, in this context, far more likely to satisfy the parties and effectuate a more permanent agreement than would most results achieved in court or in adversarial negotiations. . . .

b. Expanding the Resources Available

Of course, the parties' needs will not be sufficiently complementary in all cases to permit direct solutions. Needs may conflict or there may be conflict over the material required to satisfy the needs. In addition to focusing on the parties' needs as a source of solutions, negotiators can attempt to expand the resources that the parties may eventually have to divide. In essence, this aspect of problem-solving negotiation seeks wherever possible to convert zero-sum games into non-zero-sum or positive-sum games. By expanding resources or the material available for division, more of the parties' total set of needs may be satisfied. Indeed, as the literature on legal transactions and the economic efficiency of such transactions makes clear, the parties come together to transact business precisely because their joint action is likely to increase the wealth available to both. To the extent that principles of wealth creation and resource expansion from transactional negotiation can be assimilated to dispute negotiation, the parties to a negotiation have the opportunity to help each other by looking for ways to expand what is available to them.

Various substantive strategies may increase the material available for distribution. Resources can be expanded by exploring what could be distributed, when it could be distributed, by whom it would be distributed, how it could be distributed and how much of it could be distributed. . . .

c. Just or Fair Solutions

For those who seek the most effective or efficient solutions from a utilitarian perspective, it is enough to settle at a point where no party can gain without hurting the other party. This is the best solution that can be reached when all preferences and needs are taken into account. But legal negotiations leave us with two special non-Pareto optimal problems. First, should the zealous advocate pursue a gain for his client that would cause a loss to the other side? Second, when might the negotiator choose to pursue less gain for his client or actually cause his client to suffer some loss so as to benefit or not hurt the other side? In some sense these questions are on opposite sides of the same coin. Without solving either definitively, the problem-solving model of negotiation may provide some avenues of inquiry.

In the first case the lawyer and client together can consider whether the pursuit of an additional gain at an equivalent or higher cost to the other side is likely to affect the result in an adverse way. The second party may be so hurt, angry or defeated that the solution will be difficult or more expensive to implement. Having answered the utilitarian question, the legal negotiator must then take into account the rules of her profession. . . .

Because problem-solving negotiations are likely to result in a greater number of potential solutions not contemplated in advance, the client in such negotiations is more likely to become involved in evaluating proposals. This will be particularly true where a client's objectives or needs may change over time, or need to be reevaluated as new proposals are forthcoming. Thus, the increased fluidity and emphasis on the parties' underlying interests may result in greater client involvement in the legal negotiation process. One of the key differences between the conventional adversarial model and the problem-solving model is the extent to which the parties and their lawyers engage in a continually interactive negotiation process, using the opportunity to seek new solutions rather than simply moving along a predetermined linear scale of compromise. . . .

Conclusion

This Article has outlined a systematic approach to legal negotiation premised on the notion that agreements will be more effective when the parties conceive of their purposes as solving the problem or planning the transaction, rather than winning or gaining unilateral advantage. The creative problem-solving approach outlined here depends on two structural components: (1) identifying the parties' underlying needs and objectives, and (2) crafting solutions, first by attempting to meet those needs directly, and second, by attempting to meet more of those needs through expanding the resources available. By utilizing such a framework for negotiations, the parties should recognize the synergistic advantage of such an approach over the adversarial and manipulative strategies of zero-sum negotiations. Parties should be able to achieve solutions to disputes that would not have been possible in court-ordered resolutions. . . .

The attraction of the problem-solving approach to negotiations is that it returns the solution of the problem to the client and forces the lawyer to perform her essential role in the legal system — that of solving problems. By using her professional expertise to canvas possible solutions to the problems and by constantly referring back to the client's real needs and objectives, the lawyer can make the negotiation process more responsive, while at the same time reducing the client's desire for potentially destructive unilateral victory. By utilizing a problem-solving approach the lawyer may be able to avoid the analog of iatrogenic illness, refusing to make worse or increase the costs of the legal problem by her intervention. The client will not, then, experience his dispute or transaction as getting worse simply because of his entrance into the legal system. . . .

Questions

10. In what ways does problem-solving negotiation differ from the cooperative techniques described in *Getting to Yes*?
11. Which of the differences you thought of are most likely to be of use in settling legal controversies?
12. Are particular skills required for problem-solving negotiation? Are these skills within the repertoire of most attorneys? Do you have these skills?
13. Do you agree that, "The attraction of the problem-solving approach to negotiations is that it returns the solution of the problem to the client"? Is this always desirable or wanted by the client? When might this not be an attraction?
14. Can problem-solving negotiation occur if only one side wants to pursue this approach? Please explain your answer.

The negotiation concepts popularized by *Getting to Yes*, whether referred to as cooperative or problem-solving, have been widely taught and very influential since the book first appeared in 1981. However, some experienced negotiators believe the underlying theory and tactics espoused by Fisher, Ury, and Patton are naive and adherents to this approach could be setting themselves up for failure. One frequently-cited critic is James White, a well-respected professor and longtime teacher of negotiation. Professor White's review, excerpted next, is followed by comments from Professor Fisher.

❖ **James J. White, *PROS AND CONS OF "GETTING TO YES"*; and Roger Fisher, *COMMENT ON WHITE'S REVIEW***

34 J. Legal Educ. 115 (1984)

Getting to Yes is a puzzling book. On the one hand it offers a forceful and persuasive criticism of much traditional negotiating behavior. It suggests a variety of negotiating techniques that are both clever and likely to facilitate effective negotiation. On the other hand, the authors seem to deny the existence of a significant part of the negotiation process, and to oversimplify or explain away many of the most troublesome problems inherent in the art and practice of negotiation. The book is frequently naive, occasionally self-righteous, but often helpful. . . .

Unfortunately the book's emphasis upon mutually profitable adjustment, on the "problem solving" aspect of bargaining, is also the book's weakness. It is a weakness because emphasis of this aspect of bargaining is done to almost total exclusion of the other aspect of bargaining, "distributional bargaining," where one for me is minus one for you. . . . [S]ome would describe a typical negotiation as one in which the parties initially begin by cooperative or efficiency bargaining in which each gains something with each new adjustment without the other losing any significant benefit. Eventually, however, one comes to bargaining in which added benefits to one impose corresponding significant costs on the other. . . .

One can concede the authors' thesis (that too many negotiators are incapable of engaging in problem solving or in finding adequate options for mutual gain), yet still maintain that the most demanding aspect of nearly every negotiation is the distributional one in which one seeks more at the expense of the other. My principal criticism of the book is that it seems to overlook the ultimate hard bargaining. Had the authors stated that they were dividing the negotiation process in two and were dealing with only part of it, that omission would be excusable. That is not what they have done. Rather they seem to assume that a clever negotiator can make any negotiation into problem solving. . . . To my mind this is naive. By so distorting reality, they detract from their powerful and central thesis.

Chapter 5, entitled "Insist on Objective Criteria," is a particularly naive misperception or rejection of the guts of distributive negotiation. Here, as elsewhere, the authors draw a stark distinction between a negotiator who simply takes a position without explanation and sticks to it as a matter of "will," and the negotiator who is reasonable and insists upon "objective criteria." Of course the world is hardly as simple as the authors suggest. Every party who takes a position will have some rationale for that position; every able negotiator rationalizes every position that he takes. Rarely will an effective negotiator simply assert "X" as his price and insist that the other party meet it.

The suggestion that one can find objective criteria (as opposed to persuasive rationalizations) seems quite inaccurate. . . . To say that there are objective criteria . . . in the case of a personal injury suit for a million dollars or an $800,000 judgment, is to ignore the true dynamics of the situation and to exaggerate the power of objective criteria. Any lawyer who has been involved in a personal injury suit will marvel at the capacity of an effective plaintiff's lawyer . . . to give the superficial appearance of certainty and objectivity to questions that are inherently imponderable. . . . Their suggestion that the parties look to objective criteria to strengthen their cases is a useful technique used by every able negotiator. Occasionally it may do what they suggest: give an obvious answer on which all can agree. Most of the time it will do no more than give the superficial appearance of reasonableness and honesty to one party's position. . . .

The author's consideration of "dirty tricks" in negotiation suffers from more of the same faults found in their treatment of objective criteria. At a superficial level I find their treatment of dirty tricks to be distasteful because it is so thoroughly self-righteous. The chapter is written as though there were one and only one definition of appropriate negotiating behavior. . . . The authors seem not to perceive that between "full disclosure" and "deliberate deception" lies a continuum, not a yawning chasm. They seem to ignore the fact that in one sense the negotiator's role is at least passively to mislead his opponent about his settling point while at the same time to engage in ethical behavior.

Finally, because the book almost totally disregards distributive bargaining, it necessarily ignores a large number of factors that probably have a significant impact on the outcome of negotiations. . . . There is evidence that the level of the first offer, and the pace and form of concessions all affect the outcome of negotiation, yet there is no consideration of those matters. Doubtless the authors can be forgiven for that. No book of 163 pages can be expected to deal with every aspect of negotiation. Yet this one suffers more than most, for implicitly if not explicitly, it seems to suggest that it is presenting the "true method." . . .

Comment by Roger Fisher

. . . White is more concerned with the way the world is, and I am more concerned with what intelligent people ought to do. One task is to teach the truth, to tell students the unpleasant facts of life, including how people typically negotiate. But I want a student to negotiate better than his or her father. I see my task as to give the best possible prescriptive advice, taking into account the way other human beings are likely to behave as well as one's own emotions and psychological state. . . .

The world is a rough place. It is also a place where, taken collectively, we are incompetent at resolving our differences in ways that efficiently and amicably serve our mutual interest. It is important that students learn about bluffing and hard bargaining, because they will certainly encounter it. It is also important that our students become more skillful and wise than most people in dealing with differences. Thus to some extent, White and I are emphasizing different aspects of what needs to be taught. . . .

The most fundamental difference between White's way of thinking and mine seems to concern the negotiation of distributional issues "where one for me is minus one for you." . . . By focusing on the substantive issues (where the parties' interests may be directly opposed), White overlooks the shared interest that the parties continue to have in the process for resolving that substantive difference. How to resolve the substantive difference is a shared problem. Both parties have an interest in identifying quickly and amicably a result acceptable to each, if one is possible. How to do so is a problem. A good solution to that process-problem requires joint action. . . .

The guts of the negotiation problem, in my view, is not who gets the last dollar, but what is the best process for resolving that issue. It is certainly a mistake to assume that the only process available for resolving distributional questions is hard bargaining over positions. In my judgment it is also a mistake to assume that such hard bargaining is the best process for resolving differences efficiently and in the long-term interest of either side. . . .

White seems to find the concept of "raw power" useful for a negotiator. I do not. For a negotiator, the critical questions of power are (1) how to enhance one's ability to influence favorably a negotiator on the other side, and (2) how to use such ability as one has. My ability to exert influence depends upon the cumulative impact of several factors: skill and knowledge, the state of our relationship, the legitimacy of our respective interests, the elegance of a proposed solution, my willingness and ability to commit myself, and the relative attractiveness to each side of its best alternative. In advance of a negotiation I can work to enhance each of those elements. . . .

Without knowing the particular subject matter of a negotiation or the identity of the people on the other side, what is the best advice one can give to a negotiator? People may prefer to ask different questions, but I have not yet heard better answers to the question on which we were and are working. . . .

Questions

15. Are you more persuaded by White or Fisher? Is Professor Fisher naive, or is Professor White too skeptical? Can they both be correct in some ways?

16. Have you experienced situations in which you were open and cooperative initially and then felt that you might have revealed too much or been too accommodating, so that you did not get what you wanted for yourself? If you were in that same situation again, would you behave differently? What are the trade-offs?

17. If a positional negotiator views the person across the table as an opponent, and if an adversarial bargainer views that person as an adversary, then what is the most apt designation for two people negotiating cooperatively?

18. Does an attorney's reputation for openness and cooperation present a particular attraction to a client willing to pay a premium for that attorney to engage in "hard bargaining" or sharp tactics on his behalf? (For an interesting real-life example, see David McKean and Douglas Frantz's *Friends in High Places: The Rise and Fall of Clark Clifford* (1995).)

19. Can "problem-solving" negotiation occur if only one side wants to pursue this approach?

C. Creating Value and Claiming Value—The Negotiator's Dilemma

The distributional bargaining to which Professors White and Fisher refer occurs when the issue being negotiated is singular or all apparent possibilities of joint gain have been exhausted. Negotiation by a tourist over the cash price of a single item from a transient merchant at a bazaar is a simple example of a zero-sum game, in which a dollar more for the seller is a dollar less for the purchaser and no future relationship is anticipated. Where the possibility exists to go beyond a zero-sum situation and create additional value, such as in the Microsoft-Stac dispute, a dilemma exists for negotiators between pursuing the cooperative moves to enhance the total value available jointly as envisioned by Fisher, and competitive behavior to individually claim increased value and gain an advantage. Understanding this dichotomy of opportunities and the choice it presents for negotiators creates a tension, because after value is created through cooperation and sharing information about interests, value claiming is likely to occur, and the information we shared could haunt us.

An influential book by David Lax and James Sebenius, introduced the "negotiator's dilemma," the tension that exists between the behaviors that tend to create value and those that individually claim the value that was jointly created. "Value creating and value claiming are linked parts of negotiation. Both processes are present. No matter how much creative problem solving enlarges the pie, it must still be divided; value that has been created must be claimed. . . . Moves to claim value . . . tend to drive out moves to create it. Yet, if both choose to claim value, by being dishonest or less than forthcoming about preferences, beliefs, or minimum requirements, they may miss mutually beneficial terms for agreement. Indeed, the structure of many bargaining situations suggests that negotiators will tend to leave joint gains on the table or even reach impasses when mutually acceptable agreements are available." (See Lax and Sebenius, *The Manager as Negotiator: Bargaining for Cooperation and Competitive Gain* (1986).)

Problem: Jack Sprat

Required for effective conflict settlement is neither cooperation nor competition, but what may be referred to as "enlightened self interest." By this I simply mean a variation on what several conflict theorists have previously described as an "individualistic orientation"—an outlook in which the disputant is simply interested in doing well for himself or herself, without regard for anyone else, out neither to help nor hinder the other's efforts to obtain his or her goal. The added word "enlightened" refers to the acknowledgment by each side that the other is also likely to be pursuing a path of self interest—and that it may be possible for both to do well in the exchange. . . . I do not have to like or trust you in order to negotiate wisely with you. Nor do I have to be driven by the passion of a competitive desire to beat you. All that is necessary is for me to find some way of getting what I want—perhaps even more than I considered possible—by leaving the door open for you too to do well. "Trust" and "trustworthiness," concepts central to the development of cooperation, are no longer necessary—only the understanding of what the other person may want or need.

A number of anecdotes have emerged to make this point. . . . Jack Sprat and his wife—one preferring lean, the other fat—can lick the platter clean if they understand their respective interests. The interesting thing about this conjugal pair is that, married though they may be, when it comes to dining preferences they are hardly interdependent at all. For Jack and his wife to "lick the platter clean" requires neither that the two love each other nor care about helping each other in every way possible; nor does it require that each be determined to get more of the platter's contents than the other. Instead, it is enlightened self interest that makes possible an optimal solution to the problem of resource distribution. . . ." (Jeffrey Rubin, *Some Wise and Mistaken Assumptions about Conflict and Negotiation* (1991).)

Can you distinguish Rubin's "*individualistic orientation*" of enlightened self-interest from greed? Is the message of the Jack Sprat parable different from the story of Gordon Gekko, a fictional character in the 1987 film, "Wall Street," and its 2010 sequel, "Wall Street: Money Never Sleeps"? (Gekko was portrayed by actor Michael Douglas, whose performance in the first film won him an Academy Award for Best Actor.) In "Wall Street," Gekko famously states, "Greed, for lack of a better word, is good. Greed is right. Greed works. Greed clarifies, cuts through, and captures, the essence of the evolutionary spirit. Greed, in all of its forms; greed for life, for money, for love, knowledge, has marked the upward surge of mankind. . . ." Was Gordon Gekko right?

Differences Can Create Joint Gains

In an article published in 2002 (19 Negotiation J. 5-28), Lax and Sebenius explain the differences that can lead to joint gains and creation of value. These differences can be summarized as follows:

- Differences in relative valuation, priorities, or taste can lead to exchanges, directly or by "unbundling" differently valued interests. Because I prefer dark chocolate to milk chocolate and you don't, we can profitably trade and create value.
- Differences in tolerance for risk and *risk aversion* suggest insurance-like risk-sharing arrangements in negotiated transactions. A risk-averse litigant may be willing to discount what she will receive or pay more as a certain amount rather than bear the risk of losing at trial. If the opposing side is more risk tolerant, they can be rewarded by paying less or receiving more because they are not so averse to the risk of trial.
- Differences in *time preference* can lead to altered patterns of payments or actions over time. If a claimant needs money immediately and a defendant has a reserve set aside for settlement of the claim, a quick payment can create value for both sides and enhance the chance of an agreement.
- Different *capabilities* can be combined. Companies with complementary capabilities can negotiate deals and mergers to create value that neither could achieve alone. For example, a company with strong production capacity can combine forces with a company that has sophisticated marketing and distribution abilities to collectively enhance profitability and create value between them.
- Differences in *cost/revenue structure* can create cost saving trades. For example, if a butcher, who gets meat wholesale, can trade meat with a shoe merchant, who gets shoes wholesale, they have created value for themselves by each getting what would not otherwise be available to them at wholesale cost.
- Differences in *forecasts* can lead to contingent agreements when the items under negotiation are uncertain and themselves subject to different probability estimates, or when each party feels that it will fare well under, and perhaps can influence, a proposed contingent resolution procedure. In a negotiation over executive compensation where the prospective executive has a more optimistic view of her abilities to produce revenue than does the company, she may agree to a lower salary with a higher bonus contingent on revenue increases. Both negotiating sides may feel better off because they have structured an employment deal based on their own forecasts and have, in effect, created value for themselves.
- Other differences (evaluation criteria, the importance of precedent, the value of personal reputation, constituency attitudes, the organizational situation, conceptions of fairness, and so on) can also be fashioned into joint gains. The authors offer as an example a law firm being threatened with a suit for sexual harassment by a former clerk who may be willing to settle a claim for much more if it is cast as payment for wrongful termination.

You will note that we have come full circle in connecting the cause of conflict—different perceptions that are all in our heads—to a suggested approach for constructively resolving conflicts by trading on these differences and, thus, transcending the choice of being competitive or cooperative. This understanding of different perceptions and how perceptions shape individual needs to allow for mutual gain may explain the difference between "enlightened self-interest" and "greed," or it may lead you to think that Gordon Gekko was right in stating that greed is good.

CHAPTER
4

Selecting a Negotiation Style
and Combining Approaches

As you read about different approaches to negotiation, you may be thinking about whether you will be most effective and comfortable choosing a more competitive or cooperative approach. Your answer will depend on your assessment of which style will work best, your personality, values, the situation, the needs and wishes of your client, as well as the way the other side negotiates.

A. Effectiveness and Style

Because negotiation is usually conducted in private and accompanied by confidentiality, there is little opportunity to compare results. How lawyers behave in negotiation and what they do is not fully known. Lawyers' accounts of negotiations are filtered through the lens of the tellers' perceptions. Unless negotiations can be systematically observed on a grand scale, we will never know what really works best to produce desired negotiated outcomes. Few lawyers ever "lose" a negotiation, or tell about it if they believe they did not do well. Spoken and written "war stories" of successful negotiations are not reliable descriptions of what typically occurs, or even of what occurred in the reported negotiation. (There do not appear to be any books on "How I Failed as a Negotiator.") Obstacles to the study and profiling of negotiations leave new lawyers little reliable guidance on what is successful in negotiation and how to weigh the polar tensions they may feel between competition and cooperation to negotiate effectively within their comfort zone.

Two studies help fill the void of information about how lawyers negotiate and which negotiation styles are effective. Both studies are necessarily limited because they rely on attorneys' responses to questionnaires and their reports of whether their opponents in recent negotiations were competitive or cooperative and if they were effective or ineffective negotiators. Nonetheless, both studies provide sources of information about how lawyers negotiate and what is considered effective, as well as ineffective, negotiation behavior.

Professor Gerald Williams conducted a study in 1976 on lawyer negotiation styles by surveying 1,000 lawyers in the Phoenix area, asking about their most recent negotiation experience. These lawyers were asked to categorize their negotiation counterparts on a scale of competitive to cooperate and then to assess their counterpart's effectiveness by choosing effective, average, or ineffective. Almost two-thirds of lawyers were classified by their counterparts as cooperative, one quarter as competitive and 11 percent were unclassified. Twenty-five percent of competitive negotiators were considered effective by their peers. Close to 60 percent of cooperative negotiators were considered effective. (See Williams, *Legal Negotiation and Settlement* (1983).)

Professor Andrea Schneider replicated Professor Williams study in 1999 with attorneys in Milwaukee and Chicago. She reported that 64 percent were classified as cooperative and 36 percent as competitive. Fifty-four percent of the cooperative attorneys were considered effective negotiators and only 9 percent of the competitive attorneys were considered effective negotiators in Professor Schneider's study. Although the studies were not identical, they are close enough to provide an interesting comparison about changes over time and perhaps differences between urban areas regarding how attorneys negotiate (Schneider, "Perception, Reputation and Reality: An Empirical Study of Negotiation Skills," 6 Disp. Resol. Mag. 24, Summer 2000).

The news from the studies is both good and bad. First the good news: For students struggling with deciding on their negotiation comfort zone, and not knowing if what they are inclined to do is the right way to negotiate, the studies show that there is no one right way to negotiate. Both competitive and cooperative styles can be effective approaches to negotiation if done well and with integrity. Being an effective competitive negotiator does not require the use of tricks or deceit. Some competitive techniques can be legitimate ways to pursue negotiation goals, provided they are not carried to extremes. Being a cooperative negotiator need not be based on naiveté or on being a pushover. Cooperative attorneys, who appear from the studies to predominate in numbers and perceived effectiveness, are most successful when they are mindful of the interests they are pursuing and set limits on their cooperation.

The studies indicate that the percentage of adversarial attorneys who are considered effective was greater in Williams's study, 25 percent in his compared with 9 percent in Schneider's. The rating of cooperative negotiators as more effective than adversarial negotiators was larger in Schneider's later sampling. Again, it should be noted that some adversarial attorneys are rated as effective, but in a much lower proportion. Some admirable behaviors of negotiators—like preparation, a focus on the client's interests, and high ethical standards—were shared by effective competitive and effective cooperative attorney-negotiators in both studies.

The bad news is that the more recent study reported that adversarial negotiators are becoming more extreme and unpleasant. The terms most frequently used to describe them are more negative than 20 years earlier. If the reports are accurate, this might not bode well for the legal profession or for clients because adversarial negotiators as a whole appear to be less effective negotiators than previously reported. Professor Schneider provides more detail about her study and a more extensive analysis in *Shattering Negotiation Myths: Empirical Evidence on the Effectiveness of Negotiation Style* (2002).

Questions

1. What do you think accounts for the finding that adversarial negotiators are growing more extreme and negative and that, overall, fewer lawyers are viewed as effective by their peers?
2. Professor Schneider's respondents were over 30 percent women, compared to only 3 percent women in Professor Williams's original study. Do you believe this difference may account for any of the different results?
3. A negotiator who believes and lives by highly competitive values may nevertheless manifest personal empathy, concern, friendliness, and warmth, and may appear to engage in problem-solving behavior. These characteristics can build trust for purposes of maximizing individual gain. Because both studies depended on assessments by opposing lawyers, is it possible that they underreported effective adversarial negotiators who were so successful that they induced opponents to see them as cooperative or problem solving when, in fact, they were not?
4. Have you known anyone who exuded a style you thought to be cooperative, but turned out to be highly competitive or to have masked her purpose, like a wolf in sheep's clothing? Have you ever tried this?

One problem with labeling negotiation styles is that categorization is based on perception. You know perception can be manipulated. A really effective competitive/adversarial negotiator can present a demeanor of cooperation. Friendly sales techniques can be mastered by competitive negotiators intent on getting what they want and closing a deal more favorable to them than you will ever know. The next reading discusses this possibility and further analyzes the Williams and Schneider studies.

❖ **Charles B. Craver,** *THE INHERENT TENSION BETWEEN VALUE CREATION AND VALUE CLAIMING DURING BARGAINING INTERACTIONS*

101 Cordozo J. of Conflict Resolution 2010

The studies conducted by Williams and Schneider suggest that most effective negotiators employ a Cooperative/Problem-Solving style which generates complete openness and an effort to maximize the joint returns obtained by the parties. Nonetheless, when their findings are examined more closely, it becomes clear that many effective negotiators are actually wolves in sheep clothing. Williams and Schneider asked the effective bargainers from both groups to disclose their primary objectives in their interactions with others. The primary goal for effective Competitive/Adversarials was to maximize their *own returns*, which is the classic objective of competitive negotiators. When effective Cooperative/Problem-Solvers were also questioned about their main objectives, they indicated that their second objective—just behind a wish to maintain high ethical standards—was the maximization of their *own side's returns*. A more comprehensive evaluation of these factors has caused Professor Williams and myself to conclude that there is a hybrid negotiating style that falls between the Cooperative/Problem-Solving and Competitive/Adversarial approaches and combines the optimal characteristics of both.

Competitive/Problem-Solvers are individuals who strive for *competitive* objectives—maximization of their own side's returns—but work to accomplish this goal in a *non-adversarial way*. Once they obtain most of what they hope to achieve for their own clients, they work to maximize the returns attained by their opponents.

These individuals are more open than Competitive/Adversarials, but less forthcoming than conventional Cooperative/Problem-Solvers. They generally disclose the terms they hope to obtain, knowing that such disclosures are important if jointly efficient accords are to be achieved, but they over- and under-state the degree to which their clients want those items for strategic purposes.

When Competitive/Problem-Solvers negotiate with naive Co-operative/Problem-Solvers, they work to exploit their opponent's openness. They actually endeavor to *create value* during the Information Stage in the *Getting to Yes* tradition, but they are not entirely forthcoming. They may over-or under-state the value of items they desire to subsequently enable them to obtain more highly valued terms for less; this may also enable them to attain more from opponents when they concede issues that side values but erroneously thinks this side also considers important. As the parties move into the Distributive Stage, they similarly employ subtle, manipulative tactics in order to enable them to *claim* more of the joint surplus than they give to their opponents. . . . [E]ven within the range of circumstances in which there are significant opportunities for integrative bargaining, the bargainer must almost always engage in distributive bargaining as well. Therefore, it is in the bargainer's self-interest not just to adopt the tactics of openness and truth telling that are said to be appropriate to integrative bargaining, but somehow also to adopt the tactics of truth-hiding and dissimulation that are said to be appropriate to distributive bargaining.

Unsuspecting negotiators do not understand how manipulative and disingenuous Competitive/Problem-Solvers can be. As a result of the apparent openness of Competitive/Problem-Solvers, their opponents usually think they are Cooperative/Problem-Solvers. Since negotiators often believe these individuals are being entirely candid, they volunteer their own confidential bargaining information without realizing that their openness is not being equally reciprocated. They are certain that these persons are working to generate "win-win" results, when they are really endeavoring to obtain "WIN-win" distributions favoring their own side. . . .

The findings by Professors Williams and Schneider strongly indicate that many lawyers who appear to follow the Cooperative/Problem-Solving approach may subtly employ Competitive/Adversarial techniques to advance their interests. Although they do not commence bargaining interactions with the more extreme positions articulated by classic Competitive/Adversarials, they do not open with the truly reasonable positions taken by real Cooperative/ Problem-Solvers. They instead start with partially overstated demands or under-stated offers, hoping to establish beneficial anchoring points. They usually acknowledge their actual objectives, but frequently over-or under-state the degree to which they desire those items. They do a good job of *creating value* by getting the underlying interests of both sides on the bargaining table. Once that is accomplished, however, they cleverly use manipulative tactics that enable them to *claim* more than their fair share of the joint surplus.

Competitive/Problem-Solvers are successful, because they recognize the fact that most negotiators judge their satisfaction with bargaining outcomes more by the degree to which they believe the *process* was fair and respectful than by the objective value of the terms obtained. Competitive/Problem-Solver negotiators are personable and respectful. They avoid overtly competitive behavior, and act as if they are Cooperative/Problem-Solvers. Their adversaries are so appreciative of their seemingly open and courteous conduct that they over-value the actual worth of the terms they obtain.

During the value creation portion of bargaining interactions, Competitive/Problem-Solvers learn more about opponent values and interests than they disclose with respect to their own values and interests. This provides them with a significant advantage once the parties begin to divide the joint surplus which has been created. Through the use of subtle distributive techniques, they are able to claim more of the surplus than their unsuspecting opponents ever imagine. . . .

After negotiators use the Information Stage to determine the divisible items and an approximate understanding of the relative degree to which each side values the different terms, they enter the Distributive Stage during which they endeavor to achieve a mutual accord. This is a highly competitive part of the bargaining process, because no clear principles dictate the manner in which the joint surplus should be divided. Should the discovered surplus be divided equally or equitably? If the participants possess identical bargaining power and equal bargaining proficiency, a relatively equal sharing of the surplus might be appropriate. The difficulty concerns the fact that opponents are rarely situated so equally. One side tends to possess more economic power than the other and/ or greater bargaining skill. In such circumstances, a truly egalitarian distribution would be a windfall to the weaker or less adroit participant.

Despite the objections of some theoretical academics, most practicing attorneys would suggest an equitable division of the pertinent items that reflects the comparative power and negotiating prowess of the interactants. Even this objective is not easily attainable, due to the use of disingenuous tactics designed to enable the more manipulative participant to claim an excessive share of the joint surplus. She may establish an artificial deadline to induce a more risk averse opponent to cave in to her demands. She may employ real or feigned threats of litigation or a cessation of talks to generate excessive opponent concessions. She may imply that she has other options she could accept if this party does not provide her side with sufficiently generous terms. . . .

During the Distributive Stage, most legal and commercial negotiators use implied or overt threats, time pressure, and various manipulative bargaining tactics to obtain more favorable terms for their own side than they might objectively deserve. I see this demonstrated regularly by students in my Legal Negotiation course and in the continuing legal education programs I conduct for state bar associations and for specific law firms. The results achieved on the distributive terms of my practice exercises vary widely. I have one exercise where the monetary payments range from $250,000 to over $2 million. I have another where the monetary range is from $0 to over $250,000.

Before readers surmise that the existence of significant differences with respect to these distributive terms means that the participants have achieved inefficient accords, I must note that my law students learn how to fight over the distributive items while they simultaneously work to achieve efficient distributions of the cooperative terms. This is true whether the negotiators are particularly cooperative or competitive. The naturally cooperative interactants strive for efficient and fair terms, while the naturally competitive individuals seek efficient, but more one-sided arrangements. Even the competitive persons realize, however, that if they are inefficient with respect to the cooperative terms, they will be less likely to obtain as much of the distributive issues. They thus work diligently to ascertain the non-distributive needs of their opponents and to satisfy those desires. They do not do this because of altruistic considerations. They instead appreciate the fact that if they provide their adversaries with what those parties require in these areas, it will be easier for them to obtain more of the distributive surplus which has been created. Although my student agreements vary widely with respect to the distributive terms agreed upon, I am amazed by their ability to divide the cooperative items in a way that generates the most joint surplus. This is a practice legal representatives should always follow if they hope to achieve fair — or even unbalanced — final terms.

An empirical study conducted by Professors Kathleen O'Connor and Peter Carnevale supports my observations with respect to my Legal Negotiation students. Their study concerned "common-value issues" that both sides wished to have resolved in the same fashion even though they were not aware of their positional overlap. Some of the bargaining pairs were entirely open and cooperative with respect to their interests, while other dyads included negotiators who could be disingenuous with respect to their true interests. O'Connor and Carnevale found that the individualistically motivated pairs achieved higher joint outcomes than the cooperatively motivated pairs. This was apparently due to the fact that individualistically motivated negotiators established higher overall objectives for themselves than did the cooperatively motivated participants, and the individualistically motivated per- sons recognized that by generating the most efficient overall agreements, they increased their chances of obtaining optimal results for themselves.

Once negotiating parties have achieved agreements, how can they be certain they have generated efficient accords? The best way is to move into the Cooperative Stage before they conclude their interactions. Prior to the time they enter this stage, however, they should be certain they have reached definitive accords. They should review the different provisions agreed upon to be sure there are no misunderstandings. Near the conclusion of the Distributive Stage, negotiating parties frequently move expeditiously to close the remaining gaps. One side may have thought the other side was conceding more than it intended or took something off the table it did not mean to eliminate. If they discover such misunderstandings now, they are psychologically committed to an agreement and will usually find a way to resolve their remaining differences. On the other hand, if they fail to discern such gaps until one side drafts the accord, there are likely to be claims of dishonesty and recriminations.

Once the basic terms have been agreed upon and confirmed, the participants should take a few minutes to see if there is any way they can further expand the overall pie and simultaneously improve their respective positions. During both the Information Stage and the Distributive Stage, most parties have over and understated the actual value of various items for strategic purposes. As a result, Side A may have obtained several provisions Side B values more highly, while Side B got some terms Side A values more. If they can discover these inefficiencies and exchange these items, both sides should be able to improve their respective situations.

During this portion of their interaction, negotiators should look for terms they suspect may have ended up on the wrong side of the bargaining table. They should consider issues they over-stated their own interest in due to the fact they thought the other side wanted them more. They should ask the opposing side if they were to concede these items, what could that side give to them. Only when it seems impossible for one side to obtain further gains without actual losses by the opposing party should the participants consider their terms final.

When negotiators explore possible exchanges during the Co-operative Stage, they should be careful not to indicate such prior deception with respect to their true values, or they risk undermining the terms already agreed upon. If their opponents begin to suspect that they misrepresented many of their interests during the earlier discussions, they may begin to think that they have been excessively dishonest. As a result, their adversaries may begin to reopen many terms and possibly destroy the opportunity for a final accord.

Conclusion

Many practitioners assume that opponents are either Cooperative/Problem-Solvers who are open, trusting, and wish to generate fair and efficient agreements, or Competitive/Adversarial who are closed, manipulative, and hope to achieve one-sided agreements favoring their own side. In reality, however, many proficient negotiators are Competitive/Problem-Solvers who work to achieve efficient accords, but who employ subtle distributive tactics designed to enable them to claim more of the joint surplus created. As a result, there is an inherent tension between *value creation* and *value claiming* in most legal negotiations.

During the value creation portion of interactions, participants should use the Information Stage to determine the pertinent items and the relative values placed on those terms by the different parties. Negotiators must be willing to indicate what they actually hope to obtain and the general degree to which they value those terms. Nonetheless, Competitive/Problem-Solvers are likely to over or understate the degree to which their clients want particular items to enable them to obtain a strategic advantage over naively open opponents.

Once negotiators have ascertained the various issues to be re-solved, they have to use the Distributive Stage to decide how they will divide those items, which tends to be the most competitive portion of bargaining interactions. Individuals should not assume that their adversaries are altruistic persons who want to divide the items fairly. Most legal representatives will endeavor to claim more of the jointly created surplus for their own clients, and persons who fail to appreciate this reality are likely to end up with less when the interaction is concluded.

B. Negotiating Within Your Comfort Zone

Choosing to be cooperative, problem solving, competitive, or adversarial is, at least in part, dependent on:

- The subject and nature of the negotiation
- The interrelation between issues
- The past or anticipated future relationship between the parties and between the attorneys
- Your counterpart's negotiation approach
- The customs and conventions where the negotiation occurs
- The amount of time available
- The amount at stake

Each of these factors may influence your approach to negotiation. The biggest factor, however, is your own comfort zone, formed by your personality and values. To the extent that how you negotiate is driven by personality and values, it may be better described as a matter of style rather than approach. Behavioral style is in large part a function of who you are. Choosing a style that does not fit your personality and values, if not a recipe for failure, is likely to make your work as a negotiator difficult and dissatisfying. To succeed as a professional and find satisfaction in what you are doing, you must negotiate within your personal comfort zone.

Defining our negotiating comfort zone is not always an easy task. It is a common desire to be liked rather than disliked. We know that we are more likely to be liked when we are cooperative and giving than when we are adversarial and taking. We also know that winners are admired, and we want to be respected for vigorously representing our clients' interests and succeeding when we negotiate on their behalf. Law students without legal experience may share the view of attorneys popularized in movies and television series as hard-charging and aggressive. Students may extrapolate from the highly adversarial scenes popularly portrayed in dramatized jury trials to all opposing lawyer interactions. As a result, many students have a latent fear that their preference for cooperation and friendliness will not serve them or their clients well in negotiation.

Other students may have thrived on competition and winning in sports and other contests. We know that law students are a self-selected group of achievers who have succeeded, at least academically, and made it into law school through a competitive admissions process. Competition appears to be encouraged by the legal system, where cooperation and generosity may be viewed as a virtuous but less-valued quality. So it is understandable that some students are conflicted about whether negotiation should be approached as a professional game in which their competitive qualities are let loose and rewarded with success.

Those of you who have enjoyed competition know from your experience that good competitors can be friendly, gracious, and ethical. Similarly, not all competitive negotiators manifest an adversarial persona. A pleasant and respectful personal style is not necessarily inconsistent with competitive negotiation, any more than being cordial in competitive sports is inconsistent with wanting to win. The style you choose in negotiation may depend on how you define the "game" and the relationship you want with your counterpart in the negotiation.

Your negotiation style may also depend in large measure on your ingrained personality pattern. If personality patterns drive how we and others approach negotiation, can we discern those patterns in ourselves and others, and how can we benefit from the information?

Because personality does matter in how we interact with others, how we deal with conflict, and how we negotiate, researchers have attempted to test and measure personality traits that influence these functions. The *Thomas-Kilmann Conflict Mode Instrument* is a tested method available to assess one's tendencies as a negotiator and is administered in some law school negotiation courses. This widely used personality instrument measures five dimensions of how individuals deal with conflict and negotiation to determine their degree of assertiveness and/or cooperation. The Thomas-Kilmann "test" asks for responses to 30 statements (for example, "I feel that differences are not always worth worrying about" or "I make some effort to get my way") and respondents self-score their answers. The results give respondents a profile of how strongly they score in all five categories: competitor, accommodator (sometimes also called cooperator), avoider, compromiser, and collaborator (sometimes called problem solver).

One of the strengths of the instrument is that it provides relative scores rather than a simple yes-no or categorical placement: When you take the test, you receive a score along a continuum from very high to very low as a Competitor, for instance. Respondents receive scores in all five categories. This provides a nuanced portrait as a composite of several, sometimes conflicting, tendencies. Each of the Thomas-Kilmann conflict management categories has advantages and disadvantages in negotiation (See R. Mnookin, S. Peppet, and A. Tulumello, "Negotiator's Empathy and Assertiveness," 14 Alternatives 133 (1996).)

The five categories of conflict management styles are:

- *Competing*—high on assertiveness and low on cooperation
- *Accommodating*—low on assertiveness and high on cooperation
- *Avoiding*—low on assertiveness and cooperation
- *Compromising*—moderate on assertiveness and cooperation
- *Collaborating*—high on assertiveness and cooperation

Another personality test is the *five-factor model* of personality, also known as the "Big Five" taxonomy. This test is used extensively in experimental psychology to determine the five major categories describing broad personality traits, and it has been applied to negotiation outcomes. (See B. Barry and R. Friedman, *Bargainer Characteristics in Distributive and Integrative Negotiation*, 74 J. Personality & Soc. Psychol. 345 (1998).) The five factors that comprise the test are:

- *Extroversion*—sociable, assertive, and talkative
- *Agreeableness*—flexible, cooperative, and trusting
- *Conscientiousness*—responsible, organized, and achievement oriented
- *Emotional stability*—secure and confident
- *Openness*—imaginative, broad-minded, and curious

The best-known and most widely referred to personality test is the *Myers-Briggs Type Indicator.* You may have taken this test. It is administered over 2 million times a year by large companies, the U.S. government, and academic institutions. It is the subject of countless research studies and articles, including ones that analyze the impact of personality variables on negotiation. (See D. Peters, "Forever Jung: Psychological Type Theory, The Myers-Briggs Type Indicator and Learning Negotiation," 42 Drake L. Rev. 1 (1993).) Myers-Briggs measures four sets of contrasting personality dimensions:

- *Introverted* or *extroverted*
- *Sensing* or *intuitive*
- *Thinking* or *feeling*
- *Perceiving* or *judging*

There is now considerable literature on the role of personality in negotiation styles and outcomes, based on studies of personality test results and experimental research. However, the utility of this literature for instructional purposes is limited because of the lack of consensus among the studies and the limitations of their methodology. The following reading recognizes those limitations, but offers answers to the questions most often asked about personality and negotiation.

❖ **Sheila Heen & John Richardson, "*I See a Pattern Here and the Pattern Is You*": *Personality and Dispute Resolution***

The Handbook of Dispute Resolution 202
(M.L. Moffitt & R.C. Bordone eds., 2005)

Anyone who has more than one child knows that differences in personality are real. The first born may be quiet, eager to please, and shy in new situations. His sister comes along and is an extrovert—smiling early and befriending strangers as a toddler. These traits may remain constant throughout life as the first-born becomes a writer and his sister makes friends easily and often as a college student, professional, and retiree.

Intuitively, we know that there are differences between individuals. Your spouse is agreeable, your brother irascible, your coworker weepy, and your neighbor hyperrational.

The hard question is this: are there ways to describe the differences in people's personalities that can be useful in conducting and advising negotiations? After all, negotiation is all about dealing with people, getting along with them, and persuading them. Shouldn't knowing how people are different (and what to do about it) be an integral part of negotiation theory and strategy?

One would think so. And yet, the intersection of dispute resolution and personality is a tangle of confusion and contradiction. It is not unexplored territory—scholars have tried to find answers. And it is interesting—there is fascinating work going on and much speculation about what is being learned. Yet there are few clear, satisfying answers to questions that interest dispute resolution professionals most: Are particular personalities better negotiators? Should I negotiate differently with different personalities? And what about when the people and their problematic personalities really are the problem?

[After reviewing the most widely used personality tests, their limitations, and the literature about the reported results, the authors list and answer six questions asked about personality and negotiation.]

1. *Is there really such a thing as personality differences?*

It certainly seems so. Whether hard wired by genes or chemical mix, prompted by experience or influenced by the context, two people in a similar situation will often respond differently. This may be particularly so in the pressurized context of a dispute.

Personality researchers attempt to identify and isolate traits that are consistent across situations and different between individuals. This is where things get tricky. Human beings are complex enough, and adaptable enough, that defining and tracking traits, particularly through the dynamic process of negotiation, has proven very difficult.

2. *Or are there particular personality traits that give better outcomes?*

With the exception of cognitive ability (more is better), there is no strong answer in the current research. Although you can find small-scale studies suggesting this or that trait is helpful, you can also find studies that say it does not improve outcomes.

3. *Okay, so should I negotiate differently with different personality types?*

The biggest obstacle to setting your negotiation strategy based on the other person's personality is figuring out what it is. Because people act differently in different situations, researchers have found that people consistently misperceive the personality traits of those with whom they negotiate or are in dispute.

The best advice is to be aware of your own tendencies, have a broad repertoire of approaches and strategies, and be able to engage difficulties constructively as they come up. Pay attention to particular behavior you see, rather than trying to globalize how the other person "is." And if one approach doesn't seem to be working, try another.

4. *Isn't it true that some disputes are hopeless because people's personalities just aren't going to change?*

It is certainly true that there are limits to what can change, and that some differences between people are harder to reconcile than others. And there are definitely limits to *your ability to change the other person's personality.*

Yet the impulse to throw up our hands and attribute the problem to the other person's personality flaws is a dangerous one. It blames the other person for the dispute, blinding us to our own contributions to the problem. It may also encourage us to give up on a relationship or dispute too easily or too quickly, when finding a way to work together with less frustration remains possible.

In addition, there are at least three paths forward that personality finger-pointing ignores. Remember that human beings' *behavior* can often change without a grand *personality* change. You might shift the context — offering a private caucus or written channel of communication, for example. You can try to influence the other person's behavior by influencing the story he or she tells about what's going on. Or you might try changing your contribution to the dynamic between you. The other person is reacting both to you and to his or her own experiences, tendencies, and stories, and that's a complex enough set of factors to suggest that progress is possible.

Finally, do not underestimate people's ability to change over time. As a person ages, encounters different life experiences, and makes the transition to new phases in life (where he or she may feel more secure or happier, or have more room for reflection for example), his or her traits and tendencies evolve. You may find that your personality gradually moves into a different era, one you would not have predicted from where you stand now.

5. *Why is personality profiling so popular, if it's so inconclusive?*

People love to talk about themselves. And they especially love to talk about other people. Personality profiling also fits our interest in simplifying the world and the infinitely complex relationships in it. Researchers have long documented the effects of the fundamental attribution error, where we believe we know why people act the way they do, and tend to attribute especially bad behavior to their problematic personality.

People are so complicated that we can't really describe them with few enough variables to meet our needs for parsimony. People can only keep about seven items in their head at one time, before they go into cognitive overload. So they make up something that they can handle in their heads, whether or not it is accurate.

6. *So why pay attention to personality at all?*

The fields of personality and negotiation are both relatively young. Our ability to map interaction in negotiation and dispute resolution, and to recommend paths of influence, is in its infancy. And our ability to isolate traits and trace them through complex interaction is still maturing.

Still, familiarity with common differences between individuals is useful. It reminds us that not every approach to influence works with every person. It can help us generate diagnostic hypotheses about why a negotiation is in trouble ("Ah! We may proceed to closure at different paces"), and come up with prescriptive advice to try out. It may also help us be more forgiving of others' seemingly crazy behavior if we can spot it as a difference in the way the two of us see and respond to the world.

Familiarity with personality differences can also be a self-reflection and coaching tool for yourself. It can help you identify and work on behavior that doesn't come naturally to you. It can also help you explain your behavior to others: "I've learned that I'm not very comfortable making commitments before I have a chance to think things through. Can you give me the weekend and we'll nail this down on Monday?" Becoming familiar with some of the traits that affect your ability to mediate, negotiate, or respond well to disputes can help you become more aware of the situations that bring out these traits, and other choices you might make.

Questions

5. Are the style categories and personality dimensions used by the three test instruments just different ways to label the same personality traits, or do they really measure different aspects of personality?
6. After 17 years or more as a student and as an experienced test taker, if your negotiation course readings and class discussion gave you the impression that your instructor valued collaboration more than avoidance or competition, do you think your responses to the 30 statements

on the Thomas-Kilmann test (e.g., "I feel that differences are not always worth worrying about" or "I make some effort to get my way") might be influenced by the instructor's values or not provide a totally accurate measure of your conflict style?

7. Given that all three of the personality tests described above rely on self-assessment, do you think the results are likely to match the assessment of your personality by opponents, family, friends, and colleagues?

8. Do you feel that personality testing is helpful as an aid to better understand and improve how you negotiate? Does your answer depend on your view of whether personality traits and behavior can be altered?

9. Do you consciously take stock of the personality type of your counterparts when negotiating? Are there ways you can find out about their personalities before engaging with them?

Problem

You are planning to buy a new car upon graduation. You are living in a metropolitan area and have many dealers to choose from. You plan to have your local mechanic service the vehicle and don't expect problems with it (if you did, you would look to the manufacturer), so you don't expect to see the dealer much after the sale. You are preoccupied with the bar exam and don't want to do the bargaining yourself. Luckily you have the option of asking either of two relatives to serve as your negotiator in this transaction. Your sister Jill is an avid shopper, who enjoys the give and take of haggling and bargains assertively for the last dollar (she can be somewhat stubborn and argumentative at times). Your cousin Brian is much more agreeable, personable, and accommodating. He thinks that it is important to meet both sides' needs in a deal, and seems more fair-minded than Jill.

1. Which would you ask to negotiate for you to buy the car?

2. Assume that you are still bargaining for a car after graduation, but your plans have changed. You will be moving to a small community in which dealers are few and far between. Moreover, you can't afford a new car yet, so you are looking for a vehicle three to five years old. You expect to return to the seller for routine maintenance and servicing. Which relative would you choose for this negotiation?

3. If your choices varied depending on the situation, or the choice was at least a much closer call in one scenario than the other, what does this say about your personal view of whether one bargaining style is more effective than another in all settings?

We have explored the choice of negotiation approaches or styles based upon effectiveness in maximizing gain, comfort consistent with our personality, and as a response to the approach of our counterparts. We can also fit our negotiating style to cultural norms and expectations. Perhaps a more compelling reason to utilize an open and cooperative negotiation approach is based on the importance of relationships and the value of honest dealing. For some, the other proffered rationales of integrative bargaining and enlightened self-interest are not necessary in making the choice to negotiate collaboratively. It is enough to do so because this approach is ethical, and will help to build a better society.

❖ **Gerald B. Wetlaufer,** *THE LIMITS OF INTEGRATIVE BARGAINING*

85 Geo. L.J. 369 (1996)

It is now conventional wisdom that opportunities for integrative bargaining are widely available, that they are often unrecognized and unexploited, and that as a result both parties to negotiations and society as a whole are worse off than would otherwise have been the case. The failure to recognize and exploit these opportunities may reflect a failure of education, curable either by reading or by attending a course or seminar. It may reflect the "I'm right, you're wrong, and I can prove it" style of discourse associated with law school education and historically male modes of moral reasoning. Or it may be the result of the "negotiator's dilemma" in which the open and cooperative tactics thought appropriate to integrative bargaining are systematically exploited and driven out by the more combative tactics generally associated with distributive bargaining—starting high, conceding slowly, concealing and misrepresenting one's own interests, arguing coercively, threatening, and bluffing.

If the problem at hand is our failure to recognize and exploit opportunities for integrative bargaining, the solution, we are told, is to shift away from the tactics of distributive bargaining and toward the tactics appropriate to integrative bargaining: cooperation, openness, and truth telling. Individual negotiators should embrace these tactics not because they are good or ethical, or because they will help to build a better society, but instead because they will promote the individual's immediate pecuniary self-interest. . . .

The proponents of integrative bargaining usually assert that opportunities for such bargaining are widely, if not universally, available. Lax and Sebenius, in the most important contribution yet made to our understanding of these matters, catalogue the opportunities for integrative bargaining. Their list includes differences between the parties in terms of (1) their interests, (2) their projections concerning possible future events (3) their willingness to accept risks, and (4) their time preferences regarding payment or performance. . . . All four of these circumstances will sometimes, but only under certain further conditions and with certain important qualifications, afford opportunities for the parties to expand the pie through integrative bargaining. . . .

[The author next argues and attempts to demonstrate that the listed differences between negotiating parties rarely provide opportunities to lastingly expand the pie and create joint, integrative gains.]

A final claim that can now be evaluated is that opportunities for integrative bargaining necessarily imply that it is in a negotiator's immediate pecuniary self-interest to engage in the tactics of cooperation, openness, truth telling, honesty, and trust. First, I have demonstrated that opportunities for integrative bargaining, especially meaningful opportunities for integrative bargaining (e.g., where the pie may be made to expand and to stay expanded), exist within a narrower range of circumstances than sometimes has been claimed. Some of the differences cited by Lax and Sebenius simply do not create opportunities for integrative bargaining. Others, namely those involving different assessments regarding future events, create opportunities to expand the pie only if the parties are willing to bet on their projections. And even when the parties are willing to bet, there will be opportunities for integrative bargaining only some of the time and only in ways that will sometimes prove self-defeating in the sense that the pie may eventually return to its original size. If the pie shrinks back, one or both of the parties will be worse off than they had expected to be and, potentially worse off than they would have been had they not entered the agreement. Other circumstances named by Lax and Sebenius—multiple issues differently valued, differing projections concerning future events, differing time preferences, differing levels of risk aversion—sometimes offer opportunities for integrative bargaining but sometimes do not. Although the general claim is made that opportunities for integrative bargaining provide a reason, based solely on immediate pecuniary self-interest, to engage in openness and truth telling, those opportunities are considerably less pervasive than has been announced. Thus, this argument for openness and truth telling is, in that degree, narrower and less persuasive.

Second, even within the range of circumstances in which there are significant opportunities for integrative bargaining, the bargainer must almost always engage in distributive bargaining as well. Therefore, it is in the bargainer's self-interest not just to adopt the tactics of openness and truth telling that are said to be appropriate to integrative bargaining, but somehow also to adopt the tactics of truth-hiding and dissimulation that are said to be appropriate in distributive bargaining. However we might manage these incompatible tactics, this situation presents at most a weak and highly qualified argument for openness and truth telling. Moreover, the argument for openness and truth telling is not an argument for openness and truth telling with respect to everything, but instead, is limited to information useful in identifying and exploiting opportunities for integrative bargaining. Thus, an opportunity for integrative bargaining will present an occasion for a certain amount of truth telling with respect to one's relative interest in various issues (or one's projections about the future or aversion to risk) without also presenting even a weak argument for truth telling with respect to one's reservation price. . . .

If there is a general case for cooperation, openness, and truth telling in negotiations, that case is multidimensional and parts of it are expressly ethical. Certainly, because there are opportunities for integrative bargaining, a measure of openness and truth telling is sometimes warranted as a matter of a negotiator's immediate pecuniary self-interest. Similarly, a negotiator's long-term pecuniary self-interest may sometimes be served by openness and truth telling because of the costs that may be associated with a reputation for sharp dealing. But it is also true that a negotiator's pecuniary self-interest is, at best, only a portion of his true self-interest. Thus, it may be in his true self- interest to accept some pecuniary costs for the sake of living in a community in which cooperation, truthtelling, and ethical behavior are the norm. Moreover, Plato's Socrates may have been right when he argued that a person who has some combination of wealth and virtue may be happier and better off than a person who has more wealth but less virtue. . . .

We have, in certain respects, allowed ourselves to be dazzled and seduced by the possibilities of integrative or "win-win" bargaining. That, in turn, has led to a certain amount of over claiming. The reason, I think, is that if we hold these possibilities in a certain light and squint our eyes just hard enough, they look for all the world like the Holy Grail of negotiations. They seem to offer that which we have wanted most to find. What they seem to offer—though in the end it is only an illusion—is the long-sought proof that cooperation, honesty, and good behavior will carry the day not because they are virtuous, not because they will benefit society as a whole, but because they are in everyone's individual and pecuniary self-interest. But however much we may want "honesty" to be "the best policy" in this strong sense, the discovery of integrative bargaining has not, at least so far, provided that long-sought proof.

Perhaps the time has finally come to consider the possibility that this proof will always elude us, for the simple reason that the world in which we live does not, in this particular way, conform to our wishes. Even if there is just the chance that this is so, and it looks much more like a certainty than a chance, it would be appropriate to acknowledge the ultimate insufficiency of understanding self-interest in narrowly pecuniary terms. It would be appropriate to attend in a systematic way to the facts that, even when it is contrary to our pecuniary self-interest, relationships matter; that we care about our reputations, not just for effectiveness but also for decency and good behavior: that we care about living in—and helping to create—communities in which pecuniary self-interest is not the only language that is spoken; and that Plato's Socrates may have gotten it right. And it would be appropriate to acknowledge the central importance of the ethical case against certain forms of competitive and self-interested behavior, especially those forms of behavior, central to the process of negotiations, that involve misrepresentations and other conduct that imposes harm upon others.

Questions

10. Professor Wetlaufer concludes that being open and cooperative in negotiations may not benefit immediate pecuniary interests, but that relationships matter and that Plato may have been correct in teaching that virtue is more important than wealth. Even if we believe this is true when we negotiate for ourselves, as lawyers who negotiate for clients, can we trade off a client's potential gain for our sense of virtue?

11. Do clients have a say in what information is voluntarily revealed and how cooperative they want their attorney to be in negotiating on their behalf?

12. Do the immediate pecuniary interests of the client and the longer-term interests of the attorney in maintaining good working relations with other lawyers or a reputation for "decency" create a conflict of interest between attorney and client?

B. Cooperation vs. Competitiveness—Who Decides?

Problem

Assume that you have established yourself as an effective attorney with a good reputation for your straightforward, cooperative style. You have been a guest lecturer at local law schools about civility in the practice of law and the importance of maintaining a credible professional reputation. Your largest individual client, the president of a regional bank, which your firm also represents, has retained you to represent him in a divorce action initiated by his wife, knowing that you have experience in domestic relations practice. He explains that his highest priority is to retain total control of the bank with no share of the bank stock going to his wife, even though the law might give her a claim to some of it. He wants you to seek for him primary custody of their two middle-school-aged children, for whom he and his wife have both been active parents, so you can use that as a bargaining chip later to assure his retention of the bank stock.

1. What would you tell him?
2. Who should decide negotiation strategies and approaches, you or your client?

Ends vs. Means

Generally clients get to choose the objective of negotiation, and lawyers use their professional judgment in selecting the means of obtaining the client's objectives. Of course, it's not quite so simple. In matters of litigation, the lawyer owes the client an ethical obligation of zealous advocacy in pursuit of a client's interests. Some scholars interpret the ethical norms to mean "the final authority on important issues of strategy rests with the client; and the client may discharge his lawyer at will, but the lawyer has only limited ability to withdraw from representation" (Gilson and Mnookin 1995, 550). Mnookin and Gilson believe that a lawyer who wishes to pursue a cooperative approach, with a sensitivity for long-term professional relationships with other attorneys, may not be able to do so in the litigation context, or at least that the client calls the negotiation shots. They also point out that the client can fire the lawyer at will if the lawyer seems more cooperative than the client wishes, but that ethical norms do not always allow the lawyer to quit if the client insists on a more aggressive strategy.

A different perspective is offered by Professor Robert J. Condlin, who points to practical norms that may differ from ethical norms for attorneys. He distinguishes between the reality of what lawyers do in negotiation and what the ethical rules appear to demand. The distinction, according to Condlin, is really between ends and means. Clients have control over the end result desired, and lawyers choose the means. "Lawyers are persons in their own right, with moral and political rights and obligations of their own, and even though they must take direction from their clients, they need not do everything asked. For example, the duty of deference distinguishes between questions of ends and questions of means, and reserves to lawyers the tactical and technical decisions of how best to advance client objectives" (Condlin 1992, 71).

According to Condlin, lawyers must be substantively competitive in negotiating for clients but can choose their own personal style. Competitive attorneys can adopt a cordial and respectful persona in their negotiations, though this can be a fine and difficult distinction. Condlin refers to this tug between a client's wishes for the lawyer to defect from a pattern of cooperation and the lawyer's desire for long-term cooperation as the "bargainer's dilemma." Like the prisoners' dilemma, different negotiation tactics may be called for if the situation is viewed as a single- or multiple-round game. Clients tend to view litigation and some deals as a one-round game. Lawyers usually view their negotiation with other lawyers as unlimited multiple rounds, where any defect will bring future retaliation and a blemished reputation. Thus, the "bargainer's dilemma."

We probe this dilemma in more depth when we examine the ethical constraints on lawyer negotiation in Chapter 10. In the meantime, assume that lawyers, when negotiating for clients, do have a choice of being more cooperative or more competitive in their negotiation approach. Also recall that the choice of how to fulfill clients' interests is not completely bipolar. Cooperation may be the best way to fill the needs of all clients in negotiation when an integrative outcome is possible that allows each party to get some of what they want. In such situations, a competitive approach may eliminate the possibility of a win-win outcome that is otherwise available; however, it may produce an outcome most favorable for the client of a successful competitive negotiator.

CHAPTER
5

Negotiation Step by Step—The Beginning

A. Negotiation Stages and Approaches

Negotiation, whether competitive, cooperative, or a mixed approach, can initially be understood as occurring in stages. Even though lawyer negotiation often is not a tidy process, breaking negotiation into stages is a way to help comprehend and analyze the process. There is, however, no script—all negotiations do not follow the same lineal staging, and each stage and set of activities will not necessarily be completed in every negotiation. After mastering the basic structure and concepts of negotiation, you may find yourself improvising in a more dynamic process of give and take or problem solving.

Listed below are the activities typically occurring in the seven stages of competitive negotiation in one column and in the other column cooperative negotiation. The activities within each stage can be mixed or alternated between competitive and cooperative, bearing in mind the warning that cooperation is commonly driven out by competitiveness. Of course, the labels "competitive" and "cooperative," like all one-word descriptions, are too simple. Adversarial and problem-solving, positional and interest-based, or distributive and integrative may better capture the behavioral contrast. Finally, note that although some of the activities and tasks within the two approaches are similar, the sequence of activities may vary between positional and interest-based approaches. For example, making demands and offers comes earlier in positional negotiation and later in interest negotiation, following the exchange of information, if at all.

Stage	Competitive/adversarial approach activities	Cooperative/problem-solving approach activities
1. Preparation and Setting Goals	➢ Interviewing and counseling client about negotiation ➢ Setting goals ➢ Assessing power of each party ➢ Planning and research ➢ Formulating positions and bottom line	➢ Interviewing and counseling client about negotiation ➢ Setting goals ➢ Assessing needs of each party ➢ Planning and research ➢ Formulating best alternative to negotiated agreement (BATNA) and reservation point

Stage	Competitive/adversarial approach activities	Cooperative/problem-solving approach activities
2. Initial Interactions	➤ Setting tone ➤ Establishing credentials/authority ➤ Making first demand or offer	➤ Setting tone ➤ Establishing rapport and trust ➤ Agreeing on agenda
3. Exchanging and Refining Information	➤ Asking questions ➤ Offering overstated or understated valuations ➤ Informational bargaining ➤ Formal discovery ➤ Stating positions (often exaggerated)	➤ Asking questions ➤ Sharing assessments or appraisals ➤ Information exchange ➤ Informal discovery (I'll show you mine, if you'll show me yours) ➤ Stating needs or interests
4. Bargaining	➤ Argument and persuasion ➤ Making concessions ➤ Forming coalitions and holding out	➤ Proposing principles ➤ Applying principled criteria ➤ Trading off priorities and brainstorming solutions
5. Moving Toward Closure	➤ Using power and threats ➤ Creating time crisis ➤ Evaluating offers	➤ Examining BATNAs ➤ Agreeing on deadlines ➤ Decision analysis
6. Reaching Impasse or Agreement	➤ Possible impasse ➤ Compromising ➤ Adding conditions	➤ Possible, but less likely, impasse ➤ Reaching mutual decisions through joint problem solving ➤ Creating alternative outcomes
7. Finalizing and Writing Agreements	➤ Preparing opposing drafts of agreement ➤ Negotiating over drafts ➤ Approval, ratification, and buy-in (if necessary)	➤ Memorializing terms ➤ Concurring on single text agreement ➤ Approval, ratification, and buy-in (if necessary)

© 2015 Jay Folberg

Note and Questions

Professor Williams, in his article "Negotiation as a Healing Process," part of which is excerpted in Chapter 1, refers to negotiation as a ritual. He goes on to say:

In law school we learn that no two cases are alike, and in our culture we assume that no two people are alike. We might surmise from this that no two negotiations are alike. Fortunately, this is only partially true. One of the defining characteristics of a ritual, including the ritual of negotiation, is that it provides an accepted structure for and sequencing of events. As a general proposition, then, we can say *the ritual of negotiation unfolds in predictable stages over time.* The predictability helps explain why so many lawyers lose patience with the process; it is highly repetitive, and thus not as stimulating as new adventures would be. This aspect of ritual is well captured by W. John Smith when he says, "*ritual* connotes . . . behavior that is formally organized into repeatable patterns. Perhaps the fundamental and pervasive function of these patterns is to facilitate orderly interactions between individuals." The point could not be more clear. Negotiation is a highly repetitive process. Without predictable patterns, the negotiators could not hope to achieve orderly interaction with each other. As Smith explains: "Ritual behavior facilitates interactions because it makes available information about the nature of events, and about the participants in them, that each participating individual must have to interact without generating chaos." The task now is to develop a working knowledge of the predictable stages of the negotiation process. (Williams 1996, 33)

1. Have you found negotiations in which you were involved to be predictable in process? What types of negotiations are most likely to follow a ritualistic or predictable pattern? Might there be different negotiation rituals depending on what is being negotiated and the setting of the negotiation?

2. Can you think of how concurring on a single text agreement, listed on the chart as Stage 7, "Finalizing and Writing Agreements," might be taken up out of order and used in earlier stages to help formulate choices, bargain, and reach decisions? For a fascinating application of the single text procedure in reaching agreement between Israel and Egypt at Camp David, see Jimmy Carter's book *Keeping Faith: Memoirs of a President* (1982).

B. Getting Ready to Negotiate

Watching a good negotiator or hearing about an effective negotiation can give the impression that it comes easily and that success is the result of intuitive ability, cleverness, and quick thinking. However, similar to trial practice, appellate advocacy, or any other disciplined endeavor, success in negotiation is in large part the result of planning, research, and preparation. The famous quote by Antoine de Saint-Exupery that "a goal without a plan is just a wish" is applicable to negotiation.

The following excerpt provides a helpful blueprint for effective negotiation preparation that is likely to maximize results in most bargaining situations by refining your BATNA and reservation point, as well as by anticipating your opponent's bargaining zone.

1. Preparation

❖ **Russell Korobkin, *A Positive Theory of Legal Negotiation***

88 Geo. L.J. 1789 (2000)

[The author posits two negotiation situations: one is a potential transaction for the purchase by Esau of Jacob's catering business, and the other is a potential settlement of a suit by Goliath against David for battery.]

All observers of the negotiation process agree that painstaking preparation is critical to success at the bargaining table. . . . "Internal" preparation refers to research that the negotiator does to set and adjust his own RP [reservation point or price]. "External" preparation refers to research that the negotiator does to estimate and manipulate the other party's RP.

1. Internal Preparation: Alternatives and BATNAs

A negotiator cannot determine his RP without first understanding his substitutes for and the opportunity costs of reaching a negotiated agreement. This, of course, requires research. Esau cannot determine how much he is willing to pay for Jacob's business without investigating his other options. Most obviously, Esau will want to investigate what other catering companies are for sale in his area, their asking prices, and how they compare in quality and earning potential to Jacob's. He also might consider other types of businesses that are for sale. And he will likely consider the possibility of investing his money passively and working for someone else, rather than investing in a business.

Alternatives to reaching an agreement can be nearly limitless in transactional negotiations, and creativity in generating the list of alternatives is a critical skill to the negotiator. The panoply of alternatives is generally more circumscribed in dispute resolution negotiations. If Goliath fails to reach a settlement of some sort with David, he has the alternative of seeking an adjudicated outcome of the dispute and the alternative of dropping the suit. Most likely, he does not have the choice of suing someone else instead of David, in the same way that Esau has the choice of buying a business other than Jacob's.

After identifying the various alternatives to reaching a negotiated agreement, the negotiator needs to determine which alternative is most desirable. Fisher and his coauthors coined the appropriate term "BATNA"—"best alternative to a negotiated agreement"—to identify this choice. The identity and quality of a negotiator's BATNA is the primary input into his RP.

If the negotiator's BATNA and the subject of the negotiation are perfectly interchangeable, determining the reservation price is quite simple: The reservation price is merely the value of the BATNA. For example, if Esau's BATNA is buying another catering business for $190,000 that is identical to Jacob's in terms of quality, earnings potential, and all other factors that are important to Esau, then his RP is $190,000. If Jacob will sell for some amount less than that, Esau will be better off buying Jacob's company than he would be pursuing his best alternative. If Jacob demands more than $190,000, Esau is better off buying the alternative company and not reaching an agreement with Jacob.

In most circumstances, however, the subject of a negotiation and the negotiator's BATNA are not perfect substitutes. If Jacob's business is of higher quality, has a higher earnings potential, or is located closer to Esau's home, he would proba-bly be willing to pay a premium for it over what he would pay for the alternative choice. For example, if the alternative business is selling for $190,000, Esau might determine he would be willing to pay up to a $10,000 premium over the alterna-tive for Jacob's business and thus set his RP at $200,000. On the other hand, if Esau's BATNA is more desirable to him than Jacob's business, Esau will discount the value of his BATNA by the amount necessary to make the two alternatives equally desirable values for the money; perhaps he will set his RP at $180,000 in recognition that his BATNA is $10,000 more desirable than Jacob's business, and Jacob's business would be equally desirable only at a $10,000 discount.

Assume Goliath determines that his BATNA is proceeding to trial. He will attempt to place a value on his BATNA by researching the facts of the case, the relevant legal precedent, and jury awards in similar cases, all as a means of esti-mating the expected value of litigating to a jury verdict. If Goliath's research leads to an estimate that he has a 75% chance of winning a jury verdict, and the likely verdict if he does prevail is $100,000, then using a simple expected value calculation ($100,000 × .75) would lead him to value his BATNA at $75,000.

For most plaintiffs, however, a settlement of a specified amount is preferable to a jury verdict with the same expected value, both because litigation entails additional costs and because most individuals are risk averse and therefore pre-fer a certain payment to a risky probability of payment with the same expected value. Goliath might determine, for example, that a $50,000 settlement would have the equivalent value to him of a jury verdict with an expected value of $75,000, because pursuing a jury verdict would entail greater tangible and intan-gible costs such as attorneys' fees, emotional strain, inconvenience, and the risk of losing the case altogether. If so, Goliath would set his RP at $50,000. On the other hand, it is possible that Goliath would find a $75,000 verdict more desir-able than a $75,000 pretrial settlement. For example, perhaps Goliath would find additional value in having a jury of his peers publicly recognize the validity of his grievance against David. If Goliath believes that such psychic benefits of a jury verdict would make a verdict worth $10,000 more to him than a settlement of the same amount (after taking into account the added risks and costs of liti-gation), he would set his RP at $85,000. . . .

Internal preparation serves two related purposes. By considering the value of obvious alternatives to reaching a negotiated agreement, the negotiator can accurately estimate his RP. This is of critical importance because without a pre-cise and accurate estimation of his RP the negotiator cannot be sure to avoid the most basic negotiating mistake—agreeing to a deal when he would have been better off walking away from the table with no agreement.

By investigating an even wider range of alternatives to reaching agreement and by more thoroughly investigating the value of obvious alternatives, the negotiator can alter his RP in a way that will shift the bargaining zone to his advantage. Rather than just considering the asking price of other catering com-panies listed for sale in his town, Esau might contact catering companies that are not for sale to find out if their owners might consider selling under the right conditions. This could lead to the identification of a company similar to Jacob's that could be purchased for $175,000, which would have the effect of reduc-ing Esau's RP to $175,000 and therefore shifting the bargaining zone lower. Goliath's attorney might conduct additional legal research, perhaps exploring other, more novel, theories of liability. If he determines that one or more alternative legal theories has a reasonable chance of success in court, Goliath might adjust upward his estimate of prevailing at trial—and therefore the value of his BATNA of trial—allowing him to adjust upward his RP.

2. External Preparation: The Opponent's Alternatives and BATNA

Internal preparation enables the negotiator to estimate his RP accurately and favorably. Of course, the bargaining zone is fixed by *both* parties' RPs. External preparation allows the negotiator to estimate his opponent's RP. If Esau is savvy, he will attempt to research Jacob's alternatives to a negotiated agreement as well as his own alternatives. For example, other caterers might know whether Jacob has had other offers for his business, how much the business might bring on the open market, or how anxious Jacob is to sell—all factors that will help Esau to accurately predict Jacob's RP and therefore pinpoint the low end of the bargaining zone. This information will also prepare Esau to attempt to persuade Jacob during the course of negotiations to lower his RP. . . .

It is worth noting that in the litigation context both parties often have the same alternatives and the same BATNA. If plaintiff Goliath determines that his BATNA is going to trial, then defendant David's only alternative—and therefore his BATNA by default—is going to trial as well. In this circumstance, internal preparation and external preparation merge. For example, when Goliath's lawyer conducts legal research, he is attempting to simultaneously estimate the value of both parties' BATNAs. Of course, just because the parties have the same BATNA, they will not necessarily estimate the market value of it identically, much less arrive at identical RPs. Research suggests that an "egocentric bias" is likely to cause litigants to interpret material facts in a light favorable to their legal position, thus causing them to overestimate the expected value of an adjudicated outcome. Consequently, it is likely that, examining the same operative facts and legal precedent, plaintiff Goliath will place a higher value on the BATNA of trial than defendant David. This difference in perception often will be offset, however, by the fact that plaintiff Goliath is likely to set his RP, or the minimum settlement he will accept, below his perceived expected value of trial to account for the higher costs and higher risk associated with trial, while defendant David is likely to set his RP, or the maximum settlement he will agree to pay, above the expected value of trial for the same reasons. As long as the parties' preference for settlement rather than trial outweighs their egocentric biases, a bargaining zone will still exist, although it will be smaller than it would be if the parties agreed on the expected value of trial. Research also suggests that both parties are likely to be more risk averse when they are less confident in their prediction of the expected value of trial. In other words, the less confident the parties are in the value that they place on the BATNA of trial, the larger the bargaining zone between the RPs is likely to be.

2. *Setting Goals*

In addition to thinking through the least you can accept, or your reservation point, it is also helpful to formulate goals and set high expectations. High expectations lead to better outcomes, as discussed in this excerpt by Richard Shell.

❖ **G. Richard Shell,** *Bargaining for Advantage: Negotiation Strategies for Reasonable People*

28 (Penguin, 2006)

Goals: You'll Never Hit the Target If You Don't Aim

In Lewis Carroll's *Alice's Adventures in Wonderland*, Alice finds herself at a crossroads where a Cheshire Cat materializes. Alice asks the Cat, "Would you tell me please, which way I ought to go from here?" The Cat replies, "That depends a good deal on where you want to get to." "I don't much care where—" says Alice. "Then it doesn't matter which way you go," the Cat replies, cutting her off.

To become an effective negotiator, you must find out where you want to go—and why. That means committing yourself to specific, justifiable goals. It also means taking the time to transform your goals from simple targets into genuine—and appropriately high—*expectations.* . . .

Our goals give us direction, but our expectations are what give weight and conviction to our statements at the bargaining table. We are most animated when we are striving to achieve what we feel we justly deserve.

So it is with negotiation. Our goals give us direction, but our expectations are what give weight and conviction to our statements at the bargaining table. We are most animated when we are striving to achieve what we feel we justly deserve. The more time we spend preparing for a particular negotiation and the more information we gather that reinforces our belief that our goal is legitimate and achievable, the firmer the expectations grow. . . .

What you aim for often determines what you get. Why? The first reason is obvious: Your goals set the upper limit of what you will ask for. You mentally concede everything beyond your goal, so you seldom do better than that benchmark.

Second, research on goals reveals that they trigger powerful psychological "striving" mechanisms. Sports psychologists and educators alike confirm that setting specific goals motivates people, focusing and concentrating their attention and psychological powers.

Third, we are more persuasive when we are committed to achieving some specific purpose, in contrast to the occasions when we ask for things half-heartedly or merely react to initiatives proposed by others. Our commitment is infectious. People around us feel drawn toward our goals. . . .

Goals Versus "Bottom Lines"

Most negotiating books and experts emphasize the importance of having a "bottom line," "walkaway," or "reservation price" for negotiation. Indeed, the bottom line is a fundamental bargaining concept on which much of modern negotiation theory is built. It is the *minimum acceptable level* you require to say "yes" in a negotiation. By definition, if you cannot achieve your bottom line, you would rather seek another solution to your problem or wait until another opportunity comes your way. When two parties have bottom lines that permit an agreement at some point between them, theorists speak of there being a "positive bargaining zone." When the two bottom lines do not overlap, they speak of a "negative bargaining zone". . . .

A well-framed goal is quite different from a bottom line. As I use the word, "goal" is your *highest legitimate expectation* of what you should achieve. . . .

Researchers have discovered that humans have a limited capacity for maintaining focus in complex, stressful situations such as negotiations. Consequently, once a negotiation is under way, we gravitate toward the single focal point that has the psychological significance for us. Once most people set a firm bottom line in a negotiation, that becomes their dominant reference point as discussions proceed. They measure success or failure with reference to their bottom line. Having a goal as your reference point, by contrast, prompts you to think you are facing a potential "loss" for any offer you receive below your goal. And we know that avoiding losses is a powerful motivating force. This power is not working as strongly for you when you focus solely on your bottom line.

What is the practical effect of having your bottom line become your dominant reference point in a negotiation? Over a lifetime of negotiating, your results will tend to hover at a point just above this minimum acceptable level. For most reasonable people, the bottom line is the most natural focal point. Disappointment arises if we cannot get the other side to agree to meet our minimum requirements (usually established by our available alternatives or our needs away from the table), and satisfaction arises just above that level. Meanwhile, someone else who is more skilled at orienting himself toward ambitious goals will do much better. Not surprising, research shows that parties with higher (but still realistic) goals outperform those with more modest ones, all else being equal.

To avoid falling into the trap of letting our bottom line become our reference point, be aware of your absolute limits, but do not dwell on them. Instead, work energetically on formulating your goals . . . . [T]est the other side's reaction to your goal. Then, if you must, gradually re-orient toward a bottom line as that becomes necessary to close the deal. With experience, you should be able to keep both your goal and your bottom line in view at the same time without losing your goal focus. Research suggests that the best negotiators have this ability. . . .

If setting goals is so vital to effective preparation, how should you do it? Use the following simple steps:

1. Think carefully about what you really want—and remember that money is often a means, not an end.
2. Set an optimistic—but justifiable—target.
3. Be specific. . . .
4. Get committed. Write down your goal and, if possible, discuss the goal with someone else.
5. Carry your goal with you into the negotiation.

Set an Optimistic, Justifiable Target

When you set goals, think boldly and optimistically about what you would like to see happen. Research has repeatedly shown that people who have higher expectations in negotiations perform better and get more than people who have modest or "I'll do my best" goals, provided they really believe in their targets. . . .

Once you have thought about what an optimistic, challenging goal would look like, spend a few minutes permitting realism to dampen your expectations. *Optimistic goals are effective only if they are feasible; that is, only if you believe in them and they can be justified according to some standard or norm.* . . . [N]egotiation positions must usually be supported by some standard, benchmark, or precedent, or they lose their credibility. . . .

Commit to Your Goal: Write It Down and Talk About It

Your goal is only as effective as your commitment to it. There are several simple things you can do that will increase your level of psychological attachment to your goal. First, as I suggested above, you should make sure it is justified and supported by solid arguments. You must believe in your goal to be committed to it.

Second, it helps if you spend just a few moments vividly imagining the way it would look or feel to achieve your goal. Visualization helps engage our mind more fully in the achievement process and also raises our level of self-confidence and commitment . . .

Third, psychologists and marketing professionals report that the act of *writing a goal down* engages our sense of commitment much more effectively than does the mere act of thinking about it. The act of writing makes a thought more "real" and objective, obligating us to follow up on it—at least in our own eyes.

Questions

1. Can you explain the difference between BATNA and RP?
2. Can you explain the difference between goals and expectations?
3. Does the advice to set high expectations work only if the other side does not follow the same advice? Will setting high expectations, particularly if done by both sides to a negotiation, likely lead to larger "negative bargaining zones," as explained by Shell, and thus more frequent impasses? Is there a way for two optimistic negotiators to deal with this and reach agreement?
4. If expectations in negotiation are, in part, a function of previous success and failure, as Shell suggests, how does a new lawyer set expectations? Would a client be well advised to seek out a lawyer who has had well-known recent success in trials and negotiations on the theory that "success breeds success"? How might you leverage someone else's success with a similar case to your advantage in a negotiation?

For an in-depth discussion of the role of aspirations in settlement negotiations, see Korobkin (2002). Korobkin concludes that high aspirations may help negotiators reach better results, but at the cost of a greater risk of impasse and personal dissatisfaction in not fully achieving the expectations created by high aspirations.

3. Negotiation Preparation Checklist

The following checklist expands on the concepts developed in the previous readings and includes some points from the selections that follow. You may want to create a personal, comprehensive checklist to use in preparing for negotiations in both litigation and transactional settings. Using a checklist is a way to discipline your thinking so you may eventually not need the list. This checklist, although longer than one you might create, provides an inventory of helpful questions from which you can choose, depending on the case and the time available. Good preparation is more than you minimally need. Thorough preparation can minimize surprises and allow you to better respond to what you can't anticipate.

I. Information and Strategy

1. Information

- ☐ What information about opposing counsel and parties might help you connect and establish rapport?
- ☐ What information will help determine your opponent's needs, interests, and objectives?
- ☐ What questions will you ask to elicit such information?
- ☐ What information is the other side likely to seek?
- ☐ What are you willing to reveal, and how do you plan to disclose it?
- ☐ What should you be careful to protect, and how do you prevent disclosure?
- ☐ Are there any advantageous trades of information?

2. Alternatives

- ☐ What is your best alternative if no agreement is reached (BATNA)?
- ☐ Can you improve your BATNA or the way it is perceived?
- ☐ What is your worst alternative if no agreement is reached?
- ☐ What are your opponent's best and worst alternatives?
- ☐ How can you change how your opponent perceives his alternatives?
- ☐ If an offered settlement is not accepted, are costs and attorneys' fees triggered?

3. Interests

- ☐ What are your client's interests and their relative importance?
- ☐ How does your opponent see your client's interests?
- ☐ What are your opponent's interests?
- ☐ How can you change your opponent's perspective about his and your client's interests?

4. Solutions and Positions

- ☐ What ideas do you have for a solution (based on what you know now)?
- ☐ Will you assert a position, and if so, what will it be?
- ☐ What is your opponent's current position or proposed solution?

5. *Principles and Standards*

- ☐ What principles can you cite in support of your position?
- ☐ Which are most persuasive?
- ☐ What principles is your opponent likely to cite?

6. *Communication*

- ☐ Should you communicate prior to a negotiation meeting?
- ☐ What theme or story will best present your case?
- ☐ What messages do you want to send?
- ☐ Are there any special communication issues to consider based on culture?

7. *Relationship*

- ☐ Who should be at the table?
- ☐ Are there any relationship problems?
- ☐ Will there be a continuing relationship?
- ☐ Is there trust between you and your opponent?
- ☐ How can you build trust and credibility?

II. *Bargaining*

1. *Process and Location*

- ☐ Should you establish an agenda?
- ☐ Are there applicable negotiation customs or rituals?
- ☐ Can you negotiate over or influence the process?
- ☐ Where do you want to negotiate?

2. *Expectations and Bottom Lines*

- ☐ What goals and objectives do you hope to achieve?
- ☐ What is the best outcome you can realistically envision?
- ☐ What minimum terms are you willing to accept?
- ☐ What is your reservation or walkaway point?
- ☐ What are your opponent's likely goals and expectations?
- ☐ What value system will your opponent use in assessing his case?

3. *Your Tactics*

- ☐ What negotiation style or approach will you take?
- ☐ Should you insist on any "preconditions"?
- ☐ What should be your first demand or offer?
- ☐ How will you support your demands and offers?
- ☐ How will you move from your starting point to where you would like to end?

4. *Your Opponent's Tactics*

☐ What is the style of your opponent?
☐ What negotiation techniques do you expect your opponent to use?
☐ What pattern or moves do you anticipate? How will you counter those tactics?

5. *Concessions*

☐ What early concession will you make, if necessary?
☐ Do you have any easy "giveaways"?
☐ Are there any non-monetary concessions you can give?
☐ Are there concessions of low cost to you and of greater value to your opponent?
☐ What messages do you want to send with your concessions?
☐ What concessions do you anticipate receiving?

III. Settlement/Deal

☐ What terms will you insist upon?
☐ Do you have specific language for a final agreement?
☐ Are there terms and provisions you anticipate your opponent will insist on?
☐ What legal requirements are there for an enforceable settlement or deal?
☐ Who must sign or approve the agreement?
☐ Will there be time factors to consider?
☐ Will you or your opponent insist that the settlement be confidential?
☐ Should the settlement/deal be publicized? If so, how?

4. Web and Computer-Assisted Preparation

The questions to ask yourself in preparation will, in part, depend on your negotiation style and the subject of the negotiation. The purposes of your negotiation preparation are to learn about opposing counsel and parties, determine your strategy, BATNA, reservation point, first offer, and management of concessions. Similarly, you will use the information generated from your preparation to anticipate what your opponent perceives, values, and will do during the negotiations.

Today's technology makes it possible to obtain from the Web information that can be plugged into a computer program to prepare, generate options, value trade-offs, and anticipate the moves of a negotiation opponent. If computers can be used to research law, play chess (calculating the probable moves of an opponent and choosing the best move from all available options), engage in sophisticated market research, anticipate terrorist attacks, and plot wars, they should be of help in preparing for negotiations.

Googling your negotiation counterparts and checking them out on social and professional networking sites is an easy way to learn about their background and experience. You can use the Web to obtain clues about how they might negotiate, the value they might place on items of potential trade, and their interests. Knowing more about an opponent can also aid in how to establish trust and rapport. Please don't forget that the people with whom you negotiate will likely use Web searches to learn all they can about you as well.

Another value of the Web is to help you calculate your BATNAs. What both sides to a negotiation previously had to guess at, and as a result probably perceived differently, can now be determined by a computer search. For example, the cost of replacing equipment or an object of art can quickly be found by a search in a truly worldwide marketplace. Thus, the creation of objective criteria to propose for resolution of an anticipated issue can be easily researched and prepared in advance. You can better research jury awards for similar injuries and court decisions on questions that might have to be judicially decided if your negotiation fails. Diligent electronic research may also reveal the outcome of similar negotiations.

Proprietary software programs can help you analyze the negotiation style that is most comfortable for you and determine the approach likely to be used by your negotiating counterpart, provided some questions can be answered about them. The programs can also assist you in designing concessions and assigning relative values to them. They collect input that is used to suggest the best opening offer and counteroffers. These programs can also formulate questions for you to ask during a negotiation and predict the actions of an opposing negotiator, along with recommended strategies for you to use. Finally, they can help you value and decide on outcomes once proposals emerge.

Although these programs are sophisticated with a type of built-in negotiation intelligence, like with any productivity software, the quality of the result ultimately depends on the input you provide. If nothing else, a good negotiation software program can provide a guide for what you should do before the negotiation to be well prepared and what strategies to use during the negotiation, as well as suggestions about what to do if the negotiation gets stuck. At the time of this writing, two software programs for negotiation preparation and planning are available at *ExpertNegotiator.com* and *NegotiatorPro.com/negpro50coms.html.* There is also a smartphone app to help you assess your negotiation style and determine after a negotiation how you can improve from the experience and what you can do better next time; look for Negotiation 360. Computer-based negotiation assistance and online dispute resolution (ODR) are covered further in Chapter 8.

C. Initial Interaction

How we feel about those with whom we negotiate is a critical element to whether an agreement will be reached. Just as you may believe you can quickly "read" the character and trustworthiness of those you face, so others are forming quick impressions of you. The maxims that "you never get a second chance to make a first impression" and "first impressions matter" need to be considered as you prepare for and commence a negotiation.

1. Trust

The impression you make on an opponent will probably be formed, in part, before you meet. If the negotiation is of significance, you and your opponent will find out what you can about one another. Your reputation will precede you into the negotiation. In addition to informal inquiries among those with whom you have previously negotiated or had other professional contact, the Internet opens your public history, both accomplishments and mistakes, for all to see. So your preparation for a negotiation, in terms of the impression you make and whether you can be trusted, involves your entire professional life. Although a misimpression can be corrected, it is an uphill struggle because of what we know about self-fulfilling prophecies and the selective way we view evidence to support earlier impressions.

By the time you are in law school, you have, no doubt, learned how to make a good impression. Little things matter, including appearance, posture, eye-contact, and how you greet someone. For example, a firm handshake, or its cultural equivalent, is generally accepted as code language to show a willingness to engage cooperatively and with trust. In a classroom study, Harvard MBA students were assigned to negotiate a real estate deal. Half of the pairs of negotiators were instructed to begin their session with a handshake; the other half were seated across the table from one another and not instructed to shake hands. Those who shook hands before commencing to negotiate were observed to be less misleading then those who did not shake. Both buyers and sellers who shook hands at the outset reported to be more content with the deal. In another study, the MBA students who shook hands prior to negotiating an employment contract were observed to be more open to the other's preferences and achieved more positive joint outcomes. (See Schroeder, Risen, Gino, and Norton 2014.)

Note and Questions

THE HANDSHAKE THAT SHOOK THE WESTERN HEMISPHERE

It was just a handshake and not even the first between Barack Obama and Raúl Castro, but when historians come to select the images that best reflect the legacy of the two leaders, this may be among the pictures that define their efforts to end half a century of Cold War animosity: The widely anticipated moment came at the inauguration ceremony for the Summit of the Americas in Panama, the first occasion for the two presidents to get together since their surprise announcement on 17 December that they would move to normalize relations between their two countries. [cnn.com/2015/04/10]

1. Does the refusal by some Saudi officials in 2015 to shake the hand of Michelle Obama indicate distrust or disrespect?
2. Are there cultural or religiously based reasons to refuse a handshake?

Trust can be thought of as a metaphorical bank account. You begin the trust account with early deposits based on a good reputation, initial positive interactions like handshakes, showing respect, acting professionally, listening, and acknowledging an opponent's perceptions. During the negotiation you may have to draw upon your trust currency when you need to persuade your counterpart that your assertions are credible and your proposals are reasonable.

The flip side of trust—distrust—inhibits negotiation. Distrust tends to be reciprocated and becomes a self-fulfilling prophecy engendering negative behavior and selective perceptions that confirm the reasons for not trusting one another. Distrust is an obstacle to the exchange of information and collaboration or joint problem solving.

Unless negotiators know one another socially or have had positive professional experiences together, mistrust may be more the norm at the beginning of a negotiation because you know the other side can prevent you from getting something you want. So, setting a positive tone and making early moves to build trust are important. If you can start on a positive note, you can build a momentum of trust that can carry the negotiations through difficult times. Trust initiated through good listening, sincere compliments, or small opening concessions builds upon itself through reciprocity.

2. Rapport and Reciprocity

Considerable research has been done on ways to build rapport and influence attitudes for purposes of marketing and sales. Much of this research has applicability to negotiation and can be put to good use, provided it is implemented subtly enough that you appear sincere and don't come across like a salesperson and arouse suspicion. All the personal skills that you have been taught, and probably admire in others, come into play in establishing rapport: listening intensely, showing real interest in others, being respectful and polite, agreeing, and saying yes when it is possible to do so honestly.

One core finding of the research is that people tend to reciprocate small favors and concessions by giving more than they receive. (See Cialdini 2008.) You have probably received in the mail solicitations from charities that enclose a small gift, like personalized address labels or a small packet of flower seeds. Experience has proven that these token gifts generate larger contributions. Our embedded sense of reciprocal obligation is the source of the old saying "Nothing is more costly than something received free of charge." Similarly, making a small concession at the beginning of a negotiation can help create rapport and trigger a tendency to reciprocate with a larger concession later in the negotiation. Saying "yes" when possible not only builds rapport but plants the seeds of reciprocity that can produce more agreement from the other side. (See Martin et al. 2014.)

Another base of rapport is finding common ground. The more you know about your negotiating counterparts and their clients, the more you might find points of interest, background, experiences, and relationships that you share. Discovering connections and commonalities is a good start to building rapport.

In our chart of negotiation stages at the beginning of this chapter, we listed first demands and offers as part of initial interactions under the competitive/adversarial approach, but omitted them in the interest-based approach. Even competitive negotiators may seek to establish a positive relationship and exchange information before discussing proposals. We will return to demands and offers after the following discussion about gathering and managing information.

D. Exchanging and Refining Information

The task of finding out all that you can about the other side, their needs, their case, their BATNA, and other factors affecting their reservation point, is a significant part of the preparation stage and pervades the entire negotiation process. Similarly, disclosing and managing information in your control that may shape the other side's perceptions or that they want to know is also a continual part of the process. Exchanging and refining information is listed as a separate step only to emphasize its importance in the process and to recognize that there are points in the negotiation where information is expected to be exchanged formally or informally. Exchanging and refining information is a dynamic that continually shapes expectations and effects negotiation and decision making. Information may be the subject of bargaining before negotiating over outcomes.

A hallmark of effective negotiators, whether competitive or cooperative, is their ability to listen, their propensity to ask questions, and their desire to continually gather information. (As will be presented later, information is power in negotiations.) Information is not limited to what is written or spoken; it is gathered through all the senses, including keen observation. This is sometimes referred to as "360° awareness," which distinguishes successful negotiators. (See Molly Fletcher, *A Winner's Guide to Negotiating* 16 (2015).)

1. Listening, Observing, and Questioning

Lawyers are often characterized as good talkers, who love to argue. In court, being a "silver-tongued" attorney may be valued. In negotiations, as in conversations, being a good listener and knowing how to obtain information through the use of questions is more important than talking. This is true in interacting with clients when preparing to negotiate for them, as well as in negotiating. The old wisdom that "we were born with one tongue and two ears so that we can hear from others twice as much as we speak," is good advice for negotiators.

The same ratio of two eyes and one tongue might also be noted to emphasize the importance of observing speakers for nonverbal cues and the information they reveal. Observing facial and body language of a person talking to you may communicate more about how they feel than their words. The dynamics between opposing counsel and her client or between members of multiple parties on the other side may offer important clues about what they might be willing to pay or accept to settle a dispute or close a deal. This is also referred to as situational awareness, which combines astute observation with interpretation based on your experience. (See Wheeler 2013.)

If you can learn what is in the brain and heart of an opponent, you can make a personal connection, satisfy their needs, and get what you want at the lowest possible cost. If you actively allow others to openly express themselves, they usually will tell you what you want to know. The more you talk, the less they can say, and the less you can listen and learn. We seldom learn anything new by speaking. The key lesson here is easy: **Talk less; listen and observe more.** When you do speak in a negotiation, do so in a way that elicits more information, directly or indirectly, or that helps shape the negotiation. Sometimes giving information is a way to get information, but know when and how to listen.

Research results confirm that effective negotiators are better at eliciting information and do more of it than less effective negotiators. Disclosing information, whether by arguing the merits of your case or asserting your position early on, generally results in worse outcomes than first asking questions and listening. Neil Rackham and John Carlisle studied the behavior of English labor and contract negotiators. The more successful negotiators asked twice the number of questions asked by less successful negotiators and spent twice as much time acquiring information. Effective negotiators tested their understanding of what was said and summarized what they heard (Rackman and Carlisle 1978).

Rackham and Carlisle's research supports what psychologists and interviewers have known: The most effective listening is active listening. Active listening is the opposite of deadpan, silent, passive listening. During active listening you focus your energy on what the speaker is communicating and provide responses that encourage the speaker to open up and say more. In active listening you hear not only the content, but also identify the emotion or sentiment expressed. You then briefly restate in your own words the feeling and some of the content you heard communicated so the speaker can confirm, clarify, or amplify. Most important, your response lets speakers know you heard what they said and that you care about how they feel.

The following selection provides a guide for active listening and purposeful questioning when you are negotiating.

❖ **Lee E. Miller & Jessica Miller,** *A Woman's Guide to Successful Negotiating*

---

66 (McGraw-Hill, 2002)

Active Listening

There are numerous ways to encourage others to talk so you can find out what their real concerns are. These techniques are referred to as active listening and include the following:

Reflect Back

Restate what the other person has said in your own words. This ensures that you correctly understand what has been said, and it also shows the other person that you are trying to see things from their perspective. For example, if someone says, "I can't understand how you could come up with such an unworkable solution to our problem," you might paraphrase that by stating, "I guess we don't understand what your real needs are here."

Clarify

When something is not clear or you want a better understanding of what has been said, you can ask for clarification. For example, in response to the previous statement, you might say, "I don't understand. What do you mean by unworkable?" Or you could ask them to explain: "Why do you think it's unworkable?" In addition to giving you additional information, clarifying signals that you care about their concerns.

Encourage

Nod and smile, lean forward when others are talking, look them in the eye, and occasionally interject phrases such as "I see," "Go on," or "Really." This will encourage those who are speaking to expand upon what they are saying. The more they speak, the more information you will get. Again, by engaging in this behavior, you signal your willingness to listen and your interest in what is being said.

Acknowledge Effort

Provide positive reinforcement when the speaker tries to work with you or says something you agree with. For example, you might respond by saying "I appreciate your efforts," or "That's a good point." This will encourage further efforts to find common ground with you.

Recognize Feelings

It often helps to address the feelings that people may be experiencing but not openly sharing. In response to the statement that "The proposal is unworkable," you could reply, "I see that you're frustrated with how the discussions are proceeding." Recognizing others' feelings often defuses anger and allows them to open up. This is frequently necessary before you can move on to problem solving.

Summarize

When you believe that you understand the other person's point of view, summarize your understanding of what has been said and ask whether your understanding is correct. Do the same when you reach an agreement on a particular issue. Summarizing helps to prevent misunderstandings, and you should use it continually throughout the course of negotiations. When done on an ongoing basis, it reinforces that the parties are making progress and encourages continued efforts toward reaching an agreement.

It doesn't do much good to listen, however, if you don't act on what you hear. Don't be afraid to stray from what you had planned to say if you get signals the other side is not receptive to the approach you are taking. Moreover, nothing works better than using what the other side says. You can achieve many of your objectives just by listening carefully to what is being said and agreeing to those points that are helpful. That is why it is always best to listen first.

Purposeful Questioning

Good negotiators ask different types of questions for different reasons, from open-ended, information-gathering questions to focused questions intended to lead someone to a specific conclusion. The two primary reasons for asking questions during negotiations are to get information or to support your argument. How you ask a question will depend on what you are trying to achieve.

Ask Open-Ended Questions

You should ask open-ended questions if your goal is to obtain information or to find out what the other person is thinking. Open-ended questions can't be answered with a yes or a no. They usually begin with "who," "what," "where," "when," "why," or "how," which allow for wide latitude as to responses. Their unstructured nature often enables you to find out what the real issues are and how you might satisfactorily resolve them. Open-ended questions such as "Tell me how you reached that conclusion" can also give you an insight into how someone else thinks.

Often, asking the right question at the right time can give you the information you need to completely turn around a negotiation. I recall one such situation. . . . I was practicing law, representing an executive who was taking a job with a new company and being asked to relocate from California to Connecticut. We had worked out the major issues—salary, bonus, stock options—to his satisfaction. The new company had a generous relocation policy, but it provided for only a 30-day temporary living allowance. My client's daughter was a senior in high school and he was not going to move his family until after she graduated. So he asked the company to pay his temporary living expenses for one year. The company representative insisted that they could not deviate from their relocation policy. My client was equally adamant and felt that if the company was taking such a bureaucratic approach to his request, it was probably not a place where he would want to work. Just when I thought the deal was about to fall through, I asked a question that allowed us to successfully conclude the negotiation. What was this brilliantly insightful question? It was simply "Why?" More specifically, I told the vice president of human resources that I couldn't understand why we were arguing about this issue. He explained that the relocation policy was written that way because the company had been burned by a senior executive who, after being paid temporary living expenses for well over a year, could not get his wife to move and rejoined his previous company. Having been embarrassed once, the vice president was not about to ask for another exception to the policy. Understanding his reasons for refusing our seemingly reasonable request enabled us to readily resolve the problem. We agreed that if my client did not move his family to Connecticut, he would repay the company for his temporary living expenses. This allowed the vice president to ask for and receive a modification to the relocation policy without the fear of looking foolish if things didn't work out. . . .

One purpose of asking open-ended questions is to keep the other side talking. The more someone talks, the more likely they are to provide valuable information. An added benefit is that it helps you develop a relationship with that person, which, in and of itself, is helpful. When you ask questions of others, people feel that you are working with them to find solutions, not negotiating against them.

Ask "Why?"

As mentioned above, often the most useful question you can ask is "Why?" Asking why works particularly well as a response to statements such as, "We can't agree to that" or "That would be contrary to policy." When you ask, "Why can't you agree to that?" or "Why do you have that policy?," you are calling for a reasoned response. After you are given a reason, you can make a case that the reason is not applicable in this instance. Alternatively, you have an opportunity to satisfy the other side's objections.

Repeat Back in Question Form

Another way to ask why is to use a variation on the reflecting back technique described above. Simply repeat what has just been said, but in question form . . . reflecting back the other side's own words when a proposal is not reasonable can be very effective. Similarly, when people make unqualified statements such as, "We never do that," a simple "Never?" will force them to either confirm that this is really the case, or, more likely, cause them to retreat to something like, "Except in very unusual circumstances." Once you get that kind of admission, you are well on your way to making your case because now you know what argument to make: that yours are unusual circumstances and require an exception to the normal practice. Once someone concedes that exceptions have been made in the past, it becomes much harder to claim that you don't deserve the same treatment.

Answer Questions with Questions

Sometimes you can answer a question with a question. If you don't want to respond to a particular question or you want to understand why someone is asking a particular question, you can respond by asking, "Well, what do you think?" If you do this too often you may appear evasive and argumentative, but using this approach sparingly can be effective.

Ask What They Would Do

Finally, if you find yourself at an impasse, you can always ask what they would do if they were in your position. This can sometimes completely change the dynamics of the negotiations by forcing the other side to come up with a solution to the problem, rather than trying to convince you that there is no problem. In doing so, a solution may emerge that would be acceptable to you or could be made so with slight modification.

Questions

5. The selection above on active listening and questioning is excerpted from a book written as a guide for women. Do you consider the advice given to be gender specific? Do you think men or women are generally better listeners? Why?
6. Are there times when active listening or responding to a question with a question should not be used? When would you find these techniques annoying or counterproductive?
7. The use of silence to elicit additional information after someone stops speaking can also be effective in situations other than negotiation. The silence should be accompanied by continued eye contact to convey an expectation or invitation for more information. Have you used this method with friends, a spouse, or children? Do you think you are susceptible to this technique when used by others?

2. Managing Information

Effective negotiators know how to manage information and thoughtfully determine what information to seek, to provide, when to provide it, and what information to guard. (Gupta 2015) Generally, it is better to receive more information than you give, but this is not an absolute. The distinction between managing information and purposely deceiving is a thin line and is examined in the section on negotiation ethics.

The following selection provides advice and discusses issues regarding obtaining and providing information. Professor Nelken first focuses on managing and bargaining for information in distributive situations and then on the benefits and concerns of sharing information in more integrative negotiations. The separation between distributive and integrative negotiation is not always clear—her comments may apply to both.

❖ **Melissa L. Nelken,** *NEGOTIATION: THEORY AND PRACTICE*

41 (Anderson Publishing, 2007)

In the course of the negotiation, you will try to learn things about the other party's case, and about his perception of your case, that you don't know when the negotiation starts. He, of course, will do the same with you. Another important aspect of preparation, then, is deciding what you need to find out before you actually make a deal. Without considering what information you need to gather in the early stages of the negotiation, you will not be able to gauge how well the actual situation fits the assumptions you have made in preparing to negotiate. You may have overestimated how much the other party needs a deal with you, or underestimated the value he places on what you are selling. Only careful attention to gathering information will enable you to adjust your goals appropriately. In addition to what you want to learn, you also have to decide what information you are willing, or even eager, to divulge to the other party—for example, the large number of offers you have already received for the subject property—and what information you want to conceal—for example, the fact that none of those offers exceeds the price you paid for the property originally. Managing information is a central feature of distributive bargaining, and you have to plan to do it well.

A beginning negotiator often feels that she has to conceal as much as possible, that virtually anything she reveals will hurt her or be used against her. . . . [Y]ou are more likely to feel this way if you have not thought through your case and prepared how to present it in the best light that you realistically can. If you choose when and how you will reveal information, rather than anxiously concealing as much as possible, you gain a degree of control over the negotiation that you lack when you merely react to what your counterpart says or does. Increasing the amount of information you are prepared to reveal, and reducing the amount you feel you absolutely must conceal, will help you make a stronger case for your client. In addition, the more willing you are to share information that the other party considers useful, the more likely you are to learn what you need to know from your counterpart before you make a deal. . . .

Bargaining for Information

A central aspect of distributive bargaining is bargaining for information. In the course of planning, you have to make certain working assumptions about the motives and wishes of the other side, as well as about the factual context of the negotiation. In addition, we all have a tendency to "fill in" missing information in order to create a coherent picture of a situation. For a negotiator, it is imperative to separate out what you know to be true from what you merely believe to be true by testing your assumptions during the early stages of the negotiation. Otherwise, you risk making decisions based on inaccurate information and misunderstanding what the other side actually tells you. . . .

Many negotiators forget that they start with only a partial picture of the situation, and they push to "get down to numbers" before learning anything about the other side's point of view. Yet the relevant facts of a situation are not immutable; they are often dependent on your perspective. Knowing the other side's perspective is a valuable source of information about possibilities for settlement. The most obvious way to gather that information is by asking questions, especially about the reasons behind positions taken by the other party. Why does a deal have to be made today? How good are her alternatives to settlement with you? What is the basis for a particular offer? Asking questions allows you to test the assumptions that you bring to the negotiation about both parties' situations. Questions also permit you to gauge the firmness of stated positions by learning how well supported they are by facts. In addition, the information you gather can alert you to issues that are important (or unimportant) to your counterpart, opening up possibilities for an advantageous settlement if you value those issues differently.

In addition to asking questions, you have to learn to listen carefully to what the other party says, to look for verbal and nonverbal cues that either reinforce or contradict the surface message conveyed. If someone tells you that he wants $40,000-50,000 to settle, you can be sure that he will settle for $40,000, or less. If he starts a sentence by saying, "I'll be perfectly frank with you . . . ," take whatever follows with a large grain of salt and test it against other things you have heard. Asking questions is only one way to gather information, and not always the most informative one. You also have to listen for what someone omits from an answer, for answers that are not answers or that deflect the question, for hesitations and vagueness in the responses that you get. There is no simple formula for what such things mean, but the more alert you are for ways in which you are not getting information in a straightforward way, the better able you will be to sort through the information that you get. . . .

One of the most effective and underutilized methods of bargaining for information is silence. Many inexperienced negotiators, especially lawyer-negotiators, think that they are paid to talk and are not comfortable sitting quietly. If you can teach yourself to do so, you will find that you often learn things that would never be revealed in response to a direct question. When silences occur, people tend to fill them in; and because the silence is unstructured, what they say is often more spontaneous than any answer to a question would be. Since you are interested in gathering new information in the course of the negotiation, it is useful to keep in mind that if you are talking, you probably aren't hearing anything you do not already know. Therefore, silence is truly golden. . . .

Sharing Information

All that has been said so far about integrative bargaining suggests that lawyers will only be able to do a good job if they share substantive information about their clients' needs and preferences and look for ways to make their differences work for them in the negotiation. According to Follett (1942, p. 36), "the first rule . . . for obtaining integration is to put your cards on the table, face the real issue, uncover the conflict, bring the whole thing into the open." This is a far cry from the bargaining for information that characterizes distributive negotiations, where each side seeks to learn as much as possible about the other while revealing as little as it can. The more straightforward and clear the negotiators' communications are, the fewer obstacles there will be to recognizing and capitalizing on opportunities for mutual gain. This means, first, that they must be clear about their clients' goals, even if they are open as to the means of reaching those goals. In addition, there must be sufficient trust between them so that both are willing to reveal their clients' true motivations. Such trust may be based on past experience, but it may also be developed in the course of a negotiation, as the negotiators exchange information and evaluate the information they have received. It does not have to be based on an assumption that the other side has your best interest at heart, but only that he is as interested as you are in uncovering ways that you can both do better through negotiation. Self-interest can keep both sides honest in the process, even where there might be a short-term gain from misrepresentation. Of course, the need to share information in order to optimize results creates risks for the negotiators as well. . . .

Flexibility, rather than rigid positions, is key to integrative bargaining, since the outcome will depend on fitting together the parties' needs as much as possible. When the negotiators share adequate information, they may end up redefining the conflict they are trying to resolve. For example, what seemed a specific problem about failure to fulfill the terms of a contract may turn out to be a more fundamental difficulty with the structure of the contract itself. A better outcome for both sides may result if the contract is renegotiated. . . .

Strategic Use of Information

There is also anxiety because the amount of shared information needed for integrative bargaining to succeed may be more than a distributive bargainer wants to reveal. For example, a distributively-inclined buyer may prefer that his counterpart think that time of delivery, which he does not care much about, is very important to him, so that he can exact concessions on other aspects of the deal by "giving in" to a later delivery to accommodate the seller. Since it is hard to know in advance what issues will be most significant to the other side, it can be difficult to decide how much information to share and how to evaluate the quality of the information you receive about your counterpart's priorities. The fear of being taken advantage of often results in both sides' taking preemptive action focused on "winning" rather than on collaborating. Sometimes such strategies are effective; but they are also likely to impede or prevent what could be a fruitful search for joint gains.

E. Opening Demands and Offers

As we noted earlier, the timing of offers and demands may vary between positional and interest-based approaches. Positional bargainers tend to make demands and offers early. Their initial interaction may commence with the presentation of a demand. The filing of a lawsuit without prior negotiation of the claim is one way to assert a demand and start negotiations. In contrast, interest-based negotiators seek information from their counterpart and prefer to establish a positive relationship before discussing proposals. One purpose of the information sought and perhaps exchanged is to discover interests that might lead to an acceptable solution that creates value, even if there might later be more competitive bargaining to allocate the added value.

Whether you prefer a competitive or cooperative approach, there will be negotiations in which you must decide if it is better to make the first offer or invite an offer from the other side. (Offers and demands are used here synonymously.) If choosing to make the first offer, should it be extreme, modestly favorable, exactly what you expect, or equitably calculated to be fair to all and maximize collective value? If the first offer is made by the other side, should you flinch, counteroffer immediately, or process the offer and come back with an exaggerated counteroffer or one closer to your reservation point? How does formulating the initial offer relate to what we have learned about perceptions, ripeness, anchoring, preparation, the role of expectations, and trust?

The negotiation guidebooks are full of advice on making offers, much of it contradictory. There appears to be consensus that in distributive negotiations more extreme or aggressive offers result in more favorable outcomes. (An exaggerated offer can come before or after learning the other side's opening position.) This consensus, focused on distributive negotiation, doesn't help you on how to start an integrative negotiation.

The selection below, which is based on Professor Williams's extensive empirical research of lawyer negotiators, weighs the advantages and disadvantages of three different opening strategies.

❖ **Gerald R. Williams & Charles Craver, *LEGAL NEGOTIATION***

79 (West Publishing, 2007)

. . . The lawyers articulate their opening positions. At this early stage in the dispute, that exchange is not as simple as it appears. The facts are not all in, the legal questions are not fully researched, and unforeseen developments loom on the horizon. In the face of these uncertainties, the negotiators must leave themselves a certain amount of latitude, yet they must develop credible opening demands and offers. . . .

[T]here are essentially three strategies that can be used in framing an opening position. . . . Negotiators may adopt the *maximalist strategy* of asking for more than they expect to obtain, they may adopt the *equitable strategy* of taking positions that are fair to both sides, or they may adopt the *integrative strategy* of searching for alternative solutions that would generate the most attractive combination for all concerned. Each strategy has its own strengths and weaknesses.

Maximalist Positioning

Arguments for maximalist positioning begin with the assumption that the opening position is a bargaining position, and that no matter how long bargainers may deny it, they expect to come down from them to find agreements. Maximalist positioning has several advantages. These position statements effectively hide the bargainer's real or minimum expectations, they eliminate the danger of committing to an overly modest case evaluation, they provide covers for them while they seek to learn real opponent positions, and will very likely induce opponents to reduce their expectations. They also provide negotiators with something to give up, with concessions they can make, to come to terms with opponents. This last factor may be especially important when opponents also open high, and negotiators are required to trade concessions as they move toward mutually agreeable terms. These advantages may lead many to believe that negotiators who make high opening demands, have high expectations, make relatively small and infrequent concessions, and are perceptive and unyielding fare better in the long run than their opponents.

The potential benefits of the maximalist position need to be weighed against its potential demerits, which are those associated with competitive/adversarial strategies. . . . The most important weakness is the increased risk of bargaining stalemates. Competent opponents will prefer their non-settlement alternatives to the unreasonable demands and supporting tactics of the maximalist negotiators, unless the opponents themselves can devise effective strategies to counter such maximalist behaviors. We observe in the data that competitive attorneys at all levels of effectiveness are rated as making high opening demands. Yet, by definition, effective competitive/adversarials use the strategy proficiently, while ineffective competitive adversarials do not. We are forced to conclude that in the legal context the maximalist strategy does not consistently bring high returns for those who use it—only for those who employ it effectively. How high demands can be without losing their effectiveness depends on several considerations. One is the nature of the remedy being sought. By their nature, contract damages are less inflatable than personal injury damages, for example, and negotiators who multiply their contract damages as they do their personal injury claims will undermine their own credibility. Another consideration is local custom. Specialized groups within the bar develop norms and customs that provide measures against which the reasonableness or extremism of demands can be evaluated. Not all high demands are the same. Some demands lack credibility on their face by their inappropriateness and lack of congruity in the context in which they are made. But the level of demands is not the sole factor. The data suggest that effective competitive/adversarial negotiators are able to establish the credibility and plausibility of high demands by relying on convincing legal argumentation. Ineffective competitive/adversarials lack the skills to do this, and, in the absence of convincing support, their high demands lack credibility.

Finally, it should be noted that the effectiveness of high demands will depend upon the opponents against whom the high demands are made. In cases where opponents are unsure of the actual case values, high opening demands by maximizing negotiators have the desired effect. The opponents, unsure of case values, use the maximizer's high opening demands as standards against which to set their own goals. However, when the opponents have evaluated their cases and arrived at appropriate value judgments, the opponents interpreted maximizer high opening demands as evidence of unreasonableness. This causes maximizer credibility to be diminished, and the likelihood of bargaining breakdowns increases.

Equitable Positioning

Equitable positions are calculated to be fair to both sides. Their most notable proponent, O. Bartos, challenged the assumption of maximalist theorists that both sides to negotiations are trying to maximize their own payoffs or benefits. He argued that a competing value is also operative—that negotiators feel a cooperative desire to arrive at solutions fair to both sides. In support of this argument, he cited not only humanistic literature defending equality as an essential ingredient of justice, but also anthropological and sociological studies confirming the widespread existence and operation in society of an egalitarian norm of reciprocity. Bartos conducted numerous theoretical and experimental negotiation studies which lead him to believe that the human desire to deal fairly with others is preferable to a more competitive strategy.

This equitable approach is considered as the most economical and efficient method of conflict resolution. It minimizes the risk of deadlock and avoids the costs of delay occasioned by extreme bargaining positions. Bartos recommended that negotiators be scrupulously fair and that they avoid the temptation to take advantage of naive opponents. He cautioned that the equitable approach requires trust, which allows both sides to believe they are being treated fairly. Nonetheless, trust must be tempered with realism. It is out of trust that negotiators make concessions, but if their trust is not rewarded or returned in fair fashion, further concessions should be withheld until their opponents reciprocate. Equitable negotiators do not always open negotiations with statements specifying their desires to achieve mutually beneficial solutions. Rather, they open with positions that show they are serious about finding fair agreement, and they trustingly work toward mid-points between their reasonable opening position and the reasonable opening positions of their opponents. Unless both sides come forward with reasonable opening positions, it will be difficult for one side to compel the other to move toward an equitable resolution. Referring back to the data on cooperative/problem-solving and competitive/adversarial negotiators, we intuitively suspect that Bartos' equitable negotiators are cooperative/problem-solvers. This observation is borne out by the extremely high ratings received by cooperative/problem-solving attorneys on characteristics such as trustworthy, ethical, honest, and fair. Just as with our analysis of maximalist positioning by competitive/adversarial attorneys, it must be pointed out that the use of equitable positioning by cooperative/problem-solving attorneys does not always generate satisfactory results. It is obviously satisfactory as used by effective cooperative/problem-solvers, but it is likely to be deficient when used by ineffective cooperative/problem-solvers. We must conclude that the positioning strategy, whether maximalist or equitable, does not guarantee success. Whichever approach is used, it must be employed with care and acumen or it will not be effective.

Integrative Positioning

Integrative Positioning involves more than opening demands and offers. It describes an attitude or approach that carries through the other stages of the negotiation, and is an alternative to pure positional bargaining. The most effective advocates of this method have been Roger Fisher and William Ury who advise negotiators to avoid positioning completely. Among business people, the method is seen as the art of problem solving. Integrative negotiators view cases as presenting alternative solutions, and they believe that chances for reaching agreements are enhanced by discovering innovative alternatives reflecting the underlying interests of the parties, and seeking to arrange the alternatives in packages that yield maximum benefit to both parties. This strategy is often identified with exchange transactions involving many variables, and is generally seen as having limited utility in personal injury actions, for example, where the fundamental issue is how much money defendants are going to pay plaintiffs—a classic distributive problem. . . .

F. To Make the First Offer or Not

In every negotiation you will need to visit anew the question of whether or not to make the first offer. The optimum decision of whether to make the first offer will depend on the subject of the negotiation, the setting, custom, and practice, and what you know about your negotiating counterpart. In some situations the first offer is, in effect, the demand stated in a served complaint or the listed price of property for sale. The principal tactical benefit of making the first offer is that it establishes an anchor by defining the favorable end of the bargaining zone. Earlier readings familiarized you with the power of an anchor number, particularly when the other party is uncertain about dollar values and there is no clear way to determine an objective value. Experiments have demonstrated that even experienced lawyers, real estate agents and appraisers are influenced by exposure to a specific number prior to formulating their expert opinion about the settlement value of a case or a fair market value. (See Northcraft and Neal 1987.)

Although making the first offer allows you to fix what you think is your most favorable number on the bargaining scale, it is advantageous only if you are sure that your best number is the other side's worst number. If you anchor the bargaining range with your best offer and later discover that your opponent was willing to pay more or accept less, you are stuck and may leave money on the table that you cannot reclaim. In other words, don't make the first offer unless you are absolutely sure that you have enough information to know that the other side would never offer what you are demanding. Just like in classroom role-plays, in real life negotiations there is often private information regarding your opponent's perceptions, needs and situation that you don't know. That is why it is sometimes advantageous to encourage the first offer from your counterpart. You may learn something surprising about their assessment or, at worst, confirm your guess about the bargaining range without risking a costly miscalculation.

Another risk of making first offers without sufficient information is that what you believe is a reasonably aggressive first offer may be so far out of their range that it drives the other side away from the bargaining table and destroys your credibility if the negotiation is resumed. Never demand so much or offer so little that you can't explain the reason for it or can state a credible justification. Be able to phrase your first offer as "I propose this because. . . ." Your first offer or demand should be favorable to you but not so aggressive that it is the end of bargaining rather than the beginning. Think of this down home negotiator's advice: "You don't want to hang the meat so high that the dog won't jump."

Even if you prefer to make the first offer, the dynamics of the interaction may result in the first offer coming from the other side. The less prepared you are regarding facts, values, and needs of the other side, the more you are vulnerable to the effects of anchoring. When a first offer is presented to you, probe to find out if there is any new information you can obtain without opening the door to an extended, preemptive argument from the other side. If what you learn doesn't change your initial analysis, then present the opening proposal you had formulated before hearing their first offer and the reasoning behind it. At this point, you must decide whether to take a hard stand at your end of the bargaining range, or to initiate a more cooperative approach by indicating that you will need to work together to bridge the gap. (See Malhotra and Bazerman 2007.)

Note and Problem

A popular book by the big-time sports agent and lawyer Donald Dell, *Never Make the First Offer (Except When You Should)* (2009, 159), asks, "Why do you want them to make the first offer? Because you are really not seeking an offer at all; you are seeking information. The first offer gives you an insight into their thought process. It crystallizes all their thinking up to that point and boils it down to a single number or a series of deal points. It also tells you what their primary issues are. Whatever terms they throw in along with their first number are often the most important issues to them."

As evident from the book's parenthetical subtitle, Dell recognizes that there are times when it may be advantageous to make the first offer. Consider the following situation and questions:

You are a new law school graduate. A three-lawyer firm is interested in hiring you as its first associate. The firm's size, areas of practice, and the personality of the partners are appealing to you. Your most viable alternative is as a staff lawyer with a government agency starting at $65,000. Large firms, which do not seem like a viable alternative, are starting associates at $165,000. You are scheduled to meet with the managing partner of the firm to discuss terms of employment, which have not previously been indicated.

1. In this situation, would you make the opening salary proposal or instead ask the partner to make a salary offer?
2. What are the advantages and disadvantages of making the first salary proposal versus allowing the managing partner to propose a salary?
3. What might it be helpful for you to know before making this negotiation decision?

CHAPTER
6

Negotiation Step by Step — The Middle

A. Bargaining

Once initial demands and offers are stated and explained, bargaining begins in an effort to close the gap. Bargaining takes many forms. The term "bargaining" is more associated with the competitive/distributive approach. Phrases like "searching for solutions" and "problem solving" are frequently used to describe a more cooperative/integrative approach. However, at some point in any negotiation there must be movement from the differences that brought the parties to the table toward the agreement that will resolve the dispute or create a deal. Whether the movement results from arguments and persuasion or from proposed principles and criteria may be more a matter of semantics and tone than of real difference. For example, lawyers in negotiating a settlement of a lawsuit may agree, expressly or implicitly, that legal principles and precedent will be the criteria for settlement. Does this reduce the role of argument and attempts at persuasion regarding what case precedent is most analogous and applicable to the matter in dispute? A hallmark of integrative negotiation is trading off a lower priority to satisfy one more personally important. Is this not a form of bargaining concession?

Some principled negotiators believe that it is best to formulate a realistic opening position and stick to it. They assume that it is unseemly to haggle and that a large gap between opening demands and offers indicates that an agreement is unlikely. It is true that in some cultures and professional settings, bargaining is not the norm and a stated offer is either accepted or no deal is made. It should not be assumed that this is true in the settlement of legal disputes are most transactions in which lawyers are involved. "No" marks the beginning of negotiations and "yes" is rarely achieved without bargaining. Getting to yes without negotiating concessions usually leaves the proposer feeling that he offered too much and the acceptor with second thoughts that she accepted too little. A respectful negotiation with reciprocal concessions can be satisfying and help build good relations, though this is not always the case.

1. Planning and Managing Concessions

Concessions are the compromises you make after your opening offer to move the negotiation forward. Usually the concessions you make are offered in return for those your negotiation opponent offers. Making concessions can be done strategically in recognition that the timing, amount, and nature of concessions are a form of communication by which each side sends signals about priorities and reservation points.

No phase of negotiation stands alone. Initial interactions and how you set the scene for exchanging demands and offers creates the context within which a concession strategy will be implemented. If continuing relationships are likely, your concession strategy and bargaining will be different than in a one-time, distributive negotiation. Developing a plan for managing the process of making concessions within the context of your relationships and your client's goals, helps to ensure that you will not give up too much too soon and that an appropriate balance will be maintained between self-interested competitiveness and relational collaboration. Whether to concede, when to concede, what to concede, and how to link concessions are among a number of important considerations. Conceding without a plan can be costly. However, the execution of your concession strategy must remain flexible in order to respond to new information and unexpected developments.

In planning concessions, prioritize and rank what you can give that might satisfy the perceived needs of the opposing side and provide the highest value to them at the lowest cost to you. Likewise, in listing concessions that you would like from the other side, consider whether any represent more value to you than cost to the other side. In other words, figure out if there are concessions that can create value by being worth more to the receiver then they cost the giver.

If possible, get the other party to move first. After a gap between demands and offers is apparent, do not fear silence. If nothing more is forthcoming, do not be afraid to ask for a concession and suggest reasons why it is appropriate for them to make a move. For example, you can explain that you are prepared to negotiate in good faith if they are first willing to show their seriousness by more realistically narrowing the gap. If you must make the first concession, be prepared to offer a rationale for why you are doing so and condition your move upon the other side conceding something.

Concessions should be made in the context of trades or exchanges rather than given simply to see if it satisfies your counterpart's expectation or if it might result in reciprocation. Demanding a concession in return both reinforces the value of what is being conceded and signals your resolve in making the concession. It also helps to bolster the norm of reciprocity and stimulate movement toward agreement. Making a concession without receiving one in return makes you vulnerable to the risk of "bargaining against yourself."

The pattern of concessions forms a message. By carefully considering what you want to communicate you can manage concessions to shape the message, particularly about how close you are to your reservation point. Significant concessions indicate that more concessions are probably available. Diminishing concessions signal that you are close to your final amount. Establishing a favorable, but not outrageous, initial value expectation with supportive reasons and then executing a plan of a moderate concession first and then progressively smaller ones often can be the most powerful pattern. It communicates resolve, then flexibility, and then diminishing returns moving toward closure.

The timing of offering concessions can also be telling and must be considered carefully. Concessions given in rapid succession early on may signal risk aversion or desperation. So, concede slowly and reluctantly. Giving away too much in the initial stages of negotiation depletes the reserve of concessions that can be offered later, when they may be more appreciated.

When negotiations involve more than the payment of money and multiple issues are on the table, concessions may take the form of issue trading or package bargaining. The greater the number of issues, the greater the opportunity for integrative bargaining and a concession pattern that involves trade-offs of higher interests for lower interests. You can then more easily concede issues of less value to you in order to gain concessions of greater value, and vice versa, thus creating value. However, the importance of planning and managing the concession process is no less in integrative negotiation. The main difference is that the plan must be all the more flexible because of the need to more deeply explore interests and creative trade-offs during bargaining. Some negotiators in an integrative situation, once they have obtained what they want, prefer to conclude bargaining by being the one to make the last small concession. They want their counterpart to walk away satisfied and with the impression that they "won." This is based on the theory that a satisfied opponent will stick with the agreement and reciprocate with generosity in future dealings. (See Lantz 2004.)

By planning and using concessions strategically, you can influence the outcome of the negotiation. The flip side of anything that can be used strategically is that a similar or counterstrategy might be used by a competitive negotiator on the other side to manipulate you. So be aware that the concession signals can be deceptive about how far an opposing bargainer will go. This is all the more reason to plan ahead, prioritize your concessions and be aware of concession patterns.

In summary, the following are helpful concession suggestions:

- Develop a plan for managing the process of making concessions
- Prioritize and rank concessions beforehand
- Create high value from low-cost concessions
- Get the other party to make the first concession
- Concede slowly and reluctantly
- Offer a rationale for why you are conceding
- Get something in return for each concession
- Use concessions strategically when appropriate

Problem

Assume you are negotiating a personal injury claim on behalf of an injured pedestrian, and liability is not clear. You have spoken with the insurance claims adjuster five times. Each time you have conceded an additional $1,000 off your initial written demand of $80,000, while offering new information or arguments in support of your claim. What do you think the adjuster might be communicating to you with each of the following concession patterns (he would use only one of these four patterns), and how would each pattern influence your recommendation to your risk-averse client about accepting a $47,000 settlement after your fifth round of negotiation?

| | | Concession Pattern | | |
Round	A	B	C	D
1.	$ 0	$ 3,000	$40,000	$47,000
2.	$ 0	$ 6,000	$45,000	$47,000
3.	$ 0	$12,500	$46,500	$47,000
4.	$ 0	$25,000	$47,000	$47,000
5.	$47,000	$47,000	$47,000	$47,000

2. Value-Creating Trades and Brainstorming

Repeating initial positions, advocating for them and engaging in a process of incremental concessions may narrow the gap, but might not close it. Brainstorming is a technique to generate value creating options and trade-offs. It is associated with a problem-solving approach, but can also be helpful in distributive negotiations. The essence of brainstorming is suspending judgment and advocacy of positions in favor of exploring possible solutions that better fill the needs of all parties. In effect, brainstorming is a timeout from negotiating and practical constraints to see what the parties might be able to do outside the box formed by their conflicting positions.

There are four requirements for brainstorming:

- Neutrally frame the issue in terms of interests (what do the parties want to accomplish);
- Freely think of all possible ways those interests can be met (be creative);
- Do not evaluate brainstormed ideas (no criticism – no praise);
- Do not assign ownership (suggesting possibilities is not advocating).

Framing the issue in terms of unmet interests can remind integrative negotiators about the needs to be filled and refocus adversarial negotiators on what they each hope to accomplish. Reframing the issue away from the amount of money to be paid and instead on how else the interests at stake can be met is the beginning of brainstorming.

Once the issue is framed in terms of interests, rather than money alone, the parties can think creatively think about ways that the identified interest can be satisfied. Two or more minds generating ideas are more likely to come up with creative possibilities than one side alone. One idea may spark others that can then be collectively refined and improved, so that new and more attractive solutions emerge.

Creative ideas are inhibited by premature judgment. Particularly in a negotiation situation where a ready solution has not emerged, one side is inclined to view suggestions from the other critically. Reactive devaluation is the enemy of brainstorming. Judgment, must be suspended during the initial phase of brainstorming, including praise as well as criticism. Gratuitously being encouraging by stating that a counterpart's suggestion is a "great idea," is an indication of judgment that can discourage other contributions to the process.

Brainstorming is also dampened by assigning ownership to a suggestion. The person proposing a possibility need not be in favor of it or held to endorse it as the solution. Explaining an idea should not be equated with advocating for it. The process is intended to create a menu of possibilities that can later be collectively refined, examined for practicability and for how various pieces of the solution can be pieced together.

   Brainstorming is used in creating solutions to all types of problems and situations, whether personal, family, business or professional. It can be successfully used in negotiation and dispute resolution. The process of brainstorming can help shape value creating opportunities and convert distributive impasses to a shared problem that can be solved. (Mnookin et al. 2000)

Problem

Assume you represent the plaintiff family suing for wrongful death of a husband/father killed by a drunk driver. Distributive bargaining has reached an impasse, with your last demand at $1 million and the defendant's last offer at $800,000 (combining a $500,000 insurance limit and defendant's personal funds). Would you consider brainstorming? If you knew that the affluent defendant was facing sentencing for vehicular manslaughter and a letter from your client could be beneficial to her, would this open the door to value creation? The following letter was written to the sentencing judge following brainstorming, which resulted in settlement of the case. (All names have been changed.) Is an ethical problem raised by the use of this letter to settle a wrongful death claim against a drunk driver?

> To whom it may concern:
> We are the mother and surviving widow of the deceased, David Baron, whose death has left us and his three young sons behind. We write this letter to request leniency for Ms. Dorian.
>   Mistakes were made by both Ms. Dorian and David, and we have all paid an enormous price. At this point, we do not believe that these consequences should be further multiplied by sending Ms. Dorian to jail.
>   We understand that this was an isolated incident of drinking and driving for Ms. Dorian and she seems truly sorry for what happened. She has taken steps to deal with the drinking problem and she has done her best to compensate us and the three boys for our loss. We believe it is time for everyone to put this tragedy behind them and to begin building new lives in its aftermath.
>   We want to ask that Ms. Dorian be placed on probation for a period of time. We would like to see her participate in programs and organizations for victims and substance abusers in the criminal justice system. We think David would agree.
>   Thank you for your time and consideration.
>
> Sincerely,
> Judith Baron and Martha Baron

---

3. Multiparty Bargaining—Coalitions and Holdouts

Legal disputes and transactions often involve multiple parties. The negotiation dynamic and trades then become more complex, and there may be sub-bargaining within the more comprehensive negotiation. In a multiparty lawsuit, a plaintiff must negotiate with the defendants and the defendants are likely to negotiate with each other. If there is also more than one plaintiff, negotiations occur on both sides of the table and across it. In multiparty transactions, there is a mix of complementary and competing interests that may require many negotiations within the larger negotiation context.

A key difference between two-party and multiparty bargaining is the formation of coalitions. A coalition forms when two or more parties discover that they have complementary interests or that they can form side deals. They can then leverage their combined bargaining strength against the others or reach a deal that leaves out another bargainer. It is the possibility of freezing someone out of participating in the deal or blocking a deal that gives a coalition leverage. The more parties, the more possible alliances or coalitions there are. The bargaining gets both more extracted and complex as each party weighs their bargaining options with each of the other parties and the possible combinations. Bargaining can become very strategic. Because there are different payoffs possible with each combination and these are not immediately known, coalitions may dissolve and change before a final agreement is reached.

An example of a classic coalition arises when an injured driver sues another driver, the dealer who sold the defendant her car, the automobile manufacturer, and the auto repair shop that last serviced the defendant's car. Although naturally allied in their defense against the injured plaintiff, because of joint and several liability each defendant has individual interests that may motivate him or her to bargain separately with the plaintiff and form a coalition against the remaining defendants. So if the auto dealership bargains with the plaintiff to pay a limited amount that caps the dealer's liability and reduces its actual payout if the plaintiff recovers full damages from the other defendants, then a coalition of interests is formed against the remaining defendants. The settling defendant may agree to stay in the case to testify favorably and also avoid creating the "empty chair" defense. (This is known as a "Mary Carter" agreement and is discussed in Chapter 11. See Abbot Ford, Inc. v. The Superior Court of Los Angeles County; Ford Motor Co., 43 Cal. 3d 858, 1987.) A similar coalition situation can occur in a breach of contract case or any other type of case involving multiple defendants or plaintiffs.

Another aspect of multiparty cases and transactions that can change the bargaining process is the prospect of one or more parties holding out from a settlement or deal knowing that the others want to close the deal and will pay proportionately more to bring in the holdout. A settlement requirement of unanimity among multiple parties in a negotiation increases the strategic motivation for one party to hold out for more and also increases the chance of a negotiation impasse. For example, one of four partners may hold out in negotiations to sell their business to a suitor unless the holdout is paid more than the other partners. One of several property owners may hold out until all other property owners have sold to a developer so he may demand more in order for the complete transaction to close. (For an analysis of the added complexities and obstacles to settlement created in multiparty situations, see Mnookin 2003.)

Multiparty disputes and transactions, which create the prospect of coalitions and holdouts, complicate the bargaining phase and require more detailed analysis of the potential payoffs and negotiation leverage. Correctly anticipating the behaviors and moves of others in multiparty bargaining situations can be particularly valuable. Game theory combines mathematical and economic concepts to calculate and quantify what others are likely to do in response to what you do. Game theory principles can be useful to systematically assess the probable actions of opponents in multiparty negotiations. Game theory was made more accessible for use by negotiators through the writing of a Harvard mathematician, Howard Raiffa, *Negotiation Analysis: The Science of Art and Collaborative Decision Making* (2002). See also Joel Watson, *Strategy: An Introduction to Game Theory, Third Edition* (2013); William Spaniel, *Game Theory 101: Bargaining* (2014).

Just as there may be a payoff for one seller in a multiple-seller situation or one plaintiff in a multiparty claim who holds out to be the last to agree, there are situations in which being the first defendant to settle is advantageous. Plaintiffs may, in effect, offer an attractive discount to the first to settle to obtain one defendant's cooperation and then leverage that agreement as pressure against the remaining defendants. The following excerpt illustrates such a situation in a class-action negotiation.

❖ John M. Poswall, *The Lawyers: Class of '69*

248 (Jullundur Press, 2003)

On Monday morning, Leon and Bishop did what appeared to be poor strategy in negotiations. They went to the turf of their opponent to talk settlement—into the luxurious 28th floor conference room of the largest defense law firm in Northern California. There, overlooking the San Francisco Bay, they met with the firm's senior litigation partner, Martin Crosby, Jr., flanked by his committee of defense attorneys representing the various levels of defendants. A number of corporate senior vice presidents were also in evidence, each being given careful deference by his representative attorney. Jack Merchant was absent. . . .

"We're all realists here," Crosby went on. "All professionals. Litigation is costly, even when we win. I'll be candid with you. I think class actions are legal blackmail and should be resisted forcefully. But my clients, our clients," he corrected himself, gesturing with his hands to the assembled group, "are willing to resolve the matter now to save the costs of litigation. Of course, if the matter proceeds, this offer will be withdrawn, and I can give you my personal assurance, Mr. Goldman, that we are prepared to spend whatever it takes to win." . . .

"We're prepared to pay your class of clients $1 million"—Crosby said $1 million very slowly to let it sink in—"for any real or imagined slight they have endured and," he looked at Leon closely, "$1 million in fees and costs to your firm for its efforts in this matter." . . .

"Marty"—he knew no one called Martin Crosby, Jr., anything but Mr. Crosby—"you invite me over here, threaten me, and then insult me and my clients, and conclude with offering me what amounts to a bribe to sell out my clients. I think I should report you to the State Bar." . . .

Leon smiled. . . . He stood up, leaned on the table with both hands, and spent a few seconds on each corporate vice president, after passing his eyes over their attorneys.

"Here's how it's going to be, gentlemen. We will settle with each group separately. The first group will pay the least; the next a bit more; and so on. The last to settle will pay the most." . . .

"You should know that I met with Jack Merchant [a defense attorney not in the room] on Saturday and Sunday, and we have arrived at a settlement, signed last night, that includes all of the provisions I just outlined. The lenders group of defendants have agreed to pay $40 million in settlement with our guarantee that each remaining group will pay more."

He shifted his eyes around the room again. He sensed the shock bordering on panic.

"So gentlemen, I suggest each of you call me when you are ready."

He turned and walked to the door. . . .

B. Moving Toward Closure

1. The Role of Power and Commitment

Negotiation is often discussed in terms of power and how each side to a negotiation can use its power to move the negotiation in the direction it desires and get what it wants from the other side. Power comes from the mind of your negotiating opponents. If they believe that you can provide them what they want or deny it to them, then relative to them, you have power. Again, perception becomes reality for purposes of negotiation. What someone wants may be material or emotional. It may be a desire to gain something new or not to lose what they have. So, you have power if you control what your opponent wants, including peace of mind, looking good, or not being harmed—provided they think you will exercise your control.

Power is linked to commitment. If it is perceived that you are committed to do what another wants, or not do it, only if they give you what you want, then you have power to obtain what you want. For example, a hostage taker may have added power if one of several hostages is shot.

Power may be a factor from the beginning to the end of negotiation. However, the perception of power often changes as the process goes forward. Because power is in the mind of the perceiver, what is communicated verbally and non-verbally during the course of a negotiation determines how power is perceived at the time decisions must be made. Both parties will attempt to display or exercise the power they have over the other to move the negotiation to a successful closure. Each may communicate their power, or attempt to create a perception of power, by threats, displays of absolute commitment, or disclosure of better alternatives for themselves and worse alternatives for the opponent.

Getting to Yes did not place emphasis on negotiation power and was criticized for not addressing the topic more. In the article that follows, Roger Fisher, the lead author of *Getting to Yes*, takes up the subject of negotiating power and ties it to commitment. He defines power and expands the traditional concepts of power in a way that makes using power consistent with being a principled negotiator.

❖ **Roger Fisher, *NEGOTIATING POWER: GETTING AND USING INFLUENCE***

Negotiation Theory and Practice 127 (J. Z. Rubin & W. Breslin eds., 1991)

Getting to Yes (Fisher and Ury, 1981) has been justly criticized as devoting insufficient attention to the issue of power. It is all very well, it is said, to tell people how they might jointly produce wise outcomes efficiently and amicably, but in the real world people don't behave that way; results are determined by power—by who is holding the cards, by who has more clout.

At the international level, negotiating power is typically equated with military power. The United States is urged to develop and deploy more nuclear missiles so that it can negotiate from a position of strength. Threats and warnings also play an important role in the popular concept of power, as do resolve and commitment. In the game of chicken, victory goes to the side that more successfully demonstrates that it will not yield.

There is obviously some merit in the notion that physical force, and an apparent willingness to use it, can affect the outcome of a negotiation. How does that square with the suggestion that negotiators ought to focus on the interests of the parties, on the generating of alternatives, and on objective standards to which both sides might defer? . . .

How Should We Define Negotiating Power?

If I have negotiating power, I have the ability to affect favorably someone else's decision. This being so, one can argue that my power depends upon someone else's perception of my strength, so it is what they *think* that matters, not what I actually have. The other side may be as much influenced by a row of cardboard tanks as by a battalion of real tanks. One can then say that negotiating power is all a matter of perception.

A general who commands a real tank battalion, however, is in a far stronger position than one in charge of a row of cardboard tanks. A false impression of power is extremely vulnerable, capable of being destroyed by a word. In order to avoid focusing our attention on how to deceive other people, it seems best at the outset to identify what constitutes "real" negotiating power—an ability to influence the decisions of others assuming they know the truth. We can then go on to recognize that, in addition, it will be possible at times to influence others through deception, through creating an illusion of power. Even for that purpose, we will need to know what illusion we wish to create. If we are bluffing, what are we bluffing about? . . .

Categories of Power

My ability to exert influence depends upon the combined total of a number of different factors. As a first approximation, the following six kinds of power appear to provide useful categories for generating prescriptive advice:

1. The power of skill and knowledge
2. The power of a good relationship
3. The power of a good alternative to negotiating
4. The power of an elegant solution
5. The power of legitimacy
6. The power of commitment. . . .

1. The Power of Skill and Knowledge

All things being equal, a skilled negotiator is better able to influence the decision of others than is an unskilled negotiator. Strong evidence suggests that negotiating skills can be both learned and taught. One way to become a more powerful negotiator is to become a more skillful one. Some of these skills are those of dealing with people: the ability to listen, to become aware of the emotions and psychological concerns of others, to empathize, to be sensitive to their feelings and one's own, to speak different languages, to communicate clearly and effectively, to become integrated so that one's words and nonverbal behavior are congruent and reinforce each other, and so forth. . . .

The more skill one acquires, the more power one will have as a negotiator. These skills can be acquired at any time, often far in advance of any particular negotiation.

Knowledge also is power. Some knowledge is general and of use in many negotiations, such as familiarity with a wide range of procedural options and awareness of national or negotiating styles and cultural differences. A repertoire of examples, precedents, and illustrations can also add to one's persuasive abilities.

Knowledge relevant to a particular negotiation in which one is about to engage is even more powerful. The more information one can gather about the parties and issues in an upcoming negotiation, the stronger one's entering posture. . . .

2. The Power of a Good Relationship

The better a working relationship I establish in advance with those with whom I will be negotiating, the more powerful I am. A good working relationship does not necessarily imply approval of each other's conduct, though mutual respect and even mutual affection—when it exists—may help, the two most critical elements of a working relationship are, first, trust, and second, the ability to communicate easily and effectively.

Trust. Although I am likely to focus my attention in a given negotiation on the question of whether or not I can trust those on the other side, my power depends upon whether they can trust me. If over time I have been able to establish a well-deserved reputation for candor, honesty, integrity, and commitment to any promise I make, my capacity to exert influence is significantly enhanced.

Communication. The negotiation process is one of communication. If I am trying to persuade some people to change their minds, I want to know where their minds are; otherwise, I am shooting in the dark. If my messages are going to have their intended impact, they need to be understood as I would have them understood. . . .

3. The Power of a Good Alternative to Negotiation

To a significant extent, my power in a negotiation depends upon how well I can do for myself if I walk away. In *Getting to YES*, we urge a negotiator to develop and improve his "BATNA"—his Best Alternative To a Negotiated Agreement. One kind of preparation for negotiation that enhances one's negotiating power is to consider the alternatives to reaching agreement with this particular negotiating partner, to select the most promising, and to improve it to the extent possible. This alternative sets a floor. If I follow this practice, every negotiation will lead to a successful outcome in the sense that any result I accept is bound to be better than anything else I could do. . . . The better an alternative one can develop outside the negotiation, the greater one's power to affect favorably a negotiated outcome.

4. The Power of an Elegant Solution

In any negotiation, there is a mélange of shared and conflicting interests. The parties face a problem. One way to influence the other side in a negotiation is to invent a good solution to that problem. The more complex the problem, the more influential an elegant answer. Too often, negotiators battle like litigators in court. Each side advances arguments for a result that would take care of its interests but would do nothing for the other side. The power of a mediator often comes from working out an ingenious solution that reconciles reasonably well the legitimate interests of both sides. Either negotiator has similar power to effect an agreement that takes care of some or most of the interests on the other side.

5. The Power of Legitimacy

Each of us is subject to being persuaded by becoming convinced that a particular result ought to be accepted because it is fair; because the law requires it; because it is consistent with precedent, industry practice, or sound policy considerations; or because it is legitimate as measured by some other objective standard. I can substantially enhance my negotiating power by searching for and developing various objective criteria and potential standards of legitimacy, and by shaping proposed solutions so that they are legitimate in the eyes of the other side. . . .

To retain his power, a wise negotiator avoids advancing a proposition that is so extreme that it damages his credibility. He also avoids locking himself into the first principle he advances that he will lose face in disentangling himself from that principle and moving on to one that has a greater chance of persuading the other side. In advance of this process, a negotiator will want to have researched precedents, expert opinion, and other objective criteria, and to have worked on various theories of what ought to be done, so as to harness the power of legitimacy—a power to which each of us is vulnerable.

6. The Power of Commitment

There are two quite different kinds of commitments—affirmative and negative:

(a) Affirmative commitments
    (1) An offer of what I am willing to agree to.
    (2) An offer of what, failing agreement, I am willing to do under certain conditions.
(b) Negative commitments
    (1) A commitment that I am unwilling to make certain agreements (even though they would be better for me than no agreement).
    (2) A commitment or threat that, failing agreement, I will engage in certain negative conduct (even though to do so would be worse for me than a simple absence of agreement).

Every commitment involves a decision. Let's first look at affirmative commitments. An affirmative commitment is a decision about what one is willing to do. It is an offer. Every offer ties the negotiator's hands to some extent. It says, "This, I am willing to do." The offer may expire or later be withdrawn, but while open it carries some persuasive power. It is no longer just an idea or a possibility that the parties are discussing. Like a proposal of marriage or a job offer, it is operational. It says, "I am willing to do this. If you agree, we have a deal." . . .

A negative commitment is the most controversial and troublesome element of negotiating power. No doubt, by tying my own hands I may be able to influence you to accept something more favorable to me than you otherwise would. The theory is simple. For almost every potential agreement there is a range within which each of us is better off having an agreement than walking away. Suppose that you would be willing to pay $75,000 for my house if you had to; but for a price above that figure you would rather buy a different house. The best offer I have received from someone else is $62,000, and I will accept that offer unless you give me a better one. At any price between $62,000 and $75,000 we are both better off than if no agreement is reached. If you offer me $62,100, and so tie your hands by a negative commitment that you cannot raise your offer, presumably, I will accept it since it is better than $62,000. On the other hand, if I can commit myself not to drop the price below $75,000, you presumably will buy the house at that price. This logic may lead us to engage in a battle of negative commitments. Logic suggests that "victory" goes to the one who first and most convincingly ties his own hands at an appropriate figure. Other things being equal, an early and rigid negative commitment at the right point should prove persuasive.

Other things, however, are not likely to be equal.

The earlier I make a negative commitment—the earlier I announce a take-it-or-leave-it position—the less likely I am to have maximized the cumulative total of the various elements of my negotiating power.

The Power of Knowledge

I probably acted before knowing as much as I could have learned. The longer I postpone making a negative commitment, the more likely I am to know the best proposition to which to commit myself.

The Power of a Good Relationship

Being quick to advance a take-it-or-leave-it position is likely to prejudice a good working relationship and to damage the trust you might otherwise place in what I say. The more quickly I confront you with a rigid position on my part, the more likely I am to make you so angry that you will refuse an agreement you might otherwise accept.

The Power of a Good Alternative

There is a subtle but significant difference between communicating a warning of the course of action that I believe it will be in my interest to take should we fail to reach agreement (my BATNA), and locking myself in to precise terms that you must accept in order to avoid my taking that course of action. Extending a warning is not the same as making a negative commitment. . . .

The Power of an Elegant Solution

The early use of a negative commitment reduces the likelihood that the choice being considered by the other side is one that best meets its interests consistent with any given degree of meeting our interests. If we announce early in the negotiation process that we will accept no agreement other than Plan X, Plan X probably takes care of most of our interests. But it is quite likely that Plan X could be improved. With further study and time, it may be possible to modify Plan X so that it serves our interests even better at little or no cost to the interests of the other side.

Second, it may be possible to modify Plan X in ways that make it more attractive to the other side without in any way making it less attractive to us. To do so would not serve merely the other side but would serve us also by making it more likely that the other side will accept a plan that so well serves our interests.

The Power of Legitimacy

The most serious damage to negotiating power that results from an early negative commitment is likely to result from its damage to the influence that comes from legitimacy. Legitimacy depends upon both process and substance. As with an arbitrator, the legitimacy of a negotiator's decision depends upon having accorded the other side "due process." The persuasive power of my decision depends in part on my having fully heard your views, your suggestions, and your notions of what is fair before committing myself. And my decision will have increased persuasiveness for you to the extent that I am able to justify it by reference to objective standards of fairness that you have indicated you consider appropriate. That factor, again, urges me to withhold making any negative commitment until I fully understand your views on fairness. . . .

The Power of an Affirmative Commitment

Negative commitments are often made when no affirmative commitment is on the table. . . . To make a negative commitment either as to what we will not do or to impose harsh consequences unless the other side reaches agreement with us, without having previously made a firm and clear offer, substantially lessens our ability to exert influence. An offer may not be enough, but a threat is almost certainly not enough unless there is a "yesable" proposition on the table—a clear statement of the action desired and a commitment as to the favorable consequences which would follow.

Conclusion

This analysis of negotiating power suggests that in most cases it is a mistake to attempt to influence the other side by making a negative commitment of any kind . . . at the outset of the negotiations, and that it is a mistake to do so until one has first made the most of every other element of negotiating power.

This analysis also suggests that when as a last resort threats of other negative commitments are used, they should be so formulated as to complement and reinforce other elements of negotiating power, not undercut them. In particular, any statement to the effect that we have finally reached a take-it-or-leave-it position should be made in a way that is consistent with maintaining a good working relationship, and consistent with the concepts of legitimacy with which we are trying to persuade the other side. . . .

Questions

Getting to Yes is one of the world's best-selling books and has been translated into every major language. Since its first publication in 1981, it has become the reference point for writing on negotiation. Other writers either agree and expand on its concepts or take issue with Fisher and Ury, as we have read in excerpts by James White and Roger Dawson. Roger Fisher has responded to some of the criticisms of cooperative/principled negotiation by either conceding that *Getting to Yes* presents abbreviated concepts that need to be further expanded and specifically applied, or by elaborating on their principled theories and countering the criticisms.

1. Does the above essay by Professor Fisher on negotiating power depart from the principles of *Getting to Yes*? How is it consistent or inconsistent?
2. Does an affirmative commitment always create more power than a negative commitment or threat? Are threats ever appropriate in negotiation? If so, when and under what circumstances?
3. Have you experienced or heard reports of threats that seemed irrational but succeeded in getting the threatening party what it wanted?

Note: Irrational Threats, Absolute Commitments, and Perception of Power

The selections you have read are all premised on rational behavior to get what your client wants through negotiation. Expressed and implied threats can also be conveyed very powerfully when viewed as irrational. Nikita Khrushchev gained immense power when, as premier of Russia, one of only two countries with a nuclear arsenal in the 1950s, he pounded his shoe on the table at the United Nations in an apparent fit of anger. An irrational, impulsive leader with his finger on the nuclear button had more power to get his way than a rational, restrained person, at least in the short run.

A threat does not become powerful unless the recipient believes the person making the threat has the capacity to carry it out. Khrushchev's behavior at the United Nations was powerful because it was known that the Soviet Union had nuclear capacity. Power can also come from creating the illusion that you have capacity to harm others. Iraq's Saddam Hussein was attributed with more power than he actually had because of our impression that he had weapons of mass destruction. This illustrates the statement that your power comes from the mind of your negotiating opponents.

A commercial negotiator can exert persuasive power by threatening to end a negotiation so that both sides will lose what they want, even if the result is irrational. The threat of going to trial over a small monetary dispute, for example, may seem irrational. However, if the commitment appears real and the means exist for the threat to proceed, the power of irrationality may prevail. The apparent irrationality may be explained by an absolute commitment to prevail, but it is no less effective. If in a game of "chicken" an opposing driver, headed toward you on a narrow road, removed her steering wheel and threw it out the window, would you get off the road? Would you be more persuaded to concede if you thought the oncoming driver was carrying a load of dynamite and you were on a road wide enough for only one vehicle?

The road-chicken example of the power of commitment and many others are discussed in an essay by Thomas Schelling, who shared the 2005 Nobel Prize in Economics for his writing on non-cooperative bargaining and game theory. Schelling provides another example of the power of irrational threats: "If a man knocks at your door and says that he will stab himself on the porch unless given $10, he is more likely to get the $10 if his eyes are bloodshot." Schelling equates bargaining power with the firmness of one's commitment as communicated to an opponent. A sophisticated, rational negotiator has difficulty appearing obstinate and may have trouble bluffing. Threats and commitment to an outcome may be more believable from a madman or from someone irrevocably locked into a position by outside influences. Schelling cites examples of leverage derived from being locked into a position, including the added international bargaining power of a U.S. president negotiating under a congressional mandate on tariffs and a labor leader's leverage in negotiating with management following a union vote to strike if a set wage limit is not met.

Schelling notes that his examples have instructive characteristics in common:

> First, they clearly depend not only on incurring a commitment but on communicating it persuasively to the other party. Second, it is by no means easy to establish the commitment, nor is it entirely clear to either of the parties concerned just how strong the commitment is. Third, similar activity may be available to the parties on both sides. Fourth, the possibility of commitment, though perhaps available to both sides, is by no means equally available; the ability of a democratic government to get itself tied by public opinion may be different from the ability of a totalitarian government to incur such a commitment. Fifth, they all run the risk of establishing an immovable position that goes beyond the ability of the other to concede, and thereby provoke the likelihood of stalemate or breakdown. (1960, 22-28)

Power need not be based on the capacity to harm others. It can come from the positive ability to help others meet their needs. If they believe that you can provide them with what they want or deny it to them, then relative to them, you have power.

We know that perceptions can be manipulated to project power that otherwise would not exist. Perception becomes reality for purposes of negotiation. A classic example of perceived power resulting from illusion is portrayed in L. Frank Baum's popular tale the *Wizard of Oz*, which was made into the classic 1939 film featuring Judy Garland as Dorothy, and more recently the Broadway musical spin-off *Wicked*. The Wizard was created by the special effects of a meek, old man to be an image of power. The sorcerer was merely a carnival huckster whose hot air balloon was blown off course and ended up in Oz. This Wizard was able to create power and meet the needs of Dorothy and her rag-tag friends by manipulating their perceptions, and thus he also fulfilled his interest in banishing the Wicked Witch of the West. If only success in life and negotiation could be as easy as following the yellow brick road. The *Wizard of Oz* illustrates how power is in the mind of the beholder and that real power comes from being able to meet the needs of others. (See Hetherington 2001.)

2. Deadlines and Final Offers

The well-known maxim that work expands to fill the time available applies to negotiation. Negotiations often continue until time runs out. As available time to conclude an agreement decreases, slow-moving or stalled negotiations seem to move toward closure. Concessions are offered and compromises are sometimes reached near the forced end of negotiations even though the same concessions would not be considered at the earlier stages. As Dawson noted in *Secrets of Power Negotiating*, quoted in Chapter 3, "the rule in negotiating is that 80 percent of the concessions occur in the last 20 percent of time available." More competitive negotiators will attempt to take advantage of any perceived need of the other side to conclude a deal, while hiding their own need for quick closure. However, creative solutions also materialize for more cooperative negotiators as available time comes to an end. Experienced cooperative negotiators will discuss their time constraints and agree on a time frame for the negotiation.

The passage of time may be associated with costs or lost opportunities. Time is money in many situations. More often than not, both sides want to conclude an agreement as soon as practical. However, time and delay may be more costly for one side in a negotiation. An injured plaintiff may not have the financial resources to hold out during a protracted negotiation for payment of a claim, whereas the insurance company on the other side may benefit from delay if its claim reserves are earning interest. It is this type of asymmetrical time pressure that gives an advantage to one side and is subject to manipulation.

When it is in one party's favor to move to closure, particularly if it believes that it is advantageous to prevent the other side from exploring other alternatives or opportunities, that party will impose an accelerated deadline. The deadline may be linked to a concession or a desired sweetener in exchange for accelerating closure. ("Order now and receive a free set of 'Ginsu' knives.") The deadline may be imposed to accept the entire last offer or end the negotiation. ("Accept this settlement amount by 5 P.M. or we go to trial.") A take-it-or-leave-it deadline proposal is referred to as an "exploding offer."

Deadlines can also be used to test if the other side is serious about settlement. Of course, any test can fail, and the side imposing the deadline must be willing to live with the consequences. Consider the use of the bold and strategic deadline imposed by the plaintiff's attorney in a class-action civil rights lawsuit brought by African-American customers against the Denny's restaurant chain.

❖ **Guy T. Saperstein, CIVIL WARRIOR: MEMOIRS OF A CIVIL RIGHTS ATTORNEY**

384 (Berkeley Hills Books, 2003)

Tom Pfister showed up with the President of Denny's and began to present Denny's offer, as we sat and listened in our conference room. He explained what corrective action Denny's was willing to undertake, and, in some cases, had already undertaken. Much of that already was required under the agreement with the United States Department of Justice and we had no quarrel with the requirements of that agreement, except that it didn't go far enough. Then

Tom addressed the damage issues, explaining that Denny's would donate $3 million to various civil rights groups. . . . I interrupted Tom before he finished, demanding, "Is that it? Is that all the money you're offering?" Tom said it was. So I said, "OK, I've heard enough" . . . .

"You indicated Denny's is willing to donate $3 million to various civil rights groups. That is fine, but as far as I'm concerned, that is your client's charity. It has nothing to do with our lawsuit. We are not seeking charity, we are seeking damages for Denny's reprehensible behavior. You can give $3 million away to any group or groups you want, but you will get no credit from us for that. Frankly, I was astonished and angered at your money offer, as it bore no relation to the seriousness of our lawsuit. Your offer left me with the feeling that time spent in settlement negotiations with Denny's is time wasted. Therefore, I am going to tell you what Denny's has to do to maintain credibility with me. By 10 a.m. tomorrow morning, Denny's has to offer a *minimum* of $20 million to settle damage claims of the class. That $20 million offer which Denny's is going to make tomorrow morning will NOT settle this case. It is only Denny's down payment—a tangible expression of good faith that will allow Denny's to continue these discussions. In the end, Denny's will have to pay far more than $20 million to settle this case."

Tom and his cohort left the room. We went back to my office. The mood was heavy with gloom. No one said a word in support of what I had done; several attorneys quietly voiced negative opinions: "We overplayed our hand"; "They won't be back"; "It'll be a long time before we have settlement discussions again in this case." I responded, "We broke them today. Just watch."

I walked into the office the next morning around 9 a.m. Tom Pfister was sitting in our reception area, waiting for me. Tom, a former USC basketball player, and still trim and athletic, rose to his full height of about 6' 3'', shook my hand, and said, "You've got your $20 million."

Negotiations in the above case continued until a settlement was reached that included the payment by Denny's of $54.4 million, then the largest settlement in a public accommodations case in American history. This example also illustrates the power of commitment, the power of legitimacy, and the power of a good alternative, all explained by Roger Fisher in the previous selection. Guy Saperstein's power to successfully make this bold demand was enhanced by Denny's lawyers' awareness that Saperstein had tried and won a total of $250 million in a class-action gender discrimination case against State Farm Insurance companies.

Note: The Effect of Scarcity and Deadlines

Moving to closure by imposing deadlines or making an "exploding offer," which becomes unavailable if not accepted by a deadline imposed by the offer, is a tactic in negotiation to take advantage of what is known as the "scarcity effect." The scarcity effect enhances the value of a desired item by making it appear less available or fleeting. We tend to pay more for something now if we believe it will not be available later. If something we want seems readily available, we tend to value it less and are less motivated to act decisively to obtain it. As examples, a New Yorker might never visit the Statue of Liberty until she discovers she must move to the Midwest, and the announced closure of a local restaurant due to slowing business may make it hard to get a reservation during the time it remains open.

Scarcity is enhanced if we discover that others want what we want, particularly if the item is limited in quantity or unique. A common ploy to close a negotiation is to suggest, directly or indirectly, that there is someone else interested in the deal if you do not accept it or that another offer is pending. (Lying about the existence of a competing offer is an ethical issue, as we will see in Chapter 10.)

Introducing deadlines into a negotiation is a way to create a vanishing opportunity or scarcity. Deadlines may be imposed by one side in the form of a threat, or created by external factors, like the end of a tax year. Time limits or deadlines can also be agreed to between the negotiating parties. Mutually imposed deadlines help structure negotiations and ensure a finite conclusion. So deadlines can be used cooperatively in negotiations, as well as in a unilateral, threatening way. Of course, agreed-upon deadlines can be extended by agreement and unilateral deadlines may also be subject to negotiation.

The "exploding offer" is an often used sales tactic and a hardball negotiating ploy. The tactic presents a false deadline, forcing the recipient of the offer to agree before he might otherwise have done so and without allowing time for the recipient to explore alternatives. "Our demand will double unless you accept it before the close of business today." The exploding offer is, in effect, a final offer with an imposed deadline.

One way suggested to deal with an exploding offer is the "Farpoint Gambit," derived from an episode of the popular science fiction television show, *Star Trek*.

> [T]he crew of the *Enterprise* (the spaceship from Earth) is put on trial by a powerful alien, "for the crimes of humanity." (The episode is called "Encounter at Farpoint," hence the name of the technique.) The alien creates a kangaroo court with himself as judge, and the captain of the *Enterprise* (Jean-Luc Picard) defends the human race. At a certain point, the alien judge becomes piqued by the captain's spirited defense, and says to the bailiff, "Bailiff, if the next word out of the defendant's mouth is anything but guilty, kill him!" He then turns to Picard and asks, "Defendant, how do you plead?" Picard thinks for a moment as the bailiff menacingly points a weapon at him, then firmly announces: "Guilty." As the courtroom gasps (and after an inevitable television commercial break), he adds, "Provisionally." This is essentially the Farpoint Gambit. . . ." (Robert J. Robinson, "Defusing the Exploding Offer: The Farpoint Gambit," 11 Negot. J. 277 (1995).)

The Star Trek captain in the TV episode accepts the coercive offer and is not shot, but he accepts it conditionally. The maker of the exploding offer will want to know what the added condition is. This opens a new line of negotiation and the deadline or other ultimatum is now considered met or is ignored. The key is to add conditions that are reasonable. Although you may not want to try this upon the threat of death, meeting a deadline with acceptance conditioned upon added terms or pending clarification of stated issues can be an effective countermove if you feel you need more time, particularly if it appears that the deadline is not issued for compelling reasons. Of course, an alternative is to ask the reasons for the deadline and state that you won't bargain under threat of an arbitrary deadline, unless a proverbial gun is pointed at you.

3. Decision Tree Analysis

Moving toward closure by evaluating offers in light of probable BATNAs and making decisions about what is on the negotiation table may be aided by the use of decision tree analysis. Decision tree analysis provides a probability tool for making decisions in a rational, methodical, quantitative way, particularly in the face of uncertainty. Regularly taught in business schools to quantify strategic business choices, decision tree analysis has more recently been adopted within the legal community as an aid to decision making in complex litigation and negotiations.

Decision tree analysis is a graphic version of the decision process we often engage in intuitively when we make common life decisions. Suppose, for example, that you are planning to go out, but it is threatening to rain. You listen to the weather report to learn the probability of rain to make a decision about taking an umbrella. After learning the percentage chance of rain, in order to calculate the probable risk and degree of getting wet, you determine how far you have to walk. Next, you weigh the discomfort and damage depending on how you are dressed. Each decision is discounted or multiplied by the next to make a rational, final choice. The higher the likelihood of rain, the less far the walk need be before deciding to carry an umbrella. The more casually you are dressed, the lower the need to take an umbrella.

Making decisions in litigation and business settings can become more complicated because of the number of choices, the number of possible consequences and their probability, and the impact of decisions at each stage on later choices. More than intuition may be needed to make a rational series of decisions and keep track of the probabilities along the way. Decision tree analysis can help with this task.

The first step in decision tree analysis is to convert a set of possible decisions into a graphic format—a decision tree graph. The decision tree displays possible decision choices and the probable consequences of each choice. The decision tree graph then leads to the next set of decision choices on a new limb of the tree and all of those probable outcomes. The decision maker works through the tree graph in sequence, one limb at a time, and makes decisions based on the most favorable probable outcomes expressed in quantitative sums. The process is both logical and intuitive.

Decision tree analysis is also helpful because it requires that we and our clients write down all the explicit factors to be considered. This methodical process discourages us from taking mental shortcuts that leave out important points and considerations that should be factored into our clients' decisions. Going through a decision tree analysis with a client, in addition to promoting rationality, prevents misunderstandings and second guessing about strategic choices.

The following explanation will help you understand how to create and read decision trees as an aid to making decisions about settlement of pending litigation, even if you went to law school because math is not on the LSAT.

❖ **Richard Birke, *DECISION TREES—MADE EASY***

(2010)

Evaluating what a lawsuit is worth is difficult. The use of decision trees can make this difficult task somewhat easier. However, much of the literature on decision trees is too complicated for the average practitioner to use. This very short piece is an attempt to make this important tool more accessible.

Every negotiation or mediation of a legal dispute involves a comparison between the last offer made by the other side and the expected value of continuing on with litigation (or arbitration). On the one hand, there is a sure thing (the offer), and on the other is a risky alternative (litigation/adjudication).

In some cases, the client is unsure of how to compare the value of an offer to settle to the value of continuing litigation. In these cases, the client would do well to understand how to use a simple decision tree. The tree would help them determine the ballpark for an appropriate settlement.

There are seven simple steps that any person can take that will enable them to set up and use a decision tree to help them evaluate their claim. These are:

1. Use numbers when speaking about probability.
2. Pare the case down to no more than four major areas of uncertainty (fewer is better).
3. Learn to set up a simple tree in a logical order.
4. Assign probabilities based on the strengths and weaknesses in the case, working from left to right.
5. Add in the financial awards associated with the various ways the case might end.
6. Do the math to solve the tree.
7. Add in costs as appropriate.

Using Numbers

When lawyers talk about the value of trial with their clients, they tend to shy away from using numbers to express probabilities. This reluctance is understandable—law is not an exact science, and lawyers fear overpromising. So instead of saying "we have a 90% chance of winning," lawyers use phrases like "we have a good shot at winning" or "our case is strong." In workshops I have run in which I ask lawyers to assign a number to these phrases, they exhibit spreads of more than 50% between the intended probability and the understood probability. That is, the lawyer could say "we have a good shot," intending to express that the case is a winner 40% of the time, and the client could understand that the lawyer expressed an 80% likelihood. Words simply do not adequately express probabilistic estimates. Lawyers have to buckle under and start using numbers.

Determining the Significant Uncertainties

Lawsuits may be complicated, but disputes about the value of these lawsuits typically boil down to a small handful of disagreements between the parties. Ask what are the areas about which the parties are really far apart, and the answers are often differences like one side believes that a motion *in limine* will be granted and the other believes it will be denied. One side believes that their client will be believed by the jury and the other side believes that the client will be easily impeached. Each side is optimistic that the judge will use their jury instruction. The potential number of such disagreements is vast, but in any particular lawsuit, the number of really significant areas of disagreement is small. These disagreements represent the significant uncertainties in the case.

Setting up Trees

I like to think of decision trees as roadmaps with a few intersections, and each intersection has some discrete number of forks in the road. The intersections represent the areas of uncertainty and the number of forks represents the number of ways the issue could come out. For example, in a simple tort case in which the uncertainties are "will plaintiff prove duty," "will plaintiff prove breach," and "will plaintiff prove causation," there are three intersections, each with two forks—one for yes and one for no. Some intersections in some cases could have more than two forks. In a case in which one of the major areas of uncertainty is the credibility of a witness, there could be a fork representing "jury believes every bit of testimony," another for "jury believes nothing," and a third for "jury believes some but not all." Similarly, an intersection representing the various monetary awards that a jury might assign could have many forks.

An easy way to make sure that the tree is set up in a logical manner is to start at the left and move chronologically through the dispute. Our tort case might have duty as the first intersection, breach as the second, and causation as the third. A tree might be set up in a different manner (perhaps in order of most contested issue to least), but a chronological effort usually yields a competent result.

Each fork in the tree will end at a terminal point, and the package of terminal points represents all the different ways that a case could come out. In our tort liability case, there are four terminal points. One is where plaintiff fails to prove duty, in which case the lawsuit is over. The second is where plaintiff proves duty, but fails to prove breach, in which case the lawsuit is over. The third is where plaintiff proves duty and breach but not causation, and the fourth is where plaintiff proves all three elements.

Probabilities

First, look at each intersection and write down all the reasons why a case may travel each fork. In the tort case, the fork labeled "plaintiff proves duty" will have a yes fork and a no fork. The reasons why the case might go to the yes fork may be that plaintiff has good witnesses, a friendly judge, a good legal ruling or case, etc. The reasons why the case might go to the no fork might be related to uncertainty about witnesses, opposing legal case law, etc.

Analyze the factors that surround each intersection and then fill in the probabilities from left to right, and be careful not to double-count factors in your analysis. For example, imagine a case in which plaintiff was very concerned that a witness who would testify about duty and about breach might not show up for the trial. This might result in plaintiff assigning a lower probability to "prove duty," and it may appear again in the "prove breach" intersection. However, it would be incorrect to discount the case two times because of this witness. If the witness doesn't show up, plaintiff will not prove duty, and the case will not ever get to the "prove breach" intersection. Put another way, if plaintiff is at the "prove breach" intersection and is assigning a probability to that intersection, plaintiff has to take into account the fact that the witness has shown up. If you fill in from left to right and you take into account what has already happened in the intersections to the left, you will not run into dependent variable problems because you will have only counted each factor one time.

Add in the Awards

The awards attached to winning a lawsuit are sometimes clear—imagine our tort case involves an insurance policy with limits far below the value of the injuries, and that there is no possibility of an award in excess of the limits. So everyone in this case would know that if plaintiff prevailed, the award would be $1,000,000. In other cases, the awards might be highly variable, and that uncertainty would be another intersection in the tree with an appropriate number of forks.

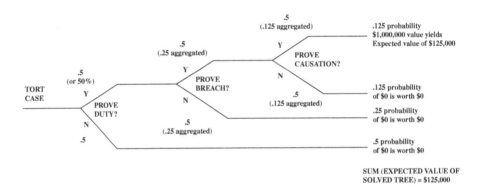

Solving the Tree

Now comes simple math. Each terminal point consists of a probability and a value. Assume for the moment that each element of our tort case has a 50/50 probability. That means that 50% of all cases result in a terminal point we can call "P didn't prove duty." The award is 0. The second terminal point "proved duty but not breach" will have a 25 percent probability (50% of 50%) and a value of 0. The third, "proved duty and breach but not causation" will have a 12.5% chance and a value of 0. The final terminal point shows a 12.5% chance of obtaining a $1,000,000 award value. A 50% chance of 0 is worth 0, a 25% chance of 0 is worth 0, a 12.5% chance of 0 is worth 0, and a 12.5% chance of a million dollars is worth $125,000. The sum is $125,000, and that is the solution of the tree.

Deduct Costs

If the trial would cost plaintiff $100,000—win or lose—we can deduct $100,000 from the solution of the tree, so that the net value of this lawsuit would be $25,000.

However, sometimes the costs vary depending on the nature of the uncertainties. For example, if the case has been tried already and is pending appeal, the uncertainties may be "will appellant win at the court of appeal" and "if they do, will they win at a new trial?" In this instance, if appellant loses at the court of appeal, they bear the costs of pursuing the appeal win or lose. If they win at the court of appeal and go to a new trial, they bear the cost of pursuing the appeal and the cost of the new trial. Thus the deductions of costs come not from the total expected value of the case, but at the end of each terminal point.

Still Not Simple Enough?

Here's a simple analogy that I like to use that helps me think of how these trees work. Imagine that there are 100 runners at the start of a race. The race course has a number of unmarked intersections. At each intersection, some number of runners will run in a way that brings them closer to the finish line, and some will turn in ways that will run them into a ditch, out of the race. Only runners who run the whole race will get a financial prize, and the rest will get nothing, and they may pay a fee for running.

Our 100 runners start, and 50 of them turn one way at the intersection of "prove duty" street and "don't prove duty" street. The 50 who run one way are still in the race with many intersections ahead, and the other 50 have run into a ditch and are out of the race. The remaining 50 split equally at the intersection of "prove breach" street and "don't prove breach" street, send 25 more into a ditch and 25 still in the race. At our third intersection, half run into a ditch and half run to the finish line where they each get a $1,000 prize. The average prize for each runner entering the race is $125, and if it cost each runner $100 to enter the race, the average take home reward is $25. If someone were to offer an individual runner $50 to buy her spot in the race, the runner would be well advised to take the money.

Of course, this assumes that the runner was in the race just for the money, and not to prove something to the defendant, or to herself, or to create a precedent. If the motivation for litigating has little to do with money, the decision tree is not a useful tool.

This is a very boiled-down discussion of a very well-studied topic. There are many wonderful, complex works on risk analysis, and the purpose of this short section is to whet your appetite. If this teaser was too much for you, then simply be aware that you can hire a consultant to help you in the appropriate case. If, on the other hand, this piece was not enough, then go to a search engine and find works by Marc Victor, Howard Raiffa, Bruce Beron, David Hofer, Marjorie Aaron, and others. They will help you get your fill.

Note: The Problem with Risk Analysis and Decision Trees

Decision trees create a mathematical model for risk analysis of a trial as an alternative to settlement. Most of us tend to give more weight to what is quantified and stated in numbers than what is stated only in words. Although decision trees can be very helpful tools, they should be used with caution. Experienced trial attorneys and judges can only guess at a party's percentage chance of prevailing on a given set of facts, which are seldom clear. As stated by Marjorie Corman Aaron and Wayne Brazil, "Even with its numerical appearance and mathematical operations, decision analysis provides no certainty. In a legal case, it is based upon human estimates. Thus, the numbers it yields are no more certain than traditional case evaluation, delivered in prose." (Aaron and Brazil, Shaking Decision Trees for Risks and Rewards, Vol. 22, No. 1, ABA Disp. Res. Mag. 12, Fall 2015)

Some risk factors (uncertainties) come from facts that we may fail to build into our risk model or decision tree, which are based only on what we know. For example, the decision tree might not factor in the possible bankruptcy of the defendant or his insurance carrier, the death of a key witness, or an earthquake postponing the trial. Nassim Taleb, in his book *The Black Swan* (2007), argues that in real-world situations there is always more that we don't know than we do, and that we tend to overvalue the known and undervalue the unknown and thereby expose ourselves to the most consequential risks when we least expect the outcome. Taleb reminds us that the "black swan" (his metaphor for highly consequential, improbable events) is produced in messy real-world circumstances where the gap between what we know and what we think we know can become dangerously wide. He postulates that our modern taste for data and "objective" decision-making models have increasingly undermined this part of the risk inquiry. The risk of "black swans" occurring between the time of settlement negotiations and trial is not easily included in decision trees. This argues for favoring a known settlement now rather than a trial later that is subject to unknown risks not represented in a decision points graph. Another approach to risk analysis applied to litigation and integrating other variables is Paul Prestia and Harrie Samaras, "Beyond Decision Trees: Determining Aggregate Probabilities of Time, Cost and Outcomes," Alternatives, Apr. 2010.

More questions about lawyer risk analysis are raised by a study of 4,532 civil litigation cases over a 44-year period. This study found that decisions to reject settlement offers and proceed to trial very often resulted in court outcomes no better than had the offer been accepted. Comparing the actual trial results with the rejected pretrial settlement offers, the study finds that 61 percent of plaintiffs and 24 percent of defendants obtained an award at trial that was the same as or worse than the result that could have been achieved by accepting the opponent's pretrial settlement proposal. Although plaintiffs experienced adverse trial outcomes more frequently than defendants, the financial costs incurred by defendants when they lost their litigation wagers were significantly higher than plaintiffs' error costs. The decision errors were worse in the most recent three years studied than in the previous 40 years, even with modern availability of jury verdict information and decision tree analysis. The average cost of "decision error," as the co-authors term these adverse trial outcomes, was $43,100 for plaintiffs and $1,140,000 for defendants during the period 2002-2005. (See Kiser et al. 2008.)

Questions

4. Is there any reason to think that the use of decision trees for case settlement would be favored more by plaintiffs or more by defendants? Why?

5. If you created a decision tree to assist you and your client in evaluating a case for settlement purposes, would you share it with the opposing side? Under what circumstances might you reveal it?

6. Are opposing sides likely to agree about the determinant events or decision points for constructing a decision tree? Are they likely to agree on the probability percentages assigned at each decision node, or the chance of the other side winning?

7. Would a decision tree be helpful in evaluating and settling a case on appeal? What would an appellate case decision tree look like, and how many branches would there be?

CHAPTER
7

Negotiation Step by Step — The End

A. Impasse or Agreement

Although a negotiation appears to be moving toward closure, progress may stall and an impasse looms. The impasse may be because of a gap between "last" offers and demands or because something else gets in the way of a final agreement. It is not always clear what that something is. Late-game impasses can occur for several reasons beside a money gap, including:

- A focus on money to the exclusion of other interests
- Misunderstanding the other side's needs or problems that must be addressed to reach agreement
- Failing to concede low-priority interests to satisfy high-priority interests
- Differing views about future events or contingencies
- Forgetting to realistically reconsider and adjust BATNAs and WATNAs (worst alternatives to a negotiated agreement)
- Decision fatigue and the perfect solution fallacy

Your preparation for negotiation should include gathering information to assess the other party's needs and what it might take to satisfy those needs in order to reach agreement. As we now know, the positions taken during a negotiation may be different than the underlying interests that need to be addressed. If the negotiation has focused exclusively on incremental compromises from initial positions, the concessions made may not meet other essential needs and the deal cannot be sealed, particularly if the concessions have only been monetary. Successfully negotiating a settlement depends on satisfying the three sets of needs—economic, emotional, and extrinsic (social)—that form the three sides of the settlement triangle presented in Chapter 1. The triangle is like a three-legged stool: If any of the three sets of needs is not addressed, the deal is likely to fail.

All sides must assess if what is on the table is or is not better than no agreement by realistically considering their BATNAs, as well as their WATNAs, in light of new information gained during the negotiation. Cooperative negotiators will see the cloud of impasse as the time for joint problem solving and the need to explore the possibility of improving the outcome for all parties in order to create an acceptable resolution. More competitive bargainers may test an opponent's resolve by threatening to end the negotiation, and adversarial negotiators may sense an opportunity and add new demands or conditions. Several endgame moves or collaborative strategies are available to bring closure. Some of these look for agreement by attending to matters beyond money and others focus on closing remaining economic gaps in the settlement or transaction. We now look at some approaches to breaking impasse.

1. Apologies

Economic needs can be quantified and satisfied with money. Emotional and extrinsic factors are more nebulous, but there are ways to satisfy emotional and social needs in a manner that creates value. Offering something other than money that fills a perceived need can be worth more to the recipient than what is given up by the offering party. An apology and its acceptance may satisfy important emotional and social needs.

The most readily identified words indicating an apology are "I'm sorry." This usually marks the beginning of an apology, but the most effective apologies contain several elements:

1. Expressing regret for the wrong suffered (I'm sorry);
2. Manifesting sympathy for the injury or hurt;
3. Admitting responsibility or blame;
4. Promising forbearance—not to do it again; and
5. Offering repair or compensation.

Saying you are sorry and showing sympathy without admitting fault is a partial apology that might help, but it can also make matters worse if perceived as insincere or a brush-off. A "full apology" would include at least the first three elements on the list. The third element, admitting fault, in many situations is the key component of an apology. However, admitting fault can be legally dangerous because the admission may be admissible evidence at trial to establish liability. The two elements of providing assurances that the wrong will not happen again and offering compensation create the perfect apology package.

The hoped-for counterpart or trade-off for an apology is forgiveness. Forgiveness may create value by filling needs for both the recipient and the forgiving party. An apology, even if not full or perfect, and expressions of forgiveness can unlock a stalled negotiation and facilitate closure. Although we have placed this material on apology at a late stage of negotiation, under the heading of "impasse," an apology that precedes negotiation or is offered in the earliest stages may be most effective. In resolving some disputes, the amount of compensation or other substantive considerations may be secondary to an apology and resulting forgiveness. In other cases, an apology might not matter or could be seen as manipulative.

The role of apologies in settling cases has become a subject of increased interest as states consider legislation providing evidentiary protection or "safe harbor" for apologies made by people who have done harm to those on the receiving end of a tort or wrong. Several significant law review articles have examined the appropriateness and effect of apologies on settlement, most drawing on psychological literature and anecdotal experience. (See, e.g., O'Hara and Yarn 2002; Taft 2000; Cohen 1999.) The following reading reports on new systematic studies using a large number of participants, presented with two personal injury factual scenarios, to gauge the effects of different types of apologies on settlement negotiations. Receipt of a full apology expressing responsibility increased the acceptability of a settlement offer. In contrast, a partial apology expressing regret and sympathy, but not responsibility, did not help, and in the case of more clear liability and greater injuries, a partial apology appears to increase the likelihood that a settlement offer will be rejected.

❖ **Jennifer K. Robbennolt,** *APOLOGIES AND LEGAL SETTLEMENT:*
AN EMPIRICAL EXAMINATION

102 Mich. L. Rev. 460 (2003)

It is often said that U.S. legal culture discourages apologies. Defendants, defense counsel, and insurers worry that statements of apology will be admissible at trial and will be interpreted by jurors and judges as admissions of responsibility. In recent years, however, several legal commentators have suggested that disputants in civil lawsuits should be encouraged to apologize to opposing parties. They claim that apologies will avert lawsuits and promote settlement. . . .

Survey research suggests that claimants desire apologies and that some would not have filed suit had an apology been offered. In addition, there is anecdotal evidence of . . . settlement negotiations coming to a standstill over the issue of apology even after agreement on an appropriate damage amount has been reached, of plaintiffs who would have preferred an apology as part of a settlement, and of occasions on which a failure to apologize promoted litigation by adding insult to injury. . . . [The author explains her experimental simulation methods for studying the role of apologies in legal settlement negotiations.]

Effects of Apologies on Settlement Decisionmaking [First Study]

The first study examined recipients' interpretations of apologies and the effects of those apologies on willingness to accept a settlement offer in the dispute. The hypothetical scenario detailed a relatively simple personal-injury dispute: a pedestrian-bicycle accident. All participants reviewed this scenario and evaluated the same settlement offer.

Control participants evaluated a version of the scenario in which no apology was offered. Additional participants evaluated versions of the scenario in which two variables, the nature of the apology offered and the nature of the applicable evidentiary rule, were varied. First, the nature of the apology offered was varied to compare the effects of a partial apology, in which the other party merely expressed sympathy for the potential claimant's injuries, with the effects of a full apology, in which he or she also took responsibility for causing the injuries. Second, the evidentiary rule described to participants was varied to examine how different evidentiary rules influence the interpretation and effectiveness of an apology, comparing respondents' reactions to an apology where the evidentiary rules protected the apology, where the evidentiary rules did not protect the apology, and where no evidentiary rule was described. Thus, there were seven

different variations of the basic scenario. One hundred forty-five people participated in the study and were randomly assigned to the experimental conditions.

Effects of Apology on Settlement

The first set of analyses compared the two different types of apology (partial
and full) to the no-apology control where no evidentiary rule was specified.
It was predicted that the nature of the apology would influence participants'
settlement decisions. Moreover, based on the previous research on the psychological effects of apologies, it was predicted that an apology would influence
settlement decisionmaking through its effects on participants' perceptions and
attributions. That is, participants' interpretations of the apology, their affective
reactions, and their evaluations of the situation and the offender were expected
to mediate the effects of an apology on their settlement decisions: the nature of
the apology would influence these perceptions and attributions, which would in
turn influence settlement decisions.

Effect of Apology on Settlement Decisions

First, even though all participants were told that they had suffered the same
injuries and received the same offer of settlement, the nature of the apology
offered influenced recipients' willingness to accept the offer. . . . When no apology was offered 52% of respondents indicated that they would definitely or
probably accept the offer, while 43% would definitely or probably reject the
offer and 5% were unsure. When a partial apology was offered, only 35% of
respondents were inclined to accept the offer, 25% were inclined to reject it,
and 40% indicated that they were unsure. In contrast, when a full apology was
offered, 73% of respondents were inclined to accept the offer, with only 13-14%
each inclined to reject it or remaining unsure. . . .

Comparing each type of apology to the condition in which no apology was
received, receiving a partial apology increased the likelihood that the respondent would be unsure about how to respond to the settlement offer, and receiving a full apology increased the likelihood that the respondent would choose
to accept the offer and decreased the likelihood that the respondent would
choose to reject the offer.

The Role of Perceptions and Attributions

Next, the study examined the effects of the nature of the apology on a number of constructs thought to underlie the effect of apology on settlement decisionmaking. Where there were differences in participants' responses across
conditions, the differences follow a strikingly similar pattern: offering no apology or a partial apology elicited equivalent responses that were both different
from the responses elicited when a full apology was offered. . . .

Thus, a full apology was viewed as more sufficient than either a partial apology
or no apology. An offender who offered a full apology was seen as experiencing
more regret, as more moral, and as more likely to be careful in the future than
one offering a partial or no apology. While an offender offering a full apology
was seen as believing that he or she was more responsible for the incident than
one who offered a partial or no apology, the conduct of the full apologizer was

judged more favorably than that of offenders who offered either a partial or no apology. Participants expressed greater sympathy and less anger at the offender who offered a full apology than they did at offenders who offered either a partial or no apology. Participants also indicated more willingness to forgive an offender who gave a full apology than they did for offenders offering a partial or no apology and expected that less damage to the parties' relationship would result following a full apology than they did following a partial or no apology. Finally, participants indicated that the settlement offer would better make up for their injuries when they had received a full apology than when they had received either a partial or no apology.

Therefore, apologies influenced the inclination to accept or reject a settlement offer. The effect of an apology on settlement decisions was complex, however, and depended on the type of apology offered. Only the full, responsibility-accepting apology increased the likelihood that the offer would be accepted. The partial, sympathy-expressing, apology, in contrast, increased participants' uncertainty about whether or not to accept the offer. . . .

Factors Influencing the Effects of Apologies [Second Study]

A second study was conducted to explore the boundaries of these findings. This study, again, examined recipients' interpretations of apologies and the effect of those apologies on willingness to accept a settlement offer in the dispute. This time, however, in addition to the nature of the apology and the type of evidentiary rule, the strength of the evidence of the offender's fault and the severity of the resulting injury were manipulated. . . .

Consistent with the results of the first study, apologies influenced participants' attributions and perceptions of the situation and the offender. Overall, full apologies improved the participants' perceptions of the situation and the offender, while partial apologies did little to alter such perceptions. Exploration of the possible moderating influences of the severity of the injury and the evidence of the offender's responsibility revealed some interesting boundary conditions on these overall results. In particular, there were patterns in the data suggesting both that partial apologies may negatively impact perceptions where responsibility is relatively clear or where the injury is more severe and that partial apologies may positively impact perceptions where responsibility is relatively less clear or where the injury is relatively minor. . . .

Defendants

In the absence of statutory protection, defendants or potential defendants who desire to apologize are faced with balancing the effects of apologies on different types of judgments—settlement decisionmaking, liability decisions, and decisions about appropriate damage awards—as well as weighing the less strategic aspects of apologizing. The results of the instant studies inform one important component of these interrelated decisions—the impact of apology on settlement decisions. An important lesson for defendants to draw from these data is that apologies can have beneficial effects on settlement, altering the injured parties' perceptions of the situation and the offender so as to make them more amenable to settlement discussions and ultimately more likely to accept an offer.

As a general matter, the results of the present study provide evidence that a full apology that both expresses sympathy for the victim's injuries and accepts responsibility for those injuries influences a variety of perceptions and attributions about the situation and the other party that might lead to a settlement or allow the parties to begin discussions. Full apologies were seen as more sufficient apologies, as evidencing more regret and a greater likelihood of care in the future, and as offered by people of higher moral character. Full apologies favorably altered assessments of the conduct leading to the injuries and changed the emotions of the injured party so as to reduce anger and increase sympathy for the offender. Full apologies were seen as mitigating potential damage to the relationship, were more likely to lead to forgiveness, and inclined injured parties to look more favorably on the settlement offer. In addition, the results of the first study demonstrated that full apologies, through these effects on perceptions and attributions, increased the likelihood that the settlement offer would be accepted.

Accordingly, full apologies that include accepting responsibility for the incident may facilitate the settling of lawsuits. These "responsibility-accepting" apologies, however, are precisely the type of apologies that most clearly raise concerns about the effects of apologizing on liability decisionmaking and are not likely to be protected by evidentiary rules protecting apologies. Making a statement that admits fault and that might be admissible at trial, while improving the prospects for settling the case, is thought to increase the risk that the offender will be found liable.

For this reason, there is growing interest in ways in which offenders can apologize without exposing themselves to the same risks attendant to a full, responsibility-accepting apology. The present research suggests that the effects of such partial apologies are complex and identifies several aspects of the case that defendants ought to take into account when considering a partial apology. First, the effects of partial apologies on settlement decisionmaking appear to be much more complicated than the effects of full apologies. On the whole, partial apologies did not appear to facilitate settlement in the ways hoped by proponents. The most consistent finding was that partial apologies tended to be no better (or worse) than not offering an apology. Across both studies, regardless of the level of responsibility and the level of injury, there were no differences between those receiving partial apologies and no apology in their evaluations of the offender's conduct, the offender's regret, the offender's belief that he or she was responsible, damage to the relationship, anger, the degree to which the offer would make up for the injuries, or forgiveness. . . . Thus, a defendant or potential defendant who wants to fully apologize may face the uncertain effects of the apology on liability and damage-award decisions if settlement negotiations fail, but may benefit from an improved settlement climate and an improved chance of avoiding litigation altogether.

Defendants contemplating a partial, sympathy-expressing apology may not face the same liability risks. The beneficial effects of such apologies are not clear, however, and there is evidence of some risk that perceptions will be negatively impacted. Thus, defendants must be carefully attuned to the types of factors identified here, in particular the severity of the plaintiff's injury and the degree to which the offender appears to be responsible, in evaluating these rules.

Plaintiffs

In contrast to defendants, plaintiffs or potential plaintiffs must determine how to respond to an apology from someone they believe has wronged them. . . . The results of the present studies suggest that plaintiffs may, in fact, be able to critically evaluate the content of an apology and to distinguish those that they find credible and that communicate the necessary information from those that do not. Participants in the studies evaluated partial apologies very differently from full apologies. Participants did not interpret partial apologies as conveying the same evidence of regret, acceptance of responsibility, or likelihood of greater care in the future as full apologies. . . . [H]owever, it is plausible that some plaintiffs would be willing to accept a smaller financial settlement if they receive an apology. If this is true, one explanation may be that they have been unfairly induced to forego their rightful compensation. An alternative explanation may be that they are more satisfied by a combination of financial compensation and the apology than they would have been with a larger monetary amount and no apology. Plaintiffs may value the apology more than or differently from financial compensation. Indeed, motivations other than legal entitlement and monetary recovery may be important to plaintiffs. While a monetary settlement may adequately restore financial losses resulting from an injury, an apology may be a better mechanism for restoring less tangible damage, expressing the proper relative moral positions of the parties, assuring the injured party that the offender will not reoffend, or achieving restorative justice. . . .

Note: Evidentiary Consequences of Apologies

Pursuant to the Federal Rules of Evidence and state evidence rules, admissions by party opponents are generally admissible at trial, as an exception to the hearsay rule. Apologies that include admissions of fault would be admissible under Federal Rule of Evidence 801(d)(2) and under state rules of evidence. However, most states now have confidentiality protections that preclude admission into evidence of what is said and done in mediation. Apologies offered as part of the mediation process are generally safe from evidentiary admission.

Several states have enacted laws intended to encourage apologies and "other benevolent gestures" on the scene of an accident and in negotiations afterwards. In 1986, Massachusetts became the first state to adopt a rule of evidence intended to preclude evidentiary admission of apologies for purposes of establishing liability. Following the lead of Massachusetts, Texas (1999), California (2000), Florida (2001), and Washington (2002) amended their evidence codes to provide some protection for certain types of apologies. Although the language varies from state to state, California Evidence Code section 1160 is typical: "The portion of statements, writings, or benevolent gestures expressing sympathy or a general sense of benevolence relating to the pain, suffering, or death of a person involved in an accident . . . and made to that person or to the family of that person shall be inadmissible as evidence of an admission of liability in a civil action. A statement of fault, however, which is part of, or in addition to, any of the above shall not be inadmissible pursuant to this section." It is important to note that the California legislation, as well as that of other states, only encourages partial apologies that do not admit fault.

Colorado has gone further to encourage full apologies in medical malpractice situations. The Colorado "I'm Sorry" rule provides: "[I]n any civil action brought by an alleged victim of an unanticipated outcome of medical care, or in any arbitration proceeding related to such civil action, any and all statements, affirmations, gestures, or conduct expressing apology, fault, sympathy, commiseration, condolence, compassion, or a general sense of benevolence which are made by a health care provider or an employee of a health care provider to the alleged victim, a relative of the alleged victim, or a representative of the alleged victim and which relate to the discomfort, pain, suffering, injury, or death of the alleged victim as the result of the unanticipated outcome of medical care shall be inadmissible as evidence of an admission of liability or as evidence of an admission against interest" (Colo. Rev. Stat. Sec. 13-25-135). Since the passage of the Colorado statute in 2003, many states have enacted legislation providing some form of protection for apologies by health care providers, including Oregon, Oklahoma, Wyoming, Ohio, North Carolina, South Dakota, West Virginia, Maryland, Georgia, and Arizona.

Questions

1. The Colorado rule quoted above was part of a tort reform campaign. Do you feel that the protection provided to health-care providers by this exclusionary rule is likely to encourage meaningful apologies? Does the rule in any way favor health-care providers at the expense of malpractice victims? (See Dauer 2005, 47.)
2. Does the California "benevolent gesture" rule go far enough? Would you support legislation that protected from evidentiary admission full apologies that refer to a tortfeasor's blame or wrongdoing? Why or why not?
3. In what type of cases would an apology be most effective to bring closure? What needs might an apology fill in such a case? Are there cases in which an apology would not work or would not be appropriate?
4. A highly publicized apology from basketball star Kobe Bryant in 2004 played a role in the dropping of criminal rape charges by the recipient of the apology and the settlement of a related civil suit. Do you think the following apology by Mr. Bryant was a spontaneous, benevolent gesture, or the result of careful drafting and negotiation by attorneys? What policy issues are raised by this apology, the subsequent dropping of criminal charges, and the negotiated settlement in 2005 that resolved the civil suit? What considerations and motivations, from both sides, prompted the inclusion of the specific wording that was used? What purpose did this apology serve?

First, I want to apologize directly to the young woman involved in this incident. I want to apologize to her for my behavior that night and for the consequences she has suffered in the past year. Although this year has been incredibly difficult for me personally, I can only imagine the pain she has had to endure. I also want to apologize to her parents and family members, and to my family and friends and supporters, and to the citizens of Eagle, Colorado.

I also want to make it clear that I do not question the motives of this young woman. No money has been paid to this woman. She has agreed that this statement will not be used against me in the civil case. Although I truly believe this encounter between us was consensual, I recognize now that she did not and does not view this incident the same way I did. After months of reviewing discovery, listening to her attorney, and even her testimony in person, I now understand how she feels that she did not consent to this encounter.

I issue this statement today fully aware that while one part of this case ends today, another remains. I understand that the civil case against me will go forward. That part of this case will be decided by and between the parties directly involved in the incident and will no longer be a financial or emotional drain on the citizens of the state of Colorado.

5. In testimony on June 17, 2010, before the U.S. House of Representatives' Energy Committee, BP's then-CEO Tony Hayward offered this apology for the worst environmental catastrophe in U.S. history: "The explosion and fire aboard the Deepwater Horizon and the resulting oil spill in the Gulf of Mexico never should have happened and I'm deeply sorry that it did." Hayward went on to detail what BP was doing to remedy the spill, and BP did pledge a fund of $20 billion to pay resulting claims. However, Hayward did not admit BP's fault. Does the Hayward "apology" help or hurt BP? Why?

2. Splitting the Difference and Leaving the Door Open

A deceptively simple concluding technique for avoiding impasse, often used in both competitive and cooperative negotiations, is "splitting the difference." The rationale for splitting the difference and a couple of caveats about agreeing to it are discussed in a negotiation guide by Richard Shell. Professor Shell also offers advice on leaving the door open and other tactics when the remaining gap causes the negotiation to reach impasse.

❖ **G. Richard Shell,** *Bargaining for Advantage:*
Negotiation Strategies for Reasonable People

---

185 (Penguin, 2006)

Perhaps the most frequently used closing technique is splitting the difference. Bargaining research tells us that the most likely settlement point in any given transaction is the midpoint between the two opening offers. People who instinctively prefer a compromise style like to cut through the whole bargaining process by getting the two opening numbers on the table and then splitting them right down the middle.

Even in cases in which the parties have gone through several rounds of bargaining, there often comes a time when one side or the other suggests that the parties meet halfway between their last position. In situations in which the relationship between the parties is important, this is a perfectly appropriate, smooth way to close.

Why is splitting the difference so popular? First, it appeals to our sense of fairness and reciprocity, thus, setting a good precedent for future dealings between the parties. . . . Each side makes an equal concession simultaneously. What could be fairer than that?

Second, it is simple and easy to understand. It requires no elaborate justification or explanation. The other side sees exactly what you are doing.

Third, it is quick. For people who do not like to negotiate or are in a hurry, splitting the difference offers a way out of the potentially messy interpersonal conflict that looms whenever a negotiation occurs.

Splitting the difference is such a common closing tactic that it often seems rude and unreasonable to refuse, regardless of the situation. This is taking a good thing too far, however. There are at least two important situations in which I would hesitate to split the difference.

First, you should be careful that the midpoint being suggested is genuinely fair to your side. If you have opened at a reasonable price and the other party opened at an aggressive one, the midpoint is likely to favor the other party by a big margin. So don't split the difference at the end if there was a lack of balance at the beginning. Second, when a lot of money or an important principle is on the line and relationships matter, quickly resorting to a splitting may leave opportunities for additional, creative options on the table. . . .

When the gap between offers is too wide to split, another friendly way to close is to obtain a neutral valuation or appraisal. If the parties cannot agree on a single appraiser, they can each pick one and agree to split the difference between the two numbers given by the experts.

What Happens If Negotiations Break Down?

The concession-making stage of bargaining sometimes ends with no deal rather than an agreement. The parties reach an impasse. In fact, a no deal result is sometimes the right answer. No deal is better than a bad deal. . . .

In addition to escalation problems, the parties may start too far apart to close the gap. Many times there are miscommunications, misunderstanding, and simple bad chemistry that the parties fail to overcome. Now what?

Jump-Starting the Negotiation Process

Perhaps the easiest way to overcome impasse is to leave yourself a back door through which to return to the table when you get up to leave it. "In light of the position you have taken," you might say as you pack your bags, "we are unable to continue negotiations at this time." An attentive opponent will pick up on your use of the words "at this time" and tactfully ask you later if the time has come to reinitiate talks. This back door also allows you to contact the other side at a later date without losing face.

If the other negotiator leaves in a genuine fit of anger, he may not be very careful about leaving a back door open. If so, you should consider how you can let him back in without unnecessary loss of face. You must, in one expert's phrase, build him a "golden bridge" across which to return to the table. Such bridges include "forgetting" that he made his ultimatum in the first place or recalling his last statement in a way that gives him an excuse for returning.

When miscommunication is the problem, a simple apology may be enough to get the parties back on track. If the relationship has deteriorated beyond apologies, changing negotiators or getting rid of intermediaries altogether may be necessary.

In America, the sport of professional baseball lost nearly two full seasons in the 1990s because of an impasse in negotiations between the players' union and the club owners. The team owners from the big cities wanted to limit the size of team payrolls. The team owners from smaller cities wanted the team owners from big cities to subsidize their franchises. The players wanted more money. It was a three-ring circus. The breakthrough came when the owners hired a new negotiator—a lawyer named Randy Levine—to represent them at the table. Levine acted in the role of mediator as much as advocate and brought a high degree of both credibility and creativity to the process that, according to one participant, "broke the dam of mistrust" that had built up between the parties. Another move that helped move the talks beyond impasse was getting all parties to agree to stop talking to the press and taking public positions that made it hard for them to compromise at the table. . . . [P]ublic commitments can help you stick to your goals, but there comes a time when it is in everyone's interest to get unstuck from their positions. In a high stakes negotiation such as a labor strike, this often means getting the parties out of the spotlight so they can work in private.

The worst impasses are the products of emotional escalation that builds on itself: My anger makes you angry, and your response makes me even angrier. . . . The solution to this sort of collision, in business deals as well as wars, is what I call the "one small step" procedure. One side needs to make a very small, visible move in the other side's direction, then wait for reciprocation. If the other party responds, the two can repeat the cycle again, and so on. Commentator Charles Osgood, writing about the Cold War in the early 1960s, created an acronym for this process: GRIT (Graduated and Reciprocated Initiatives in Tension Reduction).

Egypt's late prime minister, Anwar Sadat, used the "one small step" technique to deescalate the Arab-Israeli conflict when he flew to Jerusalem on November 19, 1977 and later met with Prime Minister Menachem Begin. By simply getting off a plane in Israel—a very small step indeed—Sadat demonstrated his willingness to recognize Israel's existence. This move eventually led to the Camp David peace accords and Israel's return of the Sinai Peninsula to Egypt.

An executive once told me a bargaining story that nicely sums up how the "one small step" process can work in everyday life. Two parties were in a complex business negotiation. Both were convinced that they had leverage, and both thought that the best arguments favored their own view of the deal. After a few rounds, neither side would make a move.

Finally one of the women at the table reached in her purse and pulled out a bag of M&M's. She opened the bag and poured the M&M's into a pile in the middle of the table.

"What are those for?" asked her counterparts.

"They are to keep score," she said.

Then she announced a small concession on the deal—and pulled an M&M out of the pile and put it on her side of the table.

"Now it's your turn," she said to the men sitting opposite.

Not to be outdone, her opponents put their heads together, came up with a concession of their own—and pulled out two M&M's. "Our concession was bigger than yours," they said.

The instigator of the process wisely let the other side win this little argument and then made another concession of her own, taking another M&M for herself.

It wasn't long before the parties were working closely together to close the final terms of the deal. Call this the M&M version of the GRIT process. Any similar mechanism that restarts the norm of reciprocity within the bargaining relationship will have a similar, helpful effect.

Overall, when parties reach an impasse, it is usually because each sees the other's demands as leaving it below its legitimate expectations. Eventually, if the parties are to make any progress, they must change their frame of reference and begin seeing that they will be worse off with no deal than they would be accepting a deal that falls below their original expectations.

Sometimes this transition takes time. The impasse must be allowed to last long enough that one or both parties actually alter their expectations. A final agreement must be seen as a gain compared with available alternatives.

Questions

7. Have you ever "split the difference" to conclude a negotiation or sale? Looking back, was that the best way to close the deal? Are you now sure you were not manipulated into an outcome or price that was more favorable to the other side? Have you used this closing tactic to your advantage?

8. If you propose splitting the difference and the other side does not immediately accept the proposal, does the added or subtracted amount from your previous position become your new, less favorable, number going forward? How can you prevent this from causing you a loss when they propose a split between your "new" proposed compromise number (the gap's mid-point) and their last number?

9. Do you agree that an impasse can be helpful? If so, when? Why would anyone plan an impasse as part of their negotiating strategy?

3. Logrolling and Packaging

You should now be familiar with the concept that value is created through negotiation when what is received in trade is worth more to the recipient than to the provider. "Logrolling" involves conceding on low-priority interests to satisfy high-priority interests. Legislators logroll when they trade their vote on a matter of little concern in their district for another legislator's vote on an important issue in their own district. For example, a congressman from Montana might agree to vote for a federal rapid transit subsidy bill in return for a New York City congressman's vote for federal animal grazing subsidies. Logrolling creates value, because both legislators are better off if both bills pass than if neither passes. The New York congressman strongly favors the rapid transit bill, while only moderately opposing the grazing bill, and the Montana legislator strongly favors the animal grazing bill and only moderately opposes the rapid transit bill.

You should also understand that the difference between overlapping reservation points, or "bottom lines," of negotiators creates a bargaining zone within which agreement is likely. Differences in the value that negotiators place on multiple items or promises allow for integrated solutions that expand the bargaining zone. Packaging multiple items, adding items to the mix, and taking advantage of an expanded zone of possible agreement can help close a deal. Packaging requires flexibility and creativity because the negotiators may have initially perceived the negotiation to be fixed on a single item or a more limited set of trade-offs. Selling a car by including a longer warranty or a reduced-price luxury package is a sales example of packaging. When negotiating for office space, the landlord may not budge on the rent but will include in the package the use of his building crew to make office improvements or the use of free conference rooms.

Packaging is also used in negotiating the settlement of lawsuits. An agreement may not be possible based on the claim in litigation, but a universal settlement that resolves other pending or potential claims between the same parties or those aligned in interest may expand the bargaining range, and allow more high-priority/low-priority trade-offs that allow an agreement to be reached. It was this type of packaging that led to the "universal" settlement of the *Microsoft v. Stac* litigation described in Chapter 3. Each side agreed to drop its claims in the lawsuit in exchange for cross-licensing all of their existing patents as well as future ones over five years, and Microsoft agreed to pay Stac license royalties totaling $43 million over 43 months, while also investing $39.9 million for a 15 percent equity stake in Stac. Although most often associated with problem-solving negotiation, packaging and logrolling are frequently utilized by competitive negotiators at the end of the day. Effective negotiators, regardless of their general approach, will do what it takes to reach a settlement or complete a deal if they end up getting more than they have to give up.

4. Agree to Disagree: Contingent Agreements

If impasse is reached because of different predictions of future events or disagreement over risks, an agreement might be structured based on these differences. In short, you can agree to disagree and write contingent outcomes into the deal.

Recognition of different views and probability assessments of uncertain events can help conclude a negotiation and result in an agreement that builds on differences by rewarding the side that most accurately predicts an unknown future event or outcome. An impasse over the amount of rent for a new restaurant can be resolved by the landlord agreeing to a lower base rent for the skeptical or risk-averse renter, with an additional amount to be determined by the restaurant's revenue. A personal injury settlement negotiation that is stalled because of different predictions about the ongoing need for medical treatment can be resolved by a lump sum amount, with a contingent amount based on the speed of recovery.

Agreeing to disagree and leaving economic questions open to uncertain results through the use of contingent agreements has a downside. The uncertainty and the temptation to manipulate the contingencies on which future rewards are based can create moral dilemmas and future disputes. The nature, potential, and dilemmas of contingent agreements are discussed in the next reading.

❖ **Michael Moffitt,** *CONTINGENT AGREEMENTS:*
AGREEING TO DISAGREE ABOUT THE FUTURE

87 Marq. L. Rev. 691 (2004)

"That won't happen." "Yes, it will." "No, it won't." "Will too." "Will not."

Negotiators generally find no shortage of things about which to disagree. For example, negotiators seeking to resolve a dispute often have sharply differing perceptions of the past. What happened? Whose decisions and actions caused the effects in question? How does their conduct compare with expectations or duties? In some circumstances, settlement is impossible without resolution of these backward-looking questions. A significant component of classical dispute resolution theory suggests that one might overcome impasse by shifting the focus of conversations toward the future. Sometimes, however, the shift to a forward-looking exploration merely provides fertile, new grounds for disagreement. Rather than arguing about what happened, the negotiators argue about what will happen. A wholesaler asserts that demand for the product will skyrocket in the future, and the retailer suspects otherwise. A defendant points to the relatively minor and temporary injuries caused in a car crash, but the victim fears that currently undetected injuries may manifest themselves down the road. Instinct may suggest that one negotiator will need to persuade the other about the likelihood of future uncertain events. Instead, genuinely held disagreements about the future present an important opportunity for negotiators to discover an attractive trade. The vehicle for capturing this potential is the contingent agreement.

Structurally, a contingent agreement is one in which the parties identify the universe of possible future conditions and agree to take on different obligations in each of those conditions. The simplest contingent deals are those in which the future has only two possible relevant conditions. X will happen, or it will not. If X happens, the terms of our deal are ABC; otherwise, we will do DEF. If I think X is unlikely to happen, I will be happy to give you terms you prefer for ABC, in exchange for terms I favor for DEF. Believing that she will get the work finished on time, an author signs a lucrative book contract with a very harsh penalty for late completion. Buyer loves Seller's house, but really wants a property with off-street parking. Seller firmly expects that the city council will approve a variance required for construction of a new garage, but Buyer is less confident about the likelihood of getting approval. Buyer agrees to purchase the property from Seller at a reduced price, with a substantial additional payment to Seller if the City Council grants a variance within the next twelve months. Negotiators can craft attractive trades by establishing obligations that are contingent on a future uncertain event that affects each side's valuation of the agreement.

Contingent agreements can also include variable terms, pegged to some benchmark to be measured in the future. I think interest rates will increase over the next few months, and you think they will go down. If I am loaning you money today, we will each be happy to agree to a deal with a floating interest rate. A school board is nervous about the future level of state funding to the districts, while the teachers' union is optimistic. The teachers' union agrees to a wage and benefit increase tied to a particular line in next year's state budget. The plaintiff believes that he may suffer long-term health effects of exposure to the defendant's product, while the defendant believes no significant health risks exist. The defendant agrees to pay specified medical monitoring expenses for the plaintiff and to assume any future medical costs associated with exposure. Parties to a joint venture agree to final, binding resolution of their intellectual property dispute by an appointed arbitrator. Without the possibility of contingent agreements, uncertainty regarding future conditions can make distributive decisions (for example, who gets how much money) difficult. By linking the allocation of resources to an externally measurable variable, negotiators can sometimes overcome otherwise paralyzing disagreements about the future.

Contingent agreements also present an opportunity to create favorable incentives. Some negotiated deals involve no future relationship between the negotiators and are self-executing. Buying a trinket in a marketplace involves a simple exchange of money for goods. In more complex circumstances, however, ongoing relationships exist and implementation of the agreement takes place over time. When the negotiated deal involves more than a simple, one-time exchange, parties' behavior after the agreement is relevant. Contingent agreements can help to create incentives for parties to behave well after the terms of the deal are fixed. A company may agree to tie a sales executive's compensation to sales performance, thus promoting sales-maximizing behavior out of the executive after the deal is signed. The health ministry of a developing country approaches a prospective donor, seeking support for particular health sector programs. Both the prospective donor and the developing country want to see multiple sources of funding. They agree to a matching program under which the donor will contribute an amount equal to the funds the ministry secures from other sources, giving the ministry officials added incentive to garner resources. In some contingent deals, one party can affect the likelihood of the contingent trigger—the salesman can make more sales calls, the ministry officials can approach more donors. Contingent agreements can affect parties' behavior after the agreement.

Precisely because contingent agreements can affect parties' behaviors, some contingent agreements risk creating conditions of moral hazard. Moral hazard is a condition in which one party, under the terms of an agreement, may undetectably or uncontrollably behave in a way that is adverse to the other party. How quickly do you take the speed bumps when you are driving a rental car? Moral hazard suggests that many drivers will drive more cautiously over the bumps if they are driving their own cars because they consider the long-term effects of their driving behavior. Athletes' contracts often contain contingent incentive clauses. If the athlete scores a certain number of points, for example, he or she receives additional money. Moral hazard arises when, toward the end of the season, a team notices that the athlete is only a few points away from the triggering contingent event. Will the team structure its play to enable the athlete to achieve the statistical goal? If an agent's contract provides for a thirty percent commission on sales this year, but only a ten percent commission in future years, the agent will have an incentive to push deals into the current year—even if the deal he or she could have struck next year would have been on terms more favorable to the company. Negotiators crafting a contingent agreement should foresee the possibility of moral hazard and, where appropriate, structure incentives and disclosures to minimize the incentive for subsequent adverse behavior. . . .

Contingent agreements may affect negotiators' perceptions of "winning" and "losing." Classical negotiation advice counsels negotiators to conceive of negotiations in terms other than win-lose, pointing to the risk that competitive behavior may cloud opportunities for joint gains. In one respect, contingent agreements may present an opportunity for negotiators to avoid the necessity of identifying a winner. Rather than forcing one side to concede on its forecast, contingent agreements permit (in fact, require) both sides to maintain their conflicting predictions about the future. At the time of the agreement, therefore, each side can declare "victory," to the extent such a declaration is important. On the other hand, contingent agreements have the nature of a wager or a bet. Unless one counts the sheer joy of gambling as a victory, both sides cannot win a wager. The contingent event either happens or it does not. Either way, one side may be disappointed. In some organizational cultures, failure is punished more harshly than success is rewarded. A negotiator fearful of identifiable failure (for example, a wager that visibly did not pay off) may forgo an elegant contingent agreement in favor of a less efficient non-contingent deal. Elegantly structured contingent deals may help to reduce the risk of visibly "losing." For example, if the plaintiff fears that a jury may award him nothing, and a defendant fears a runaway jury award of millions, the two could agree to a small guaranteed recovery in exchange for a cap on the maximum recovery. The losing party at trial will then be grateful to have made the contingent agreement, and the winner's regret will be dampened by having won a favorable verdict. . . .

A final, often overlooked, factor dissuading parties from crafting contingent deals is that parties place some value on certainty and finality. Particularly for negotiators embroiled in a dispute, achieving resolution may have an inherent value independent of the terms of the deal. Many disputants find it emotionally costly to carry around uncertainty. A contingent agreement does not represent complete finality, as at least some of the terms are yet to be determined. Uncertainty also can be costly for economic reasons. A company with an uncertain liability or benefit on its books faces considerable challenges in planning appropriate reserves of money, for example. If a company has a large collection of similar contingent agreements, it may be able to spread the risks and allocate money accurately in the aggregate. Similarly, some circumstances may permit parties to manage risks through the use of hedging instruments such as futures or options. Such allocations are not generally available to all individual negotiators, potentially making contingent agreements less attractive. For a contingent

agreement to be appropriate in a given context, therefore, the perceived benefit it captures for each negotiator must exceed the transaction costs of discovering and implementing the agreement.

Negotiators arguing about the past sometimes "agree to disagree," preferring
instead to focus on what they will do moving forward. Negotiators with differing
perceptions of the future should similarly agree to disagree — using contingent
agreements to capture the potential benefits of their differences.

5. Realistically Reconsider and Adjust BATNAs and WATNAs

You know it is important before commencing a negotiation to consider all of the
information available to you in determining realistic best and worst scenarios
if no agreement is reached. It is also crucial to process additional information
gleaned during the negotiation in order to compare what is on the table at the
end of negotiation with your readjusted BATNA and WATNA. The new information may be provided directly by the other side during the negotiation or by
a refinement of your pre-negotiation perceptions based on interactions, nonverbal cues and changing circumstances. The information available near the
end of the negotiation is more current, reality-tested, and accurate then what
you knew prior to negotiating. Too many negotiators cling to their pre-negotiation assessments and reservation points in deciding whether to accept or reject
a concluding proposal, which can create an impasse that may later be regretted.
We are all subject to the confirmation bias, discussed in Chapter 2, and tend
to give credit only to information that is consistent with our preexisting beliefs
and predictions rather than information that challenges or contradicts them.
In addition to the realistic reconsideration of your client's no-agreement alternatives, it may be necessary to remind your counterparts that their rejection of
your final offer does not factor in new information that you have provided during the negotiation or changes in circumstances.

6. Decision Fatigue, Glucose, and the Nirvana Fallacy

After intense negotiations and the multiple decisions often necessary to reach
a final agreement, a relatively small issue or the necessity of approving a comprehensive package of the component parts of a comprehensive settlement
may be the "straw" that blocks agreement and causes impasse. Recent research
has confirmed the deteriorating quality of decisions made after a long session
of decision-making and the depletion of mental energy resulting from sustained decision making. Decision fatigue is different from ordinary physical
fatigue — you're not consciously aware of being tired, but you do become low
on mental energy. The more choices you make throughout the day, the harder
each one becomes for your brain and it looks for shortcuts. You might become
reckless and act impulsively instead of expending energy to think through the
consequences. ("If you won't pay an additional $2,000, I will see you in court!")
The other shortcut is the inability to decide — decision paralysis. ("I just can't
agree to that!") (John Tierney, "Do You Suffer From Decision Fatigue?," New
York Times, Aug. 17, 2011.) Because decision fatigue correlates with low energy

and glucose levels, the anti-dote may be to take time for a sweet bite or a night's rest before declaring impasse. (See Danziger et al., *Extraneous Factors in Judicial Decisions*, Proceedings of the National Academy of Sciences 2011, www.pnas.org/content/108/17/6889. See also Baumeister et al., "The Glucose Model of Mediation," 15 Pepp. Disp. Res. L. J. 377 (2015).)

The perfect solution standard, or the "nirvana fallacy," can cause us to reject a mutually advantageous settlement because we can imagine something better, even though we might not be able to ever obtain it. It is a similar message to Voltaire's admonition that "perfect is the enemy of good." Comparing a realistic settlement agreement negotiated to provide much, but not all of what each party most wanted, and then rejecting it because it was not quite as good as an idealized but untested BATNA is an example of the nirvana fallacy creating impasse.

> **Problem**
>
> Assume you are negotiating with a small law firm interested in hiring you as an associate. The firm is offering you a lower salary than larger firms are paying new associates. You do not want to accept a lower salary, but you prefer a smaller firm and believe that you will be able to generate some new business. Based on the above readings, what terms of agreement might you suggest that could benefit you and be attractive to the firm?

7. *Win with a Shrug, Lose with a Smile*

Never celebrate a victory, at least not in the presence of the other side. If you can leave your counterpart convinced he did well, there will be fewer issues going forward and less likelihood that the other side will back out of the deal. The relationship between negotiators is strengthened if no one feels they were beaten. There is value in the rapport established for future negotiations. Conversely, if an opponent or his attorney loses face, he may feel compelled to "get even" at the next opportunity.

One of the authors remembers this example of never celebrating a victory from observing his father in action at the family's pawnshop at the end of vigorous bargaining over the price of an electric fan on a hot summer day.

> *"Glen you drive a hard bargain. You can take the fan for $17 on one condition; don't tell anyone how little you paid for it. I'm losing my shirt to you."*
> *"Stop your bellyaching Lew. You gotta' be making money. How else do you stay in business and feed your family when you always lose money selling this stuff?"*
> *"You're right. I lose money on almost everything I sell, but I sell so much I can afford to lose more money. It's a matter of volume!"*

Glen left the shop feeling like he had bargained well. The person you negotiate with should always feel they got a good deal. A positive experience prevents buyer's remorse and may bring them back for more. When appropriate, congratulate your counterpart on the agreement achieved, but not too much. When negotiators lavish effusive praise on their opponents, they have reason to become suspicious and think they may have been taken. (See Folberg 2008.)

B. Finalizing and Writing the Agreement

After you reach decisions about how a case will be settled or a deal will be structured, your work as a lawyer is not complete. The relief you feel in reaching an agreement can induce you to neglect the important task of attending to how the agreement will be worded and how the remaining details will be determined. Issues of implementation and execution may remain to be determined. The old maxim that "the devil is in the details" is an apt warning. Often, a negotiated settlement about the amount to be paid or an agreement "in principle" triggers another set of negotiations, this time over the formal terms of the settlement agreement itself. Lack of clarity about the terms of the agreement can result in perceptual differences about what was decided and the unraveling of the agreement. Inattention to how the agreement is written can also put your client's interests at risk of intentional overreaching by the other side or unintentional differences of interpretation that do not favor your client. Not memorializing the agreement in writing as quickly as possible can lead to unnecessary expenses if more time is required to reconstruct exactly what was agreed upon or if uncertainty develops about the outcome. If you did well negotiating, the favorable result for your client can lead to buyer's remorse, causing the other side to look for ways to change the non-finalized terms or reject the not-yet-enforceable agreement.

A negotiated business transaction is usually memorialized in the form of a written contract that incorporates the terms of the deal and follows general contract principles. An agreement to settle a legal claim may have different characteristics and requirements. A release of claims, a dismissal or other disposition of the underlying lawsuit, enforceability by entry of judgment or liquidated damages, how and when money will be paid or performance of obligations will occur, costs, expenses, and tax aspects—all of these issues must be considered when writing an agreement to settle a lawsuit. Ambiguities must be avoided; a settlement document is written to resolve an existing dispute, not foster a future one.

It is also important to attend to the psychological and relationship aspects of closing the deal. As illustrated in the pawn shop scenario, never gloat unless it is truly felt by all to be a mutually successful outcome. The relationship is strengthened if no one feels they were bested and if clients on both sides have reason to think they were well represented. (It is for this reason that a good negotiator on the other side will not give you an honest critique or tell you that you could have done better.) Even if the parties will not have an ongoing relationship, the attorneys may have future professional contact. There is value in the rapport that carries forward to future negotiations when each side is satisfied with the outcome and great cost if an opponent feels compelled to "get even" at the next opportunity because of regret over an outcome.

We present below the basics involving release of claims, structured settle-ments, ratification, and the use of single text agreements. Then relationship and practical issues involved in finalizing negotiated agreements, whether trans-actional or settlement based, are addressed. Tax considerations, which may affect some settlement terms and how the settlement agreement is written, are discussed in Chapter 11.

1. Release of Claims

If the settlement agreement resolves a legal dispute between parties, the agree-ment should contain a clause mutually releasing one another from future legal claims, either in general or relating specifically to the present controversy. The release-of-claims clause can be broad or narrow, depending on the case, but most settlement agreements should contain mutual releases. In tort cases, the release clause usually releases the defendant from all future claims by the injured party. It may narrowly release the defendant from claims arising out of the facts alleged, or more generally from all claims arising before the settle-ment date. If you represent the defendant, failing to obtain such a release in the settlement agreement could expose your client to future liability. You will want the broadest release possible. If you represent the plaintiff, especially in a personal injury case where the full extent of injury and complications may not be known, you will negotiate the narrowest release possible so that damages not now known may be sought later.

A tort defendant will usually seek a settlement provision that the settlement is not an admission of liability, which could be used in actions by other parties, particularly in product liability settlements. In many cases, the defendant, par-ticularly in employment and sexual harassment claims, will want a confidential-ity provision with liquidated damages. Such a provision may be the subject of added negotiation. In product liability and malpractice cases, confidentiality provisions may raise public protection, ethics, and policy issues (addressed in Chapter 10).

In settlement agreements between businesses, your client may not want to release the other parties from all claims arising before a certain date, since the business relationship may have ongoing conflicts, and some potential future claims may not be apparent. A blanket release may not take into account real-ities of the continuing relationship and latent claims, so it may be wise to pro-pose and, if necessary, negotiate a limited release.

2. Structured Settlements

Structured settlements are commonly used where damages are substantial or otherwise difficult to meet in one lump-sum payment, and in cases of cata-strophic injury or in significant settlements where the plaintiff is a minor. In a structured settlement, the amount recovered by the plaintiff is paid over time in installments. The defendant funds the payments by purchasing an annuity or bond, or by establishing a trust from which the plaintiff receives periodic payments. The structure can be tailored to meet a variety of circumstances.

For example, an injured child whose future earning capacity is impaired by an accident may receive a sum now for medical expenses and escalating monthly payments beginning at age 18 for supplemental income. Experts and annuity representatives are readily available to help structure the future payments and offer annuities for a time-discounted payment.

3. Ratification

There are many situations where final authority to sign an agreement rests with someone not directly part of the negotiation. This can result in another opportunity to reopen negotiations to obtain approval of an absent author- ity and, in the process, for one side to "nibble" at what was thought to be an agreed deal. They might take advantage of asymmetrical timing needs or an opponent's investment in the anticipated outcome. Clarification of who has ultimate authority and whose signature is necessary to create an enforceable agreement should occur before the negotiation begins. (Issues of enforcement and defenses are covered in Chapter 11.)

The settlement of some disputes or transactions requires ratification by a constituent group. For example, the resolution of labor-management contro- versies may require ratification of union members. Some corporate issues may require a vote of stockholders. Disputes involving municipalities and other pub- lic bodies may rest upon final approval of elected councils or boards. Again, it is helpful to agree at the outset of negotiations on the approval/ratification pro- cess and on mechanisms to help ensure that those engaged in the negotiation have the confidence of the final decision makers. Good faith deposits or penalty provisions if approval is not forthcoming may help guard against last minute manipulations and disappointments.

The most effective way to ensure approval and ratification of "stakeholders" or interested parties not at the table is to involve those who hold final authority in the negotiation or to structure steps that require interim approval or endorse- ment along the way. If the stakeholder group becomes invested in the process and aware of the value being created, as well as the BATNAs involved and the concessions leading to the proposed agreement, its members are more inclined to concur with what they feel part of than if presented with an up-or-down vote on what appears to be a fait accompli. A gradual "buy-in" is more likely to result in endorsement than an after-the-fact request, even if a group process compli- cates the negotiation.

4. Single Text Agreements

One method used by mediators can also be of help in direct negotiation, partic- ularly when ratification may be required. The single-text approach of building an agreement by writing the provisions or sections together at the table and then circulating that section for approval before the next section is written was made famous by President Jimmy Carter during the Camp David negotiations between Egypt and Israel. (See Carter 1982.) The resulting document grows section by section with the buy-in of all approving parties along the way. The completed agreement then reflects a joint effort that was grown to maturity by those who feel an ownership of what was built together. Of course, the pieces of an agreement are interrelated and final approval must await the completed document, so there is no guarantee that the end terms of a single text agreement will be accepted. However, using a single-text approach and getting buy-in along the way makes it more likely that there will be concurrence on the cumulative final document that represents the resulting agreement.

> Questions
>
> 10. Can you identify additional situations that may require ratification, formal or informal, of a negotiated settlement or deal?
> 11. What are the potential advantages and disadvantages of a structured settlement?

5. Memorializing the Agreement

❖ **Charles B. Craver,** *EFFECTIVE LEGAL NEGOTIATION AND SETTLEMENT*

212 (Lexis, 2001)

Take Time to Review Agreement

When bargaining interactions are successfully concluded, many participants are anxious to terminate their sessions and return to other client matters. As a result, they fail to ensure a clear meeting of the minds. If both sides are not in complete agreement, subsequent misunderstandings may negate their bargaining efforts. To avoid later disagreements, the participants should take the time to review the specific terms agreed upon before they adjourn their discussions. In most instances they will encounter no difficulties and will merely reaffirm the provisions they have achieved.

Endeavor to Draft Final Agreement

Once the Competitive/Distributive, Closing, and Cooperative/Integrative Stages have been completed and a final accord has been achieved, many negotiators are readily willing to permit opposing counsel to prepare the settlement agreement. While this may save them time and effort, it is a risky practice. It is unlikely that they and the opponent would employ identical language to memorialize the specific terms agreed upon. Each would probably use slightly different terminology to represent his or her own perception of the matter. To ensure that their client's particular interests are optimally protected, bargainers should always try to be the one to draft the operative document.

No competent attorney would ever contemplate the omission of terms actually agreed upon or the inclusion of items not covered by the parties' oral understanding. Either practice would be wholly unethical and would constitute fraud. Such disreputable behavior could subject the responsible practitioner and his or her client to substantial liability and untoward legal problems. Why then should lawyers insist upon the right to prepare the final accord? It is to allow them to draft a document that unambiguously reflects their perception of the overall agreement achieved by the parties.

Each provision should be carefully prepared to state precisely what the drafting party thinks was mutually agreed upon. When the resulting contract is then presented to the other party for execution, it is quite likely that it would be reluctant to propose alternative language, unless serious questions regarding the content of particular clauses were raised. Doubts tend to be resolved in favor of the proffered document. This approach best ensures that the final contract will most effectively protect the interests of the party who drafted it.

Review Opponent's Draft Carefully

If negotiators are unable to prepare the ultimate agreement, they should be certain to review the terms of the document drafted by the other side before they permit their client to execute it. They should compare each provision with their notes and recollections of the interaction, to be positive that their understanding of the bargaining results is accurately represented. They should be certain that nothing agreed upon has been omitted and that nothing not agreed upon has been included. If drafters suggest that certain new terms are mere "boilerplate," reviewers should make sure those terms do not alter the fundamental substantive or procedural aspects of their agreement.

Unabashed Questioning of Drafts

Agreement reviewers should not hesitate to question seemingly equivocal language that may cause future interpretive difficulties or challenge phrases that do not appear to describe precisely what they think was intended by the contracting parties. Since practitioners now use word processors to draft contractual documents, it is easy to accommodate additions, deletions, or modification. Bargainers should never permit opponents to make them feel guilty about changes they think should be made in finally prepared agreements. It is always appropriate for non-drafting parties to be certain that the final language truly reflects what has been achieved through the negotiation process. If the other side repeatedly objects to proposed modifications because of the additional work involved, the participant suggesting the necessary alterations can quickly and effectively silence those protestations by offering to accept responsibility for the final stages of the drafting process. It is amazing how expeditiously these remonstrations cease when such an easy solution to the problem is suggested!

Tact in Questioning

When negotiators reviewing draft agreements discover apparent discrepancies, they should contact their opponents and politely question the pertinent language. They should not assume deliberate opponent deception. It is always possible that the persons challenging the prepared terminology are mistaken and that the proposed terms actually reflect what was agreed upon. The reviewers may have forgotten modifications quickly accepted near the conclusion of the negotiation process. It is also possible that the drafting parties made honest mistakes that they would be happy to correct once they have examined their notes of the bargaining interaction. Even when document reviewers suspect intentional deception by drafting parties, they should still provide their opponents with a face-saving way out of the predicament. The best way to accomplish the desired result is to assume honest mistakes and give the drafters the opportunity to "correct" the erroneous provisions. If reviewers directly challenged opponent integrity, the dispute would probably escalate and endanger the entire accord.

Vigilance Against Underhanded Tactics

In recent years, a few unscrupulous practitioners in the corporate area have decided to take advantage of the drafting stage of large documents to obtain benefits not attained during the negotiation process. They include provisions that were never agreed upon, or modify or omit terms that were jointly accepted. They attempt to accomplish their deceptive objective by providing their opponents with copies of the agreement at the eleventh hour, hoping that time pressure will induce their unsuspecting adversaries to review the final draft in a cursory manner. Lawyers who encounter this tactic should examine each clause of the draft agreement with care to be certain it represents the actual accord achieved. If necessary, they should completely redraft the improper provisions. If their proposed terms are rejected by opposing counsel, they should insist upon a session with the clients present to determine which draft represents the true intentions of the parties. When this type of meeting is proposed, deceitful drafters are likely to "correct" the "inadvertent misunderstandings" before the clients ever get together. If a client session were to occur and the other side enthusiastically supported the deceptive drafting practices of their attorneys, it would be appropriate for the deceived lawyers to recommend that their client do business with another party.

Addressing Unforeseen Ambiguities and Problems

On some occasions, ambiguities or actual disagreements may be discerned during this stage. Negotiators should not allow these difficulties to destroy their previous progress. When good faith misunderstandings are found, the advocates should strive to resolve them before they terminate their current interaction. At the conclusion of the Closing or the Cooperative/Integrative Stage, the parties tend to be in a particularly accommodating frame of mind. They feel good about their bargaining achievements and are psychologically committed to a final accord. It is thus a propitious time to address newly discovered problems. If they do not deal with these issues now, they are likely to encounter greater difficulties when these questions arise at a later date.

Writing and Signing Items as Safeguard

A few unscrupulous negotiators attempt to obtain a tactical advantage by deliberately creating "misunderstandings" as final agreements are being drafted. They hope to extract additional concessions from unsuspecting opponents as these seeming ambiguities are being resolved. Individuals who suspect that their adversaries may employ this tactic should insist on a careful review of the basic terms at the conclusion of the bargaining process. They should write out these items and have their opponents sign the draft to indicate their concurrence. This practice makes it difficult for adversaries to later create disingenuous "misunderstandings" that can be used to obtain unreciprocated benefits for their own side.

CHAPTER
8

Telephone and Cyber Negotiation

Effective negotiators use multiple forms of information gathering as the basis for formulating strategy and shaping responsive communication. All of our senses are put to use in determining the needs, feelings, resolve, strengths, and vulnerabilities of our negotiation counterparts. We also convey messages by nonverbal means, such as gestures and body language, to construct a desired context, shape perceptions and build rapport. Therefore, face-to-face negotiation is the gold standard to get and give information and pursue agreement. Meeting in person provides an opportunity to establish a relationship before jumping into negotiation details. Social psychologists and communication theorists refer to face-to-face discussions as a "rich medium," providing synchronous or "real-time" communication.

Our schedules, time restraints, distance, limited resources, and changing norms may require that we use telephone communications, e-mails, and text messages to initiate, conduct, or conclude negotiations. These methods of communication limit nonverbal cues and other information. They are more "lean" forms of communicating than face-to-face negotiation. Thus, we must employ a different skill set and approach to achieve effective negotiation results and avoid the potential traps of relying only on telephone and cybercommunication.

A. Negotiating by Telephone and Video Communication

Before the ubiquitous use of e-mail and text messages (discussed in section B), telephones were the efficient substitute for face-to-face negotiations and still serve an important role. Like in-person communications, the telephone allows for real-time conversation. The use of voice messaging adds to the efficiency factor by allowing sequential messages, or "asynchronicity," when it is not practical for negotiating counterparts to be on the phone at the same time. Negotiation communication by telephone, rather than face-to-face meetings, may be a necessity when geographical distance or busy schedules prevent meeting in person. Teleconferencing or videoconferencing in multiple-party negotiations offers exponential economies and convenience compared to getting several lawyers physically in the same room together.

Although negotiating by telephone strips us of visual cues, some audible cues beyond the words chosen can provide a richer medium of negotiation than the written word. Tone of voice, inflection, pitch, pace, volume, pauses, breathing, and sighs provide audible cues. These audible cues may be more pronounced with the elimination of visual distractions in face-to-face discussions. We also feel we can "read" meanings like friendliness, hostility, fear, and other emotions based on what we hear from others over the telephone. Telephonic communication may be less personal than face-to-face negotiation, but the use of the telephone is generally more personal than the written word alone. It is more common to engage in "small talk" and other ice-breaking or rapport-building communication by telephone than in e-mails. We previously studied the role of trust in successful negotiations (see Chapter 5). Trust is fostered by getting to know a negotiating counterpart through conversation and identifying common interests before "getting down to business."

Telephone negotiations may be advantageous in some situations. It may be helpful to have your notes, concession points, and other reminders in front of you when negotiating by telephone. The use of outlines and prompts cannot so easily be relied upon in face-to-face talks. If your client is present with you when you are negotiating by telephone, you can visually communicate together in private in a way that cannot be done in face-to-face meetings with the other side. If you need to take time to gather your thoughts prior to making an offer or deciding what to do next, it is easier to interrupt the telephone conversation and offer to call back than it is to excuse yourself from a face-to-face negotiation.

Telephoning a negotiation opponent offers the caller a degree of control beyond that provided by scheduling a negotiation meeting. Calling when you are prepared and ready may provide some advantage over the person who answers the call when she is not as focused as you are on the topic. (Courtesy and custom, however, may require scheduling the telephone conversation in advance.) In a significant negotiation, it may be easier to say no or be more insistent on favorable terms when negotiating by telephone than when facing a forceful opponent in person. It is also easier to strategically conclude a telephone negotiation that is not going well than to leave a negotiation meeting, particularly if it is in your office. Of course, an opposing lawyer might do the same or more easily use deceptive and strategic tactics on the telephone, including hanging up. Every advantage can be a double-edged sword.

Telephone follow-up to an in-person negotiation is common and presents fewer of the disadvantages and dangers noted above. If rapport and trust are established in face-to-face negotiations, communicating by telephone or videoconferencing to conclude the deal or settlement can be a cost-saving convenience.

Video technology is further transforming how we communicate and negotiate. Virtual meetings and teleconferencing through immersive telepresence, possibly even in 3D and with holographic technology, is becoming more of a reality to replace long-distance travel and scheduling of in-person negotiations. Tablet devices and smart phones with two-way cameras are becoming so ubiquitous that electronic video communication is an expanding alternative to in-person negotiation. Skype, FaceTime, Tango, Zoom, and other visual-plus-voice forms of cybercommunication may become the negotiation media of choice, just as e-mailing and texting became more convenient and popular than telephone conversation. All of these technologies, present challenges that person-to-person negotiations behind closed doors do not. (See Ebner and Thompson 2014.)

Take the Deal!

Sports agents and others who negotiate for a living spend a lot of time on the telephone negotiating deals. Leigh Steinberg is a legendary lawyer-agent, who, in his book, *Winning with Integrity*, discusses his use of telephone follow-up and other electronic aids to negotiation. Steinberg states that he could easily make a hundred telephone calls in a day. He cautions about the need to protect against invasions of privacy and eavesdropping. An interesting example provided is a contract he negotiated for Troy Aikman to become the star quarterback for the Dallas Cowboys. The negotiations began in a face-to-face meeting in Texas of Steinberg, Aikman, Cowboys owner Jerry Jones, the head coach, and others.

> This was a get to know you meeting. A lot of the conversation was about hunting and fishing. Everyone in that room, with the exception of me, was from Arkansas, Texas, or Oklahoma. I soon felt that I was the one with a heavy accent. . . . When I finally left Dallas that day and flew back home, we were far from finished. But the groundwork had been laid. . . . [W]e were on the phone constantly. . . . I had a particularly intense car phone conversation with Jerry Jones. I was stuck in the infamous Los Angeles rush-hour traffic on the San Diego Freeway, and Jerry was stuck at his offer of 10 million.
> "Jerry," I told him, "we've got to have eleven and a half."
> "Son," he said, "that dog won't hunt."
> "Jerry," I said, "this is fair."
> "Son," he answered, "we passed *fair* about eight million dollars ago." Back and forth it went, until suddenly a third voice came on the line, a stranger who had crossed cell phone signals with us.
> "Listen, buddy," the voice said, addressing me with a Texas drawl, "if you don't want the 10 million, I do. Take the deal."
> This deal was finally closed through a two-way telecommunications link-up between Los Angeles and Dallas as the parties sat in their offices watching one another on widescreen television.

B. E-Mail and Text Message Negotiation

E-mail is commonly used for purposes of conducting all types of negotiation or following up negotiations started through in-person or telephone discussions. We explore below some of the issues raised by e-mail negotiation.

This discussion of e-mail negotiation should be placed in generational perspective. For many law students, e-mail, text messaging, and the use of social media might serve as your primary mode of communication. However, some older attorneys and clients may not be as comfortable or knowledgeable about cybercommunication. The law relating to negotiation and the enforcement of negotiated agreements is, by nature, slow to catch up to technological advancement, as are some older lawyers.

As you know from your own experience, the ease and informality of e-mail and texting can be both a blessing and a curse. Experienced users of e-mail and text messaging develop shortcuts and abbreviations that among friends may be understood as acceptable conventions but can appear to others to be curt, abrupt, and sloppy. An informal choice of words may create misunderstandings and further disputes. Although e-mails and texts used in negotiation can and should be composed with care, it is easy to lapse into "cybermode." As a "lean" form of communication, electronic words are not readily put in context by facial expressions, like a smile, and by posture or body language, like a shrug or a nod. The speed, convenience, and economy of electronic communication must be balanced against the risk of misinterpretation and the bareness of the medium.

The following reading is based on the assumption that digital negotiation is now mainstream and will continue to expand. It presents eight major challenges of negotiating online and offers practical advice about how to capture its advantages and avoid its pitfalls.

❖ *Noam Ebner,* NEGOTIATION VIA (THE NEW) EMAIL

**Negotiation Excellence: Successful Deal Making
(M. Benoliel ed. 407-436, 2014)**

With the explosive increase in internet usage and online communication, and the surge in e-commerce, online negotiation can be expected to continue to gain traction as one of the most widespread methods of interaction. As the world goes increasingly mobile, we find ourselves with a range of communication devices scattered about our persons, vying for our attention and rendering us susceptible to interaction at unexpected moments. Negotiating in this environment presents many challenges. However, as opposed to several years ago, when students and clients would regularly inform me that they would *never* negotiate anything important by email, today this statement is rarely voiced—and with good reason. . . .

Negotiating Online is Unavoidable—and Unavoidably Different

The proliferation of e-communication media has presented us with a world of opportunity for negotiation interactions. So many of our interactions are now conducted online, that isolating negotiation activity as something to *avoid* online might seem unnatural to people. . . . However, the ease with which so many people have transferred so many of their interactions online conceals a hidden, yet crucial, truth: online negotiation is significantly different from face-to-face negotiation. While many people intuitively recognize this, the differences are either ignored and dismissed as inconsequential; alternatively, they are seen as insurmountable, a cause to avoid negotiating any significant matter online at all. However, in today's world, we can neither bury our heads in the sand, nor can we avoid online negotiation—we need to understand it, and learn how to conduct it well. . . .

Using Email: A Moving Target

Hailed as the fastest spreading technology in human history, the introduction of the smartphone has caused substantial upheaval in our communication habits. This tool has affected society in many ways, but for the purposes of this [article], I will stress one in particular: A major feature of the smartphone, as opposed to a regular mobile phone, is its capacity for accessing web and client-based email while on the move, via cellular or wireless connections, rather than requiring a physical connection to a static modem. In turn, this capacity has significantly affected our negotiation habits. . . .

Communicating via email no longer conjures a more-or-less uniform picture of a person seated at her desk or in her home office, typing on her computer, or even of her ordering a cappuccino and summoning up sufficient attention to work on her laptop at a café. Emails are read and written on buses and trains; while watching the kids at the playground or in-between turns of playing a game with them; during classes, rock concerts and movies; and even—even though most of us would never admit to this—while driving. The smartphone has introduced new elements of accessibility, distraction, environment, timing and technical limitations to email communication. . . .

Negotiating via email: Eight major challenges

Building on this understanding of media effects on communication, and awareness of the potential effects of communication media's constant shifts, we can now examine specific media effects affecting negotiation dynamics. We will focus on eight major elements:

1. *Increased contentiousness*
2. *Diminished information sharing*
3. *Diminished inter-party process cooperation*
4. *Diminished privacy*
5. *Diminished trust*
6. *Increased effects of negative attribution*
7. *Diminished party commitment and investment*
8. *Diminished focus*

1. Increased contentiousness

Communication at a distance is more susceptible to disruption than face-to-face dialogue Parties communicating via telephone have been found more prone to distrust, competition, and contentious behavior than those in comparable face-to-face interactions. These findings are intensified in e-communication, which tends to be less inhibited than face-to-face communication due to physical distance, reduced social presence, reduced accountability and a sense of anonymity. The lack of social cues in e-communication causes people to act more contentiously than they do in face-to-face encounters, resulting in more frequent occurrences of swearing, name calling, insults, and hostile behavior.

Early research on negotiation showed the same tendency for parties-at-a-distance (such as parties negotiating over the phone) to act tough and choose contentious tactics Examinations of e-negotiation brought to light the effects of further-diminished media richness: the social presence of others is reduced and the perceived social distance among negotiators increases. This might explain why e-negotiators seem less bound by appropriate, normative behavior than face-to-face negotiators. This translates into an increased tendency to threaten and issue ultimata; to adopt contentious, "squeaky wheel" behavior; to lie or deceive; to confront each other negatively, and to engage in flaming. In short: email negotiation is a rough playing field!

Getting practical:

1) Unmask yourself: The mutual invisibility inherent in email negotiation facilitates adversarial, contentious behavior. It is easier to cause damage to a faceless other—particularly when one feels protected by a shield of anonymity and physical distance. This can cause people to assume that they can get away with this behavior, and lower moral inhibitions they might have against doing so. By adopting a proactive agenda of unmasking ourselves—making ourselves human, present, and real in the other's eyes—we can protect ourselves from these dynamics. This unmasking process can include sharing personal information, building rapport, and reducing the perception of distance through shared language, or shared geographical or cultural references.

2) In the unmasking process, decide carefully what to share about yourself, taking advantage of the masking effect to avoid any anticipated bias.

3) Unmask the other: Remember, there is a person behind the other screen as well, whether they have had the foresight to engage in unmasking themselves or not. They are not computers or inboxes—they will respond to your messages on emotional, cognitive and behavioral levels which you will then have to deal with.

4) Use email's potential for asynchronicity in order to think and work proactively: Read a received message twice instead of banging out an angry reply. When you do write a response—delay sending it, and read it again before clicking send. Be extra careful on this front while communicating via smartphone; the fact that you can now answer instantly in more cases than ever before doesn't mean that you should!

2. Diminished inter-party process cooperation

As we've noted, information exchanged in email negotiations is likely to be constrained, analytical, and contentious. This might explain why email negotiators suffer from reduced accuracy in judging the other party's interests. Such reduced accuracy would reduce negotiators' ability to accurately assess differential preferences and identify potential joint gains—and therefore, one might posit, their desire to engage in this type of cooperative activity in the first place. Reduced social awareness in lean media causes parties to engage more heavily in self-interested behavior when negotiating by email. Focused inwardly, negotiators may simply ignore or fail to elicit important information regarding the other party's interests and priorities. The use of email may, therefore, accentuate competitive behavior in negotiations. Email communication is conducive not only to parties acting uncooperatively, but to parties feeling *justified* for choosing this pattern of behavior. Combine this with increased contentiousness, and with the comparative ease of walking away from the process (see below), and we are faced with a recipe for diminished process cooperation.

Getting practical:

1) Use interest-related language intentionally, and often, when discussing your own position and inquiring about theirs. Use process-cooperative language

overtly, and try and set the tone for others to do so. This might give process-cooperation a much-needed boost.

2) Take the stage: You have the opportunity to speak your mind, state what you want and explain why you should get it. No one can shout or shut you down. Utilize this clear stage.

3) In a multi-party interaction, if one party is dominating the conversation and others are quiet, you might invite them in, either in a "Let's hear what some others have to think" email to the group, or in a private, behind-the-scenes message to reticent parties.

4) Use bundling intentionally, highlighting connections between the issues, and perhaps using language you feel might trigger similar thinking in your negotiation opposite.

5) A familiar source of confusion in email negotiation occurs when your opposite party relates to some of the issues you raised in a letter, but not to other issues raised. This might not be a deliberate, contentious omission — it may simply be information overload. Consider whether you want to call their attention to this as an oversight, before assuming there is some underlying meaning in the omission.

6) Some people may find writing long, well thought-out messages on the small screen and keyboard or touchpad provided by a smartphone to be a daunting task; cooperative, information sharing messages may sometimes fall into this category. Rather than discard such opportunities, you might give more careful thought to the question of which machine you would best type your message on.

3. Reduction in integrative outcomes

The potential for email negotiation to result in lower rates of integrative outcome is partially connected to the previous challenge of reduced process cooperation. Indeed, many experiments measuring these two indicators illustrate significant challenges: First, that e-negotiation entails lower rates of process cooperation, and lower rates of integrative outcomes, when compared to face-to-face negotiation. Second, that the potential for impasse appears to be greater than in face-to-face negotiation.

These findings don't clearly explain *why* email negotiation results may be less integrative. Is it an outcome of reduced process cooperation? Of increased contentiousness? Of the difficulty of establishing rapport in email? Of reduced inter-party trust? Or, perhaps of a combination of some or all of these elements? . . .

Getting practical:

Most of the suggestions made above (regarding process cooperation) apply here as well. In addition:

1) Consider using the multimedia potentialities used in e-mail in order to portray integrative offers or ideas. Charts, graphs, presentations — all easily attached to an email — are powerful tools for overcoming the challenges of lean media.

2) Frame: In email negotiation, every message is an opportunity to set a new frame around the interaction, much more so than rapid-fire statements and

reactions in face- to-face processes. Intentional and repeated integrative framing might have an effect on the outcome.

4. Diminished privacy

Maintaining a negotiation process' privacy is never an easy task. In face-to-face negotiation, in the absence of a confidentiality agreement (and too often, in practice, even when one exists!) parties can, and do, share information about the negotiation with their friends, families and colleagues, and occasionally with wider circles. However, you can meet in a private setting, physically shut out the rest of the world, or relate something confidentially in a lowered voice. Anything shared with external parties will always be subjective, after-the-fact, secondhand (and in legal terms, hearsay). In email negotiation, by contrast, you never know who is "in the room" with you. Is your opposite showing your letter to their boss, to their colleagues or to your competition? The messages you transmit are recorded, and forever archived somewhere beyond your control; they can be adjusted or tampered with, altering what you wrote. Personal or proprietary information you send might be exposed to wider circles than intended, whether due to the other's bad intentions or their technical shortcomings. Who among us has never clicked "reply all" instead of "reply", thereby sending a personal message into a public domain?

Getting practical:

1) Consider each address field carefully. To whom should a message be sent? Should anyone appear in the "cc" field? Do you want anyone invisibly lurking on the conversation, from the "bcc" field?

2) Use the lack of privacy to your advantage: Record the interactions, return to them when things get unclear, and relate to them when it seems the other party is being inconsistent. Share messages with anybody you feel you need to share them with, and consult—often—about the process.

3) Increasingly, individuals' online activities are becoming public, widespread, sought out by future opponents and admissible in court. Be cautious of what you write in an email, particularly before trust is established. A good rule of thumb might be: Don't write anything in an email that you wouldn't want shown on the news.

5. Diminished degree of inter-party trust

Diminished privacy is but one factor that affects the much wider issue of inter-party trust. Trust has been identified as playing a key role in enabling cooperation, problem solving, achieving integrative solutions, effectiveness and resolving disputes.

Communicating via email, negotiators must cope with threats to trust that are inherent in the medium and in its employ. Email negotiators trust their counterparts less than negotiators in similar face-to-face interactions—at all stages of the process. Before the process' inception, e-negotiators report a comparatively low level of trust in their opposite. This low trust-level persists throughout the course of the negotiation, resulting in diminished process cooperation and information sharing. Even after reaching deals with their opposites, e-negotiators trust their opposites less than participants in face-to-face negotia-tions, manifesting in lower degrees of desire for future interaction with them. Why do people distrust each other online—or, more to the point, what is it they are worried about? It may be that they are specifically concerned about inten-tional deception.

Getting practical:

The following practices are helpful for building trust in email interactions:

1) Build rapport: Try to "bond", building an instant relationship with your opposite.

2) Apply social lubrication: Take the time, at the beginning of a negotiation and throughout its course, for light conversation. While this does not come as naturally by email as it does face-to-face, email doesn't make icebreaking or small talk superfluous—the contrary is true. Even minimal pre-negotiation, socially-oriented contact, such as preliminary email introductory messages, can build trust, improve mutual impressions, and facilitate integrative outcomes.

3) Mix media, when possible: Holding a preliminary face-to-face meeting can assist in setting the stage for a trust-filled e-negotiation. Meeting face-to-face in the middle of the process can also be beneficial. Remember that the smart-phone you are reading the email on can also be used to call the other person for a conversation through a media that is at once more synchronous and rich, injecting cue multiplicity into the interaction.

4) Show e-empathy: Showing empathy performs multiple roles in negotia-tion, including trust building. E-negotiators who show empathy are trusted by their negotiation opposites more than those who do not. This cannot be neglected just because the medium seems to be "cold" and impersonal. Utilize email's characteristics which allow considered, careful language to intentionally show e-empathy.

6. Increased attribution, increased misinterpretation

Communicating through lean media increases the tendency toward the fun-damental attribution error: parties perceive negative actions or statements on their opposite's part, and interpret these as outgrowth of the other's negative intentions and character—rather than as unintended results of circumstance. Reduced social presence and few contextual cues lend a sense of distance and vagueness to the interaction. The media richness element of interactivity com-pounds this: E-negotiators ask fewer clarifying questions than face-to-face nego-tiators—leaving more room for assumptions to form and take root. Attribution dynamics will cause these assumptions to tend toward the negative. Analysis of failed email negotiations shows that they tend to include unclear messages, irrelevant points, and long general statements, each of which provides ample breeding ground for attribution.

Getting practical:

1) Increase your social presence: constantly remind the other of the real per-son opposite them.

2) Write clearly, taking into account negative interpretations. Clarify much more than you do face-to-face. Here are several rules of thumb for enhancing email clarity:

a) Avoid unnecessary length—don't overload your opposite.

b) Use "In summary" sentences to highlight your main points.

c) Use the subject field intentionally. This introduces your letter (preparing your opposite for the content), provides a frame through which it will be read (diminishing negative interpretation), allows your opposite to find it when they want to review it for clarity before responding, and helps organize messages bundling multiple issues.

d) Avoid use of emoticons—particularly in early message exchanges.

e) If you are writing your message on a smartphone, be aware to the changes this causes in your writing style. If it causes you to respond in short messages, or constrains the way your email is laid out, consider how that might look through the eyes of your negotiation opposite. You might hold off and respond on a different machine, or you might simply let them know that you are responding to them via smartphone, which will explain issues of style and stave off negative attribution.

3) Waiting and perceived delay cause anxiety, which is conducive to negative attribution. Manage both sides of this cycle: Don't expect immediate answers to your own letters, and do your best to provide prompt responses to your opposites. Consider how use and expectations of smartphones—your own, or your counterpart's—may have affected your expectations on this issue. Knowing you read mail on your smartphone, certain opposites might get uptight if you don't respond within a few minutes! Conversely, accustomed to a couple of days typically passing before hearing from your opposite, you might be surprised to get a near-instant response from her—and read meaning into that haste. In reality, she may have just happened to have her smartphone in her hand when your message arrived and responded on the spot. Remember that you and your opposite might use multiple machines for email, each with its own nature with regards to message reading, message writing and other timing issues.

4) Be very careful when using humor: While humor has been shown to be a valuable tool in online negotiation, leading to increased trust and satisfaction levels, higher joint gains and higher individual gains for the party who initiated the humorous event, humor is often misunderstood, misinterpreted and misattributed—and can easily backfire.

5) If you are concerned that all this mindfulness and caution might not suffice, don't leave it to email: Recognize situations in which you need to pick up the phone and call, or meet in person with your negotiation opposite.

7. Diminished party commitment and investment

Parties to e-mail negotiation might be less motivated than face-to-face negotiators. They have not displayed the minimum commitment of getting up, getting dressed and coming to the table; indeed, there might not be any sunk costs at all. Smartphones have compounded this issue by reducing even the value of the time invested in writing the email, given that they allow people to do so during what might be "garbage time" to them—commuting, waiting for someone to show up, etc. Email may be the easiest medium there is for making "shot in the dark" approaches (perhaps best exemplified by the 62 trillion spam e-mails sent yearly, most of which are "shot in the dark" scamming or marketing efforts). This might provide partial explanation for reports of higher rates of impasse in email negotiation (see above), and for the familiar phenomena of email negotiations simply evaporating, with one party simply dropping out of the conversation, either disappearing in a whiff of smoke or dissolving into a cloud of "I'll get back to you".

Getting practical:

1) Stay on top of things: Provide regular contact, keeping your counterpart engaged—without getting pushy.

2) Bridge time gaps: Try to create the illusion or experience of an uninterrupted conversation. For example, write "As I wrote you . . . ," and then copy and paste a quote from your previous letter.

3) It could happen to you: The implications of this section are not only about roping in and maintaining contact with your opposite. You yourself might be prone to underinvestment and a low level of commitment. Email negotiation tends to confuse us in this regard; keep a constant eye on your motivation level, and make sure it matches your commitment and the resources you invest.

8. Diminished party focus

E-negotiators, even if they are committed and invested at the same level one might encounter in face-to-face negotiation, are likely to suffer media-related effects including confusion, low cognitive retention of previous messages, and diminished concentration. This is due to several factors, including time passage between information exchanges, the tendency to answer emails in spurts and sections rather than finding the time to write full messages, and the tendency to answer emails in less-than-optimal surroundings and circumstances. In addition, email is often not something we train our full attention on, but rather something we do as part of our media multitasking. We check our email as we surf the web, and we surf the web as we read or reply to our email—perhaps holding in-person or phone conversations at the same time. Recent research addressing this issue indicates that we are not as good at multitasking as we like to think we are. Heavy multitaskers suffer a range of shortcomings as opposed to "focusers", many of which are pertinent to negotiation: They are not good at filtering out irrelevant information, and are easily distracted. They tend to have low detail recall, and despite their tendency to switch between tasks rapidly—they are not skilled at this, as their brain is always somewhat focused on the task they are *not* doing. Negotiators suffering from any of these, due to their multitasking tendency, work surroundings, or email-management habits, might be confused and unfocused. Similar adjectives might be suitable for negotiators communicating via smartphone in noisy or crowded environments, without taking care to consider the effects their surroundings may have on their capacity to focus.

Getting practical:

1) Stay focused: The greater the importance of the negotiation to you, the more it pays to concentrate on it. Read and write messages in an environment

that allows you to concentrate. One simple rule of thumb to follow would be to close your Internet web browser while reading and writing email.

2) Be very aware of the costs of distraction. Negotiating via email on your smartphone might seem like a good way to make the most of your train ride into the office in the morning—but you may be setting yourself up for poor negotiation performance.

3) Go mobile—intentionally: Conversely, being able to take your negotiation to a place in which you feel comfortable, empowered, and competent might enable you to do your best. If you feel this is the case, grab your smartphone or tablet and go! The key is in making the choice to go mobile consciously and intentionally.

Conclusion:

Already a challenging medium to negotiate through, email has recently developed into a semi-synchronous communication channel and continues to evolve rapidly. Communicating by email, negotiators face a rougher playing field, a more contentious opposite, and numerous process-challenges. The good news is, that armed with some knowledge and a healthy dose of awareness, negotiators can navigate these challenges and even turn the use of the media to their advantage. Given the anticipated increase in e-negotiation processes, and the increasing sophistication and variation of the tools for engaging in it, the sooner negotiators get started on improving their skills and awareness in this area, the better.

Questions

1. Do you believe that negotiating by e-mail or text message is significantly different in terms of necessary preparation, strategic considerations, or ethical issues than face-to-face or telephone negotiations? How so?
2. Is it necessary to get client approval for negotiating by e-mail before the process begins?
3. Should clients be copied on all negotiation e-mails?
4. Need you check with clients about system compatibility, encryption programs, and metadata scrubbing mechanisms?
5. In the course of a negotiation, you receive an e-mail from opposing counsel with an attachment containing a proposed settlement amount. Can you ethically send the electronic proposal to your IT department with the request that the electronic file be mined for embedded metadata that might reveal hidden information, like other amounts they had considered offering and erased? Are you aware of the practice of mining electronic documents for metadata? (See *ABA Formal Opinion 06-442*, 2006.)

1. Talk First

When lawyers know one another, either socially or from past dealings, the use of text messaging may have fewer disadvantages than when they do not have a relationship. Research indicates that the existence of a prior relationship between opposing counsel favorably affects the likelihood that they will settle a lawsuit. In a study of thousands of cases filed in federal courts, it was discovered that attorneys were less likely to go to trial and could settle cases more quickly when they had faced each other in the past than when they had not. (See Johnston and Waldfogel 2002.) One explanation of this tendency is that those who know one another, even as opponents, are better able to communicate and know what to expect based on past interactions. They are able to put their communications in context more easily based on past experience together.

How can lawyers who do not know one another tap the advantages of e-mail for negotiation while minimizing the risks inherent in the "lean" nature of digital communication and the absence of social cues? This question is answered by the empirical research described in the next reading. As explained by Professor Nadler, law students were assigned to negotiate a commercial transaction with counterparts at a different law school using e-mail as the mode of communication. Negotiators who spoke together in an introductory telephone call established a relationship that tended to create rapport and trust, which aided them in reaching agreement in the subsequent e-mail negotiation and created positive feelings about one another. By contrast, those who began e-mail negotiation without first engaging in telephone "small talk" were over four times as likely to reach impasse and tended to end up feeling resentful and angry about the negotiation. Professor Nadler concludes by discussing implications of this experiment for lawyers who use e-mail to negotiate.

❖ Janice Nadler, *Rapport in Legal Negotiation: How Small Talk Can Facilitate E-Mail Dealmaking*

Harv. Negot. L. Rev. 223 (2004)

A. Procedure

The negotiation exercise used in the experiment involved the purchase of a new car. Participants consisted of 146 law students, half of whom were students at Northwestern University School of Law and half of whom were students at Duke Law School. The students participated as part of a class assignment in a Negotiation course. Thirty-five randomly selected Northwestern students were paired with thirty-five randomly selected Duke students and were assigned to the "Small Talk" condition. The remaining thirty-seven Northwestern students were randomly paired with the remaining thirty-seven Duke students and were assigned to the "No Small Talk" control condition.

Participants were given confidential role instructions which specified that they were to conduct a two-party negotiation exclusively via electronic mail. Each student received a packet of materials that contained a page of general confidential instructions and guidelines, an e-mail address for their counterpart, and pre- and post-negotiation questionnaires. Participants were given one week to complete the negotiation and questionnaires, and were specifically instructed to not discuss the negotiation or procedures with their classmates.

Unbeknownst to participants in the "No Small Talk" control condition, the participants in the "Small Talk" condition received an additional special instruction: they were to have an initial "getting to know you" telephone conversation lasting five to ten minutes with their partner before they began negotiating. Directions specified that participants should not talk about business (i.e., the negotiation) in this initial conversation, ensuring that it was a strictly social conversation. The goal was to have negotiators "break the ice." Regardless of group assignment, all negotiations took place exclusively via e-mail.

The negotiation itself involved the purchase of a new company car by a manager at a software company. The negotiation contained both distributive and integrative elements. Whereas both parties were motivated to claim as much value for themselves as possible, parties had different priorities; hence concessions by Party A on a given issue could be traded for gains on another issue which Party A values more but Party B values less. This type of logrolling increases the joint value of the agreement, creating more profit that can be allocated between the two parties. . . .

B. Results

"Small Talk" negotiators who had a brief "getting-to-know-you" telephone conversation prior to negotiating via e-mail reached superior economic outcomes and markedly better social outcomes than negotiators who did not talk on the phone. Differences between the "Small Talk" and "No Small Talk" conditions in economic and social outcomes are described below.

1. Economic Outcomes — Small Talk Led to More Negotiated Agreements

"Small Talk" negotiators were over four times as likely to reach an agreement as "No Small Talk" negotiators. Only three out of thirty-five "Small Talk" pairs (less than 9%) failed to reach an agreement, whereas fourteen out of thirty-seven "No Small Talk" pairs (nearly 40%) failed to reach agreement. The high percentage of "No Small Talk" pairs that were unable to reach agreement is especially noteworthy in light of the fact that a positive bargaining zone existed, making it economically desirable for each party to reach a negotiated agreement. Interestingly, the value of the outcome (measured both in terms of joint outcome and individual outcome) for the pairs that did reach agreement appears to be unaffected by small talk. . . .

An examination of precisely what occurred between negotiators who reached impasse is revealing. Because parties negotiated via e-mail, the transcripts of unsuccessful negotiations indicate the last offer on the table prior to the point at which impasse was declared. For all three "Small Talk" negotiators that failed to reach agreement, the last offer on the table had a value below the reservation price of one of the parties. In other words, none (0%) of the "Small Talk" pairs walked away from an offer that was more profitable than their outside option. For all three pairs, given the value of the last offer, it is understandable that one of the parties would refuse to agree to it. But the story for the "No Small Talk" pairs was quite different: the value of the last offer on the table exceeded both parties' reservation price for nine out of the fourteen pairs (64%). Thus, these eighteen negotiators (none of whom engaged in small talk) failed to reach agreement despite the fact that the last available offer would have made all of them better off than impasse. . . .

2. Social Outcomes

What accounts for the huge differences between the "Small Talk" and "No Small Talk" negotiators in their propensity to reach a mutually beneficial agreement? Prior to negotiating (but after the phone call, if there was one) negotiators indicated on a scale from one to seven (1 Not at all; 7 Quite a bit) how "competitive" they were feeling toward their counterpart as they entered into the negotiation. They also indicated how "cooperative" they were feeling toward their counterpart. Negotiators who did not engage in small talk with their counterpart prior to negotiating reported feeling more competitive and less cooperative toward their counterpart than negotiators who did engage in small talk.

3. Negotiation Processes

Why would negotiators who adopt more cooperative, less competitive attitudes toward the negotiation achieve greater success economically than negotiators who adopt the opposite attitudes? After all, one might expect a negotiator who is too nice and unwilling to be tough to do poorly in a negotiation. By contrast, in this simulation, the cooperative attitude adopted by negotiators who engaged in small talk led them to come away from the negotiation in a position that was substantially more favorable economically than those who did not engage in small talk.

a) Small Talk Negotiators Shared More Information

. . . Consistent with their cooperative mental model of the negotiation process, negotiators who engaged in telephone small talk prior to negotiating exchanged significantly more information relating to their relative priorities on multiple issues compared to negotiators who did not engage in small talk. Thus, negotiators who established initial rapport with a brief telephone chat felt more cooperative in the negotiation and trusted the other negotiator enough to share the kind of information necessary to reach an efficient solution.

b) Small Talk Negotiators Engaged in More Reciprocity

In addition to offering more freely their own information about relative priorities, information sharing was reciprocated more often for negotiators in the "Small Talk" condition than for negotiators in the "No Small Talk" condition. That is, compared to negotiators who did not engage in small talk, negotiators who chatted with their counterpart prior to negotiating were more likely to receive multiple issue priority information from their counterpart immediately following their own provision of such information. Negotiators who engaged in small talk expected more strongly to cooperate, did cooperate by sharing more relevant multiple-issue information, and received more cooperation in return from their counterpart. This pattern of multiple-issue information sharing is necessary for negotiators to avoid impasse by recognizing numerous, mutually beneficial solutions in the negotiation. In this mixed motive negotiation, failing to exchange information resulted in negotiators failing to integrate their interests, leaving little or no joint surplus to share.

c) Small Talk Negotiators Made Fewer Threats

The negotiation transcripts were also analyzed to examine whether negotiators provided information that related to one's own alternative, because such a reference can be akin to a threat to walk away from the table (e.g., "I can buy a similarly equipped car much more cheaply at another dealership"). Compared to negotiators whose initial contact was strictly business-like, negotiators who engaged in small talk before negotiating were less likely to reference their own alternative. Thus, in the absence of an initial getting-to-know-you telephone conversation, negotiators assumed a competitive mental model and behaved competitively during the negotiation by making subtle (or not so subtle) threats to walk away from the table. . . .

d) Small Talk Negotiators Developed More Respect and Trust

Negotiators who did not chat beforehand ended the negotiation with a substantially different attitude toward both the process and their counterpart than the negotiators who did chat initially. . . . Negotiators who did not chat found the process of e-mail communication more difficult. They ended up feeling significantly more angry, annoyed, and cold toward their opponent, as well as less friendly and pleasant, compared to negotiators who had the opportunity to chat with their opponent. These feelings are consistent with the competitive mindset and inferior economic outcomes of negotiators in the "No Small Talk" condition. The increased cooperation and trust that the telephone chat engendered led to smoother interactions and a friendlier attitude toward the opponent after the negotiation concluded. This attitude was also associated with respect—negotiators who engaged in small talk formed an impression of their counterpart as significantly more accomplished, skilled, effective, and perceptive than the impression formed by negotiators who did not engage in small talk. . . . Finally, this experiment also measured the extent to which negotiators came away trusting their counterparts. One of the many ways to define trust is the expectation that the other person will cooperate with you when you are in a vulnerable position. In legal communities, lawyers who face each other in one negotiation often can expect to cross paths again in the future. If trust is eroded during negotiation in one matter, this is likely to affect the way the lawyers approach the negotiation in the next matter when they meet again. To explore the question of whether engaging in small talk prior to negotiating would increase trust, negotiators in this experiment answered two questions relating to trust. First, they were asked to suppose that they and their counterparts were in the position of working together on a future project and to rate how smoothly such a project would go. . . . Second, negotiators were asked to imagine that sometime in the future, they were in a vulnerable position in a dispute with their counterpart's firm. Would they prefer to negotiate with the same counterpart, or some other unknown attorney. . . . Negotiators who had an initial chat with their opponents left the negotiation with significantly more trust in their counterparts than did negotiators who did not chat initially.

C. Discussion

In the negotiation simulation involved in this experiment, a seemingly trivial intervention—a preliminary, brief, and informal chat on the telephone—increased the likelihood that the e-mail negotiations that followed would be characterized by cooperation, information exchange, reciprocity, liking, trust, and ultimately, agreement. These negotiators had the opportunity to establish common ground with the other negotiator through small talk, even if the basis for common ground was exceedingly trivial (e.g., "The weather is nice here in Chicago." "Yes, it is nice here, too."). Engaging in small talk enabled negotiators who were strangers to get to know one another and to connect in a fashion that did not spontaneously occur during the process of e-mail exchange. The seemingly inert act of small talk encouraged negotiators to adopt a cooperative mental model in the negotiation, leading to the sharing of crucial information with the other party. Negotiators who engaged in small talk were more willing to take the chance that the other negotiator would reciprocate and share their own private information, which is precisely what happened. This resulted in favorable impressions of the counterpart after the negotiation. Negotiators who engaged in small talk placed their trust in the ability of their counterpart to recognize the mutual benefit of information exchange. When the counterpart successfully recognized these benefits and shared crucial information, their abilities and skills were respected, and they were generally held in high regard.

By contrast, negotiators who did not have an opportunity to chat with their counterpart prior to e-mail negotiation approached the negotiation with a competitive mental model, and either failed to exchange the kind of information that would lead to identification of mutually beneficial solutions, or failed to recognize as beneficial the solutions which arose, leading to greater likelihood of impasse. In the absence of the phone call, the two negotiation counterparts were complete strangers, never having seen one another or heard one another's voice. Because the other person was, in this sense, an unknown quantity, negotiators could not be sure of the other person's motives. These circumstances were associated with negative impressions of the other person, as evidenced by negotiators' ratings of their opponents as less accomplished, skilled, effective, and perceptive than negotiators who engaged in small talk. In short, negotiators in the "No Small Talk" condition were less likely to reach agreement, which made them angry and annoyed and for which they blamed the other negotiator. . . . The failure to reach an economically advantageous outcome is even more remarkable when one considers the circumstances under which this occurred—a substantial portion of the "No Small Talk" negotiators who reached an impasse did so despite an offer on the table that would have made both negotiators better off than impasse.

One reason that a cooperative mental model served negotiators well in this simulation (while an overly competitive mental model served negotiators poorly) is that cooperation helped participants solve the "negotiator's dilemma." This getting-to-know-you telephone call made e-mail interaction proceed more smoothly by creating rapport before the negotiation began. This rapport helped negotiators approach the negotiation with a more cooperative mental model, thereby trusting in each others' good intentions. This mental model, in turn, led to a successful negotiation that concluded with a contract and engendered positive feelings about one another. The negotiators who engaged in small talk solved the "negotiator's dilemma" by agreeing (albeit tacitly) to share enough information to determine what kind of agreement would satisfy their needs simultaneously.

Sharing information was crucial in the negotiation simulation used in this experiment because of the mixed motive nature of the exercise. While some issues were purely distributive, others could be profitably logrolled in a manner that inured to the benefit of both parties simultaneously. To successfully expand the pie of available resources (as opposed to simply compromising and "splitting the difference"), it was crucial for negotiators in this experiment to exchange enough information to allow them to determine, for example, that both parties preferred all airbags and yellow color, that financing was an especially important issue for the seller, but warranty was especially important for the buyer, etc. Without communicating this information in some form, negotiators were unable to maximize the joint value of the agreement. Adopting an attitude that was more cooperative than competitive allowed negotiators to trust the other party enough to share with them relevant private information, and to expect the other party to reciprocate by sharing their own relevant private information, which in turn resulted in identification of and agreement to efficient solutions. Because lawyers are repeat players within a legal community, and often expect to interact with each other again in the future, it is important to observe here that one deal that sours because of misunderstandings in the course of e-mail negotiations can affect the tenor of future negotiations—whether conducted via e-mail or more traditional means. . . .

This study documents the importance for lawyers of establishing rapport when negotiating with another lawyer who is an "unknown quantity." When face-to-face contact between negotiators is not possible, it is important to find an alternative method of building rapport. This study demonstrates that a social, personalizing communication via telephone is one way to restore some rapport that may be missing from electronically mediated negotiations. . . .

Questions

6. Nadler's study appears to confirm the often repeated traveler's story of being invited to sit down for a cup of tea by a Turkish rug dealer before talking business or being asked by a Balinese beach peddler, how do you like Bali, and where are you from? What is the purpose of these benign gestures, and how do they relate to the previously described experiment?

7. If "schmoozing" is the social grease that makes deals happen, are there ways other than a preliminary telephone conversation to schmooze or create rapport and promote cooperation before engaging in e-mail negotiations? In her article, Professor Nadler suggests the following:

> [A]n initial, non-business, getting-to-know-you chat over e-mail prior to beginning e-mail negotiations has been shown to increase the likelihood of reaching a mutually beneficial agreement. Moreover, outside of the negotiation context, social psychologists have shown that using flattery (even when

> people suspect the flatterer has ulterior motives) and humor, and mention-
> ing points of similarity, can facilitate good feelings and relationship building,
> thereby engendering the kind of cooperation and trust that leads to discov-
> ery of mutually profitable negotiated solutions. (Nadler 2004, 11 n.250.)

8. How might the increasing affordability and use of digital video cameras
   and voice technology change the way we negotiate? Will the use of these
   technologies equate digital means of negotiation with in-person negotiation, or will differences remain? What might such differences be?

2. Avoiding Costly E-Mail Mistakes

No doubt you have either experienced or heard e-mail horror stories. Knee-jerk
reactions or damaging, unfiltered thoughts hastily entered via the computer
keyboard and sent instantly through cyberspace without the benefit of delay or
having to write them down longhand can cause long-lasting mischief. Hitting
the "reply to all" button when sensitive information was intended only for the
original sender can cause embarrassment and resentment. Misaddressing an
e-mail that contains confidential or revealing information creates breaches
of confidentiality, and the leaked information cannot be erased. Having an
important message go unread because the subject line did not accurately indicate the content may result in a missed deal, or at least misunderstanding. The
recipient taking offense because an abbreviated term was misinterpreted or an
attempt at humor was misunderstood or coolly read out of context may be hard
to turn around. These mistakes can be costly if committed in the course of
e-mail negotiations. Why do people communicate differently in digital mode,
and how can mistakes be avoided?

First, be aware of the false anonymity shield, or what has been referred to as
"online disinhibition effect." We tend to believe that we are more anonymous
in cyberspace and that we will not be held accountable in the same way as in
face-to-face exchanges. Many people state in e-mails what they would not say
face-to-face. When you are stuck in a room with a negotiation opponent, you
see her reactions and the consequences of your comments. With e-mail, you
can, in effect, hit and run without staying around to see emotional reactions.
Responses can only come later in digital form, so we tend to be bolder and less
inhibited. However, if your name or e-mail address is on the message, you are
not anonymous; you are accountable and can be held legally liable for what you
send. E-mails also satisfy the writing requirement for a binding contract under
the Statute of Frauds, because the Uniform Electronic Transactions Act provides that a "record or signature may not be denied legal effect or enforceability
solely because it is in electronic form." See, e.g., International Casings Group,
Inc. v. Premium Standard Farms, Inc., 358 F. Supp. 2d 863 (W.D. Mo. 2005).

Second, e-mail communication can be highly "flammable." That is, without the schmoozing and face-to-face social lubrication that can soften spoken
words, e-mail messages can be read with the most harsh and inflammatory interpretation. Devoid of eye contact, facial expressions, voice inflection, and body
language, e-mail offers a "narrow bandwidth" or undressed mode to convey

meaning. The flammable potential of naked e-mail, combined with the "hit-and-run" factor, is reason for caution and restraint in negotiating by e-mail.

Third, when representing clients, lawyers tend to write more formally and precisely because we understand the legal consequences of words and the downside of ambiguity. As agents of clients, we have a responsibility when negotiating not to be careless or sloppy in the words and phrases we use. If the medium is the message, as Marshall McLuhan said, then e-mails may not be an easy medium for lawyers to use in negotiating. The common style and "netiquette" of e-mail is informal and highly abbreviated. Although conventions of abbreviation and new definitions may be emerging, e-mail syntax remains idiosyncratic and rapidly evolving, particularly with the advent of handheld digital devices. Lawyers can use the speed and economy of the digital world to negotiate with composed and clear messages and more formally drafted attachments. Combining e-mail with other forms of communication, as we saw in the pre-negotiation telephone schmoozing experiment described above, allows for the best use of different media. The use of e-mail to negotiate need not be all or nothing.

The following checklist will help you avoid common e-mail and texting traps when negotiating, as well as when using digital communication generally. (See Jay Sullivan, "Lawyers and Technology: A Crash course in Writing Effective E-Mails," 229 N.Y. L.J. 5, Feb. 2003.)

✓ **Use proper grammar, spelling, and punctuation.** Never send a message with an incomplete sentence, a misspelled word, or referring to yourself as "i" because besides deleting them, people often forward or print e-mails.

✓ **Never send negative feedback or criticism through e-mail.** Criticism sent through an e-mail can come across like a slap in the face. It is always received more harshly than intended. At the very least, the recipient will feel as if you should have picked up the phone to deliver your message, and you will appear to be "hiding behind your e-mail."

✓ **Refrain from humor and sarcasm.** The nuances of face-to-face or spoken communication are lost with the written word. It is very hard to be funny in an e-mail. People who are humorous in person cannot necessarily write humor well. It requires a different discipline. Sarcasm, in particular, does not translate well through e-mail, and it is often taken literally, with potentially disastrous consequences.

✓ **Think before sending an e-mail.** This requires more than proofreading: It requires giving your brain a break between drafting and sending. Very few e-mails require an immediate response, so you can build in a delay to improve the quality of your communication.

✓ **Put substance in the "subject" line.** It is always easier to hit "reply" than to start a new message, but consider changing the subject to better reflect your reply. Also, do not start your message in the subject line and continue it within the body. It is disconcerting to the reader and almost always requires that the recipient read the sentence twice.

✓ **Use a salutation.** E-mail is generally an abrupt way of communicating, but by starting a message with the recipient's name, the tone is softened. It is especially important to use a salutation when copying someone on a message.

✓ **Get to the verb.** Use short sentences and direct language in the body of the message. Avoid the passive voice. Do not begin a professional e-mail with "How was your weekend?" or the recipient may think the message is more personal and never get to the meat of the message. This does not mean you should eliminate all niceties. Just keep them short.

✓ **Make it clear how you want the recipient to respond.** People tend to respond to a particular communication in the same form they receive it. If we get a voicemail, we tend to reply by phone. When someone gets your e-mail, the instinct is to hit the "reply" button. However, if you are inaccessible for the next few hours or days, make that known and indicate the best way for the reply to be delivered. For example, "Please respond by phone. I will not be able to check my e-mail for a few hours."

✓ **Review your "cc:" list.** Who is on it and why? Is there a legitimate reason for including each individual? Do not include someone just to keep him or her "in the loop" unless it is appropriate and you have first asked that person if they want to be included. The courtesy will be appreciated.

✓ **Be careful.** Do not gossip, make off-color jokes or comments — they will come back to haunt you.

✓ **Remember, e-mail does not get deleted, only subpoenaed.** Deleting it from the hard drive does not "destroy" it. The message is still floating around somewhere in your devise or in cyberspace.

✓ **Apply the Golden Rule.** Only send e-mails you would like to receive.

Questions

9. Can you add any cautionary or advisory items to this checklist?

10. Are the potential mistakes noted previously and those in the checklist equally applicable to all forms of negotiation communications? What is truly unique about e-mail communications?

11. Have you negotiated electronically? Looking back on that experience, would you have done anything differently?

12. Given the "lean" nature of e-mail communication and that the digitally transmitted word need not reveal the sender's gender, race, or ethnicity, does negotiation only via e-mail eliminate any influence of these factors? Why or why not?

13. Can you think of ways in which e-mail communication might exacerbate cultural differences and create obstacles to successful negotiation?

14. Can you think of any worse e-mail blunder than the one below, attributed to a Harvard summer associate at Skadden Arps by the *New Yorker* on June 30, 2003? First, he made the mistake of sending the message to everyone in the law firm rather than just to the friend he intended as the sole recipient, and then it was posted worldwide:

> "I'm busy doing jack shit. Went to a nice 2hr sushi lunch today at Sushi Zen. Nice place. Spent the rest of the day typing e-mails and bullshitting with people." He signed off, "So yeah, Corporate Love hasn't worn off yet. . . . But just give me time."

A helpful guide to business and legal use of e-mail is David Shipley and Will Schwalbe, *Send: The Essential Guide to Email for Office and Home* (2007).

C. Computer-Based Negotiation Help and Online Dispute Resolution

Today's negotiation software programs are not your parents' calculator, spreadsheets, and word processors. The power of the computer to process information is now combined with the Web-based power of the Internet and computer networks to transmit information. The ever-improving resources of cyberspace, initially used to assist traditional, face-to-face negotiation processes, have evolved to offer alternative ways of negotiating to reach a settlement online. So now an attorney can tap into the Internet to take advantage of sophisticated, programs and databanks to prepare, strategize, and improve their negotiation effectiveness, or use online dispute resolution platforms (ODR) to resolve money claims, as well as more complex issues in cases involving multiple parties.

Two of the software programs to aid in planning and preparing for negotiations were described in Chapter 5 (*ExpertNegotiator.com* and *NegotiatorPro.com/negpro50coms.html*). There is also a smartphone app to help you assess your negotiation style and determine after a negotiation how you can improve from the experience and what you can do better next time. (See *Negotiation 360.*) Another intriguing program available as software or as a tablet app is designed to help lawyers plan a specific negotiation strategy, including how much to demand or offer at the beginning of a negotiation and at each successive round to reach a target amount. *PictureItSettled.com* uses predictive analytics based on statistical studies of thousands of negotiated settlement histories by case categories and other distinguishing inputs to predict the behavior of opposing negotiators. This information is analyzed to graph the probable monetary moves necessary to reach an optimum settlement. It was initially designed to help in-house lawyers plan a negotiation strategy calculated to induce cooperative behavior and to reach settlements at favorable numbers.

The above programs are designed to help negotiators on one side optimize their outcomes. Another category of Web-based computer programs exists to provide all sides with an alternate way to reach a mutually satisfactory outcome online. There are cybernegotiation sites that conduct monetary negotiations using sophisticated algorithms to match demands and offers in a double-blind bidding process. (See *Cybersettle.com* and *Fairoutcomes.com.*) Although initially created to be used to settle insurance claims, these blind bidding platforms can be used in any negotiation involving a single variable, like the amount to be paid in settlement of a contested medical bill, which now appears to be the primary use of Cybersettle.

Lawyer Negotiation Meets High Tech

The story of how *Cybersettle.com* was created to resolve insurance claims by computer blind bidding is an interesting tale combining lawyer negotiation, tech start-up, and maybe a little urban legend. In 1995 two seasoned New York City trial attorneys, Charles Brofman and James Burchetta, were representing opposing sides in an insurance claim and met in the courthouse in an attempt to settle their case. They were tens of thousands of dollars apart, but they each felt they knew roughly the amount for which the case would eventually settle; they just didn't want to show their hand to the other side and risk paying more than necessary or leaving money on the table.

The lawyers agreed to write down their bottom-line numbers on a piece of paper and hand them to a clerk, who was instructed to indicate if the numbers were within $1,000. If they weren't, the clerk would destroy the papers and neither side would know what had been written. If they were within the range, they would split the difference. The numbers were in range and the case settled in minutes. The paper process used by those New York attorneys is now automated through a double-blind computer bidding program, which preserves the secrecy of the demands and offers. Brofman and Burchetta obtained a patent for the process, created Cybersettle and later sold the company for millions of dollars, before engaging in litigation with the off-shore purchaser.

Cybersettle became a go-to resource for the Association of Trial lawyers of America, the New York State Trial Lawyers Association, and the American Arbitration Association. It has counted among its clients Wal-Mart, General Electric, and Zürich Insurance, along with the city of New York's Office of the Comptroller. When a claim is filed against a Cybersettle client, the client receives an electronic request to settle the matter online. Both parties log in to the system and submit three different amounts of money for their demands or offers. Neither side knows what dollar amounts were submitted during the online process. Whenever the competing numbers come within a certain range, as determined by the Cybersettle program, both sides are alerted and a live person steps in to finalize the amount to be paid. That payment is made online through the Cybersettle site. Although mostly used for smaller cases, the company has reported online settlements as high as $12.5 million. (See Douglas S. Malan, "A Numbers Game," 36 Conn. L. Trib. No. 4 (2010).)

There are secure, Web-based platforms to facilitate communication between negotiators that go beyond quantitative monetary claims to resolve qualitative issues based on prioritizing interests (see *Smartsettle.com*). Smartsettle offers an unattended, automated process for simple cases, and a facilitated process for more complex ones, including multi-party matters. The platform moves disputants through several stages that clarify the issues in dispute, guage how strongly the parties feel about these issues, and prioritize acceptable outcomes. Parties are asked to place values on their different interests and demands. In this process, Smartsettle provides a structure to clarify and assess issues that, by itself, can help parties reach consensus. Smartsettle works to combine interests and issues into packages so that the parties can see the impact of various decisions, enabling them to reach an agreement that meets their needs. A successful end result will involve trade-offs by each party. A novel feature offered by Smartsettle, is that it can take a tentative agreement and, based on information obtained, suggest other possibilities that may give each party a more favorable, or optimal, outcome.

ODR has had its greatest success in resolving disputes arising from e-commerce and online marketplaces, which generate a tremendous number of long-distance conflicts that can best be settled online using cloud-based programs to automate the dispute resolution process between sellers and buyers. In 1999, eBay decided that having a dispute resolution process might strengthen trust between buyers and sellers. eBay selected an Internet startup, SquareTrade, to be its dispute resolution provider. Before providing a human mediator, SquareTrade used the Web, rather than e-mail, as the means for communicating and working with disputants. SquareTrade recognized that almost all eBay disputes fell into eight to ten categories, allowing it to create forms that clarify and highlight both the parties' disagreements and a choice of solutions. If Web-based negotiation failed, SquareTrade provided a human mediator for a modest fee. The negotiation was then individually facilitated by the mediator using the Web interface so they did not all need to participate at the same time. SquareTrade resolved millions of eBay disputes and put ODR on the global map. More advanced electronic platforms now offer automated cyberresolution of all types of claims that arise from e-commerce. (See *Modria.com.*) These computerized settlement functions for consumer online disputes reduce the need for customer care personnel or call center involvement, as well as the assistance of lawyers.

Professor Ethan Katsh, a leading authority on ODR has stated, "ODR will grow in importance as offline activities migrate to the Web. The growth of ODR is partly a recognition that disputing is a kind of growth industry on the Internet. ODR is also, however, a sign or indicator that cyberspace is maturing. Many of the same tools that built such online venues as auctions, stores, and casinos can contribute to building online civic institutions such as courts and dispute resolution systems." (Katsh, Online Dispute Resolution, in *The Handbook of Dispute Resolution* 425 (Moffitt and Bordone eds., 2005).)

Problem

Assume you are consulted by a business client who purchased a computer server system from an out-of-state supplier in a private transaction for $80,000. The system is dysfunctional, and the client believes that the seller defrauded him by not revealing that the system would function only with customized software, which would require an additional $17,000 to create. Even with this software, the client says, the system probably will not handle the volume of data that he has to process, contrary to assurances given during the sales process. He wishes to revoke the transaction. He has heard about the Cybersettle system and wonders if it would make sense to use it. What would you advise your client and why?

CHAPTER
9

Gender, Culture, and Race

Most of us find it easiest to negotiate with those we perceive as similar to us and with whom we can identify. Gender, culture, and race are only a few of the distinguishing characteristics with which you and your negotiation counterpart may identify. Where you were born, the schools you attended, your political affiliations, religion, sexual orientation, age, hobbies, and attire may also distinguish you and create a positive connection or noted difference between you and others. However, gender, race, and cultural backgrounds are core elements associated with identity and are frequent subjects of analysis. These are the three distinctions on which we focus in this chapter, but only as a starting point for understanding the influence of commonalities and differences as a factor in negotiation. It all comes back to perceptions and mental shortcuts, like stereotyping. Self-fulfilling prophesies can turn stereotypes into our reality during negotiations and create obstacles to assessing individual interests and reaching optimum settlements.

A. Moving Beyond Gender Stereotypes

A generation or two ago, the issue of gender in negotiation was addressed as a question of how women should approach bargaining in a male-dominated profession. Although this issue has not totally disappeared, it is no longer the central question. More than half of law students are women, and quantitative gender balance among attorneys is approaching parity. If there is a "male" model of practice, it is no longer necessary that women conform to it. Nor is it any longer necessary to ask whether women can succeed as negotiators. Experience and research have clearly shown that women can excel in all lawyering roles, including negotiation. We have seen that effective negotiation draws on an expanded set of qualities and skills—including listening, trust building and problem solving—than just those associated with stereotypical "male competitiveness." The game, as well as the players, has changed.

The fact that women have taken their place at the negotiation table does not necessarily mean that gender is irrelevant in negotiation. Questions remain about whether men tend to negotiate differently than women, whether negotiating with someone of the other gender is different than negotiating with someone of the same gender, and whether any differences can be used to advantage or disadvantage. There is also a question of whether men and women tend to communicate differently—whether we speak the same language.

In considering matters of gender, as well as culture and race, it is important to note that there are no generic beings—no common man or woman. Every individual is unique, defined by genetic makeup, environment, and personal experience. Emphasizing gender differences detracts from considering women and men across culture, class, race, ethnicity, age, and gender orientation. However, culture and perhaps chromosomes foster some associated behaviors that identify us with our gender and set us apart. The phenomenon of selective perceptions, and its children, stereotyping and self-fulfilling prophecies, along with attribution errors, magnify these differences and create cognitive traps that may shape and limit how we interact with those of the other gender when negotiating. The way to avoid these traps is to understand our individual uniqueness, as well as our gender differences, and work with them. Even if there are no actual differences, the belief by some that differences exist between male and female approaches to bargaining can be as important as reality in driving behavior. Gender stereotyping may not influence a new generation of enlightened lawyers who experience and assume more equality than previous generations, but implicit gender bias may be more ingrained in older lawyers and clients.

Carol Gilligan has written about a theory of moral development, which has been much cited and discussed in negotiation literature. Her theme is that men and women think and speak differently when confronted with ethical dilemmas. Gilligan distinguishes a feminine "ethic of care" with a masculine "ethic of justice" and believes that these gender differences in moral perspective are due to contrasting images of self:

> My research suggests that men and women may speak different languages that they assume are the same, using similar words to encode disparate experiences of self and social relationships. Because these languages share an overlapping moral vocabulary, they contain a propensity for systematic mistranslation, creating misunderstandings which impede communication and limit the potential for cooperation and care in relationships. (Gilligan 1982, 173)

Several more recent books provide guides for women on how to succeed at negotiating in what is assumed to be a male-dominated environment. Deborah Kolb and Judith Williams describe the "shadow negotiation"—the often determinative negotiation within a negotiation. In their book, *The Shadow Negotiation: How Women Can Master the Hidden Agendas That Determine Bargaining Success* (2000), they advise:

> This shadow negotiation takes place below the surface of any debate over problems. As bargainers try to turn the discussion of the problem to their advantage or persuade the other side to cooperate in resolving it, they make assumptions about each other, what the other person wants, his or her weaknesses, how he or she is likely to behave. They size each other up, poking here and there to find out where the give is. They test for flexibility, trying to gauge how strongly an individual feels about a certain point. . . . How you resolve the issues hinges on the actions you take in the shadow negotiation. If you don't move to direct the shadow negotiation, you can find the agreement tipping against you. The shadow

negotiation is no place to be a passive observer. You can maneuver to put yourself in a good position or let others create a position for you. Your action—or
inaction—here determines what takes place in the negotiation. . . . Active positioning is critical to how you negotiate the issues. The impressions you create in
the shadow negotiation determine how much give and take there will be over the
issues. If you are unsure of yourself or doubt whether your demands are justified
or legitimate, you will have a tough time convincing others to give them much
weight. Bargainers are quick to ferret out points of weaknesses, where you are
tentative or vulnerable. You must be ready to move in the shadow negotiation not
just to promote your interests but to block any attempt to undermine your credibility. . . . Almost without exception, the women we interviewed could analyze a
problem or a situation with great skill. Yet they stumbled in the shadow negotiation. (Kolb and Williams 2000, 21-23.)

Some critics have questioned categorizing negotiators by gender and juxta-
posing behaviors of men and women on a binary scale of male-female distinctions. The following reading raises some of these issues.

❖ **Amy Cohen,** *GENDER: AN (UN) USEFUL CATEGORY OF*
PRESCRIPTIVE NEGOTIATION ANALYSIS

13 Tex. J. Women & L. 169 (2003)

. . . [R]epresentations of gender as either male-female difference or male-
female similarity, as the basis for describing interpersonal skills and theoretical analysis, draw artificial parameters around the range of behavioral and
communicative capabilities available to us each to imagine and perform.
Naming negotiating skills and analysis as "masculine" versus "feminine" in
the first instance is of little, if any, pedagogical advantage and potentially
considerable pedagogical harm insofar as such binary coding works to narrow and normalize the emancipatory possibilities inherent in the process of
learning and achieving. In arguing for a pedagogy of negotiation that decodes
behaviors and skills as masculine and feminine, I begin with a detailed look
at Deborah Kolb and Judith Williams' construction of gender and women bargainers in *The Shadow Negotiation: How Women Can Master the Hidden Agendas
that Determine Bargaining Success.* I focus on *The Shadow Negotiation* because it
presents a recent, widely acclaimed, and perhaps the most extensive attempt
to link feminist theory and empirical research with prescriptive negotiation
advice. . . . Much of their advice is written in second person—the "you" is
presumably female throughout. Kolb and Williams begin by critiquing conventional "rational" (read: masculine) negotiation advice to "take the people
out of the problem" and suggest that as individuals bargain over issues, they
are simultaneously negotiating the terms of their relationships, albeit in the
"shadow." Thus, Kolb and Williams propose we learn to focus on active interpersonal positioning—both assertive and collaborative—within the "shadow
negotiation" in order to best resolve the issues that form the substance of the
"real" negotiation.
Unsurprisingly, if not ironically, the "shadow" is also the location of gendered expectations and frustrations. In aiming to allow women a nonessential-
ized space to overcome stereotypical gender barriers, Kolb and Williams reject

paradigmatic, if purposefully oversimplified, liberal feminist . . . and cultural feminist . . . attempts to resolve the tension they assume exists between women and negotiation. Namely, they discount conventional wisdom suggesting that with equal access to personal and institutional resources, individual women will negotiate just like individual men. Instead, they remind us "she will always play the game as a woman." Alternatively, they admit there is a risk of unqualified praise of women as empathic and relational that may cloud differences among women. Nonetheless, they conclude that even though "many" women do have "these special qualities," such feminine skills become structural liabilities in real world negotiations where yardsticks of success are typically correlated with "masculine" experience and standards.

Ultimately, "the effective negotiator," they tell us, "turns out to look remarkably like a man": independent, self-confident, active, objective, and unruffled by pressure. Kolb and Williams are correct in their observation that this reified model hurts men and women alike—men when they show their "feminine" side and women when they fall short of the "masculine" ideal, for "no woman, however competent, can pull off what is essentially a male performance." Thus, their prescription is not a matter of choosing between masculine and feminine styles, but rather encouraging women to draw on "all our skills" as we learn to recognize and manage gendered behavioral patterns and expectations in the shadow negotiation.

However, in maintaining a binary distinction between what is feminine and what is masculine as the basis for prescriptive negotiating advice, as well as in creating a "shadow" as the locus of the interpersonal that can be analyzed separately from the substance of the problem, Kolb and Williams solidify the categories of analysis they in fact attempt to discredit. Perhaps even more importantly, by encouraging women to place "ourselves" in negotiations based on descriptive assumptions about the way we as women are, they draw unnecessary parameters around their own useful and seasoned interpersonal negotiating advice that limit our range of imagining the ways in which individuals and groups might communicate with each other. . . .

The challenge for women, then, is to "learn how to use their strengths and manage the dual impressions of femininity and strategic resolve." Thus, for women learning the art and science of negotiation, gender is the point of entry; it is the preexisting condition we bring to the table and then use to position ourselves as we interact with other parties. However, the conclusion that women do not fare as well as men, Kolb argues, follows not from our skills or abilities, but rather from the technical and rational prescriptions underlying conventional negotiation advice that excludes a "subjective and embedded feminine approach." . . .

Thus, "as women," Kolb and Williams tell us in *The Shadow Negotiation*, "we take our differences and our competence into every negotiation. These can be turned to our advantage, but they have to be recognized as valuable. . . . We need, in effect, to revise the standard." Using gender both as a descriptive indicator of women bargainers and as a method of feminist critique, Kolb, together with Williams, provides a series of behavioral and analytical skills to help women negotiate effectively in a feminine voice. . . .

Questions

1. Is the legal negotiation table still slanted against women? Are there situations in which it might be slanted against men? Can you give examples?
2. Are female law students a self-selected group that does not reflect the characteristics described by Kolb and Williams? (See note below.) For a general report on gender differences in negotiation, see Babcock and Laschever, *Women Don't Ask: Negotiation and the Gender Divide* (2003). See also Korobkin and Doherty, *Who Wins in Settlement Negotiations?* (2009)
3. If relationships matter and effective negotiation results from making connections and problem-solving skills, could men benefit by signing up for seminars on how to negotiate like a woman?
4. The above selection and the literature on gender and negotiation focuses on male perceptions of females and, to a lesser extent, on female perceptions of males. Isn't the perception that women have of women, and that men have of men, just as important in explaining our negotiation approaches and behaviors? Do you believe from what you have read and experienced that patterns between women negotiating with one another would be significantly different than negotiations between men? If so, how?
5. Do you agree with the statement by Kolb and Williams that "a woman quite simply has to work harder than a man to get what she wants at a negotiation"?

Note: Good News

This book has emphasized that lawyers negotiate as agents for others. Our role and style as agents may be different than how we approach negotiations on our own behalf. Research has confirmed that women perform significantly better in competitive negotiations when they are negotiating on behalf of another person rather than for themselves. In these studies, men did not differ much in their negotiating performance when they were negotiating for themselves or for someone else. When acting as agents, general negotiation outcomes were similar for men and women. (See Amanatullah and Morris 2010; Bowles et al. 2005.) A newer study found that if a female negotiator prepared for a negotiation on her own behalf by *imagining* that it was actually a negotiation for someone else, but then proceeded to negotiate for herself, her negotiated results were improved relative to the results for male negotiators. (See L. Babcock and J. Bear, "Gender Relevant Primes and Negotiation," unpublished paper, Aug. 2015.) Pretending can become reality! This intra-psychic method to improve results is recommended both by negotiation researchers and in the popular book by Babcock and Laschever, *Ask for It: How Women Can Use the Power of Negotiation to Get What They Really Want* (2009). *Ask for It* provides compelling evidence that women do not ask for what they want with the same frequency as men and offers practical advice on how women can get what they want and deserve by knowing how to ask for it.

Most of the studies comparing the negotiation outcomes and differences in style between men and women do not involve law students or lawyers. Female law students and lawyers may be a self-selected group that does not reflect the general population characteristics described by Kolb and Williams and by Babcock and Laschever. This distinction is supported by an article that examines a dilemma often faced by women in the professional world: a double bind between being perceived as competent or as likeable, but not both.

> "Both qualities are imperative for success but professional women generally are either seen as likeable, but incompetent, or as competent, but unlikeable. Interestingly, lawyers do not seem plagued by this same double bind. . . . In a study of lawyers rating other lawyers in their most recent negotiation, female lawyers were described in terms that were similar to their male colleagues (ethical, confident, and personable) and both were equally likely to be judged as effective in general. In fact, women lawyers were rated more highly in assertiveness than their male counterparts, and yet did not seem to suffer negative consequences for violating feminine proscriptions. . . . Female lawyers are effective negotiators, perceived as both assertive and empathetic. This result is because of at least three factors: the high status of lawyers, their role expectations, and the fact that these negotiations are on behalf of others. Women lawyers and other professionals can use this information to continue their success on behalf of clients and themselves in a variety of ways. Lawyers need to make the most of their lawyer status and their training in advocacy. They can remind themselves that they are fighting for their clients, as well as for their gender, when they negotiate. They should maintain their femininity while cuing themselves to fight the stereotypes and negotiate hard. (Schneider, Tinsley, Cheldelin, and Amanatullah, "Likability v. Competence: The Impossible Choice Faced By Female Politicians, Attenuated by Lawyers," 17 Duke J. of Gender L. & Policy 363 (2010).)

The effectiveness of female law students as negotiators has been a topic of discussion at conferences of law professors. Our teaching experience does not support gender-specific negotiation outcomes. Charles Craver, one of our most experienced negotiation teachers and trainers, has studied the results from his decades of using scoreable negotiation exercises. His conclusions confirm that although there may be stylistic differences between men and women, the negotiated outcomes when clients are represented by female law students do not differ statistically from outcomes obtained by male law students.

❖ **Charles B. Craver, *The Impact of Gender on Negotiation Performance***

14 Cardozo J. of Conflict Resolution 339 (2013)

For the past thirty-five years I have taught Legal Negotiation courses to several thousand second and third-year law students. I have also taught Effective Legal Negotiation skills to 90,000 practicing attorneys in Continuing Legal Education courses and in-house programs in over forty states and in countries around the world. While in these sessions . . . I conducted several studies comparing the male and female stylistic differences, and the results achieved by students in my Legal Negotiation class exercises.

My previous studies found no statistically significant differences with respect to the average results achieved by male and female students, or with respect to the standard deviations involved. . . . I thought it would be beneficial to explore the results achieved by my students in negotiation exercises, since my last study was published in 1999. . . .

[T]here were no differences in the negotiation exercise results based upon gender. There is not a single year for which any male or female mean score difference was statistically significant at even the 0.10 level, let alone at the preferred 0.05 level. The only two years for which t-probability values approached the 0.10 level were 2008, when the male mean was higher, and 2009, when the female mean was higher. When the data for all sixteen years is considered, male and female means are almost identical, with a t-probability of 0.9731. . . .

Many people continue to believe that men are more proficient negotiators than women. They may consciously — or even subconsciously — think that males are more assertive and more competitive than females. . . . The data from my Legal Negotiation class over the past sixteen years clearly contradicts the validity of such stereotypical beliefs. There are no statistically significant differences with respect to the average results achieved by my male and female students on course negotiation exercises, or with respect to the standard deviations. While it is true that some male and female differences may continue to exist,

These findings should unequivocally demonstrate that any such differences do not influence the results of bargaining interactions. . . .

Problem — The Power of Underestimation

In a paper on the subject of gender in negotiation, a female law student argued that being underestimated as a woman negotiator was an advantage. Do you agree with what she states below? Is advantageous use of an opponent's underestimation of your negotiation savvy an acceptable manipulation?

Both men and women underestimate women in male-dominated settings, particularly if the female is young. People tend not to expect women to be highly competitive or manipulative. This works to the advantage of the female negotiator. She can not only perform beyond her employers' or colleagues' expectations, but more importantly, she can also outsmart her opponents without their even realizing it. For example, if a male negotiator feels less intimidated by the young female negotiator, he may not fully engage his competitive skills and simply give her his "bottom line." The young female negotiator may then use that figure as the starting point for her negotiations. Being underestimated can also be a great psychological motivator for women. Such offensive attitudes can act as a powerful catalyst to prove their opponents wrong. From this vantage point, women can see how being underestimated can be a highly underrated advantage.

B. Cultural Differences, or Why the World Is Not Boring

*"Culture is the collective programming of the mind which distinguishes the
members of one group or category from those of another"*

— *Geert Hofstede, Dutch cultural anthropologist*

Negotiating with people from other cultures can be challenging because rapport and trust affect negotiations, as do cultural values and traditions, which influence what we perceive. As noted, we tend to be most comfortable and trusting among people like ourselves, with similar appearance and mental software, and we are most fascinated with those who are different.

Cultural differences are difficult to discuss and apply to negotiation because the meaning of "culture" is elusive. Like gender, focusing on culture or ethnicity lends itself to stereotypes and creates a risk of substituting categorical norms for the uniqueness of individuals. Cultural considerations are so complex and ever-changing in our globalized, increasingly blended world that defining a person by culture and using that cultural identity to predict values or behavior is inviting error.

However, because it is helpful to have clues about how our negotiating counterparts perceive the world and perhaps value things differently than we do, cultural variations should be considered. Sensitivity to cultural differences can assist in preparing for negotiations, interpreting behavior, and providing ideas for how impasse can be avoided and value might be created in a negotiation. Cultural awareness can also help us avoid unintended consequences of what we say and do, as well as alert us to what others may anticipate from us because of our own cultural identity.

We use cultural labels for categories of people, although we know that the common characteristics attributed to the group are not distributed or shared uniformly. In addition, few people are part of only one cultural identity. So we can never be sure which of several cultural influences will be most applicable. Will the culture of a person's national origin, ethnicity, religion, schooling, professional identity, or economic class predominate in a particular situation? Also, can we ever know if the culture of the last generation, when cultural norms for that group may have been identified or popularized, is the same behavioral or value norms of that group today? We know that cultural generalizations, although convenient, are inherently unreliable. In constitutional parlance, they are necessarily underinclusive and overinclusive.

With all of these caveats, cultural considerations are of great interest because we need all the help we can get in better understanding others. Effective negotiation depends on accurately reading the real meaning of the other negotiator's verbal and nonverbal communications regarding needs, offers, and concessions. Cultural differences can create misunderstandings and disastrous results because we see others through our own cultural lens. A negotiator from India may shake his head in a manner understood by an American to mean no, when in India moving the head up-and-down with a slight twist means yes. A Japanese negotiator, who feels it is impolite to say no, may well think that saying yes under the circumstances has a clear meaning of no.

Even negotiators with the same native language may impute certain words with opposite meanings. British linguist Neil Payne tells about U.S. and British negotiators who found themselves at a standstill when the American company proposed that they "table" particular key points. In the United States, "tabling a motion" means to not discuss it, while the same phrase in Great Britain means to "bring it to the table for discussion."

These are some examples of what can go wrong cross-culturally. This text cannot attempt to catalog what you need to know in order to negotiate in all of the countries in the United Nations and in the multiple cultures within most countries. Country-specific preparation and research is required. In addition to the Internet, most travel guides feature a section on the culture you will encounter in another country. One book claims to provide clear and concise information on how to negotiate in 50 different countries that account for 90 percent of the world economy (Llamazares 2008).

Sociologists, anthropologists, and linguists, among others, study the impact of culture and describe cultural behavior and norms. Many books on negotiation include their research and offer advice on how to utilize cultural awareness and knowledge to improve negotiation results. The next article explains both the value and shortcomings of using categorical cultural norms. The perception errors referred to by Professor Sebenius should, by now, be familiar to you.

❖ **James K. Sebenius,** *CAVEATS FOR CROSS-BORDER NEGOTIATIONS*

18 Negot. J. 122 (2002)

While some of the work on culture and negotiation is at best superficial, much of the relevant academic literature is well grounded and accompanied by careful statements as to its limits and the conditions under which it should apply. While holding on to the truth that some characteristics do systematically vary across national borders, however, there is often a general uneasiness about unwarranted use of purported cross-cultural insight. . . . My objective is to make analysts and negotiators more sophisticated consumers of this advice by suggesting four classes of caveat, each with a slightly tongue-in-cheek name that will, I hope, be usefully evocative.

1. The John Wayne v. Charlie Chan Fallacy: Stereotyping National Cultures

Start with the obvious: All American negotiators are not like John Wayne and all Chinese negotiators are not like Charlie Chan. . . . In the face of such internal variation, we wisely caution ourselves against mindless stereotyping by nationality (as well as by gender, religion, race, profession, or age). Even so, in many situations it remains all-too-common to hear offhand remarks such as "all Chinese negotiators . . ." (as well as generalizations about "women" . . . or "engineers"). To combat this, a strong version of the anti-stereotyping prescription calls for ignoring nationality altogether in preparing for negotiation.

That advice is too strong. Nationality often does have a great deal to do with cultural characteristics, particularly in relatively homogeneous countries like

Japan. The careful work of many researchers confirms significant associations between nationality and a range of traits and outcomes. . . . It would be foolish to throw away potentially valuable information. But what does information on a particular group's behavioral expectations or deeper cultural characteristics really convey? Typically, cultural descriptions are about central *tendencies* of populations that also exhibit considerable "within-group" variation. . . .

Inferences about individuals from central tendencies are often misleading or wrong. *You negotiate with individuals, not averages.*

But viewing the world without the aid of stereotypes is difficult. Forming stereotypes is a natural reflex that helps order the overflow of information that barrages people. Social psychologist Ellen Langer argues that a solution to the negative effects of stereotyping is "mindfulness," which she defines as a willingness to create new categories, an openness to new information, and an awareness that more than one perspective exists. Rather than straining against forming stereotypes, a more realistic strategy is to allow stereotypes room to change, multiply, and adapt to new information.

In sum, remember that "national traits"—as well as traits supposedly associated with gender, ethnicity, etc.—are *distributions* of characteristics across populations, not blanket descriptions applicable to each individual. Be very cautious about making inferences about characteristics of specific individuals from different groups—even where the groups are, on average, sharply different. Avoid stereotyping and the "prototypicality" error of assuming an individual will exhibit the most likely group characteristic. Even if U.S. negotiators are on average more impatient, deal-focused, and individually oriented than their Chinese counterparts, be careful not to help amplify that stereotype in the mind of the other side. . . .

2. The Rosetta Stone Fallacy: Overattribution to National Culture

National culture clearly matters. But there is a tendency to see it as the Rosetta Stone, the indispensable key to describe, explain, and predict the behavior of the other side. Of course there are many possible "cultures" operating within a given individual. . . . National culture can be highly visible but, obviously, it is only one of many possible influences. For example, Jeswald Salacuse surveyed executives from a dozen countries to determine national tendencies on ten important bargaining characteristics, such as negotiating goal (contract v. relationship), orientation (win-win v. win-lose), formality level, communication style, risk-taking, etc. While his results showed significant national differences, he also analyzed the data according to profession and occupations of the respondents such as law, engineering, marketing, the military, diplomacy, accounting, etc. These categories, too, showed systematic association with different bargaining styles. Finally, Salacuse could also differentiate many of these characteristics by gender. Other extensive studies extend and elaborate analogous findings. Nationality often matters when considering someone's bargaining characteristics but so too does gender, ethnicity, functional specialty, etc. . . . [N]ational culture is but one of many "cultures" that can influence bargaining behavior. . . .

3. The "Visual Flying Rules" at Night Fallacy: Falling Prey to Potent Psychological Biases

Self-Serving Perceptions of Our Own Side

There is a powerful tendency, formally studied as "biased assimilation," for people to interpret information in negotiation self-servingly. For example, experiments give a number of people identical information about a pending court case but randomly assign them to the role of plaintiff or defendant. When each person is asked for his or her private assessment of the probability that the plaintiff will win, those assigned the role of plaintiff on average give much higher odds than those (randomly) assigned to the role of defendant (but, again, on the basis of identical information). People tend to "believe their own lines" or self-servingly interpret information, . . . researchers conducted an experiment at a boy's camp, sponsoring a jelly bean hunt among the campers. After the hunt, the boys were shown an identical picture of a jar of jelly beans. Each boy evaluated the total number of beans in the jar according to whether he was told the jar belonged to his own team or to the other side. The same photograph was estimated to contain many more beans when it was presented as "your team's" and far fewer when it was alleged to be the "other side's."

Partisan Perceptions of the Other Side

If our capacity to process information critical of our own side is flawed, it is even more the case for our assessments of the other side in a conflict or negotiation. In part, this stems from the in-group/out-group phenomenon. Persons from different cultures, especially on the opposite side of the bargaining table, are more readily identified as belonging to an out-group, or the Other. Once that labeling is in place, powerful perceptual dynamics kick in (beyond the tendencies toward stereotyping and overattribution). Robert Robinson describes extensive research over the last 40 years, documenting an unconscious mechanism that enhances "one's own side, portraying it as more talented, honest, and morally upright" while simultaneously vilifying the Other. This leads to a systematic exaggeration of the other side's position and the overestimation of the extent of the actual conflict. As a result, negotiators are often unduly pessimistic about their ability to find common ground, and can be unwilling to pursue it.

Self-Fulfilling Prophesies

Such partisan perceptions hold the power to change reality by becoming self-fulfilling prophesies. The effects of labeling and stereotyping have been documented thoroughly to show that perceptions have the power to shape reality. . . . At the negotiating table, the same principle holds true: Clinging firmly to the idea that one's counterpart is stubborn, for example, is likely to yield intransigence on both sides, precluding the possibility of a compromise that might have occurred had the label of "obstinacy" not been so rigorously affixed.

In short, just as a pilot trying to navigate by visual flight rules [VFR] at night or in a storm is prone to dangerous misjudgments, the psychology of perception in cross-cultural situations is rife with biases. Not only do we stereotype and overattribute to nationality, we are also poor at interpreting information on our own situation, vulnerable to partisan perceptions of the other side, and likely to act in ways that become dangerously self-fulfilling.

4. St. Augustine's Fallacy: "When in Rome . . ."

Assume that you have undertaken a full analysis of the culture of the person you will meet on the other side of the bargaining table. St. Augustine gave the classic cross-cultural advice: When in Rome, do as the Romans do. While this admonition certainly has merit, it is not always good advice . . . much better options may be available. For example, learning that the Chinese, on average, are more hesitant than North Americans to take risks is only a first step. Clearly, a responsive strategy would not mimic this hesitancy, but effectively anticipate it.

Rather than learning to behave as the Romans do (while in Rome or elsewhere), strategies should accommodate the degree of cross-table understanding each side has of the other. For example, consider the best approach for a U.S. manager on his first visit to Japan dealing with a Yale-educated Japanese executive who has worked extensively in Europe and North America. Here it would be sensible to let the Japanese take the lead. If a negotiator is far more familiar with a counterpart's culture than vice versa, the best strategy might be to embrace the counterpart's negotiating "script." If both sides are equally "literate," an improvisational and mutually-accommodating approach might be most appropriate. A lower degree of familiarity dictates bringing in locally familiar expertise, perhaps on your side and perhaps even as a mediator.

A great deal depends on how familiar you are with "Roman" culture and how familiar your "Roman" counterpart is with your culture. And of course you want to avoid the previous fallacies as well. The nationalities across the table from each other may be Chinese and U.S., but both players may be regulars on the international business circuit, which has its own, increasingly global negotiating culture. Again, assess—etiquette, deeper traits, negotiation-specific expectations, and caveats; do not assume and project your assumption onto your counterpart.

Note: Research on Culture and Negotiation

Professor Sebenius provides important caveats about the limits of cultural references. He also concludes that cultural analysis offers insight into systematic differences about how people from different cultures negotiate. We now turn to some of the salient features that research indicates do distinguish the way people from different cultures negotiate.

The negotiation approaches and behaviors common within a culture are related to other aspects of that culture and are based on societal values, social structure, and modes of communication. The three distinguishing features most often mentioned in relation to negotiation norms within a culture are the value of individualism versus collectivism, egalitarianism versus hierarchy, and direct versus indirect modes of communication. Understanding these norms is helpful in forming working assumptions about different cultures and also in understanding our own values. The sharpest differences between societal values are often framed as differences between Eastern and Western cultures; however, the counter-posed sets of values summarized below is not limited to East versus West. The juxtapositions could be applied to the United States and Cuba, or Albania and Serbia.

- *Individualism versus collectivism:* Some societies appear to value individual needs over the collective needs of the group. Economic rewards, as well as social standing, are based on individual accomplishments. Individual autonomy is more important than societal interests. Individual rights tend to be most highly valued. In contrast, other societies place a higher priority on the interdependence of individuals and their social obligations to one another. Collective interests are valued more highly than individual rights.
- *Hierarchy versus egalitarianism:* This cultural juxtaposition distinguishes societies in which power and status are seen as vertical rather than horizontal. In hierarchical societies, social superiority is based on others being socially inferior and deference is given to those who are higher on the social and economic ladder. In egalitarian societies, there are no social castes and social status is undifferentiated.
- *Direct versus indirect communication:* In more direct-communicating societies, information is explicit, with minimum nuance, and can be readily understood regardless of the context. Meaning is on the surface rather than embedded in other layers of pretext or context. People in societies with more indirect communication embed the meaning of their words in the context of the situation. Meaning must be inferred to be fully understood.

Interdisciplinary research is increasingly focusing on cultural variations in negotiation. Although very interesting, much of the research is highly theoretical and is written in research parlance. Practical application of the research findings is just starting to emerge and should be of considerable value to negotiators, subject to the limitations explained by Professor Sebenius. The following excerpt, written more for practitioners, is from an extensive volume of research findings on negotiation and culture.

❖ **Wendy L. Adair & Jeanne M. Brett,** *CULTURE AND NEGOTIATION PROCESSES*

**The Handbook of Negotiation and Culture 158
(M. Gelfand & J. Brett eds., 2004)**

Culture is a distinctly group construct. Individuals have personalities; groups have cultures. Culture consists of group members' shared beliefs, attitudes, norms, and behaviors, and the group's social, political, economic, and religious institutional structures. . . . Social institutions carry culture in their ideology and reinforce it by rewarding and sanctioning social interaction within the group. . . . [We] use national boundaries to identify cultures, because national boundaries define institutional boundaries, and as a result provide an objective way to distinguish cultural groups. . . .

Culture and Beliefs about Negotiation

People from Western cultures tend to have independent, also called individualistic, self-construals. They understand themselves as independent or detached from the social groups to which they belong and view themselves as agents free to focus on personal goals to self-actualize rather than on social obligations. People from Eastern cultures tend to have interdependent, also called collectivist, self-construals. They tend to understand themselves within the context of the social groups to which they belong and view themselves as agents constrained by social obligations to maintain harmony and preserve "face" within their social groups.

An independent self-construal seems to be a worldview that is naturally associated with the perspective that negotiation is about distributing resources, not so much about relationships. An interdependent self-construal seems to be a worldview that is naturally associated with the perspective that negotiation is about relationships first, and then about distributing resources. This is the first distinction reflected in our model of culture and negotiation processes. . . .

This leads us to predict that a relationship frame will be more salient for negotiators in Eastern cultures, while a resource distribution frame will be more salient for negotiators in Western cultures. This implies that negotiators in Eastern cultures are more likely to think about negotiation in terms of relationships and that this frame should influence their negotiation goals. Negotiators in Western cultures are more likely to think about negotiation in terms of outcome, and this frame should influence their negotiation goals.

Culture and Negotiators' Goals

Because negotiation is a mixed-motive, cooperation and competition are both central elements of negotiation in the East and the West. Cooperative goals focus negotiators on integrative outcomes or joint value creation, while competitive goals direct the distributive or value-claiming aspects of negotiation. We propose that the normative behaviors that negotiators from different cultures use to enact cooperative and competitive goals are different and can be predicted from cultural differences in goals and how negotiation is framed in Eastern and Western cultures.

If people from Eastern cultures believe negotiation is more about relationships, the interplay between cooperative and competitive goals may represent an attempt to create a long-term relationship that is not too cooperative but has enough social distance to justify claiming value. For example, the primary cooperative goal may be to build trust, and the primary competitive goal may be to establish dominance. If people from Western cultures believe negotiation is more about the distribution of resources, the interplay between cooperative and competitive goals may represent an attempt to both create joint gains and claim the largest possible portion of that gain. . . . Thus, although negotiators from Eastern and Western cultures have both cooperative and competitive goals, the meaning of those goals may be different and may be one factor affecting normative negotiation behavior.

Culture and Negotiators' Norms

Norms are standards of appropriate behavior in social interaction. As with negotiation beliefs and goals, we argue that culture affects negotiation norms and therefore the behaviors that negotiators are more or less likely to use. In addition to cooperative and competitive goals, another major difference between Eastern and Western cultures that may affect negotiation behavior is low-versus high-context communication. In Eastern cultures that tend to be high context (e.g., Japan and China), meaning is communicated not just by a person's words or acts, but also by the context in which those words or acts are communicated. High-context communication is indirect and requires considerable familiarity with the cultural meaning conveyed by various contexts. In Western cultures that tend to be low context (e.g., the United States and Germany), meaning is embedded in words or acts. Low-context communication is direct, and although it requires familiarity with words and acts, it does not require familiarity with contexts.

Discussions of low- and high-context communication emphasize the differences between direct and indirect communications, but the dimensions on which high- and low-context communication cultures differ go beyond directness. For example, a negotiator from a low-context culture might suggest that his company is so financially weak that without a good price, his company will not be able to buy the product at all. In the same situation, a negotiator from a high-context culture might appeal to sympathy: "We've had a bad quarter, and our acquisitions budget is extremely limited." In the first example, the negotiator's message is explicit: "If you do not give us a good price, we will not be able to buy from you." In the second example, the negotiator's message is implicit; the other negotiator has to infer that a sale depends on an especially competitive price. The appeal is different in each case, too. In the first example, the appeal is to fact: "If you do not give us a good price, we will not be able to buy." In the second example, the appeal is to a more general principle: you are stronger, and you should take care of us. Logic in low-context communication therefore tends to be linear, developed in "if-then" terms. Logic in high-context communication tends be more amorphous and may require the listener to infer the focus of the argument.

Several research studies on negotiation processes support the low- and high-context communication distinction in the East and West. In low-context cultures, persuasion makes appeals to rationality; and in high-context cultures, persuasion makes appeals to emotions and affect. For example, in a content analysis of U.S.-Taiwanese cross-cultural negotiation transcripts . . . U.S. negotiators used more analytic statements, relying on logic and reasoning to persuade. In contrast, Taiwanese negotiators used more normative statements, relying on social roles and relationships to persuade. Other research has found U.S. negotiators using more commitments, a form of rational persuasion, than Chinese negotiators, and making more promises, a form of rational persuasion, than Soviet negotiators. In low-context cultures, information sharing is explicit and direct, whereas in high-context cultures, information sharing is implicit and indirect. For example . . . U.S. negotiators used more no's, a direct form of information exchange, than Chinese negotiators. Our own research also reveals that negotiators from low-context cultures engage in more direct information sharing, whereas negotiators from high-context cultures favor more indirect, implicit communication. . . .

In sum, our model implies an East-West distinction in negotiation with respect to beliefs, goals, and norms. Negotiators from the East tend to frame negotiation as a relationship. They have both cooperative trust goals that we propose are enacted through indirect information sharing behaviors, and competitive dominance goals that we propose are enacted through affective influence behaviors. Negotiators from the West tend to frame negotiation as a distribution of resources. They have both cooperative joint-gain goals that we propose are enacted through direct information sharing behaviors, and competitive claiming goals that we propose are enacted through rational influence behaviors. . . .

Of course, the East-West divide is not a dichotomy, but rather a continuum representing cultures that are more high-context on one side and more low-context on the other. Culturally normative behaviors occur in degrees of more or less, and contextual cues less subtle than culture may cause the frame to flip from what is culturally normative to what is not. For example, even high-context culture conflict avoiders may make a direct refusal in a competitive negotiation situation. . . .

Culture and Negotiation Process

In a study comparing negotiation behaviors and six cultures (the United States, Russia, France, Brazil, Japan, and Hong Kong), we looked at behavioral differences along a low-high context culture continuum (Adair, Brett, Lempereur, Okumura, Shikhirev, Kinsley, and Lytle, 2004). U.S. negotiators used relatively more direct information sharing than negotiators from the other five cultures. Russian, Japanese, and Hong Kong Chinese negotiators were more likely to use indirect information sharing than other negotiators, and, Russian and Japanese negotiators were more likely to use both rational and affective influence than negotiators from the other four cultures. These results confirm a relatively consistent low-high context continuum, with the U.S. negotiators more low context, Japanese and Russian negotiators more high context, and French, Brazilian, and Hong Kong Chinese negotiators somewhere in the middle of the continuum. . . .

Conclusion

Because researchers are just beginning to study culture and negotiation processes, the research . . . is not yet cumulative. Thus, our model of culture's effect on negotiation behaviors and sequences is tentative; our understanding of how negotiators in a cross-cultural setting can most effectively adapt their behaviors to maximize effective communication is limited; and, our evidence for what patterns of adaptation lead to joint satisfaction and joint gain is restricted. . . .

Much of the research and writing on culture as a factor in negotiation focuses on cultural norms as traits we should be aware of in those with whom we negotiate, particularly across borders. If the research on cultural norms is reliable, our own cultural identity can offer clues to others about our negotiating tendencies and can provide us with personal insight into our negotiating behaviors and responses, both domestically and cross-border. Even though our own cultural or group identity may influence how we perceive ourselves and how others view us, these categorical attributes are subject to error and oversimplification to the point of being misleading and insulting. This limitation will not stop others with whom we negotiate from generalizing about us in a way that might affect their behavior toward us. Just as important, our self-identity helps shape our beliefs, emotions, and behaviors. This can have an impact on how we negotiate.

If you would like to test your own cultural, gender, or racial sensitivities and biases online, go to *https://implicit.harvard.edu/implicit/*, where you have the opportunity to participate in a Web-based research study. The results can be revealing and might be discussed in class.

Questions

6. What is the dominant culture with which you identify? Is this the same culture that those who do not know you well would assume you belong to? Are there other cultural subgroups that help define who you are? Are there stereotypes that opposing negotiators might have about you? Is there any way you can use those likely stereotypes to your advantage?
7. Does the downside of thinking about people as part of a cultural group outweigh the possible benefit of grouping people to help understand their values and anticipate their behavior?
8. Does the Adair and Brett writing contrasting Eastern and Western cultural differences to negotiating contradict Sebenius's warning about cultural stereotyping? Do you find Adair and Brett's report on cultural research helpful?
9. Do you agree that "culture is the lens through which we make sense of the world"? If so, is there any doubt that people of different cultures will see the world so differently that world conflict is inevitable? Is conflict and how to deal with it culturally defined? For a comprehensive and instructive collection of provocative readings on both culture and gender as they relate to conflict, see Chew (2001).
10. Based on selection, training, and shared values, do lawyers constitute a cultural subgroup that helps others understand them and predict their behavior? Is your answer the same for doctors, accountants, or clergy?

C. Is Race a Factor in Negotiations?

If gender and culture are nebulous categories, race is even more difficult to clearly define and discuss. More than 70 years ago, M. F. Ashley Montagu questioned the concept of "race" in his book, *Man's Most Dangerous Myth: The Fallacy of Race* (1945). Nevertheless, distinctions are drawn on the basis of race as a social construct, even though "from an evolutionary standpoint, we are all Africans." (Shea 2011.)

We live in an age in which an African-American was twice elected U.S. president, an increasing number of professionals are people of color, and many more people identify themselves as interracial or blended race—or choose not to identify with any racial classification. Although some may feel that we have moved beyond race, we cannot ignore the pervasive role of race in the lives of people of color or the implicit bias of those with whom they interact, including other negotiators and mediators. As a Mexican-American colleague commented, "I can't help but think about and experience my race every day." Unspoken and sometimes unrecognized racial prejudices and misperceptions alter intrapersonal responses and interpersonal interactions in negotiations. (See Izumi 2010.)

It is interesting to note that the U.S. Census Bureau adheres to the 1997 Office of Management and Budget (OMB) standards on race and ethnicity, which permit the reporting of more than one race. An individual's response to the census question about race is based upon self-identification. The OMB-listed definitions of race and ethnicity are:

White—A person having origins in any of the original peoples of Europe, the Middle East, or North Africa.

Black or African American—A person having origins in any of the Black racial groups of Africa.

American Indian or Alaska Native—A person having origins in any of the original peoples of North and South America (including Central America) and who maintains tribal affiliation or community attachment.

Asian—A person having origins in any of the original peoples of the Far East, Southeast Asia, or the Indian subcontinent including, for example, Cambodia, China, India, Japan, Korea, Malaysia, Pakistan, the Philippine Islands, Thailand, and Vietnam.

Native Hawaiian or Other Pacific Islander—A person having origins in any of the original peoples of Hawaii, Guam, Samoa, or other Pacific Islands.

Hispanic or Latino—A person of Mexican, Puerto Rican, Cuban, South or Central American, or other Spanish culture or origin, regardless of race. The term "Spanish origin" can be used in addition to "Hispanic or Latino".

Even though discrimination still exists and race matters in important social justice issues, does it make a difference in negotiating? Published studies on race as a factor in negotiation outcomes appear to focus on differences between Caucasians and African-Americans. One set of studies (Ayers 1991, 1995) compared prices arrived at for new cars in the Chicago area between white and black testers posing as otherwise similar buyers. Although cited in negotiation literature and texts as disturbing evidence that African-Americans "often get worse outcomes in negotiations," this evidence cannot be extrapolated to indicate that race is a predictor of negotiation skill. These studies documented discrimination in the offers that sales personnel made to African-American versus Caucasian testers, rather than differences in negotiating ability among the testers. (The tester's bargaining approaches were similar and each was prepped from the same bargaining script.) Indeed, the studies were later introduced as evidence of discrimination in a class-action lawsuit against General Motors Acceptance Corporation. (See Hawkins 2004.)

Similar to the question raised about negotiation studies concerning women, does evidence about lesser outcomes for African-American negotiators (or buyers) in the general population indicate any distinctions among lawyers, who are a self-selected group of achievers with similar training? Professor Charles Craver, who was cited earlier in this chapter regarding his studies showing that negotiated outcomes obtained by female law students are equal to outcomes obtained by male law students, also tracked negotiation outcomes among his students by race. Professor Craver indicated that he published the negotiation outcome statistics comparing black and white law students because of his concern about the relatively low percentage of black sports agents. "In professional football, sixty-nine percent of the players are black, but black agents comprise only fourteen percent of the registered agents with active files. Worse yet, more than eighty percent of the NBA's players are black, but less than ten percent of them have black agents." He found no significant statistical difference between negotiation results achieved by black and white law students.

> "The nine years of Legal Negotiation course data evaluated by me indicates the absence of any statistically significant correlation between student race and the results achieved on negotiation exercises. These findings would suggest that even if cultural and behavioral differences between black and white students exist, those differences have no impact on students' ability to achieve beneficial negotiation exercise results." (Craver, "Race and Negotiation Performance: Does Race Predict Success as a Negotiator?" 8 ABA Disp. Resol. Mag. 22, Fall 2001.)

We asked a colleague, who is an African-American law professor, to review and comment on Professor Craver's study:

> As a law professor, and as a teacher of ADR, I was interested in what Professor Craver had learned in 16 years of teaching negotiations (9 years of which constituted the basis of his study). What I wonder, however, for your readers, is what his student negotiations in mock exercises in law school tells us about negotiations among lawyers and clients in the real world of sports negotiation. In my mind, the more interesting question concerning race has to do with the perception among many black athletes that they would do better with white lawyers (and some would say Jewish lawyers) serving as their agents. There are interesting questions about the impact of race and how that perception gets internalized in the individual coming into a world with which he or she did not have prior experience. What goes on in the world of high-level (i.e., a great deal of money involved) sports negotiations that leads to the perception in the NBA and NFL that a black athlete needs a white lawyer (agent) to be truly successful in the negotiations with the owners?
>
> I appreciate the fact that Professor Craver has used his experience in teaching Legal Negotiation in law school to provide some empirical data about race and its impact on student results in law school negotiations. I think that Professor Craver may agree that his study tells only about law students in mock legal negotiations in law school. Does the study reliably tell us much about perceptions and actions among black and white negotiators serving as agents for athletes and representatives of owners in sports negotiations?

Questions

11. In a multicultural, increasingly blended society, is race relevant in the study of negotiation? Why?
12. Is race distinguishable from culture for purposes of negotiation? If so, what is the difference?

13. In discussions of race as a factor in negotiation, why is the focus more on distinctions, if any, between Caucasians and African-Americans and not between Asians and other races?

14. What might explain the disproportionate number of African-American sports agents?

15. Is there any different explanation for the relatively few female sports agents?

CHAPTER
10

Negotiation Ethics

As a lawyer, you will find yourself pulled between serving your client's particular interests and the public's interest in justice. There is also the often-unspoken concern about your own interests and "serving your soul." This set of tensions results in constant and challenging choices facing attorneys in terms of ethics, morality, and negotiation effectiveness.

Because negotiation occurs in private, usually without clients present, there is little check on what is said or not said in negotiation between lawyers. Ethics rules attempt to provide guidance on how to balance your obligation of vigorous advocacy and the integrity of the profession in a negotiation, but the specifics of applying the rules are elusive, especially regarding what must be revealed to an opposing party and whether that decision is made by you or your client.

A. Deception vs. Disclosure

Ethics codes forbid you from lying in court but permit you to lie in negotiation, at least as most non-lawyers would define lying. Even if you would not deceive or lie on your own behalf, the classic obligation to be a zealous advocate for clients, now described as a duty to act with "commitment and dedication to the interests of the client," will confront you with the dilemma of deciding how far to go in gaining a negotiation advantage for your client by misstating or not disclosing information.

Ethical limits can be found in each state's Rules of Professional Conduct or Code of Professional Responsibility and in its case and statutory law. The American Bar Association's (ABA's) Model Rules of Professional Conduct are the basis for most state ethics rules. The beginning point is Rule 4.1, which states that a lawyer shall not "knowingly (a) make a false statement of material fact or law to a third person; or (b) fail to disclose a material fact to a third person when disclosure is necessary to avoid assisting a criminal or fraudulent act by a client, unless disclosure is prohibited by Rule 1.6."

A serious limitation in knowing what should or should not be revealed is the qualification that only "material" facts must be revealed. The official comment to Rule 4.1 states that "under generally accepted conventions in negotiation, . . . estimates of price or value placed on the subject of the transaction" are not considered material, nor are "a party's intentions as to an acceptable settlement of a claim" covered by Rule 4.1's prohibitions against making false statements. (See Comment 2.)

To complicate matters, Rule 1.6 protects client confidences. So an attorney whose client reveals a bottom line, or any other information that the client regards as confidential, cannot disclose that information, unless the client authorizes the disclosure. In effect, the requirement that a lawyer may not reveal client confidences swallows the rule requiring disclosure, except for continuing criminal conduct.

The net result of the ethical rules is that lawyers in negotiation can lie about some things, but not others. You can puff and bluff because that's the expected convention. So, as a lawyer you can tell the other side that "this is a seven-figure case if it gets to a jury," even though you believe a verdict would not exceed $500,000, or that your client's bottom line is $100,000 when it is really $80,000. However, you cannot say your client sustained a broken neck, knowing that she did not. In other words, deception is considered an acceptable aspect of negotiation, but only to a point. (See Chapter 11 for the limits imposed by contract law.) This creates a dilemma for the ethical negotiator and tension between service to your client and service to justice.

The next article explains why rules for lawyer negotiations are "morally complicated" and reports on a survey of 734 practicing lawyers in Phoenix and St. Louis who were asked if they would agree to a client's specific request to engage in a fraudulent pre-litigation negotiation scheme if a client asks them to do so.

❖ **Art Hinshaw and Jess K. Alberts,** *Doing the Right Thing: An Empirical Study of Attorney Negotiation Ethics*

16 Harv. Negot. L. Rev. 95 (2011)

Rule 4.1(a)

[Tension exists] because Rule 4.1(a)'s prohibition applies only to "material" facts or law. However, the Model Rules fail to define the term "material," instead explaining that what constitutes a material fact "depends on the circumstances." Generally, a statement of fact is considered material if it is significant or essential to the negotiation, but Comment 2 explains: "Under generally accepted conventions in negotiation, certain types of statements ordinarily are not taken as statements of material fact."

It then provides examples of statements that ordinarily fall into this immaterial fact category, including estimates of price or value and a party's intentions as to an acceptable settlement of a claim, arguably the two most material matters during bargaining interactions. The Comment's phrasing also suggests that this is not an exclusive list, and many authorities have surmised that other types of statements must not be material facts because they fall into the "generally accepted negotiation conventions" category However, it is unclear what those other statements might be.

Defining the Rule's determinative principle by explaining what it is not leads to difficulties in interpretation. When grappling with this problem, only one court has defined the term "material fact" using verbiage other than what appears in the Rule's Comments, and it did so in positive terms: "A fact is material to a negotiation if it reasonably may be viewed as important to a fair understanding of what is being given up and, in return, gained by the [deal]."

This definition underscores the breadth of the term "material fact," which explains why Comment 2 narrows it. The two keys to determining whether a fact is material in the context of Rule 4.1 are: (a) whether the fact has a reasonable effect on one party's understanding of what is being negotiated, and (b) whether the statement is an estimate of price or value on the subject of a transaction or a party's intentions as to an acceptable settlement of a claim.

Rule 4.1(a) forbids false statements of material law as well as false statements of material fact. The Rule's Comments do not address what constitutes "material law," leaving lawyers with a dictionary definition: law that is either significant or essential to the negotiation. Rule 4.1's prohibition regarding material law is most often germane when a statement is addressed to a non-lawyer, but it applies to opposing counsel and judges as well.

Thus, when speaking to others about material issues, Rule 4.1(a) simply requires lawyers to speak the truth as they understand it without engaging in any misrepresentations. However, a lawyer is not prohibited from making deliberate misrepresentations about non-material facts or law to anyone.

Rule 4.1(b)

Generally, lawyers have no duty voluntarily to inform an opposing party of relevant facts when negotiating. Under the auspices of Rule 4.1(b), however, a duty to disclose material facts or law arises only if doing so avoids assisting in a client's criminal conduct or fraud. In other words, the lawyer's silence may cause the lawyer to be complicit in a fraudulent misrepresentation by omission. In instances where nondisclosure constitutes a fraudulent misrepresentation, such as when the lawyer finds that her work has unwittingly been used to further an ongoing fraud, the lawyer has a duty to correct the misapprehension.

Yet the Rule provides that disclosure is proper only if it does not violate the duty of maintaining client confidences stated in Rule 1.6. This would appear to vitiate the duty of disclosure, allowing lawyers to participate in a client's crime or fraud. However, reading Rule 4.1(b) with Rule 1.6 and with the values behind the Model Rules negates such a conclusion. Rule 1.6 contains several discretionary exceptions permitting disclosure with respect to criminal or fraudulent conduct in order to prevent, mitigate, or rectify injuries due to conduct for which the lawyer's services have been unwittingly used. But these permissive reporting requirements become mandatory . . . "when disclosure is necessary to avoid assisting a criminal or fraudulent act by a client." Similarly, the general requirements of Rule 1.6 have always been subject to Rule 1.2(d)'s prohibition against knowingly participating in a client's criminal or fraudulent conduct. Thus, the reference to client confidential information in Rule 4.1(b) does not modify the duty to disclose material facts when doing so would avoid assisting the client's criminal conduct or fraud.

If a client asks an attorney to engage in criminal or fraudulent acts, the attorney and client should first discuss the consequences of the client's request and, if the client refuses to reconsider the action, the lawyer should withdraw from the representation. If the lawyer withdraws, she may still be required to disaffirm any fraudulent statement with which she might be deemed to be associated by reason of the prior representation.

Rule 4.1's regulation on attorney negotiation behavior is modest notwithstanding its prohibition of fraudulent conduct and assisting in a client's fraudulent conduct. The Rule allows attorneys to be deceitful about opinions and non-material facts and law, which allows for puffing and bluffing. Furthermore, technical violations of Rule 4.1 where no one is harmed are unlikely to be the subject of disciplinary proceedings or court sanctions. In practice, Rule 4.1 does little other than proscribe fraudulent misrepresentations in negotiation.

Rule 3.3(b) and Rule 8.4(c)

Rules 3.3 ("Candor Toward the Tribunal") and 8.4 ("Misconduct") are not specifically tailored to negotiation. However, both do affect the negotiation arena. Rule 3.3 contains several relevant prohibitions in the litigation context including one in Rule 3.3(b) against engaging in criminal or fraudulent conduct related to a proceeding. This Rule extends to settlement negotiations in litigation, because the resolution of disputes short of trial is an integral part of the judicial process. Essentially, Rule 3.3(b) provides courts with another weapon to discipline lawyers who participate in fraudulent settlement negotiations.

Rule 8.4 applies broadly to all lawyering contexts. Specifically it defines professional misconduct to include any violation of the professional norms set forth in the Model Rules, attempting to violate the Model Rules, aiding or abetting another in violating the Model Rules, or violating the Model Rules through the use of a surrogate or agent. In the negotiation context, the Rule defines misconduct as engaging "in conduct involving dishonesty, fraud, deceit or misrepresentation," which puts Rule 8.4 at odds with Rule 4.1's legitimizing certain misleading and deceptive negotiation tactics. Since Rule 4.1 provides specific exceptions to the general rule of Rule 8.4, rules of statutory interpretation require the dictates of Rule 4.1 to take precedence. However, Rule 8.4(c) often is used to bolster disciplinary claims against those who are charged with violating Rule 4.1.

The Negotiation Scenario [for the Survey]

The hypothetical used in the study centers on a pre-litigation settlement negotiation where the participant attorney represented a client who believed his former girlfriend had infected him with the DONS virus, a hypothetical sexually transmitted disease which is fatal and for which there is no cure. In response to a letter from his former girlfriend admitting she had had the disease for the duration of the relationship, the client took two DONS home tests, both of which were positive. After he threatened to sue her, the former girlfriend suggested their respective attorneys meet to negotiate the appropriate amount of damages

The DONS Negotiation places the attorney in the moments before the settlement negotiations are about to begin. At that time the client reveals a critical new fact to his lawyer. The results of his two earlier DONS tests turned out to be false positives and he does not have the disease after all. The client, still angry with his former girlfriend, wants to punish her for the agony caused by her reckless behavior. As a result, he asks his attorney to refrain from revealing the fact that he does not have the disease during the negotiation. At this point, the questionnaire begins.

Lawyers' Responses to Client's Requests to Withhold Information

The hypothetical scenario presents the respondent with an ethical dilemma: to go along with the client's desire to engage in fraudulent behavior or to follow the dictates of Rule 4.1. The study approached the question in two separate ways — first, respondents were presented with the client's "unconditional request", and if they refused the unconditional request, a follow up "conditional request" was offered.

A. Client's Unconditional Request

The client's initial request to the attorney to refrain from disclosing his actual DONS status was simple and straightforward. It contained no reservations or conditions which would allow for disclosure of his actual condition. The lawyers were asked whether they would agree to this request. In an attempt to keep from prompting a socially desirable response, withdrawing from the representation as a response to the client's request was not given as an available option.

In response to the client's request, 62% of the respondents (452 respondents) said that they would not agree to such a request, while 19% (142 respondents) said they would agree with the client's request, and the remaining 19% (140 respondents) were not sure how they would respond. Thus, almost one-fifth of the respondents reported that faced with the client's request, they would be willing to engage in the client's fraudulent settlement scheme in violation of Rule 4.1. However the majority of respondents reported that they would comply with the dictates of Rule 4.1 and would not agree to join in the fraudulent scheme.

Under tort law, the client himself has a duty to correct his former girlfriend's mistaken belief. Going forward with the negotiation without disclosing that he does not actually have the DONS disease would constitute fraudulent misrepresentation. By extension, the client's request that his lawyer refrain from disclosing his actual DONS status to induce a settlement would constitute a request to engage in a fraudulent settlement scheme on his behalf.

Any attempt by the attorney to knowingly assist the client in the commission of a fraudulent settlement agreement is fraught with serious problems. If in the negotiation the lawyer were to make an actual misrepresentation of the client's DONS status or request money as reimbursement for any future DONS-related symptoms, the lawyer would violate Rule 4.1(a). If the lawyer made no attempt to correct the former girlfriend's mistaken belief, the lawyer would violate Rule 4.1(b). Thus, under the Rules, the only proper course of conduct in the hypothetical scenario was to refuse the client's request to conceal his DONS status in settlement negotiations.

B. Client's Conditional Follow-up Request

Lawyers who either refused to follow the client's initial request or were not sure what they would do in response to the client's request (a total of 592 respondents) were asked a follow-up question in which the hypothetical situation was changed slightly. In this instance, the client requested that the attorney disclose his true DONS status only if directly asked about it. Thus, if opposing counsel specifically questioned whether the client had DONS, the lawyer had the client's permission to disclose the truth.

While this condition allowed for disclosure of the critical fact in a limited circumstance, it did not change the basic analysis of the appropriate course of conduct for the lawyer heading into the negotiation. The primary negotiation strategy still required going forward without correcting the opposing party's mistaken belief and the lawyer still had the duty to correct the adverse party's mistaken belief. As discussed earlier, doing otherwise would be a fraudulent mis-representation. As with the initial request, failure to disclose the client's DONS status would still induce a negotiated settlement based on a false premise, in vio-lation of Rule 4.1. Again, the only proper course of conduct in the conditional disclosure scenario was to refuse the client's request.

When this subset of 592 respondents was presented with the conditional request to refrain from disclosing the truth unless asked directly, 64% indicated they would refuse to comply, 13% indicated that they would agree, and 23% replied that they were not sure what they would do. Over one-third of this subset of respondents indicated that they either would definitely or potentially violate Rule 4.1 in this situation.

C. Summary

When faced with a client's request to engage in a fraudulent settlement nego-tiation scheme, 30% of the entire set of respondents agreed to do so in one of the two situations—both a clear violation of Rule 4.1. Only 50% followed the proper course of action and refused both client requests, and the remaining 20% were not sure how they would respond to one or both requests. . . . [T]he fact that nearly one-third of the respondents agreed to engage in sanctionable professional misconduct is unacceptable. Moreover, the fact that only one-half of the respondents properly applied Rule 4.1 is alarming. . . .

For several reasons our findings likely under-represent the number of attor-neys who would violate the Rule during actual negotiations. First, if those respon-dents who responded that they were uncertain were forced to make a choice, it is possible that a fair number would choose to violate the Rule. Moreover, some of those who indicated that they would follow the Rule might make a different choice in practice, where clients exert pressure and lawyers may be tempted to place their ability to achieve results with the resulting financial gains over adherence to the Rule. It is unlikely, however, that those who agreed to join the client's scheme would do otherwise in actual negotiations; in the pressured world of practice, adherence to ethical rules tends to decrease rather than rise.

The results of the survey were disturbing to Professors Hinshaw and Alberts. The apparent willingness of so many attorneys to perpetuate fraud in behalf of a client confirms that there is considerable confusion about what the ethics rules permit or require regarding preserving client confidences and the duty of pursuing a client stated interests. The results may also indicate that many lawyers believe that the type of fraud presented in the scenario is commonplace in practice and generally accepted behavior among attorneys when confronted with client expectations of lawyer complicity. Indeed, lawyers' answers to ques-tions about common practices included in the survey demonstrated this belief. The perception that such lawyer behavior is widespread normalizes conduct and perpetuates it. Hinshaw and Alberts later in their article propose clarifying changes in the ethics rules, as well as greater enforcement and continuing education of lawyers.

In the absence of these suggested reforms, what is an attorney to do when asked by a client to mislead the other side in a negotiation? This is the question addressed in the next excerpt.

❖ **Robert H. Mnookin, Scott R. Peppet & Andrew S. Tulumello,** *Beyond Winning: Negotiating to Create Value in Deals and Disputes*

282 (Harvard University Press, 2000)

What If My Client Wants Me to Mislead the Other Side?

Seek to Understand the Client's Choice

If a client is asking you to mislead the other side, the first step, as always, is to try to understand why. In what ways does this request make sense for the client? Put yourself in her shoes. If you were the client, would you propose the same thing that she's proposing?

By identifying the incentives that motivate your client to ask you to mislead the other side, you may be able to relate better to the client as you talk about his request. The key is to learn why the client thinks you should manipulate the truth. What does he see as the advantages? What does he see as the risks? What are the client's concerns? By listening and demonstrating understanding, you can often draw out the client to talk about the underlying choice of strategy.

Raise Your Concerns Explicitly

Lawyers also must learn to discuss ethical dilemmas explicitly. You can find yourself in a very uncomfortable situation if neither you nor your client is willing to discuss ethical conflicts. Learning to have such conversations productively is a critical skill.

If your client asks you to mislead the other side, you should negotiate with her and try to help her understand your views. You must explain that you don't want to violate established rules of professional responsibility, and that you don't want to do something that isn't in your client's best interests. You don't want to go against your personal beliefs, and you don't want to do something that hurts your reputation. By explaining your interests and perspective—while continuing to demonstrate understanding for the client's views—you can begin a conversation about the dilemma you face.

Ed's lawyer, for example, would want to explain that in the face of questioning by Mr. Jenks he would either have to tell the truth about a competing offer or refuse to answer a direct question. "That would probably give away the issue right there," Ed might say. "Couldn't you just say 'No, he has no other offers'?" "No," his lawyer might explain. "I can't lie about a material piece of information like that. And I've got to tell you, it would probably amount to fraud. Given that sooner or later he's going to find out whether you're working again, lying about it could cause serious problems later."

Remember That Your Reputation Is a Valuable Asset

Clients sometimes want to use a lawyer's reputation for honesty as a cover for their own unethical behavior. If a lawyer is known for telling the truth, this reputation can be a perfect smokescreen for throwing the other side off track. If your client persuades you to lie, however he may take advantage of your reputation for his own short-term gain, disregarding the long-term effect on your career and well-being.

We learned of a recent example in a divorce case. After discovering that his wife had hired an attorney, the husband hired an outstanding family lawyer—known in his community as an honorable problem-solver. The two lawyers had done many divorce cases together in the past and had built up a great deal of trust. Ordinarily they did not rely on formal discovery procedures, choosing instead to exchange information informally. This saved their clients a great deal of time and money.

The husband in this case insisted that his lawyer not disclose certain financial information to the other side unless forced to do so through formal discovery. The husband's lawyer faced a real ethical dilemma. When his colleague proposed that they informally exchange information as they had in the past, what was he to do? He knew that if he disclosed partially but withheld the information in question, it would go against his counterpart's clear expectation and would ultimately hurt his own reputation as an honest negotiator. At the same time, he was obligated to obey his client's wishes not to disclose the financial information.

Ultimately, he chose to refuse to engage in the informal information exchange process with the other attorney. This implicitly signaled, of course, that this divorce was unlike the others they had negotiated together before. Many lawyers had told us that in such situations they are likely to signal to the other side that the normal rules of play are suspended and that the baseline professional ethics rules are all that should be expected. One lawyer told of a case in which he entered the room where the negotiation was to occur, sat down across the table from a long-time colleague, and simply said "On guard." Both knew immediately that their normal collaborative rules of engagement were temporarily suspended.

Such signaling raises difficult ethical issues, of course. On the one hand, why should a client be able to gain distributive advantage by hiding behind his lawyer's reputation? Doesn't that disserve the attorney's other clients who rely on his problem-solving abilities? By refusing to engage in the informal discovery process that was based on trust, doesn't the lawyer merely give his client what the client would get from any other attorney that *didn't* have a reputation for honesty? On the other hand, is it ever legitimate for an attorney *not* to do something that would maximize the distributive benefit for a given client? If a lawyer's approach conflicts with his client's, would the best approach be simply to withdraw?

In our view, withdrawal is one possible solution. In practice, as we've discussed, however, lawyers *and clients* face real financial and logistical constraints that may make withdrawal unattractive. Once an attorney has worked with a client over time, the lawyer has built up a store of knowledge and experience relevant only to that client, and the client has invested time and money in educating his lawyer about the particulars of the case. Under such circumstances, rather than withdraw, it seems reasonable for an attorney to signal to the other side that for this negotiation they should not expect anything beyond what the formal discovery rules require.

The lesson we draw, however, is that lawyer-client preparation is essential. As a lawyer-client relationship begins, an attorney must be clear with his client about his problem-solving orientation and what that requires. If a lawyer is unambiguous about what he will and won't do, the client can make an informed choice about which lawyer to retain. Such ethical conflicts are thus much less likely to arise.

Problem—Hiring a Lawyer to Hide the Truth

Assume that you are a third-year law student who has landed a plum job as an associate with a boutique intellectual property law firm to commence after graduation. You were to be paid $160,000 a year. The written offer, which the law firm prepared and you accepted, was an absolute commitment on the part of the firm with no conditions. Since your acceptance, economic conditions have worsened and the type of litigation in which the firm primarily engages has declined. A couple of weeks ago you met with the managing partner, Bob Higgins, who cordially explained the circumstances and indicated that the firm needed to cancel the employment arrangement but wanted to be fair with you. You indicated that you relied on the early offer and turned down other employment offers during the law school interview season, which is now concluded. You also truthfully revealed that you had rented a new apartment and purchased a car in reliance on the employment agreement. You acknowledged that economic conditions have tightened since you accepted the offer, but pointed out that the offer was unconditional and that the bad economic times would make it difficult for you to find a comparable position.

You agreed that you would meet again with Mr. Higgins in a few weeks to discuss severance terms. While discussing your situation with your intellectual property law professor, he told you of an alum who recently was appointed as general counsel for a tech startup and asked him for a recommendation of a graduating student who might be interested in working with him. He passed on your name, and you have been offered the position at a starting salary of $120,000 to commence immediately following the Bar exam. Although the position pays less than the law firm job, you are thrilled because of the excitement of the startup and the unique opportunity it presents, as well as the fact that the other job offer was withdrawn. You plan to accept the associate general counsel position. However, you first want to talk with Mr. Higgins to see what you can work out with him regarding the breach of your employment contract by his law firm. You are truly concerned about your immediate economic needs and your heavy student loan debt. Although Higgins's law firm may not be expanding, you are aware of its high per-partner income and the firm's solid economic base. You would like to get as much from them as you can. You know that if you personally negotiate with Mr. Higgins, you will feel compelled to tell him about your new job offer, even if he doesn't ask. If you do that, though, your severance package won't be worth much.

Can you hire a lawyer to negotiate for you and not tell the lawyer about your pending job offer? If you do tell the lawyer about the other job offer, would she be acting unethically not to disclose it if Higgins does not ask if you have other offers? If Higgins does ask about what you have done to mitigate damages, then must your attorney reveal the other offer? Can your lawyer insist on revealing the terms of the other job offer even if you instruct her not to do so? If you were to switch roles, would you agree to negotiate on behalf of someone in these circumstances? What would you advise your client to do and why?

Professor Longan, in the next reading, provides hypotheticals that highlight some of the ethical issues in negotiation. In considering these hypotheticals, he analyzes the ABA Model Rules and opinions on point, but goes beyond these in urging consideration of both what is wise and most effective in the long run.

❖ Patrick E. Longan, *ETHICS IN SETTLEMENT NEGOTIATIONS: FOREWORD*

52 Mercer L. Rev. 810 (2001)

A. The Limits of Representations

You represent the plaintiff in a breach of contract action. You are seeking lost profits. What can you say in negotiations about the lost profits if:

1. Your expert has come to no conclusion about their cause.
2. Your expert has told you the breach did not cause the lost profits.
3. Your expert has given you a range between $2,000,000 and $5,000,000 for the lost profits.
4. Your expert says the maximum lost profit is $2,000,000.
5. You do not have an expert; your client says the loss was $5,000,000.

It is common in negotiation for each side to emphasize the strength and persuasiveness of its evidence. On the other hand, each side in discovery has the opportunity to explore the other side's evidence. In this scenario, each side would be entitled to a report and a deposition of the other's testifying expert. Any statement about the expert would be a statement of fact. Because of the importance of expert testimony to this case, any statement of this sort would be material. The lawyer must be careful to tell only the truth to avoid violating Rule 4.1. Good lawyers, however, will test the assertions in discovery, consistent with the now-famous Russian proverb, "Trust, but verify."

Beyond the rules of ethics, however, it is proper to ask what the best strategy is for a lawyer in this negotiation. Here, any statement about the expert's conclusions probably will be the subject of discovery. If the statement is found to be false, the lawyer who made it will lose some credibility. That loss, which will likely survive the conclusion of this particular case and affect negotiations with the other lawyer in future cases, will cause these future negotiations to be more strained, more lengthy, and probably less fruitful. To the extent that the lawyer gains a reputation for untruthfulness as a result of statements about the expert, the lawyer may be impeding all his or her future negotiations. In other words, this hypothetical involves a happy situation in which it is both the right strategy and the smart strategy to tell the truth. . . .

In this breach of contract action, can you:

1. tell opposing counsel that you will not settle for less than $3.5 million when you have authority to settle for $2 million?
2. tell opposing counsel that five major buyers stopped buying from your client after the breach, knowing that they stopped buying for other reasons?

[C]omment 2 to Model Rule [4.1] defines statements about settlement authority not to be material. Technically, therefore, the lawyer should feel free to lie about his or her authority. Another strategy, however, and one that may be more effective in the long run, is simply to deflect any questions of authority with statements such as, "You know neither one of us can discuss our authority—let's talk about a fair settlement of this case." The reason a deflection may be more effective in the long run is the same reason exaggerations about the expert's conclusions may cause long term harm. You may be ethically permitted to lie about your authority, but if you do it, and the other lawyer catches you at it, he or she will not trust you again.

The misleading statement about the lost customers raises a persistent and subtle issue for lawyers about the use of language. The statement is literally true. These customers have left, and they did so at a time after the defendant's breach. The only reason the statement is made, however, is in the hope that the defendant will make the leap and conclude that the customers left because of the breach or, at least, that the plaintiff will attempt to prove that they did. The statement is, therefore, an intentionally misleading, sly use of language. It is reminiscent of former President Clinton's response to a question before the grand jury about his deposition testimony: "It depends on what the meaning of is is." The lawyer who engages in this type of deception is more clever, perhaps, than a straightforward liar, but the lawyer is no less worthy of condemnation. Once again, however, we can rely on the power of reputation to deter lawyers (at least those who care about their reputations) from engaging in these tactics. Word gets around.

B. Disclosure of Factual Errors

The second hypothetical concerned a duty to disclose facts when the other lawyer has made a settlement offer containing obvious mistakes:

You represent the husband in a divorce action. You receive from opposing counsel a proposed property settlement with the following errors: (1) a transcription error that undervalues an asset; (2) an arithmetical error that undervalues an asset; (3) a valuation by purchase price of an asset when market value is much higher. All the errors work to your client's advantage. What, if anything, should you do about them?

To the extent that the first two errors are "scrivener's errors" (the other lawyer missed a typographical error or failed to add the numbers correctly), the lawyer has the duty to correct the mistakes. The third problem may raise more difficult issues because the error may come from opposing counsel's conscious but erroneous judgment about what valuation is best for his or her client. Can the lawyer in the hypothetical take advantage of his or her adversary's error in judgment?

The question is a species of a fundamental, recurring question in an adversarial system. The lawyer owes a primary duty of loyalty to the client. In most respects, the lawyer is not expected to be his or her brother's keeper. One answer to the particular ethical question presented is to say that it is not the interesting or important question. The client is not perpetrating a fraud or a crime by taking advantage of a bad lawyer on the other side. There is no duty to disclose under Rule 4.1.

Abiding by the rules of ethics, however, is necessary but not always sufficient for good lawyering. Ethically, the lawyer need not correct every misstep of opposing counsel. But sometimes correcting the mistake would be the wise thing to do. For example, if the mistakes involved in the proposal were fundamental mistakes, ones that under the law of contract the opposing party would provide grounds later to void the transaction, then the lawyer may best serve his or her client by alerting opposing counsel to the mistakes now. If the parties to the transaction will have a continuing relationship, such as shared responsibility for minor children, the best strategy might be to correct the mistakes and buy some trust, which may be sorely needed later. Here, as in many situations, ethics tells you the options available, but the lawyer must still exercise good judgment among the options.

C. Disclosure of Legal Errors

The final hypothetical . . . highlighted the fact that Model Rule 4.1 forbids a lawyer from making a material misrepresentation about the law. The hypothetical does so in the context of an interaction with a young lawyer who is operating under a mistake about the state of the law:

> You represent the defendant in a personal injury case. In negotiation with plaintiff's counsel (a young, relatively inexperienced lawyer), it becomes clear to you that this lawyer believes his or her client's potential recovery is limited by a tort reform statute. You know that this statute has been found unconstitutional by the state supreme court. May you, and should you, correct opposing counsel's mistake about the law?

Most practicing lawyers would not think twice about taking advantage of this younger lawyer. Again, the client is not perpetrating a fraud or a crime, and the client might be very happy to save some money because his or her adversary's lawyer is clueless. No rule of legal ethics requires the lawyer to be the opposing party's lawyer also. No rule requires that lawyers settle cases only on "fair" terms.

Again, however, the strictly ethical inquiry cannot end the discussion. For example, lawyers might find that taking advantage of the mistake in particular circumstances, such as a horrific injury to a young child, would be morally wrong although ethically permissible. The lawyer is free to counsel the client about nonlegal matters, such as the morality of leaving the injured child unable to obtain the life-long care the child needs. The lawyer is even free to seek to withdraw if assisting in a settlement under these circumstances would be repugnant to the lawyer. Here, as in the prior examples, the best lawyers consider all the circumstances and determine first whether the rules of ethics require a particular course of action and, if they do not, what under all the circumstances is the wisest choice. . . .

Questions

1. Assuming that a lawyer can lie about a client's bottom line and matters of value in negotiation without violating ethical rules, when might doing so be a good tactic, and when not? What is the tactical advantage of candor? If there is reason to be candid when not ethically required, should it be selective candor depending on the situation or is a uniform policy of candor more advantageous? Why?
2. Should the client have a say in what is revealed in the above hypotheticals? If you disagree with your client, must the client's wishes govern? (See the next section, Client Control vs. Lawyer Integrity, for discussion of these issues.)
3. Is there any reason to behave differently toward people in negotiation than you would in other interactions? In other words, what distinguishes negotiation from interpersonal interactions generally? (For an interesting analysis of this question, see Cohen 2001.)
4. If you are representing a client injured in an automobile accident, need you reveal the client's death following the filing of the claim, but prior to finalizing settlement? Why or why not? (See Kentucky Bar Assn. v. Geisler, 938 S.W.2d 578 (1997).)
5. How does what Rule 4.1 requires of lawyers compare with your personal moral values? If your personal ethics are more restrictive than the rules, is there a risk that your interests might conflict with those of your client? This topic is covered in the following section.

Problem

You are defending an insured driver in a serious auto accident that injured the plaintiff, a young man in his late teens. You properly insisted that the plaintiff be examined by a doctor of your choosing paid by your client, the insurance company. Your doctor discovered something that the youth's own physician had missed: a life-threatening aortic aneurysm that could burst at any time, and had likely been caused by the accident. Revealing the results of a physical exam obtained by the defense is not generally required in your jurisdiction. If the plaintiff learns about the aneurysm it will result in a much higher settlement to be paid by your client. Your client instructs you not to reveal the aneurysm.

Do you have an ethical obligation to reveal the aneurysm? (See Spaulding v. Zimmerman, 263 Minn. 346, 116 N.W.2d 704 (1961).)

B. Client Control vs. Lawyer Integrity (Conflicts of Interest)

Ethical issues in negotiation are often compounded for lawyers because their interests are seldom in complete congruity with those of their client's. When lawyers are employed to negotiate for principals, the interests in the timing, costs, trade-offs, goals, and relationships involved in a settlement may be different for the lawyer than for the client. However, lawyers work for clients and, at least to some extent, clients get to call the shots. ABA Model Rule 1.2(a) states that "[a] lawyer shall abide by a client's decisions concerning the objectives of representation . . . and shall consult with the client as to the means by which they are to be pursued. A lawyer shall abide by a client's decision whether to accept an offer of settlement of a matter." This rule distinguishes the end goal, decided by the client, from the means of achieving it, decided by the lawyer in consultation with the client. The rule is clear that the decision whether to settle and under what terms is the client's choice. The application of the rule to how lawyers should negotiate is less clear.

We suggested earlier, in discussing cultural identities, that being a lawyer identifies you with what may be considered a cultural subgroup. Another way to view the relationship between lawyers is to analogize the relationship among lawyers to a "community." Whether viewed as a community or a subculture, lawyers have long-term relationships with one another and repeatedly interact in ways that have their own norms of behavior and shared expectations. This may be in contrast to the relationship of clients to the legal/judicial system, which is likely to be a one-time occasion. A potential conflict exists between the client's interest in maximizing gain from a one-time transaction or settlement and a lawyer's longer term interest in maintaining credible and amicable relations with other lawyers. The gain from deceit and lying may benefit a client at the expense of the lawyer's reputation and relationships within the community.

Both economic and ethical considerations, as well as the priorities and cultural values of your client, may conflict with your ideals and commitment to self-defined professional integrity and honesty. Preserving your client's confidences may prevent you from candidly discussing with an opposing lawyer how your client has asked you to negotiate or giving your counterpart warning that she should be cautious.

Questions

6. If a client you represent in the sale of a business instructs you to make a first offer of $1 million to eventually sell for his target of $500,000, can you refuse because you feel the bloated offer compromises your integrity? If you do refuse, over the client's objection, is the representation necessarily ended? Can you make the first offer to opposing counsel with a wink and not be breaching a client confidence?
7. Does Model Rule 1.2(a), which divides bargaining decision responsibilities along an end-means line (client decides the end goal, lawyer decides the means of obtaining client's goal), provide a helpful distinction for you?

8. Is there a cleaner end-means line when representing an injured tort claimant than when representing a businessperson in a commercial transaction? Is an insurance company that retains a lawyer to defend a personal injury claim more likely to control the means of lawyer negotiating than is an injured plaintiff? Do different ethics rules apply to lawyers depending on who employs them?

A conflict may also exist between a client's personal economic needs, which drive her to value an attractive settlement offer more than societal interests, and a lawyer's ideals, which may focus more on broader policy concerns. This conflict can cut the other way if an idealistic client wants to reject a settlement on principle when the lawyer covets the immediate fee payoff.

Consider the settlement situation described in the following problem and the conflicts it raises.

Problem — Secret Settlements

E.J. Boyette was a forty-eight-year-old computer programmer when he died, leaving a wife and five kids. . . . Shortly after his forty-seventh birthday he noticed that he was getting tired easily and was often short of breath. He made an appointment with his doctor, who referred him to a cardiologist. After extensive tests, the cardiologist recommended surgical placement of a new kind of heart valve . . . that had been highly praised in all the medical journals.

At first everything seemed fine. Boyette was released from the hospital, . . . But after three months Boyette's physical condition began deteriorating quickly. In another month he was dead. His widow consulted attorney Andrea Hardy, partner in a small firm that represents plaintiffs in injury cases. . . .

Now eighteen months later, after extensive discovery and a review of thousands of documents, Andrea and her paralegal have just found a memo that seems to show that the company knew its first-generation heart valves had design flaws that could cause some patients to get worse and even die. . . . They quickly draft a new and very specific demand for the other side to produce more documents, which Andrea believes will include the smoking gun she can use to prove that the manufacturer knew the heart valves were defective. . . .

On the appointed day for delivery, Andrea is surprised to find Burger himself [chief defense counsel] at her office. He asks if they can talk.

"Look," he says, "I'll hand over these documents in a minute. I think you know what's in them. But there's something I'd like you to consider. We'll offer you five million dollars right now to settle the case. There are just two conditions: the amount we pay must be secret, and the documents you've gotten from us must be returned. All of them, including copies." Andrea is dumbstruck. Until this moment Burger had maintained his client's innocence and never breathed a word about settlement. She knows $5 million is a lot more than she's likely to get for the case at trial, even with punitive damages. And the fee would easily be the largest her firm has ever received. She's sure the documents in George Burger's briefcase include the smoking gun she'd been looking for.

> Andrea tells Burger that she'll have to review the documents and discuss things with her client before making a decision. . . . Andrea reads three memos . . . that conclusively prove that the manufacturer knew that the heart valve's design was defective before Mr. Boyette's valve was implanted. One memo summarizes 107 incidents in which the valve was considered a contributing cause in a patient's death. The other two discuss how the company should deal with the design flaw, eventually concluding that nothing should be done to take it off the market until a new product could be developed to replace it. (See Richard Zitrin and Carol M. Langford, *The Moral Compass of the American Lawyer* 183 (1999).)
>
> What would you do, if you were Andrea?

Some state laws ban secret settlements to prevent protection of public health and safety. What are the arguments for and against statutory restrictions on secret settlements involving claims of defective products, fraud, and malpractice? Should lawyers be required to report such settlements? Why or why not? (See Doré 1999; Zitrin 1999.)

C. Fee Arrangements and Settlement

Attorneys' fees and how they are determined may influence how lawyers negotiate on behalf of both plaintiffs and defendants. Throughout this book we have emphasized the importance of determining and satisfying needs in order to reach agreement. Although attorneys are ethically bound to put the needs of clients first and avoid conflicts of interest, an attorney's economic needs and fee arrangements may play a role in settlement negotiations. Fees contingent on a negotiated outcome, whether calculated as a percentage of the amount a plaintiff obtains, or a reverse contingency based on the amount the defendant saves, can effect decisions. Fees based on time spent can also influence the pace of negotiations and the appeal of a speedy outcome. Client and attorney interests regarding settlement may be incongruent.

Professor Herbert Kritzer has written extensively about lawyer practices and the effect of contingency fee arrangements. He interviewed attorneys in Toronto, Canada, and analyzed data from a survey of 1,382 lawyers in multiple jurisdictions in the United States regarding the impact of fees on settlement negotiations. He observed that to understand the dynamics of the settlement process, the interests of all involved in the litigation must be considered. A number of responding attorneys mentioned the importance of taking into account the interest of the opposing lawyer. For example, a litigation partner in one large firm explained that "[i]f you can satisfy the lawyer with regard to his fee, you'll be a lot closer to settlement." Another lawyer was quoted as stating that to achieve settlement, "you need to provide an incentive for the opposing lawyer." (Kritzer 1987 342)

Kritzer is careful to mention,

> I am not suggesting that lawyers engage in questionable actions for financial gain. The argument is more subtle: Lawyers, like all of us, when forced to make a choice for which there is no definitive answer, will tend to select the option that is in their own interest. In other words, the financial incentives of their work will often influence the decisions, and it is not coincidental that they will personally benefit from these choices. Thus, although the plaintiffs' bar may truly believe that the contingent fee is the poor man's key to the courthouse door, this belief is shaped by the fact that the key to the courthouse also brings clients—and therefore a livelihood—to the plaintiffs' lawyers. Elsewhere I have pointed out that the relationship between lawyers and clients is shaped by professional, personal, and business considerations, the last, at their most basic, meaning income (and income streams.) (Kritzer 1987 342)

His interviews and observations lead him to raise a caution about a potential conflict of interest between contingent fee attorneys and their clients.

> Contingent fee lawyers in cases with modest amounts at stake have an incentive to arrive quickly at a settlement, even if that settlement is not the best for the client. Whether this means that the fee arrangement directly affects the amount of time the lawyer spends on settlement negotiations (although I could in fact find no systematic difference in time spent on such activities between hourly and contingent fee lawyers), the same theoretical considerations apply to the content of the actual negotiation. Specifically, since the contingent fee lawyer is to receive a share of the ultimate recovery, she has an incentive to see to it that the recovery can in fact be shared.

One of the effects of a contingent fee arrangement on the scope of the settlement agreement is that the non-monetary settlement possibilities may be limited because the contingent amount is derived from a percentage of the monetary recovery. A contingent fee lawyer who sought nonmonetary resolutions of her clients' cases, even if those resolutions were better from the clients' perspective, would have difficulty collecting a fee unless some alternate payment method were available for such settlements. In other words, a contingent fee based on a percentage of the amount received only works if the negotiated settlement is quantifiable and devisable. As a means to counter this limiting influence on creative, problem-solving approaches, Kritzer suggests the possibility of fee shifting, whereby the defendant pays the plaintiff's attorney for his time, or a central fund, created by taxing contingent fees, from which the lawyer could receive compensation. (See Herbert M. Kritzer, "Fee Arrangements and Negotiation," 21 Law & Society Rev. 341 (1987); see also Kritzer, *Risks, Reputations and Rewards: Contingency Fee Legal Practice in the United States* (2004).)

Questions

9. What types of non-monetary settlements might be better from the client's perspective, but not necessarily in the economic interests of the contingent fee lawyer? What is the meaning of the saying that "all contingent fee settlements need to be divisible by three"?

10. Would Kritzer's suggestion that contingent fees be replaced by a fee shifting method where the defendant pays the plaintiff's attorney for time spent or that a tax on contingent fees be collected to create a central lawyers' fee fund eliminate attorney-client conflicts of interest in settlement negotiations or create new ones? Would you support these "reforms"?

11. Are ethical concerns any less when a client seeks the most speedy, least costly resolution of a dispute and is represented by a litigator who bills by the hour? How might these potential attorney/client conflicts be addressed in a negotiation?

D. Good Faith vs. Threats, Exposure, and Coercion

Although it can be hoped that lawyers will be retained to negotiate only when the client desires to reach an agreement and bargain in good faith, there may be occasions when settlement is not the goal or when compromise for purposes of agreement is not an option. On occasion a client may pursue negotiation for purposes of delay or distraction, to obtain information from a competitor, or to harass. As previously discussed, clients have the right to decide the purpose and objectives of negotiation, but lawyers can usually decline to represent a party or can withdraw. Indeed, ethical rules may require the lawyer to withdraw if continued representation will result in violation of ethical rules. (See ABA Model Rule 1.16(a)(1).)

There is no general ethical duty to bargain in good faith, but if the parties have agreed by contract to negotiate in good faith, for example, before ending a business relationship or going to court, they may be held to their bargain. In some labor management disputes under the National Labor Relations Act, 29 U.S.C.A. 158(d), there may be a good faith negotiation requirement. Rules of court and court orders may also require "good faith" negotiation or mediation before a dispute will be heard.

Even if good faith in negotiation is not required, ethical rules and contract law limit certain types of "bad faith" bargaining. A prohibition against bad faith negotiation is indicated by ABA Model Rule 4.4, which states:

> *Respect for Rights of Third Persons:* In representing a client, a lawyer shall not use means that have no substantial purpose other than to embarrass, delay, or burden a third person, or use methods of obtaining evidence that violate the legal rights of such a person.

In addition, Model Rule 4.1, *Truthfulness in Statements to Others,* and Model Rule 3.1, *Meritorious Claims and Contentions,* also provide ethical limits on the use of threatening criminal prosecution.

Tort law, contract law, and criminal law may further restrict the use of threats, extortion, and some forms of coercion. However, threatening to file a civil lawsuit to resolve the matter in dispute when the lawyer has a good faith basis for the claim is not prohibited. (See *Restatement, Second of Contracts,* Sec. 175, Comment (b) (1981).) Indeed, every legal negotiation carries, at least, an implicit threat that if agreement is not reached, further action will be taken or alternatives will be pursued. Adversarial negotiations and pressure from clients may tempt lawyers to go further and use threats of unrelated legal action or exposure of wrongdoing if negotiation demands are not met. The law, rather than ethical rules, may be used to decide when threatening exposure of wrongdoing or a ruinous lawsuit becomes criminal extortion, and also when lying becomes fraud.

A threat by a lawyer to punch an opponent in the nose if a demand is not met is clearly unethical and criminal. A threat to do something adverse to your opponent, even if not unlawful, only for the purpose of gaining an advantage in a negotiation, presents more challenging issues. For example, deciding to expose or not expose an opposing lawyer's unethical behavior in conjunction with a negotiation may place you between the proverbial "rock and a hard place." If, after calling the lawyer on the bad conduct, you do not report it and obtain a favorable outcome, opposing counsel or his client with second thoughts about the settlement, may claim you threatened to report only to obtain a negotiation advantage. (You and opposing counsel may both have to answer to the Bar.) Power imbalances may also create questions of intimidation in the negotiation process, as might the otherwise-legitimate threat of filing a class action against a modest-sized company if monetary demands are not met. In addition to being ethically risky, threats may jeopardize the enforceability of a settlement because of duress or other contract grounds for voiding or rescinding agreements.

The article that follows addresses some of these issues and is included to help you understand that even though the ethical limits of what lawyers can do in negotiations are murky, tort, contract, and criminal law impose outer limits on negotiation conduct and communications. It explains negotiation constraints, particularly where there is unequal power.

❖ **Robert S. Adler & Elliot M. Silverstein,** *WHEN DAVID MEETS GOLIATH: DEALING WITH POWER DIFFERENTIALS IN NEGOTIATIONS*

5 Harv. Negot. L. Rev. 1 (2000)

Although the superior bargaining power of one party, standing alone, does not generally provide the basis for invalidating an agreement, the law does set limits within which bargainers must operate. These limits apply both with respect to the terms that can be negotiated and to the methods one can use to influence an opponent to agree to the terms. They are premised on the assumption that at some point in the bargaining process, power advantages can produce inequities so pronounced that the law must step in to protect the weak. In negotiations involving power imbalances, most abuses arise when the stronger party, either through threats or other overt displays of power, intimidates the other into entering an agreement so one-sided that it offends reasonable sensibilities. Of course, not all bargaining abuses result from overt power displays. Some arise from shifting the balance of power by exploiting trust or employing deceit.

Depending on the nature of the abuse, the law may take different approaches—regulating modestly where "arm's length" conditions exist or expansively where a "special relationship" requires protection for particularly vulnerable individuals. Where special relationships exist, special protections apply.

A. Undue Influence

When a relationship of trust and dependency between two or more parties exists, the law typically polices the relationship closely and imposes especially stringent duties on the dominant parties. . . . Contract law imposes . . . duties in the case of agreements involving undue influence in special relationships. Where one party—because of family position, business connection, legal authority or other circumstances—gains extraordinary trust from another party the courts will scrutinize any agreements between them with great care to ensure fairness. Common examples of special relationships include guardian-ward, trustee-beneficiary, agent-principal, spouses, parent-child, attorney-client, physician-patient, and clergy-parishioner. To treat negotiations in these settings as arm's length interactions would invite "unfair persuasion" by the dominant parties either through threats, deception, or misplaced trust. Accordingly, the law imposes special obligations on those who play the dominant role in such relationships, requiring them to exercise good faith and to make full disclosure of all critical facts when negotiating agreements with dependent parties. In determining whether a dominant party in a special relationship exerted undue influence, the courts generally look to the fairness of the contract, the availability of independent advice, and the vulnerability of the dependent party. An agreement entered into as a result of undue influence is voidable by the victim.

B. Protections in Arm's Length Transactions

Under the "bargain theory" of contracts, parties negotiate at arm's length to exchange consideration. An arm's length transaction is one in which the parties stand in no special relationship with each other, owe each other no special duties, and each acts in his or her own interest. The vast majority of contracts fall within the arm's length category, which means that no special obligations of disclosure, fair dealing or good faith are generally required. This is not to suggest that parties are free to operate without rules, but it does mean that they are accorded substantial leeway in negotiating contracts. They certainly maintain the freedom to assume even foolish and shortsighted contractual obligations, so long as they do so knowingly and voluntarily. Once one of the parties acts in a patently abusive manner, however, the law does provide protection, as, for example, with fraud, duress, and unconscionability.

1. Fraud

Negotiated agreements, to be binding, must be entered into by the parties in a knowing and voluntary manner. Lies undermine agreements by removing the "knowing" element from the bargain. That is, one induced by misrepresentations to purchase a relatively worthless item of personal property typically buys the product "voluntarily"—in fact, eagerly—with enthusiasm generated by the false promise of the product's value. The catch is that because of the defrauder's lies, the victim has unfairly lost the opportunity to "know" the precise nature of what he or she has bought. Lies of this nature clearly alter the normal contractual dynamic, unfairly shifting power from the victim to the defrauder. Because of the dramatic impact that fraud has on the power balance in negotiations, we necessarily review this doctrine.

In its classic formulation, common law fraud requires five elements: (1) a false representation of a material fact made by the defendant, (2) with knowledge or belief as to its falsity, (3) with an intent to induce the plaintiff to rely on the representations, (4) justifiable reliance on the misrepresentation by the plaintiff, and (5) damage or injury to the plaintiff by the reliance. Fraud entitles the victim to void the transaction and permits him or her to pursue restitution or tort damages. A false representation may be made in several ways—through a positive statement, through misleading conduct, or by concealing a fact that the defrauder has a duty to disclose. . . .

2. Duress

Coercion, whether express or implied, takes many forms. One party, for example, might threaten to take its business elsewhere if its terms are not met. Another might threaten to file suit if its financial claims are not resolved. Still another might insist that it will no longer provide a discount or expedited delivery if a deal cannot be struck. These threats, designed to exert pressure on an opponent to secure his or her cooperation, generally fall into a category that the law would consider to be hard bargaining, but not illegal. At some point, however, coercion becomes objectionable. How does one distinguish between proper and improper behavior? Unfortunately, there is no clear dividing line. As various commentators and courts have stated, threats per se are acceptable; only wrongful threats are forbidden. What makes one threat "wrongful" and another not depends on the circumstances of each case. To constitute duress, threats must be of a particularly virulent nature. . . .

Threatened action need not be illegal—even acts otherwise legal may constitute duress if directed towards an improper goal. For example, a threat to bring a lawsuit—normally a legitimate form of coercion—becomes abusive if "made with the corrupt intent to coerce a transaction grossly unfair to the victim and not related to the subject of such proceedings." Similarly, a threat to release embarrassing, but true, information about another person, although abhorrent, would not constitute duress (in the form of blackmail) unless accompanied by an improper demand for financial or other favors.

Should negotiators with a decided power advantage feel inhibited from pushing for as hard a bargain as they can in light of the law of duress? Generally, no. Judging from the language in the courts' opinions, hard bargainers should have little to fear from the doctrine of duress. Nothing in the law of duress prevents negotiators from pushing to the limits of their bargaining power or from taking advantage of the economic vulnerabilities or bad luck of their opponents. Trouble arises only when a party makes threats that lapse into the illegal, immoral and unconscionable. Of greater impact on negotiators concerned about legal protections is the law of unconscionability, to which we now turn.

3. Unconscionability

The doctrine of unconscionability functions to protect bargainers of lesser power from overreaching by dominant parties. Invoked in a variety of cases under the Uniform Commercial Code and elsewhere, the term has never been precisely defined, no doubt to provide greater flexibility in its use. . . .

What is an unconscionable contract? Given that the UCC drafters deliberately avoided an explicit definition, one cannot simply and easily capture the concept. At a minimum, an unconscionable contract is one "such as no man in his senses and not under delusion would make on the one hand and no honest and fair man would accept on the other." Unconscionability seeks to prevent two evils: (1) oppression and (2) unfair surprise. In a seminal analysis, Professor Arthur Allen Leff labeled these two concepts "substantive" and "procedural" unconscionability, respectively. Substantive unconscionability includes the actual terms of the agreement; procedural unconscionability refers to the bargaining process between the parties. . . .

Virtually all cases in which unconscionability arises as an issue involve significant disparities in bargaining power, but that, standing alone, rarely justifies a finding of unconscionability according to most courts and commentators. What draws judicial fire is when the party endowed with superior bargaining power imposes an extremely unfair and one-sided agreement on the weaker. In effect, the stronger party oppresses the weaker party through the application of brute power, thereby removing any real "choice" from the victim. Accordingly, inequality of bargaining power seems a generally necessary, but not sufficient, condition of unconscionability. . . .

How concerned should a negotiator be—especially one with superior bargaining power—that pursuing an advantage in a contract will result in a court ruling that the agreement is unconscionable? Our best answer: some, but not much. For the most part, the courts have taken a cautious approach to finding unconscionability in negotiated agreements. The vast majority of successful unconscionability claims involve poor, often unsophisticated, consumers challenging oppressive adhesion contracts foisted on them by retail merchants or credit sellers. . . . No doubt this reflects the general view that persons of greater sophistication suffer less contractual abuse and need less protection. . . .

Questions

12. If you become aware that an opposing lawyer is lying about a material fact, like the amount of medical damages incurred by a client, what should you do? Must you report the lie to the Bar? Should you first confront the lawyer or state your intent to report? Might this be considered a threat? Must you wait until after the negotiation is completed to report the ethical breach?
13. Suppose during a lawsuit you receive a copy of a letter from your opponent instructing one of their witnesses to lie under oath. May you use

this letter in settlement negotiations? May you use the threat of a Bar disciplinary proceeding or a criminal prosecution for obstruction of justice? In exchange for a favorable settlement, may you agree not to report the opponent's instructions? (See ABA Comm. on Ethics and Professional Responsibility, 1992.)

14. There is a generally recognized privilege for statements made in the course of judicial proceedings. (See Silberg v. Anderson, 50 Cal. 3d 205 (1990), holding that a letter with threats of criminal prosecution sent in the course of judicial proceedings is privileged.) Should a threat of physical violence be covered by this privilege?

15. Assume a client asks you to represent her against a prominent, wealthy man she claims had forced sex with her. She wants you to inform him that if he reasonably compensates her, she will not "go public." Would you accept this assignment, and, if so, how might you proceed? Do you risk criminal prosecution or a civil action against you for extortion? (See Flatley v. Mauro, 18 Cal. Rptr. 3d 472 (2004).)

16. The greatest power differentials in negotiation are associated with consumer cases and bargaining where one side is not represented by an attorney. Can undue influence and unconscionability in negotiations occur when all parties are represented by competent lawyers? By definition, if undue influence or unconscionability is found to void a settlement or transaction negotiated by lawyers, do incompetence and malpractice exist?

Problem

Your client is a small business tenant who is involved in a civil dispute with his landlord regarding whether the lease entitles him to use certain space in the basement of the building for the storage of inventory items. You have requested that the landlord give your client access to the space, but the landlord will not agree unless your client pays significantly more rent. During the course of negotiations you discover that the landlord has failed to maintain the property in accordance with local building codes, and this may subject him to criminal prosecution. Can you inform the landlord that you intend to report him to the appropriate authorities if he fails to agree to your settlement terms? (See Peter H. Geraghty, *Making Threats*, ABA 2008, *www.americanbar.org/content/newsletter/publications/youraba/201205article11.html.*)

D. Ethics Reform and New Forms of Practice

1. Reform Proposals and Guidelines

The absence of a rule explicitly prohibiting deception by lawyers during negotiation has disturbed many who feel that a change in lawyer ethics is necessary to promote honesty and correct the lawyer-as-liar image. For decades there has been a debate within the Bar about prohibiting false statements of fact in negotiation, whether material or not. The ABA, when drafting the Model Rules in the early 1980s, considered requiring that lawyers be "fair" in negotiations and not permit "unconscionable" agreements, but these requirements, following much debate, were rejected as untenable. Some believe the ethics requirements should be enhanced to promote honesty and professional integrity. For others, requiring truthfulness in all matters relating to negotiation would be naive and undermine the enforceability of negotiated agreements, particularly when truthfulness regarding nonmaterial facts is not required of those who are not lawyers. An array of proposals has been urged to formally change Model Rule of Professional Conduct 4.1, which prohibits only lying about material facts, and Comment 2, which acknowledges and does not disapprove the use of deception about bottom lines and puffery about value. The rule would be easy to rewrite, but the revisions could be difficult to garner approval and to enforce. (For a specific proposal, see Alfini 1999.)

The Litigation Section of the ABA in 2002 approved Ethical Guidelines for Settlement Negotiations. Although the Guidelines do not change the ABA Model Rules, they do suggest best practices and aspirational goals that go beyond the rules regarding honesty in negotiation. (See *www.americanbar. org/content/dam/aba/migrated/2011_build/dispute_resolution/settlementnegotiations. authcheckdam.pdf.*)

The work of the ABA's Commission on Evaluation of the Rules of Professional Conduct, known as the "Ethics 2000 Commission," resulted in a slight change to Comment 2 of Rule 4.1. The official comment now states that "a party's intentions as to an acceptable settlement of a claim are *ordinarily* not in the category of facts" where candor can be expected. (See Mahoney 2002.)

The prevailing view is opposed to requiring fairness as a matter of lawyer ethics and against prohibiting lawyers from making false statements regarding "nonmaterial" facts. This practical, minimalist view of regulating lawyer negotiation is rooted in our adversary legal system and a lawyer's duties to his client of loyalty and confidentiality. It is also justified by the recognition that the ethical rules serve as a floor of acceptable conduct—not as an ideal or ceiling of civil behavior by lawyers. (See Peter Reilly, "Was Machiavelli Right? Lying in Negotiation and the Art of Defensive Self-Help," 24 Ohio St. J. on Disp. Res. 481 (2009).)

2. Collaborative Law, Cooperative Practice, and Mindfulness

a. Collaborative Law

A movement by some lawyers to commit to a nonadversarial, interest-based approach and increases openness in how they represent clients may have a more profound impact on lawyering ethics and the negotiation of disputes than changes in ethics rules alone. The discontent with the practice of adversarial law, fueled in part by the tension created between the expectation of zealous representation and the desire for personal integrity, has caused some lawyers to explore other models of practice. These efforts have been thoughtful and courageous, as well as controversial. Individual lawyers have reshaped their practices by emphasizing aspects of representation that they find more comfortable and rewarding. We have previously covered the problem-solving approach in contrast to adversarial negotiations. This approach changes the practice paradigm and has implications for personal standards of professional integrity.

Some lawyers have gone further, forming regional groups of practitioners who pledge between them to abstain from litigation and adhere to enhanced standards in their interactions. The most notable example is the collaborative law (CL) movement in domestic relations, where subscribing lawyers contract with clients about standards and limits of representation. A collaborative lawyer will not represent the client if the case goes to court and will not mislead another lawyer during negotiations. (For an explanation of the collaborative practice model see Lawrence 2003.)

The basic elements of CL, as explained by Pauline Tesler one of its founders, are:

- Each party is represented by separate counsel specially trained to provide effective collaborative representation.
- All parties and attorneys sign a binding participation agreement providing that the attorneys are retained solely to facilitate reasonable, efficient settlement of all issues (a "limited purpose" retention).
- The agreement commits all participants to good-faith negotiations, without the threat of or resort to litigation during the pendency of the collaborative process. All parties agree to provide early, voluntary, continuing disclosure of all information that a reasonable decision maker would need to make an informed decision about each issue in the dispute. If a party refuses to disclose information that counsel considers relevant and material to the dispute, collaborative counsel commit to withdraw and/or terminate the process. In other words, although collaborative lawyers remain bound by attorney-client privilege, they will not assist a client to participate in bad faith in the collaborative process or to misuse the process for undue advantage.
- Clients are free to terminate the process at any time and seek third-party dispute resolution, including litigation, but if any party does so, all attorneys are disqualified from participating in any way in nonconsensual third-party proceedings brought by any party to the dispute against any other party or parties.
- If the process is terminated and litigation follows, the collaborative agreement may give the court jurisdiction to make awards of attorneys' fees and costs against any party who has misused the collaborative process for delay, deception, or other bad-faith purposes. The collaborative lawyers, however, could not be witnesses in such proceedings. (See Tesler 2008.)

CL practice is designed to encourage parties to stay in the negotiation process, but this may cause some clients to feel stuck, having invested time and money and then being at risk of losing their lawyer if the collaborative process terminates and the conflict continues. Ethical issues have been raised about attorneys limiting their practice to provide clients with representation only if the other side collaborates. Several states, including Kentucky, Pennsylvania, and New Jersey, have examined CL practice in light of Model Rule of Professional Conduct 1.2(c), which requires informed client consent before lawyers can limit the scope of their practice, and Rule 1.7, which prohibits representation if there is a conflict of interest with the lawyer's responsibilities to others. The CL lawyer's commitment to other CL attorneys, as well as her own interest in a limited practice, raises conflict of interest questions. Several ethics opinions have found that these two provisions create a duty for a CL lawyer to assess whether the limitation and commitment are in the client's best interest and screen cases for CL appropriateness. Clients must be clearly informed about the risks of the process. Although considerable effort has been made by proponents of CL to expand the practice to non-family civil matters, the effort has not met with much success. (See Lande and Mosten 2010; Peppet 2008.) The Colorado Bar Association's Ethics Committee ruled in 2004 that the disqualification provision, a hallmark of CL, violates the lawyer's duty of client loyalty and creates a non-waivable conflict of interest:

> It is the opinion of this Committee that the practice of Collaborative Law violates Rule 1.7(b) of Colorado Rules of Professional Conduct insofar as a lawyer participating in the process enters into a contractual agreement with the opposing party requiring the lawyer to withdraw in the event that the process is unsuccessful. The Committee further concludes that pursuant to Colo. RPC 1.7(c) the client's consent to waive this conflict cannot be validly obtained.

The comment to Rule 1.7 explains:

> Loyalty to a client is also impaired when a lawyer cannot consider, recommend or carry out an appropriate course of action for the client because of the lawyer's other responsibilities or interests. The conflict in effect forecloses alternatives that would otherwise be available to the client.

Despite the controversy over the withdrawal aspect, or perhaps because of it, the Uniform Law Commission in 2009 voted to adopt the Uniform Collaborative Law Act. The Act recognizes CL as an ADR process. It also articulates requirements for informed client consent to participate and a duty upon lawyers to protect the safety of clients from domestic violence during the collaborative process. (See Schepard 2009, *http://lawprofessors.typepad.com/family_law/2009/week30/index.html.*) At the time of this writing, the UCLA has been adopted in Alabama, Arizona, District of Columbia, Hawaii, Maryland, Michigan, Montana, Nevada, New Jersey, Ohio, Texas, Utah, Washington, and introduced in Florida and Massachusetts.

b. Cooperative Law

A variant on CL is known as "cooperative law." Interestingly, the Colorado ethics opinion distinguished cooperative law from CL. It found that cooperative law is not per se unethical because it "lacks the disqualification agreement found in Collaborative Law." As explained by Professor John Lande, its principal advocate, cooperative practice also involves a "participation agreement" between lawyers and parties setting out a negotiation process with a goal of reaching a resolution that is fair for all parties. These agreements vary and may include terms committing to negotiate in good faith, act respectfully toward each other, disclose all relevant information, use jointly retained experts, protect confidentiality of communications, and refrain from formal discovery and contested litigation during negotiation. The participation agreement may provide for use of a mediator or a "cooling off" period before engaging in contested litigation. It may also state that if the parties do litigate, the lawyers would focus solely on the merits of the issues. The process generally begins before the parties file a lawsuit or soon afterward. The process typically involves "four-way meetings" with the parties and lawyers, although some negotiation may be directly between the lawyers or parties when appropriate.

The main difference between cooperative practice and CL, as noted in the Colorado ethics opinion, is that the participation agreement in cooperative practice does not include a "disqualification agreement" or "withdrawal agreement," so that if any party chooses to litigate (or threatens litigation), the lawyers are not disqualified from representing the parties, and there is no need to hire new lawyers. In addition to this distinction, there may be other differences in tailoring the procedure to the particular circumstances. For example, cooperative practitioners may not use four-way meetings as much or involve as many other professionals in the meetings as in collaborative practice. (See Lande 2009.)

c. Mindfulness

Another developing concept and practice that may influence how some lawyers negotiate is "mindfulness" in lawyering. Although difficult to simply describe and pigeonhole, mindfulness derives from meditative qualities that put immediate demands in a larger perspective. Mindfulness builds individual capacity for non-judgmental awareness of ourselves and all around us. It amounts to paying attention, being present, and developing insight through concentration. It is a way of being that focuses the practitioner on the big picture and not only on the discrete transaction of the moment. Mindfulness redirects the context of practice to the integrity of the person and the system, rather than the immediate needs of the situation. Mindfulness focused on ethical decision making and compassion is not necessarily the opposite of being adversarial, but they may be difficult to reconcile. (See generally Riskin 2012.)

Mindfulness is finding its way into law school curriculums, law firm programs, and legal publications. A magazine, *Mindful*, is devoted to it. Some lawyers believe that mindful meditation improves their capacity to practice law and serve clients more effectively and ethically. (See Magee, Making the Case for Mindfulness and the Law, 68, No.3, NWLawyer, Apr/May 2014) In an issue of the *Harvard Negotiation Law Review* dedicated to ADR and mindfulness, Scott Peppet takes on the logical extension of mindfulness, perhaps tongue in cheek, to reach an analogy between the mindful lawyer and a saint or holy man, and then questions whether two saints could negotiate. His article helps put our earlier consideration of Model Rule 4.1 in perspective and recasts the question of whether a lawyer can reconcile personal integrity with the conduct allowed, if not required, by Model Rule 4.1.

❖ **Scott R. Peppet,** *Mindfulness in the Law and ADR: Can Saints Negotiate?*

7 Harv. Negot. L. Rev. 83 (2002)

[I]magine that, at the extreme, a diligent mindfulness practitioner might eventually reach a state of complete dedication to an ethical life. I will call this person a "saint" because she adopts a more conscientious stance toward her relations with the world and others than most of us will ever achieve. Our saint would also have to be sufficiently strong-willed to live up to her moral commitments. She must have developed herself to the point that the contingencies of her life—her history, attachments, psychology, and emotions—no longer lead her to act against these deeply-held beliefs. She is so mindful as to be somewhat frightening.

What sort of ethical commitments would our saint adopt? For the sake of argument, I will assert that at the very least such a person would commit to both honesty and fairness, resolving neither to deceive nor to take advantage of other human beings for her own ends and to respect and take others' interests into account. There is good reason to believe that a very mindful person would adopt such a saintly view of life. Even without turning extensively to religious doctrine, one can imagine that our saint would be consistently non-partisan when it came to her own and others' interests. . . .

Consider the negotiating standards of two holy men, one a willing buyer and the other a willing seller. If their personal commitments to holiness prevented them from making the slightest misrepresentation or from engaging in any abuse of their bargaining positions, how would the ultimate outcome of their negotiations differ from the outcome achieved by two lawyer negotiators? If deceit truly is inherent to negotiation, the outcome achieved by the holy men could not be defined as the product of a negotiation. . . .

Not everyone agrees with this characterization, but it is certainly common. Perhaps the best example of this sort of thinking is, again, Model Rule 4.1's permission of misrepresentations about reservation price. According to the Rule's Comments, misleading statements of this sort are permitted because "under generally accepted conventions in negotiation, certain types of statements ordinarily are not taken as statements of material fact." Although the Rules do not say so explicitly, this Comment seems to imply that barring all types of misrepresentation would demand too much—it would make negotiation as we normally understand it impossible.

I disagree with this view. . . . Although many negotiators may deceive and manipulate, I see nothing that requires one to do so, nor do I think that one can be effective only by doing so. Negotiation requires parties to manage different and sometimes conflicting interests to determine whether a jointly-created outcome can be found that is more satisfying than any self-help alternative. Two saints could honestly disclose their alternatives and reservation values, their interests and priorities, and still face a variety of challenging decisions regarding how best to maximize achievable joint gain and divide the pie. Even for the enlightened there would likely be no easy answer as to whether to give more of the economic surplus in a transaction to the person who needed it more, wanted it more, or deserved it more. Two saints might disagree about how to classify a used car in the "blue book" scheme, or about when an employment agreement should vest an executive's stock options. I see no reason to redescribe their interaction over these matters as something other than negotiation merely because they chose to avoid dishonesty or manipulation.

I must make one caveat, however. One can imagine a person who becomes so universal in her views—so detached from the particulars of her individual position—that she no longer values her own interests at all. Her only interest becomes to serve others' interests. Although it is difficult to imagine how two such people could interact (wouldn't they merely circle each other endlessly, each trying to help the other?), I think the introduction of even one such person into what would otherwise be a negotiation does require redescription of the interaction as something other than bargaining. In this extreme circumstance there would not be two people with differing or conflicting interests; only one with interests and another with a desire to serve. There would be nothing to negotiate about—person A would express needs and person B would satisfy them to the best of B's ability.

Finally, one might object that lawyers have a duty to compete. If a lawyer refuses to do so because of ethical commitments that include consideration of an opponent's interests, then even if we cannot redescribe that lawyer's interactions as something other than negotiation, perhaps we should simply decide that the person can no longer be a lawyer. Robert Condlin, for example, has written that lawyers "must use any legally available move or procedure helpful to a client's bargaining position. Among other things, this means that all forms of leverage must be exploited, inflated demands made, and private information obtained and used whenever any of these actions would advance the client's stated objectives. . . ." If negotiating lawyers will not play the game, they should be disqualified as players.

Although it opens yet another difficult line of argument, I think it unlikely that a saint, or even just a very reflective person, would decide, like Condlin, to prioritize client loyalty over the saint's already-discussed ethical commitments. As Riskin explains, mindfulness loosens one's attachments—one's loyalties. This is, again, what suggests that these practices might aid in adopting a more universal perspective on moral questions. It also suggests, however, that a loyalty-driven ethic, peculiar to one's particular duties to a particular client, will be relatively unpersuasive to our saint as compared to the basic obligations to honesty and fairness. . . .

Questions

17. How might a "disqualification agreement," as used in collaborative practice, benefit a client?
18. What might be the barriers to the acceptance of collaborative law in general civil cases?
19. If cooperative practice does not involve a disqualification agreement, how does it differ from more traditional practice by competent attorneys, who attempt to negotiate settlements before initiating litigation?
20. Would a "saint," as described by Judge Peppet, who negotiates on behalf of a client, be subject to discipline by the Bar for failing to make the client's interests a priority and for not being a zealous advocate? Would you retain such a saint as your lawyer for purposes of negotiation?
21. Would you change Rule 4.1 and the comments to it? If so, what would you change and why?
22. A corporate defendant may desire to restrict a plaintiff's lawyer from representing other plaintiffs with similar claims or may feel vulnerable to future lawsuits based on information the plaintiff's lawyer obtained through discovery. As part of a negotiated settlement, the defendant in this situation may request that the plaintiff's attorney agree not to represent other plaintiffs with similar claims. Such a provision would contravene Model Rule 5.6, which provides, "A lawyer shall not participate in offering or making . . . an agreement in which a restriction on

the lawyer's right to practice is part of the settlement. . . ." What do you think is the rationale and justification for this prohibition?

23. Is the "mirror test" the ultimate guide for negotiation ethics? That test takes into account your own values following a completed negotiation by asking, "Can you look at yourself in the mirror and feel okay?"

CHAPTER
11

The Law of Negotiation

A. How Law Impacts Negotiation

Most negotiation by lawyers occurs in the "shadow of the law." Bargaining is influenced by the prospect of the law of the case and what would happen in court if the claim or business dispute is not successfully negotiated to a conclusion. (See Mnookin and Kornhauser 1979.) The substantive law of the matter being negotiated affects lawyer negotiations and forms the backdrop for bargained outcomes. So, the entire law school curriculum bears in some way on the process, substance, and outcomes of negotiations by lawyers.

Areas of Law Included Here.   We focus on six areas in which the law may shape negotiation conduct.

- Because a settlement agreement is a contract, this chapter examines how the law may limit the extent to which the settlement can be enforced if it is the result of fraud, misrepresentation, or duress.
- The law can impact negotiations by encouraging settlement discussions and offers of compromise with rules barring use of such offers as evidence in subsequent legal proceedings if the negotiation fails to produce a settlement. The evidentiary protection available to promote settlement offers and communications is summarized.
- Negotiated settlements can be encouraged by allocating attorneys' fees and litigation costs based on the reasonableness of rejected settlement offers, so statutory and case law regarding fee shifting through offers of settlement is presented.
- Strategic moves by lawyers to settle with only some of several defendants who share joint and several liability have spawned appellate decisions about the consequences when some defendants settle and others do not, therefore we look at "Mary Carter" agreements, as these secret, selective settlements have become known.
- The tax aspects of settlements can influence negotiation tactics and results, so we provide a primer on tax considerations in negotiating settlements.

- Finally, lawyers must be aware that what they do or fail to do as negotiators for clients can lead to charges of professional malpractice—we include material on potential claims by disappointed clients against their lawyers after the negotiation is concluded.

Areas of Law Not Covered.   Other areas of law related to negotiation that cannot adequately be presented in a general negotiation course, but should be noted include:

- Insurance coverage issues and the role of insurance in paying settlement agreements that looms in the background of tort and other lawsuit settlement negotiations.
- Questions about a lawyer's authority, as agent, to represent a party's interests in settlement negotiations and bind the client can surface when a settlement or transaction is challenged.
- Class actions create unique issues about class representation, conflicts of interest, lawyer's fees, the fairness of settlements, and the need for court approval.
- Distinct legal issues and possible reporting requirements regarding settlements when bankruptcy lurks in the shadows or when the negotiation may impact publicly traded securities of a company.
- Unique requirements, of which negotiators must be aware, that may exist in domestic relations, environmental, and civil rights cases, particularly when courts must approve the settlement.
- Settlement discussions may postpone filing an action and a question may arise about whether negotiation can stop a statute of limits from running and barring the claim. Although negotiation does not generally stop the statute from running, there are exceptions.

What follows is intended to help familiarize you with a few critical areas in which the law does matter in lawyer negotiations and to help you spot red flags calling for research on the current state of the applicable law or consultation with specialized experts.

B. Common-Law Limits—Fraud, Misrepresentation, and Duress

The purpose of most negotiation by lawyers is to reach an agreement to settle a claim or transact a business deal. The resulting agreement is a contract intended to bind the parties to each do something—like paying money to dismiss a lawsuit or appeal—or refraining from actions—most often from pursuing a lawsuit. Therefore, contract law is in play during negotiations and becomes the focus when enforcing or challenging a negotiated agreement. The basic contract principles of offer, acceptance, and consideration are the foundation of understanding the law of negotiated agreements. When a negotiated agreement is challenged, it is most often for contract-based failure of consideration, fraud, misrepresentation, or duress.

Problem

Your client successfully sued Goodyear for damages resulting from a defective hose and valve that they manufactured. The verdict was for $1.3 million, but you appealed because the award did not grant prejudgment interest. The Court of Appeals remanded to the trial court for determination of interest. The parties agreed as to the dates from which interest should be calculated, but their calculations about the amount of interest owed were apart by several hundred thousand dollars. Goodyear sent an e-mail offering to negotiate a settlement, in which it accidentally overstated the damages it owed by $550,000. You accepted immediately. While Goodyear was drafting the satisfaction of judgment, it noticed its mistake and sent a revised document, with $550,000 deducted. You refused to sign and instead moved the district court to enforce the "settlement agreement." The district court did so, and Goodyear appealed.

What argument might Goodyear make to overturn the district court decision? What would you argue in support of the favorable ruling? Are some things really too good to be true? (See Sumerel v. Goodyear Tire & Rubber Co., 232 P.3d 128 (Colo. App. 2009).)

Courts, in applying the common law when enforcing or declining to enforce settlement agreements, set limits on bargaining behavior. Those limits are discussed in the following reading. (Footnotes have been retained to provide helpful case and source references.)

❖ **Russell Korobkin, Michael Moffett & Nancy Welsh, *The Law of Bargaining***

87 Marq. L. Rev. 839 (2004)

When a negotiated agreement results from false statements made during the bargaining process, the common law of tort and contract sometimes holds negotiators liable for damages or makes their resulting agreements subject to rescission.[1] The common law does not, however, amount to a blanket prohibition of all lying. Instead, the common law principles are subject to the caveats that false statements must be material, the opposing negotiator must rely on the false statements, and such reliance must be justified. Whether reliance is justified depends on the type of statement at issue and the statement's specificity. A seller's specific false claim ("this car gets 80 miles per gallon gas mileage") is actionable, but his more general claim ("this car gets good gas mileage") is probably not, because the latter statement is acknowledged as the type of "puffing" or "sales talk" on which no reasonable buyer would rely.

---

1. *See generally* Restatement (Second) of Torts §525 (1986), Restatement (Second) of Contracts §164 (1982).

While it is often said that misrepresentations of fact are actionable but misrepresentations of opinion are not, this statement is not strictly accurate. Statements of opinions can be false, either because the speaker does not actually have the claimed opinion ("I think this Hyundai is the best car built in the world today") or because the statement implies facts that are untrue ("I think this Hyundai gets the best gas mileage of any car"). But statements of opinion are less likely to induce justified reliance than are statements of specific facts, especially when they are very general, such as a claim that an item is one of "good quality." [2]

Whether reliance on a statement of fact or opinion is justified depends significantly on the context of the negotiation and whether the speaker has access to information that the recipient does not. A seller "aggressively" promoting his product whose stated opinions imply facts that are not true is less likely to find himself in legal difficulty if the veracity of his claims are easily investigated by an equally-knowledgeable buyer than if his customer is a consumer unable to evaluate the factual basis of the claims.[3] The case for liability is stronger still when the negotiator holds himself out as being particularly knowledgeable about the subject matter that the expressed opinion concerns.[4] Whether a false statement can be insulated from liability by a subsequent disclaimer depends on the strength and clarity of the disclaimer, as well as on the nature of the false statement. Again, the standard is whether the reasonable recipient of the information in total would rely on the statement at issue when deciding whether to enter into an agreement.[5]

It is universally recognized that a negotiator's false statements concerning how valuable an agreement is to her or the maximum she is willing to give up or exchange in order to seal an agreement (the negotiator's "reservation point," or "bottom line") are not actionable, again on the ground that such false statements are common and no reasonable negotiator would rely upon them. So an insurance adjuster who claimed that $900 was "all he could pay" to settle a claim is not liable for fraud, even if the statement was false.[6] The law is less settled regarding the status of false statements concerning the existence of outside alternatives for a negotiator. A false claim of an offer from a third-party is relevant because it implies a strong reservation point, so a negotiator might logically argue that such a claim is no more actionable than a claim as to the reservation point itself. But courts have occasionally ruled that false claims of a specific outside offer are actionable, on the ground that they are material to the negotiation and that the speaker has access to information that cannot be easily verified by the listener's independent investigation.[7]

---

2. *See* Royal Bus. Machs., Inc. v. Lorraine Corp., 633 F.2d 34, 42 (7th Cir. 1980) (calling such statements "'puffing' to be expected in any sales transaction").

3. *See, e.g.,* Vulcan Metals Co. v. Simmons Mfg. Co., 248 F. 853 (2d Cir. 1918).

4. *See* Pacesetter Homes v. Brodkin, 85 Cal. Rptr. 39, 43 (Cal. Ct. App. 1970).

5. *See, e.g.,* In re Trump, 7 F.3d 357, 369 (3d Cir. 1993) (finding that repeated warnings of risk meant that "no reasonable investor could believe anything but that the . . . bonds represented a rather risky, speculative investment," despite other optimistic claims about the financial stability of the issuer).

6. Morta v. Korea Ins. Corp. 840 F.2d 1452, 1456 (9th Cir. 1988).

7. *See, e.g.,* Kabatchnick v. Hanover-Elm Bldg. Corp., 103 N.E.2d 692 (Mass. 1952) (falsely claiming a "bona fide offer from one Melvin Levine . . . of $10,000 per year"); Beavers v. Lamplighters Realty, 556 P.2d 1328 (Okla. 1976) (falsely claiming a prospective buyer was willing to pay the asking price for a house and would be delivering a check that same day).

The most inscrutable area of the law of deception concerns when a negotiator may be held legally liable for failing to disclose information that might weaken his bargaining position (rather than affirmatively asserting a false claim). The traditional laissez-faire rule of caveat emptor eroded in the twentieth century, with courts placing greater disclosure responsibility on negotiators. It is clear that any affirmative action taken to conceal a fact, including the statement of a "half-truth" that implies a false fact, will be treated as if it were an affirmative false statement. Beyond this point, however, the law becomes murky. Although the general rule is probably still that negotiators have no general disclosure obligation, some courts require bargainers (especially sellers) to disclose known material facts not easily discovered by the other party.[8]

Just as the law places some limits on the use of deceptive behavior to seal a bargain, so too does it place some limits upon negotiators' ability to use superior bargaining power to coerce acquiescence with their demands. In general, negotiators may threaten to withhold their goods and services from those who will not agree to their terms. Courts can invoke the doctrine of duress, however, to protect parties who are the victims of a threat that is "improper" and have "no reasonable alternative" but to acquiesce to the other party's demand,[9] such as when one party procures an agreement through the threat of violence,[10] or through the threat to breach a prior agreement after using the relationship created by that agreement to place the victim in a position in which breach would cause noncompensable damage.[11] Judicial intervention is most likely when the bargaining parties' relationship was not arms-length. For example, the common law provides the defense of undue influence to negotiators who can show that they were dependent upon and thus vulnerable to the other, dominant negotiator.[12] . . .

C. FRE 408 and Mediation Confidentiality

The first sentence of this book defined negotiation as, "the process of communication used to get something we want when another person has control over whether or how we can get it." What you communicate during an unsuccessful negotiation can become evidence involving the underlying subject of the negotiation, like liability for an injury or the amount of damages or other values in dispute. In order to promote communication for the purpose of settlement, case law and rules of evidence make offers of compromise made during settlement negotiations inadmissible in legal proceedings. Federal Rule of Evidence

8. *See, e.g.,* Weintraub v. Krobatsch, 317 A.2d 68 (N.J. 1974) (sellers must disclose known insect infestation of house).

9. *See* Restatement (Second) of Contracts, §175(1) (1982).

10. *See, e.g.,* Rubenstein v. Rubenstein, 120 A.2d 11 (N.J. 1956); Restatement (Second) of Contracts §176(1)(a) (1981).

11. *See, e.g.,* Austin Instruments, Inc. v. Loral Corp., 272 N.E.2d 533 (N.Y. 1971).

12. *See* Restatement (Second) of Contracts §177 (1979).

408, originally adopted in 1975, along with similar state rules, expands on the protection offered by the common law against the use at trial of conduct or statements made during compromise discussions. Rule 408 excludes from admissible evidence the settlement offer itself and any information about settlement negotiations.

In addition, in order to promote mediated settlement negotiation, most states have evidentiary rules broadly shielding what is communicated during mediation from being introduced into evidence in any legal proceeding. The Uniform Mediation Act (UMA), promulgated by the National Conference of Commissioners on Uniform State Laws in 2001, is intended to protect the confidentiality of mediation proceedings. The central rule of the UMA is that a mediation communication is not subject to discovery or admission into evidence in any formal proceeding. At the time of this writing, the UMA has been adopted in ten states and the District of Columbia and has been introduced in a few other states. States not adopting the UMA have their own approach to encouraging settlement by protecting mediation confidentiality. (See, e.g., Mass. Gen. Laws ch. 233; Cal. Code Evid. §§1115-1128.) Although most state laws and the UMA prevent parties from using mediation communications in adjudicatory proceedings, they leave them free to make disclosures outside of litigation. Evidentiary exclusions only apply to court proceedings, discovery, and other formal hearing situations. For example, the parties or their lawyers may hold a press conference or otherwise reveal to the public the negotiations that occurred in mediation. In order to protect the confidentiality of negotiation communications and settlement agreements outside of court proceedings and discovery, the parties must enter an enforceable confidentiality agreement. Parties may also apply for protective orders under Federal Rule of Civil Procedure 26(c) and state counterparts to assure that information such as trade secrets and sensitive settlements are non-disclosable. It is important to note these evidentiary exclusions, although we do not include here the case law on point because this will probably be covered in your course on evidence. A related area of law on the inadmissibility of communicated apologies was presented in Chapter 7. A non-evidentiary use of offers of settlement is discussed next.

D. Offers of Settlement and Fee Shifting

1. The American Approach

The attorneys' fees and costs of bringing or defending a lawsuit are a major factor in negotiating settlement of a dispute. Whether legal action is threatened or pending, each side must consider in its risk analysis the potential costs of court proceedings. Favorable verdicts must be discounted by the amount required to obtain them; a defendant's exposure to loss is enhanced by the amount required to defend. Modest victories in court can be dwarfed and losses magnified by the costs expended, particularly for attorneys' fees. Anticipation of litigation costs affects reservation price calculations and can have a profound influence on negotiations.

In the United States the general rule is that each party pays its own legal expenses. This rule is modified by statute for some causes of action, like civil rights cases, or by pre-dispute contractual agreements. In contrast to the "American rule," England and most of Europe impose costs on the losing party by awarding costs to the prevailing party. The "English rule," as this approach is known, tends to discourage litigation, particularly for those of limited means, by increasing the costs of losing. The leverage of increased costs on the loser increases the incentive for settlement. "Loser pays" legislative proposals in the United States have been favored by business defendants as part of "tort reform" to discourage frivolous lawsuits.

One problem with "loser pays" is identifying who is the "loser." Is the person who obtains a verdict of $10,000, after bringing a lawsuit claiming damages of a million dollars and rejecting an offer of $100,000, the winner or loser? To more clearly define a court "win" for purposes of determining who pays the costs of a suit, a modified "loser pays" approach is to allow a defendant to offer a judgment against itself for a designated amount. This offer, if not accepted, then becomes the benchmark to decide who the winner is relative to the money put on the table before the trial begins. This approach, known as an "offer of judgment," is embodied in Federal Rule of Civil Procedure 68, which has many state counterparts and variants. Pursuant to this rule, a plaintiff who rejects the defendant's formal, unconditional settlement offer, made within a specified time prior to trial, and is then awarded less than the offered amount, is responsible for the defendant's court costs and fees incurred after the date of the offer. It is important to note that court costs and fees, as used in the rule, do not include actual attorneys' fees, but may include certain discovery expenses incurred after the offer is made, as well as filing fees and other statutory costs. Although the cost-shifting mechanism of Rule 68 is only available for defendants, it is thought to provide an incentive for both sides to make more reasonable offers of settlement. (See Robert G. Bone, "To Encourage Settlement: Rule 68, Offers of Judgment, and the History of the Federal Rules of Civil Procedure," 102 Nw. U. L. Rev. 1551 (2008); Edward F. Sherman & Christopher M. Fairman, "Interplay Between Mediation and Offer of Judgment Rule Sanctions," 26 Ohio St. J. on Disp. Res. 327 (2011).)

2. Rule 68 and Its Application

There are explicit and implicit requirements for making a Rule 68 offer of judgment. Failure to follow the requirements can defeat the recovery of costs and have other adverse consequences. The principal requirements to invoke Federal Rule 68 and most of its state counterparts include the following:

- The offer must be in writing.
- The offer must be served more than 14 days before the date set for trial, although the time requirement varies state by state.
- The terms and amount of the offer must be clear.
- The offering defendant must agree to have a formal judgement entered on the record.
- The acceptance must be in writing and unconditional.

Once an offer of judgment is made, it is irrevocable until the trial begins, and it is then considered withdrawn and inadmissible as evidence at trial. Because the offer is treated as unconditional, there is no relief to a defendant for a unilateral mistake or misstated offer. On occasion this can result in a windfall for an accepting plaintiff, as in the following case of the free BMW.

❖ *BMW of North America, INC. v. KRATHEN*
-----

471 So. 2d 585 (1985)

HURLEY, Judge.

BMW appeals from an order of the circuit court denying its motion to vacate judgment and, alternatively, its motion for relief from judgment. We affirm.

The Krathens filed suit against BMW, seeking money damages for breach of express and implied warranties under the Uniform Commercial Code, and for alleged violations of the Magnuson-Moss Warranty Act . . . . The gravamen of the complaint was that BMW sold the Krathens an automobile, at a purchase price of $26,534.13, (with a deferred payment price of $32,501.88), which had a shimmy in the front end that could not be corrected.

BMW responded by mailing an offer of judgment to the Krathens which reads, in its entirety: Pursuant to Fla. R. Civ. P. 1.442, Defendants hereby offer to allow the Plaintiffs to take judgment against them in the amount of Twenty Thousand Five Hundred ($20,500) Dollars, plus reasonable attorneys fees and costs heretofore accrued.

The Krathens promptly mailed their acceptance of the offer "as written" pursuant to rule 1.442, Fla. R. Civ. P. After the offer of judgment was filed, the clerk of the court entered judgment against BMW for "the total sum of twenty thousand five hundred ($20,500) dollars, plus reasonable attorneys fees and costs."

BMW thereafter filed a motion to clarify the offer of judgment and to vacate judgment by the clerk of the court and, alternatively, a motion for relief from judgment pursuant to rule 1.540, Fla. R. Civ. P. Essentially, BMW argued that "return of the vehicle was always a condition precedent to all settlement negotiations with the plaintiffs," and that the offer of judgment should therefore be clarified to reflect that understanding. In its motion for relief from judgment, BMW further argued that even if return of the vehicle were not a condition precedent to the offer, it should be granted relief under rule 1.540, Fla. Civ. P., because the offer "was made as a result of mistake, inadvertence, or excusable neglect on the part of [BMW's] counsel." Both motions were denied and this appeal ensued.

As to the denial of the motion to vacate and clarify, the trial court properly refused to look at the pleadings in this case for purposes of interpreting the offer of judgment which unambiguously states that $20,500 is offered "to allow the Plaintiffs [the Krathens] to take judgment against them." The Krathens accepted the offer "as written"; BMW therefore cannot now be heard to complain that a condition precedent should be read into the offer merely because the attorney who drafted the offer "assumed" that both parties contemplated return of the vehicle in exchange for the $20,500.

A judgment entered pursuant to rule 1.442, Fla. R. Civ. P., may properly be analogized to a consent judgment, which is in the nature of a contract. As such, the construction of a rule 1.442 judgment should be governed solely by the language employed by the parties if it is without ambiguity. When contractual language is clear and unambiguous, courts cannot indulge in construction or interpretation of its plain meaning. Further, where a contract is silent as to a particular matter, courts should not, under the guise of construction, impose on parties contractual rights and duties which they themselves omitted.

Thus, in construing the rule 1.442 judgment at issue in this case, the trial court properly refused to look to the pleadings for evidence of the parties' intent because the offer and acceptance were unambiguous on their face.

Next, we turn to BMW's assertion that the judgment should have been vacated because it was the result of a mistake. Under the rule in most states, a contract cannot be opened, changed or set aside without the assent of the parties in the absence of fraud, *mutual mistake*, or actual absence of consent. Florida, however, follows the minority rule which permits a contract to be set aside on the basis of *unilateral mistake* unless (a) the mistake is the result of an inexcusable lack of due care or (b) the other party has so changed its position in reliance on the contract that rescission would be unconscionable.

The facts in the case at bar provide ample support for the trial court's implied finding of inexcusable lack of due care on the part of BMW's counsel. The offer of judgment did not involve a complex transaction. The terms were few and easily understood. Thus, the omission of what is now claimed to be an essential term, cannot be characterized as a minor, inadvertent error. On the contrary, it evidences a total lack of forethought and such poor draftsmanship as to be well below accepted professional standards. Accordingly, the trial court was justified in refusing to grant relief from a unilateral mistake which resulted from an inexcusable lack of due care. . . .

Under rule 1.540(b), the trial court is authorized to relieve a party from a final judgment or decree on grounds of "mistake, inadvertence, surprise or excusable neglect." A party to a consent judgment who files a rule 1.540(b) motion is not entitled to relief because he misunderstood the legal effect of his consent, nor is a party to a stipulation for dismissal entered after a negotiated settlement entitled to relief on grounds of inadvertence or excusable neglect where a belated discovery of a more serious injury sustained by one plaintiff is discovered, even though the defendants were in possession of a physician report describing said injury, where plaintiffs failed to avail themselves of available methods for obtaining the report. Neglect of counsel amounts to excusable neglect sufficient to warrant relief from judgment only where it is the result of generally accepted practices and amenities among the local bar. In this case, the omission of a key contractual provision simply cannot be classified as a generally accepted practice among the local bar.

Therefore, we find that the trial court acted well within its discretion by denying BMW's motion for post-judgment relief.

In *Randle-Eastern Ambulance Service, Inc. v. Vasta*, 360 So. 2d 68 (Fla. 1978), the supreme court observed:

> It has never been the role of the trial courts of this state to relieve attorneys of their tactical mistakes. The rules of civil procedure were never designed for that purpose, and nothing in Rule 1.540(b) suggests otherwise. . . .

Similarly, we hold that the court below correctly concluded that it was without authority to grant relief under rule 1.540(b) in order to relieve BMW's counsel

of his mistaken assumptions and neglect in failing to specifically provide for return of the vehicle as a condition precedent to its offer of judgment. The trial court's denial of BMW's motion is
AFFIRMED.

Questions

1. Who is likely to pay for the BMW car the plaintiffs are allowed to keep, along with return of $20,500, attorneys' fees, and costs? (Negotiation malpractice is presented in more detail later in this subsection.)
2. Why did the trial court refuse to look at the pleadings for purposes of interpreting the offer of judgment? Does the appellate court's decision not to discern the intent of the parties based on the pleadings seem correct? Why?
3. If the negotiations preceding the offer of judgment in *BMW of North America v. Krathen* were clearly premised on Krathen returning the BMW in exchange for repayment of the purchase price, would you as Krathen's attorney have any ethical obligation to have corrected the wording of the plaintiff's offer of judgment or advised your client to return the car?

When the plaintiff brings a cause of action pursuant to a statute that provides attorneys' fees if the plaintiff "prevails," is the right to statutory attorneys' fees lost when the judgment obtained is less than the rejected Rule 68 offer? This important question, and the settlement-promoting rationale for Rule 68, are considered by the Supreme Court in the opinion that follows.

❖ *Marek v. Chesny*

473 U.S. 1 (1985)

Justice BURGER delivered the opinion of the Court.

We granted certiorari to decide whether attorney's fees incurred by a plaintiff subsequent to an offer of settlement under Federal Rule of Civil Procedure 68 must be paid by the defendant under 42 U.S.C. §1988, when the plaintiff recovers a judgment less than the offer.

Petitioners, three police officers, in answering a call on a domestic disturbance, shot and killed respondent's adult son. Respondent, in his own behalf and as administrator of his son's estate, filed suit against the officers in the United States District Court under 42 U.S.C. §1983 and state tort law.

Prior to trial, petitioners made a timely offer of settlement "for a sum, including costs now accrued and attorney's fees, ONE HUNDRED THOUSAND ($100,000) DOLLARS." Respondent did not accept the offer. The case went to trial and respondent was awarded $5,000 on the state-law "wrongful death" claim, $52,000 for the §1983 violation, and $3,000 in punitive damages.

Respondent filed a request for $171,692.47 in costs, including attorney's fees. This amount included costs incurred after the settlement offer. Petitioners opposed the claim for postoffer costs, relying on Federal Rule of Civil Procedure 68, which shifts to the plaintiff all "costs" incurred subsequent to an offer of judgment not exceeded by the ultimate recovery at trial. Petitioners argued that attorney's fees are part of the "costs" covered by Rule 68. The District Court agreed with petitioners and declined to award respondent "costs, including attorney's fees, incurred after the offer of judgment." The parties subsequently agreed that $32,000 fairly represented the allowable costs, including attorney's fees, accrued prior to petitioners' offer of settlement. . . . [The first question addressed was whether the rejected lump sum offer, which included attorney fees to that point, was "more than" the judgment obtained for damages alone. The Court held the Rule 68 lump sum offer was more than the judgment.]

The second question we address is whether the term "costs" in Rule 68 includes attorney's fees awardable under 42 U.S.C. §1988. By the time the Federal Rules of Civil Procedure were adopted in 1938, federal statutes had authorized and defined awards of costs to prevailing parties for more than 85 years. Unlike in England, such "costs" generally had not included attorney's fees; under the "American Rule," each party had been required to bear its own attorney's fees. The "American Rule" as applied in federal courts, however, had become subject to certain exceptions by the late 1930's. Some of these exceptions had evolved as a product of the "inherent power in the courts to allow attorney's fees in particular situations." But most of the exceptions were found in federal statutes that directed courts to award attorney's fees as part of costs in particular cases. . . .

The authors of Federal Rule of Civil Procedure 68 were fully aware of these exceptions to the American Rule. The Advisory Committee's Note to Rule 54(d), 28 U.S.C. App., p. 621, contains an extensive list of the federal statutes which allowed for costs in particular cases; of the 35 "statutes as to costs" set forth in the final paragraph of the Note, no fewer than 11 allowed for attorney's fees as part of costs. Against this background of varying definitions of "costs," the drafters of Rule 68 did not define the term; nor is there any explanation whatever as to its intended meaning in the history of the Rule.

In this setting, given the importance of "costs" to the Rule, it is very unlikely that this omission was mere oversight; on the contrary, the most reasonable inference is that the term "costs" in Rule 68 was intended to refer to all costs properly awardable under the relevant substantive statute or other authority. In other words, all costs properly awardable in an action are to be considered within the scope of Rule 68 "costs." Thus, absent congressional expressions to the contrary, where the underlying statute defines "costs" to include attorney's fees, we are satisfied such fees are to be included as costs for purposes of Rule 68.

Here, respondent sued under 42 U.S.C. §1983. Pursuant to the Civil Rights Attorney's Fees Awards Act of 1976, 90 Stat. 2641, as amended, 42 U.S.C. §1988, a prevailing party in a §1983 action may be awarded attorney's fees "as part of the costs." Since Congress expressly included attorney's fees as "costs" available to a plaintiff in a §1983 suit, such fees are subject to the cost-shifting provision of Rule 68. This "plain meaning" interpretation of the interplay between Rule 68 and §1988 is the only construction that gives meaning to each word in both Rule 68 and §1988.

Unlike the Court of Appeals, we do not believe that this "plain meaning" construction of the statute and the Rule will frustrate Congress' objective in

§1988 of ensuring that civil rights plaintiffs obtain " 'effective access to the judicial process."' Merely subjecting civil rights plaintiffs to the settlement provision of Rule 68 does not curtail their access to the courts, or significantly deter them from bringing suit. Application of Rule 68 will serve as a disincentive for the plaintiff's attorney to continue litigation after the defendant makes a settlement offer. There is no evidence, however, that Congress, in considering §1988, had any thought that civil rights claims were to be on any different footing from other civil claims insofar as settlement is concerned. Indeed, Congress made clear its concern that civil rights plaintiffs not be penalized for "helping to lessen docket congestion" by settling their cases out of court.

Moreover, Rule 68's policy of encouraging settlements is neutral, favoring neither plaintiffs nor defendants; it expresses a clear policy of favoring settlement of all lawsuits. Civil rights plaintiffs—along with other plaintiffs—who reject an offer more favorable than what is thereafter recovered at trial will not recover attorney's fees for services performed after the offer is rejected. But, since the Rule is neutral, many civil rights plaintiffs will benefit from the offers of settlement encouraged by Rule 68. Some plaintiffs will receive compensation in settlement where, on trial, they might not have recovered, or would have recovered less than what was offered. And, even for those who would prevail at trial, settlement will provide them with compensation at an earlier date without the burdens, stress, and time of litigation. In short, settlements rather than litigation will serve the interests of plaintiffs as well as defendants.

To be sure, application of Rule 68 will require plaintiffs to "think very hard" about whether continued litigation is worthwhile; that is precisely what Rule 68 contemplates. This effect of Rule 68, however, is in no sense inconsistent with the congressional policies underlying §1983 and §1988. Section 1988 authorizes courts to award only "reasonable" attorney's fees to prevailing parties. In *Hensley v. Eckerhart*, [*supra*], we held that "the most critical factor" in determining a reasonable fee "is the degree of success obtained." We specifically noted that prevailing at trial "may say little about whether the expenditure of counsel's time was reasonable in relation to the success achieved." In a case where a rejected settlement offer exceeds the ultimate recovery, the plaintiff— although technically the prevailing party—has not received any monetary benefits from the postoffer services of his attorney. This case presents a good example: the $139,692 in postoffer legal services resulted in a recovery $8,000 less than petitioners' settlement offer. Given Congress' focus on the success achieved, we are not persuaded that shifting the postoffer costs to respondent in these circumstances would in any sense thwart its intent under §1988. . . .

Justice BRENNAN, with whom Justice MARSHALL and Justice BLACKMUN join, dissenting.

. . . I dissent. The Court's reasoning is wholly inconsistent with the history and structure of the Federal Rules, and its application to the over 100 attorney's fees statutes enacted by Congress will produce absurd variations in Rule 68's operation based on nothing more than picayune differences in statutory phraseology. Neither Congress nor the drafters of the Rules could possibly have intended such inexplicable variations in settlement incentives. . . . Finally, both Congress and the Judicial Conference of the United States have been engaged for years in considering possible amendments to Rule 68 that would bring attorney's fees within the operation of the Rule. That process strongly suggests that Rule 68 has not previously been viewed as governing fee awards, and it illustrates the wisdom of deferring to other avenues of amending Rule 68 rather than ourselves engaging in "standardless judicial lawmaking."

. . . The Court argues, however, that its interpretation of Rule 68 "is neutral, favoring neither plaintiffs nor defendants." This contention is also plainly wrong. As the Judicial Conference Advisory Committee on the Federal Rules of Civil Procedure has noted twice in recent years, Rule 68 "is a 'one-way street,'" available only to those defending against claims and not to claimants. Interpreting Rule 68 in its current version to include attorney's fees will lead to a number of skewed settlement incentives that squarely conflict with Congress' intent. To discuss but one example, Rule 68 allows an offer to be made any time after the complaint is filed and gives the plaintiff only 10 days to accept or reject. The Court's decision inevitably will encourage defendants who know they have violated the law to make "low-ball" offers immediately after suit is filed and before plaintiffs have been able to obtain the information they are entitled to by way of discovery to assess the strength of their claims and the reasonableness of the offers. The result will put severe pressure on plaintiffs to settle on the basis of inadequate information in order to avoid the risk of bearing all of their fees even if reasonable discovery might reveal that the defendants were subject to far greater liability. Indeed, because Rule 68 offers may be made recurrently without limitation, defendants will be well advised to make ever-slightly larger offers throughout the discovery process and before plaintiffs have conducted all reasonably necessary discovery.

This sort of so-called "incentive" is fundamentally incompatible with Congress' goals. Congress intended for "private citizens . . . to be able to assert their civil rights" and for "those who violate the Nation's fundamental laws" not to be able "to proceed with impunity." Accordingly, civil rights plaintiffs "'appear before the court cloaked in a mantle of public interest'"; to promote the "*vigorous* enforcement of modern civil rights legislation," Congress has directed that such "private attorneys general" shall not "be deterred from bringing good faith actions to vindicate the fundamental rights here involved." Yet requiring plaintiffs to make wholly uninformed decisions on settlement offers, at the risk of *automatically* losing all of their postoffer fees no matter what the circumstances and notwithstanding the "excellent" results they might achieve after the full picture emerges, will work just such a deterrent effect. . . .

Questions

4. Does the Court's holding in *Marek* seriously impair the incentive to bring civil rights cases, as intended by Congress when it provided for recovery of plaintiffs' attorneys' fees?

5. In Chapter 2 you read about risk averseness and the role of this concept in negotiation. Professor Ed Sherman suggests "that a well-heeled defendant is less likely to be deterred from defending a weak suit by the threat of having to pay its opponent's attorneys' fees than a plaintiff from prosecuting a possibly meritorious suit. Since plaintiffs are generally more

risk averse than defendants, a 'loser pays' rule impacts disproportion-
ately on plaintiffs' access to the courts" (Sherman 1998, 1863). Is it convincing to you that well-heeled defendants are less risk averse than less
financially well-off plaintiffs? Why might or might not this be correct?

6. You also read previously about the tendency of parties and lawyers to be
overly optimistic about the strength of their cases and their chances of
winning. If both sides in a case are confident about their chance of prevailing, does a "loser pays" rule promote or impede settlement? Are both
sides likely to insist on more in their negotiations because each believes
the other will have to pay all costs and fees following trial?

7. Often, attorneys negotiate the amount of statutorily allowed fees at the
same time that they seek substantive payments for their clients. The
defendant may seek trade-offs of lower attorneys' fees, or waiver of fees,
in exchange for a higher payment to the client. This principal-agent conflict can pit client interests against those of the lawyer. The Supreme
Court addressed this issue in Evans v. Jeff D., 475 U.S. 717 (1986), and
held that the plaintiff lawyer's waiver of statutory attorneys' fees to
obtain a better settlement for his client would not be set aside and that
the trial court could consider the propriety of such a trade-off on a case-
by-case basis. Is the ethical dilemma greater for the plaintiff's attorney
confronted with a coercive offer to waive or reduce fees to obtain a better settlement for his client, or for the defendant's attorney whose client
insists that the trade-off be proposed? Do you feel that such proposals
for a fee waiver or reduction should be ethically prohibited?

Justice Brennan in his dissent in *Marek* notes that the Judicial Conference,
which proposes the wording of the Federal Rules, and Congress have on multiple occasions considered amending Rule 68 to include attorneys' fees and
to make the Rules mechanism available to plaintiffs as well as defendants.
Congressional bills continue to propose expansion of Rule 68 to increase its
impact on promoting settlement. This ongoing interest in amending Rule 68
is prompted, in part, by a sense that in its current form Rule 68 is not enough
of an incentive in the negotiating process to make a meaningful difference in
settlement rates and fails to shift enough expense risk to plaintiffs if they reject
an offer. Although the frequency with which Rule 68 is invoked in negotiating
lawsuit settlements is not regularly tracked, its effectiveness in settling cases is
thought to be relatively low. On the other hand, there is concern that increasing the economic risks for plaintiffs to proceed to trial may diminish access to
courts by plaintiffs attempting to right wrongs or pursue public interest causes.
This concern, along with the complexities of expanding Rule 68, has defeated
attempts to broaden the Federal Rule.

Consider a recent gender discrimination case in which an offer of judgment
was rejected by the plaintiff at great cost. This case illustrates that negotiation
may continue after a jury verdict.

Problem — Pao v. Kleiner Perkins Case

Ellen Pao is a Chinese American woman from New Jersey who has a bachelor's degree in Electrical Engineering from Princeton, and JD and MBA degrees from Harvard. She worked as a junior partner at Kleiner Perkins Caufield & Byers, a top venture capital firm in Silicon Valley. Pao filed a gender discrimination lawsuit against her former employer, alleging, among other counts, retaliation by another married junior partner with whom she had a consensual affair. She sought $16 million in compensatory damages plus punitive damages. Three months prior to the start of trial the defendant offered entry of judgment for $1 million under California Code of Civil Procedure §998. Pao declined the offer. In a 2015 highly publicized San Francisco Superior Court trial lasting 24 days, the six-woman/six-man jury returned a verdict in favor of the defendant. The defendant moved for recovery pursuant to §998 of expert witness fees of $900,000 and court costs of $72,814, all of which it offered to waive if plaintiff did not appeal the jury verdict. The judge found the settlement offer by Kleiner was made in good faith but reduced the requested amount of fees and costs, ordering the plaintiff to pay defendant Kleiner $276,000. The judge noted Pao, who during the law suit was employed as interim CEO of on line discussion site Reddit, had the resources to pay the ordered fees. Pao filed a notice of appeal, which she offered to drop if Kleiner paid her $2.7 million. Kleiner refused. Pao later withdrew her appeal, stating "I cannot afford the risk of even more costs to fight against a firm with tremendous financial resources and massive legal and PR armies." (See San Francisco Chronicle, C1, Sep. 11, 2015.)

1. Do you think Ellen Pao, who was a highly paid Silicon Valley executive, would have been more likely to accept the $1 million dollar offer of judgment if the California code section would have subjected her to the risk of paying Kleiner's multimillion dollar attorneys' fees were she not to prevail at trial?
2. Assuming that her complaint withstood a motion for summary judgment before the offer of judgment and appeared to be credible, would it be a good policy to put more teeth in the offer of judgement law to make the risk of going to trial greater for those alleging gender discrimination or who bring other civil rights cases?
3. Are you comfortable with the continuing post-trial negotiation by both sides over pursuing an appeal? Does this raise any policy concerns in high profile civil rights cases?

Note: Does FRCP 68 Create More Risk Taking Rather Than Less?

The study referred to in Chapter 6 of 4,532 civil litigation cases over a 44-year period where offers of judgment were rejected was based on California Code of Civil Procedure §998, the California equivalent of Rule 68, intended to encourage settlement by financially penalizing parties whose trial result is worse than the settlement offer made by an adversary. That study shows that §998-inspired offers, available to both plaintiffs and defendants, could be counterproductive. Parties who received settlement offers under §998 were more likely to take aggressive settlement positions, resulting in financially adverse outcomes, than were those in the study who didn't receive such offers. The decision error rate (defined as getting less at trial than the pretrial offer) for plaintiffs who risked the imposition of statutory financial penalties for not accepting written settlement offers was 83 percent, compared with 61 percent for plaintiffs who did not receive such offers. Similarly, defendants faced with statutory penalties for unreasonable settlement positions exhibited a decision error rate of 46 percent, compared to an error rate of 22 percent for defendants who did not negotiate under the threat of statutory penalties. These findings complement other empirical and experimental studies indicating that legislation intended to increase settlement rates or curb risk-taking settlement negotiation behavior may be ineffective. Whether this particular California statutory procedure provokes risk-taking behavior, the co-authors caution, is unclear, as other factors may cause the high decision error rates associated with the procedure. (See Kiser et al. 2008.)

The beat goes on to promote more negotiated settlements by increasing settlement incentives and litigation disincentives. The issue is sometimes framed in terms of putting more "teeth" in Rule 68 in order to create disincentives for bringing frivolous suits—one of the goals of the rule. Federal rule-makers have not amended the substance of Rule 68 since 1946. In contrast, state lawmakers have been more responsive to criticisms of the rule. Many states have either amended their versions of Federal Rule 68 or have completely rewritten the rule. It is thought that state rules which have beefed up the incentives to settle, for example by adding attorneys' fees and allowing the offers to be made by plaintiffs, as well as defendants, may serve as useful models for amending Federal Rule 68 to better serve the rule's twin goals—those of encouraging settlement and deterring frivolous litigation. (See Anna Aven Sumner, "Is the Gummy Rule of Today Truly Better Than the Toothy Rule of Tomorrow? How Federal Rule 68 Should Be Modified," 852 Duke L.J. 1055 (2003).)

E. Mary Carter Agreements

Negotiation between a plaintiff and multiple defendants can be legally and ethically complex. When one or more of multiple defendants with joint and several liability settles with a plaintiff and the others do not, it is commonly referred to as a "Mary Carter" or sliding-scale agreement. The settling defendant typically makes a deal with the plaintiff about the maximum amount that the defendant will pay, regardless of the trial outcome or later settlement by the plaintiffs with other defendants. The agreement also allows a decrease in the settling defendant's payment if the plaintiff obtains more from all the defendants combined than the total amount of damages (sliding scale). In other words, the settling defendant caps his liability and potentially benefits from the plaintiff's success against the remaining defendants. It is possible that the settling defendant will pay nothing if the plaintiff collects the full amount of damages from the other defendants (a "zero bottom" settlement.)

Mary Carter agreements are named after the Florida case Booth v. Mary Carter Paint Company, 202 So. 2d 8 (Fla. App. 1967), in which the plaintiff, Booth, brought a negligence action against multiple defendants for the motor vehicle death of his wife. During settlement negotiations, the defense counsel for two of the defendants made a deal with the plaintiff, separately from Mary Carter Paint Company, also a defendant in the case, about the maximum amount that they would pay. The signing defendants were not released from liability and remained in the case tried to a jury, which was unaware of the settlement agreement. In essence, the settling defendants switched to the plaintiff's side while seeming to the jury to still be defendants. The Carter Paint Company lost its post-trial objections to the secret settlement deal, which could have resulted in it paying the entire settlement (but did not). The Florida Court of Appeal confirmed the ruling and upheld the partial settlement agreement.

Mary Carter agreements classically involve four major features:

1. The plaintiff is guaranteed a certain amount of recovery from the settling defendants.
2. The dollar liability of the settling defendants is limited to the guaranteed amount and may be reduced by the plaintiff's recovery from other defendants.
3. The agreement between the settling defendant and the plaintiff is kept secret from the jury and often from the non-settling defendants.
4. The settling defendant remains in the lawsuit.

Although a few states have banned Mary Carter agreements as collusive and against public policy, most allow some form of this negotiated partial settlement in cases involving joint and several liability, even if only on a case-by-case basis or referred to by another name. In Arizona, this type of selective settlement is known as a "Gallagher covenant," from the case City of Tucson v. Gallagher, 14 Ariz. App. 385, 483 P.2d 798 (1971). A majority of states now require Mary Carter agreements to be disclosed to co-defendants and the jury. (See Hodesh v. Korelitz, 123 Ohio St. 3d 72, 2009.)

California relies on the wording of a state statute (Cal. Civ. Proc. Code 877 and 877.6) to allow "sliding scale recovery agreements," provided the amount of the settlement indicates it was entered into in "good faith." The negotiated cap amount and other financial obligations must be within a reasonable range of the settling defendant's proportional share of comparative liability among the tortfeasors. Abbot Ford, Inc. v. The Superior Court of Los Angeles County; Ford Motor Co., 43 Cal. 3d 858 (1987).

Questions

8. What are the policy reasons that justify the approval of Mary Carter agreements by most courts that have considered challenges to them?
9. Do Mary Carter agreements promote settlement or promote trials? Is a trial more or less likely to continue to conclusion if one of several defendants has negotiated a Mary Carter type settlement? Why?

10. Does the California requirement of "good faith," linked to proportion-ality of the settling defendant's comparative fault, improve or unduly complicate assessment of Mary Carter or sliding-scale settlement agreements? Does the California "case-by-case" determination of good faith promote negotiated settlements?

11. Why would the plaintiff want to keep secret from the jury that one of multiple defendants has settled or capped his payment to the defendant? Is the settling defendant then adverse to the plaintiff, or are their interests aligned? Should the jury know this? (See Alcala Co., Inc. v. Sup. Ct., 49 Cal. 4th 1308, 1317, 57 Cal. 2d 349, 354 (1996).) What difference might this information make to the jury?

12. Does proposing, negotiating, or fulfilling a Mary Carter agreement kept secret from the judge, jury, or other defendants raise any ethical questions for lawyers? If so, what are they? Should other defendants be informed of Mary Carter agreements? (See Cal. Civ. Proc. Code 877.5(c) for one statutory solution to this question.)

F. Tax Considerations

Knowing the rudiments of how taxes impact settlement outcomes can help you create value and enhance what your client ends up keeping. Early identi-fication of tax liabilities and likely tax treatment of what is paid and received, or agreed to be done, in settlement allows you to favorably shape negoti-ation strategy and better frame issues for negotiation. Tax considerations are important in negotiating business deals, contract disputes and corporate conflicts, as well as in settling tort and employment claims. The next arti-cle presents a basic primer on what you need to know about the tax conse-quences of settlements. This summary of tax considerations for plaintiffs and for defendants is the most helpful we have seen but is subject to the caveat that tax laws, regulations, and interpretive decisions must be checked for changes and updates.

❖ Robert W. Wood, *Taxing Matters in Settling Cases*

27 Cal. Law. 41 (June 2007)

Even practitioners who have assiduously avoided concentrating on the intrica-cies of tax law still need to be aware of the possible tax ramifications in case settlements before finalizing them. Luckily, if you keep in mind a few basic principles, you should be in a position at least to help assess the risks, and to know when to get or recommend outside tax advice.

First, consider whether your client is receiving money or paying money. Receiving income is usually more important from a tax perspective, so most plaintiffs are more worried about tax issues than most defendants.

Tax Concerns for Plaintiffs

The overarching rule is that the origin of your client's claim will determine the tax consequences of a settlement The U.S. Supreme Court laid down that rule more than a half century ago in *Arrowsmith v. Commissioner* (344 U.S. 6 (1952)). For example, if your client's claims are for wages, a settlement will generally be treated as wages for both income tax and employment tax purposes. *(See* Rev. Ruling 78-336, 1978-2 C. B. 225.) And if a business sues for harm to its goodwill, the resulting settlement should be treated as a recovery of goodwill, which usually means a capital gain.

Another fundamental tax rule is that all income is taxable unless there is a special rule to the contrary. In other words, you and your client should assume everything is taxable as a starting point. The biggest statutory exception to this rule is section 104 of the Internal Revenue Code, which states that damages for "personal physical injuries or sickness" are tax-free. . . .

Unfortunately, it is not clear what constitutes physical injury or sickness under the codes. The IRS view of physical injury is that there must be serious physical contact involved, such as an auto accident or battery. And the resulting injury needs to be serious enough to see — broken bones or bruises, for example. Prior to 1996, emotional-distress damages were tax-free, but the Internal Revenue Code was amended that year to add the "physical" requirement, dramatically tightening the scope of this exclusion. (I.R.C. §104(a)(2), as amended by the Small Business Job Protection Act of 1996.) The primary target of the 1996 amendment was employment litigation, in which plaintiffs generally excluded from income emotional-distress and discrimination recoveries.

Figuring out what is excludable is tough. The legislative history of the 1996 Act indicates that mere symptoms of emotional distress, such as headaches, insomnia, and stomach aches, do not qualify as physical injuries or sicknesses, so recoveries for such items are not excludable. (H. Conf. Rept. 104-737 at 301 (1996), 1996-3 C.B. 741, 1041.) However, it is not clear whether an ulcer would be treated as a mere symptom of emotional distress and taxable, or as a bona fide physical injury or sickness, and therefore tax-free.

Not surprisingly, much of the relevant case law comes from employment claims, in which employees often allege that some portion of their recovery relates to physical injuries or sickness. The IRS is strict in imposing limits. However, when there is actual physical contact, such as sexual assault in a sexual-harassment case, it may be appropriate to claim some exclusion. In such cases, it is usually wise to get a tax professional involved for specific guidance.

The language of the settlement agreement is also important. Ideally, the plaintiff and the defendant should agree on what a settlement payment represents. The IRS and the California Franchise Tax Board will usually ask for a copy of the complaint in an audit to see the genesis of the claims and will also request a copy of the settlement agreement. And though government auditors are not bound by the agreement, they do consider it. A plaintiff who fails to include tax allocation and characterization language in a settlement agreement misses an opportunity to help mold the tax treatment of the recovery.

Another matter of critical importance is how the payments to the plaintiff are reported. IRS Form W-2 is used to report the wages paid to an employee each year; Form 1099 is used for most other payments.

If a payment is excludable from income, it should not be reported on a 1099. Virtually every business issues 1099s for payments made in the course of business. The 1099 forms reporting all payments made in the prior year are due to the taxpayer who receives the payment by January 31 of the following year. Then, the business must send copies of all of its 1099s, along with transmittal Form 1096, to the IRS before the end of February, leaving a one-month delay between the time Forms 1099 are due to the taxpayer and the time they must be sent to the IRS. That delay may provide a tactical advantage for your clients. If a client receives a Form 1099 that is incorrect, and immediately notifies the payer, there may be enough time to change it before the IRS receives it.

Returning to the primary precept that all settlements are taxable unless you can prove otherwise, it is also important to recognize that section 104 does not shield all damages from taxation, even in a case indisputably involving physical injury. For example, if a plaintiff is injured and rendered a quadriplegic, punitive damages awarded for the injury are still taxable. (*O'Gilvie v. United States*, 519 U.S. 79 (1996).) The same is true for prejudgment and postjudgment interest. (*Kovacs v. Commissioner*, 100 T.C. 124 (1993).) So if your client recovers money in a personal injury case, you still need to differentiate between damages for physical injuries and any amount awarded for interest or punitive damages in determining whether the money is excludable.

The toughest calls in determining the treatment of punitive damages or interest are in cases that settle on appeal. For example, suppose that an auto accident case in which your client was awarded $500,000 in compensating damages and $2 million in punitives settles for $1 million pending appeal. Some portion of that settlement might be allotted to interest or punitive damages at trial. (*Rozpad v. Commissioner*, 154 F.3d 1 (1998).) It may be appropriate to seek the advice of competent tax counsel if you have a case involving such issues, preferably before the case settles.

Tax reporting rules are one reason to expressly address tax issues in a settlement agreement. For example, if your client's settlement agreement says nothing about IRS Form W-2 or 1099, and those forms are incorrect when issued, you may have little recourse. You can contact the defendant and plead your case, but very few defendants take such requests seriously.

In contrast, if the settlement agreement is specific—for example, there will be a W-2 for $500, a Form 1099 for $20,000, and a Form 1099 to the attorney for $10,000 you have something specific to address. If the forms come in any other manner, you can contact the defendant and assert that the settlement agreement was breached. Such discussions generally lead to corrections.

Other plaintiff recoveries. In addition to the tricky personal injury area, tax considerations play a part in virtually all other kinds of recoveries too. Again, assume everything is taxable.

You may also face the question of whether a recovery is ordinary income or a capital gain. The top tax rate for ordinary income is 35 percent while the top capital gain rate is 15 percent, so clients have big incentives to try to characterize their recovery as capital gains. In general, a recovery for a capital asset such as a business, a personal residence, or shares of stock follow a particular pattern. If the case you are handling relates to damages to assets, you must be mindful of the distinction between ordinary income and capital gains.

Intellectual property is another area ripe for tax planning. An intellectual property recovery may be treated as lost profits, such as lost royalty income on a patent license. It may also be treated as harm to the patent itself, in which case the recovery may be viewed as a capital gain, or even as a recovery of the patent holder's basis in the patent, and not taxable at all. Plainly, there can be huge tax savings depending on the characterization. It may also be wise to get tax counsel involved when you are handling an intellectual property case—again, preferably before the case is settled.

As added complications, there are special tax rules that apply when property is damaged, and unique provisions for gain on the sale of a personal residence, as well as tax provisions applying when property is involuntarily converted, for example, by fire or condemnation.

Attorneys fees. Finally, when considering awards to plaintiffs, be wary of the tax treatment of attorneys fees. In 2004, the tax law was amended to expressly allow an "above-the-line" deduction for attorneys fees in employment cases. (I.R.C. §62, as amended by the American Jobs Creation Act of 2004.) The tax issue here is a fundamental one. Suppose you handle contingent-fee litigation for a client and recover $100,000, and your fee is 40 percent. Does the client have gross income of $60,000, or gross income of $100,000, followed by a $40,000 deduction? Economically, this may sound like a distinction without a difference, yet these two alternatives generally do not mean the same thing from a tax standpoint,

Resolving a vehement split in the circuit courts, the U.S. Supreme Court ruled in 2005 that a plaintiff in contingent-fee litigation generally must be treated as receiving 100 percent of the recovery for tax purposes, regardless of how the checks are cut or whether the plaintiff's lawyer is paid his or her share directly. (*Commissioner v. Banks*, 543 U.S. 426 (2005).) The statutory change, made a few months before the Supreme Court's holding, allows employment plaintiffs an above-the-line deduction so that, in effect, they are not taxed on the money paid to their lawyers.

However, excluding employment litigation, the client in the example above generally will have gross income of $100,000 and will have to find a way to deduct the $40,000 in legal fees. Usually those fees can be deducted only as a "miscellaneous itemized deduction," which means there are limitations and restrictions. In particular, the client will often be stung by the dreaded alternative minimum tax, or AMT.

Deductibility for Defendants

If you are representing a defendant, tax worries are less obvious than those of plaintiffs. But there are a few key rules to keep in mind. First, nearly all defendants want to make sure they can deduct a payment as a business expense. In business litigation, this is usually not a problem, but it still merits close consideration. Some defendants get stung by capitalization rules, having to add the cost of a settlement to their tax basis, so they get no current deduction. That can occur in litigating environmental matters and in settling title to assets.

For example, if your client pays a settlement to resolve a dispute over who owns the land under an office building, that settlement payment will probably

be viewed for tax purposes as a payment to quiet title. As such, the client probably cannot deduct it as an ordinary business expense, but instead would have to
add it to his or her basis for tax purposes. Although the client would eventually
receive a tax benefit for this payment when he or she sold the building, that
may be a long wait. A current tax deduction is always better than a delayed tax
benefit.

The tax treatment of attorneys fees generally follows the tax treatment of the
underlying settlement or judgment. So, if your defendant client must capitalize,
rather than deduct, a settlement payment, the attorneys fees the defendant pays
will likely face the same unfavorable treatment.

Sometimes, tax planning at settlement time can help ameliorate these harsh
tax consequences. Still, most settlement payments in a business context are tax-
deductible, even punitive damages. Generally, a defendant wants to make sure
to get a current deduction, even where there is some delay in getting the money
to the plaintiff.

A larger topic relates to tax reporting and withholding. Business clients are
subject to strict rules. If you are a defense lawyer, when the plaintiff's lawyer asks
for certain tax language to be included in the agreement, review it carefully
before incorporating it. If the plaintiff asks your client to characterize a patent
royalty payment in a settlement agreement as "personal physical injury damages," don't do it. It may be tax fraud, and it is certainly inappropriate. However,
if the plaintiff asks your defendant client not to issue a Form 1099 for one-third
of a sexual harassment settlement, this may be perfectly fine, depending on the
facts. Consider whether that third of the settlement payment represents a fair
allocation.

Probably the biggest exposure defendants face is for failure to withhold
on taxes. If it is an employment case and the amounts paid to settle the case
are wages, the defendant's liability for failing to withhold can be serious. For
example, if your client is an employer and the case involves a claim for back
wages, what if the plaintiff asks that there be no withholding on the settlement
payment? If the case is 100 percent about wages, then under the origin-of-the-
claim doctrine, the settlement payment should likewise be 100 percent wages.
Wages are subject to withholding—and an employer that fails to withhold
is liable for the taxes the employee does not pay, as well as for penalties and
interest.

Thus, a plaintiff's seemingly simple request not to withhold taxes can result
in major liability if the defendant agrees and the characterization is later determined to be improper. Often, a plaintiff will offer to indemnify the defendant
for any tax problems as a way to get the tax language the plaintiff wants into the
settlement agreement. But don't simply rely on the plaintiff's indemnification
obligation, because those are rarely enforced. If your client is making a wage
payment, but the plaintiff insists that it not be reported as wages, beware.

A defendant in a case that involves damages for personal injury or sickness
can legitimately agree not to issue a Form 1099 for a portion of the settlement
that is fairly allocated to such claims.

The attorneys fees tax-reporting rules are also highly complex. In general,
in contingent-fee litigation, the defendant must issue a Form 1099 to both the
plaintiff and to the plaintiff's lawyer.

G. Negotiation Malpractice

Client dissatisfaction, after the fact, with claim settlement and transactional agreements negotiated by their attorneys, is not uncommon. An agreement that seemed appealing at the time it was obtained—when uncertainty, fear of the worse alternatives, and time pressure drove acceptance—may, in hindsight, be unsatisfactory. A good negotiated result is attributed to a strong case and a resolute client; a marginal result, after the dynamics and trade-offs of the negotiation are forgotten, is attributed to poor representation.

The frequency of complaints filed against attorneys for malpractice in negotiations is not precisely known but is thought to be high, as noted by Professor Epstein in a reading that follows. Even though there is a general requirement that clients must agree to a negotiated settlement or transaction before it becomes final, consent to the result is not a total barrier to a claim of malpractice. Clients have reason to rely on the professional expertise, skill, and integrity of the attorney negotiating on their behalf and may sue when that reliance is misplaced.

Malpractice is grounded in tort and requires proof of the classic tort elements:

- Duty to the plaintiff
- Breach of that duty
- Causation
- Damages

Proving causation and damages is difficult in claims of negotiation malpractice because, as we have presented throughout this text, there is no one right or sure way to negotiate. Damages cannot be easily established by comparing a negotiated outcome to a trial result that did not occur or to another negotiation with all the same variables. Richard Posner, Chief Judge of the Seventh Circuit, stated the issue and the challenge succinctly:

> Proof of causation is often difficult in legal malpractice cases involving representation in litigation—the vast majority of such cases—because it is so difficult, yet vital, to estimate what difference a lawyer's negligence made in the actual outcome of a trial or other adversary proceeding. . . . Proof of causation is even more difficult in a negotiating situation, because while there is (at least we judges like to think there is) a correct outcome to most lawsuits, there is no correct outcome to a negotiation. Not only does much depend on the relative bargaining skills of the negotiators, on the likely consequences to each party if the negotiations fall through, and on luck, so that the element of the intangible and the unpredictable looms large; but there is no single right outcome in a bargaining situation even in principle. Every point within the range bounded by the lowest offer that one party will accept and the highest offer that the other party will make is a possible transaction or settlement point, and none of these points is "correct" or "incorrect". (Nicolet Instrument Corp. v. Lindquest & Vennum, 34 F.3d 453 (7th Cir. 1994)).

Even though Judge Posner recognized the difficulty of proof of damages, the decision went on to reverse summary judgment and required the alleged negligent law firm to defend itself at trial and argue the question of damages there.

Note: Gravamen of Malpractice

Lawyers have both procedural and substantive duties when advising and representing clients in negotiations. Breach of the procedural duties, as well as the substantive ones, result in malpractice. The procedural duties reflect ethical responsibilities that lawyers have toward clients. These responsibilities were discussed in Chapter 10. Procedural requirements that are often the gravamen of malpractice claims against attorney negotiators include the following:

- Duty to communicate settlement offers to client (see ABA Model Rule 1.4(a))
- Duty to not exceed authority given by client in making or accepting offers (see ABA Model Rule 1.2(a))
- Duty to be diligent (see ABA Model Rule 1.3)
- Duty to reveal conflicts of interest (see ABA Model Rule 1.7) and not to trade off clients' interests to cover up attorney error (see ABA Model Rule 1.7(2))

Substantively, lawyers owe their clients the duty to know the law and properly advise clients about how law and practice affect their situation. Accurate information is necessary for clients to make informed decisions about settlement. The test for purposes of malpractice is commonly stated as whether the attorney exercised that degree of skill, prudence, and diligence in investigating facts, in legal research, and in giving legal advice that lawyers of ordinary skill and capacity would do in similar situations.

Only disappointed clients sue their lawyers. Domestic relations is an area of legal practice in which client expectations are often unrealistically high, as are emotions. It is not unusual for clients to have second thoughts and be disappointed with a negotiated settlement. "Buyer's remorse" can lead to claims against lawyers following an accepted settlement, particularly in divorce. Consider the following malpractice case and the lessons you can learn from it.

❖ *Ziegelheim v. Apollo*

128 N.J. 250, 607 A.2d 1298 (1992)

HANDLER, J.

... In September 1979, Mrs. Ziegelheim retained defendant, attorney Stephen Apollo, to represent her in her anticipated divorce action. Because this appeal relates to the trial court's granting of summary judgment against plaintiff, we assume for the purposes of our decision that all of the facts she alleges relating to Apollo's handling of her divorce are true. According to Mrs. Ziegelheim, she and Apollo met on several occasions to plan various aspects of her case. She told him about all of the marital and separate assets of which she was aware, and they discussed her suspicion the Mr. Ziegelheim was either concealing or dissipating certain other assets as well. In particular, Mrs. Ziegelheim told Apollo that she thought her husband had $500,000 hidden in the form of cash savings and bonds. Accordingly, she asked Apollo to make a thorough inquiry into her husband's assets, including cash, bonds, patents, stocks, pensions, life insurance, profit-sharing plans, and real estate. . . .

According to Mrs. Ziegelheim, Apollo failed to discover important information about her husband's assets before entering into settlement negotiations with Mr. Ziegelheim's attorney, Sheldon Liebowitz. Apollo hired an accountant who valued the marital estate at approximately $2,413,000. Mrs. Ziegelheim claims that the accountant substantially underestimated the estate because of several oversights by Apollo, including his failure to locate a bank vault owned by Mr. Ziegelheim; to locate or determine the value of his tax-free municipal bonds; to verify the value of his profit-sharing plan at Pilot Woodworking, a company in which he was the primary shareholder; to search for an estimated $500,000 in savings; to contact the United States Patent Office to verify the existence of certain patents he held; to inquire into a $1,000,000 life insurance policy naming an associate of his as the beneficiary; to verify the value of certain lakefront property; and to verify the value of his stock holdings. She alleges that had Apollo made a proper inquiry, it would have been apparent that the marital estate was worth approximately $2,562,000, or about $149,000 more than the accountant found. . . .

In sum, Mrs. Ziegelheim was to receive approximately $333,000 in alimony, $6,000 in contributions to insurance costs, and $324,000 in property, the last figure representing approximately fourteen percent of the value of the estate (as appraised by Apollo and the accountant). Mr. Ziegelheim was to receive approximately $2,088,000 in property, approximately eighty-six percent of the value of the estate.

When testifying before the court immediately after the settlement was read into the record, both Mrs. Ziegelheim and Mr. Ziegelheim stated that they understood the agreement, that they thought it was fair, and that they entered into it voluntarily. Mrs. Ziegelheim now asserts, however, that she accepted the agreement only after Apollo advised her that wives could expect to receive no more than ten to twenty percent of the marital estate if they went to trial. She claims that Apollo's estimate was unduly pessimistic and did not comport with the advice that a reasonably competent attorney would have given under the circumstances. Had she been advised competently, she says, she would not have accepted the settlement. . . .

The trial court ruled in favor of defendant on all counts. It noted that Mrs. Ziegelheim had stated on the record that she understood the settlement and its terms, that she thought the terms were fair, and that she had not been coerced into settling. . . .

In accepting a case, the lawyer agrees to pursue the goals of the client to the extent the law permits, even when the lawyer believes that the client's desires are unwise or ill-considered. At the same time, because the client's desires may be influenced in large measure by the advice the lawyer provides, the lawyer is obligated to give the client reasonable advice. As a legal matter progresses and circumstances change, the wishes of the client may change as well. Accordingly, the lawyer is obligated to keep the client informed of the status of the matter for which the lawyer has been retained, and is required to advise the client on the various legal and strategic issues that arise.

In this case, Mrs. Ziegelheim made several claims impugning Apollo's handling of her divorce, and the trial court dismissed all of them on Apollo's motion for summary judgment. As we explain, we believe that the trial court's rulings on several of her claims were erroneous. . . .

On Mrs. Ziegelheim's claim that Apollo negligently advised her with respect to her chances of winning a greater proportion of the marital estate if she proceeded to trial, we conclude, as did the Appellate Division, that there was a genuine dispute regarding the appropriate advice that an attorney should give in cases like hers. According to the expert retained by Mrs. Ziegelheim, women in her position—who are in relatively poor health, have little earning capacity, and have been wholly dependent on their husbands—often receive upwards of fifty percent of the marital estate. The expert said that Mrs. Ziegelheim's chances of winning such a large fraction of the estate had she gone to trial would have been especially good because the couple had enjoyed a high standard of living while they were together and because her husband's earning capacity was "tremendous" and would remain so for some time. Her expert's opinion was brought to the trial court's attention, as was the expert report of Mr. Ziegelheim. If plaintiff's expert's opinion were credited, as it should have been for purposes of summary judgment, then Apollo very well could have been found negligent in advising her that she could expect to win only ten to twenty percent of the marital estate.

Apollo urges us to adopt the rule enunciated by the Pennsylvania Supreme Court in *Muhammad v. Strassburger, McKenna, Messer, Shilobod and Gutnick*, 526 Pa. 541, 587 A.2d 1346 (1991), that a dissatisfied litigant may not recover from his or her attorney for malpractice in negotiating a settlement that the litigant has accepted unless the litigant can prove actual fraud on the part of the attorney. Under that rule, no cause of action can be made based on negligence or contract principles against an attorney for malpractice in negotiating a settlement. The Pennsylvania Supreme Court rationalized its severe rule by explaining that it had a "longstanding public policy which encourages settlements."

New Jersey, too, has a longstanding policy that encourages settlements, but we reject the rule espoused by the Pennsylvania Supreme Court. Although we encourage settlements, we recognize that litigants rely heavily on the professional advice of counsel when they decide whether to accept or reject offers of settlement, and we insist that the lawyers of our state advise clients with respect to settlements with the same skill, knowledge, and diligence with which they pursue all other legal tasks. Attorneys are supposed to know the likelihood of success for the types of cases they handle and they are supposed to know the range of possible awards in those cases.

As we noted in *Levine v. Wiss & Co*, 97 N.J. 242, 246, 478 A.2d 397 (1984), "One who undertakes to render services in the practice of a profession or trade is required to exercise the skill and knowledge normally possessed by members of that profession in good standing in similar communities." We have found in cases involving a great variety of professionals that deviation from accepted standards of professional care will result in liability for negligence. . . . Like most courts, we see no reason to apply a more lenient rule to lawyers who negotiate settlements. *After all, the negotiation of settlements is one of the most basic and most frequently undertaken tasks that lawyers perform* [emphasis is court's]. . . .

The fact that a party received a settlement that was "fair and equitable" does not mean necessarily that the party's attorney was competent or that the party would not have received a more favorable settlement had the party's incompetent attorney been competent. Thus, in this case, notwithstanding the family court's decision, Mrs. Ziegelheim still may proceed against Apollo in her negligence action.

Moreover, another aspect of the alleged professional incompetence that led to the improvident acceptance of the settlement was the attorney's own failure to discover hidden marital assets. When Mrs. Ziegelheim sought to reopen her divorce settlement, the family court denied her motion with the observation that "[a]mple opportunity existed for full discovery," and that "the parties had their own accountants as well as counsel." The court did not determine definitively that Mr. Ziegelheim had hidden no assets, but stated instead that it "suspected that everything to be known was known to the parties." The earlier ruling did not implicate the competence of counsel and, indeed, was premised on the presumptive competence of counsel. Hence, defendant cannot invoke that ruling now to bar a challenge to his competence. Mrs. Ziegelheim should have been allowed to prove that Apollo negligently failed to discover certain assets concealed by her former husband. . . .

In holding as we do today, we do not open the door to malpractice suits by any and every dissatisfied party to a settlement. Many such claims could be averted if settlements were explained as a matter of record in open court in proceedings reflecting the understanding and assent of the parties. Further, plaintiffs must allege particular facts in support of their claims of attorney incompetence and may not litigate complaints containing mere generalized assertions of malpractice. We are mindful that attorneys cannot be held liable simply because they are not successful in persuading an opposing party to accept certain terms. Similarly, we acknowledge that attorneys who pursue reasonable strategies in handling their cases and who render reasonable advice to their clients cannot be held liable for the failure of their strategies or for any unprofitable outcomes that result because their clients took their advice. The law demands that attorneys handle their cases with knowledge, skill, and diligence, but it does not demand that they be perfect or infallible, and it does not demand that they always secure optimum outcomes for their clients. . . .

Questions

13. The Supreme Court of New Jersey's opinion in *Ziegelheim v. Apollo* states that, "In holding as we do today we do not open the door to malpractice suits by any and every dissatisfied party to a settlement." Does the New Jersey court, in reviewing the summary judgment for the defendant and allowing the negligence action against the attorney to proceed, shut the door or, rather, leave it open?

14. The court advises that "[m]any such claims could be averted if settlements were explained as a matter of record in open court in proceedings reflecting the understanding and assent of the parties." This advice may be practical in divorce cases, where the court is asked to approve and incorporate the marital settlement agreement into a court judgment, but is this cautionary step of making a court record practical as a conclusion to other lawsuit settlements? Does this help explain why settlement agreements prepared by attorneys often recite the facts, premises, and underlying reasons for the settlement?

15. Is *Ziegelheim v. Apollo* likely to be tried following this remand? If you represented defendant Apollo, how would you negotiate a final settlement of the Ziegelheim claim, and what amount would you anticipate it would take to conclude this matter?

16. If prior to finalizing the divorce settlement agreement that lawyer Apollo obtained for Ms. Ziegelheim, she fired him and retained another lawyer who negotiated a substantially similar settlement that was approved and adopted by the court following Ms. Ziegelheim's testimony that it was fair, would she be estopped from suing Apollo? (See *Puder v. Buechel*, 183 N.J. 428, 2005.)

The New Jersey Supreme Court in the *Apollo* case expressly rejects the reasoning of the Pennsylvania Supreme Court in *Muhammad v. Strassburger et al.*, which barred a client who accepted a negotiated settlement from suing his attorney in the absence of fraud. The *Muhammad* decision has been rejected by other courts, as illustrated by *Apollo*. In the following article, Professor Epstein explains why courts have rejected the *Muhammad* opinion reasoning and then contrasts malpractice actions arising from the negotiation process with other types of malpractice cases. She also offers advice on how to defend and avoid malpractice claims when clients initially accept the negotiated settlement.

❖ Lynn A. Epstein, *POST-SETTLEMENT MALPRACTICE: UNDOING THE DONE DEAL*

46 Cath. U. L. Rev. 453 (1997)

Clients voice their approval to mediators and judges as a settlement agreement is reached. A release is signed, the file is closed, and from the lawyer's perspective, another case ends. The settled case joins an overwhelming majority of civil cases that are resolved in pretrial settlement. Buried within this figure, however, is a more troubling statistic: Over twenty percent of civil cases will be resurrected in the form of malpractice actions initiated by dissatisfied clients. In those instances, and for various reasons substantiated by expert opinions, the client will charge that they could have received a better result in the settlement even though the client knowingly and willingly agreed to end the case.

In every state except Pennsylvania, a client is permitted to proceed with the theory that his attorney negligently negotiated an agreement despite the fact that the client consented to settlement. In *Muhammad v. Strassburger, McKenna, Messer, Shilobod & Gutnick*, the Pennsylvania Supreme Court determined that an attorney is immune from malpractice based on negligence where the client consented to settle. Court decisions after *Muhammad*, however, have uniformly rejected immunity for the attorney, permitting post-settlement malpractice actions to proceed in the same manner as the prototypical malpractice case.

This Article analyzes the Pennsylvania Supreme Court's decision to bar malpractice lawsuits based on settled cases. This Article then contrasts the opinion with the contradictory majority rule in other states. Next, this Article addresses the difference between mainstream malpractice actions and those malpractice actions arising from the negotiation of settled cases. . . .

Muhammad and its Successors

Conventional wisdom dictates that attorneys settle cases effectively, as an estimated ninety-five percent of civil cases are resolved by settlement. Yet, an emerging trend of post-settlement malpractice claims threatens the integrity of the settlement negotiation process. While malpractice actions are on the rise, most attorneys reasonably believed they were insulated from liability because the client had consented to settlement, and because there was no affirmative wrongdoing by the attorney. Because so many factors influence a client's decision to settle, and because so many individuals, such as judges and mediators, are a part of the process, it would appear fundamentally unfair to hold the attorneys solely responsible for such malpractice claims. This is buttressed by a majority viewpoint which looks unfavorably upon malpractice claims that require the judiciary to infiltrate the negotiation process, a process traditionally viewed as immune from judicial scrutiny.

Balancing these competing interests, the Pennsylvania Supreme Court barred such malpractice actions to foster the negotiation and settlement process. In *Muhammad*, the Pennsylvania Supreme Court held that, absent fraud, an attorney is immune from suit by a former client dissatisfied with a settlement that the former client agreed to enter.

Pamela and Abdullah Muhammad sued the firm of Strassburger, McKenna, Messer, Shilobod, and Gutnick for malpractice arising from the settlement of an underlying medical malpractice suit. In the underlying action, the Muhammads sued the physicians and hospital that performed a circumcision on their son who died as a consequence of general anesthesia used during the procedure.

The Muhammads retained the Strassburger law firm. The physicians and hospital offered to settle the malpractice claim for $23,000, which was subsequently increased to $26,500 at the suggestion of the trial court. The Muhammads accepted the settlement offer. The Muhammads later grew dissatisfied with the amount received in settlement and instructed the Strassburger law firm to communicate this discontent to defense counsel. An evidentiary hearing ensued where the court upheld the settlement agreement, reasoning that the Muhammads agreed to the settlement amount and, thus, there existed a binding and enforceable contract.

Unable to reopen the medical malpractice proceeding, the Muhammads initiated a claim against the Strassburger law firm alleging legal malpractice, fraudulent misrepresentation, fraudulent concealment, nondisclosure, breach of contract, negligence, emotional distress, and breach of fiduciary duty. The court dismissed the fraud counts because the Muhammads had not pled fraud with specificity. Surprisingly, the court then barred the Muhammads from proceeding with their remaining negligence claim against the Strassburger firm, based on articulated public policy encouraging civil litigation settlement. In granting immunity, the court wrote:

> [W]e foreclose the ability of dissatisfied litigants to agree to a settlement and then file suit against their attorneys in the hope that they will recover additional

monies. To permit otherwise results in unfairness to the attorneys who relied on their client's assent and unfairness to the litigants whose cases have not yet been tried. Additionally, it places an unnecessarily arduous burden on an overly taxed court system.

The court emphasized that this immunity extends to specific cases where a plaintiff agreed to settlement in the absence of fraud by the attorney. This is distinguished from the instance when a lawyer knowingly commits malpractice, conceals the wrongdoing, and convinces the client to settle in order to cover up the malpractice. According to the court, in this instance, the attorney's conduct is fraudulent and actionable. . . .

Muhammad has suffered widespread criticism and is uniformly rejected in every reported opinion reviewing post-settlement legal malpractice litigation. . . . While most courts are expeditious in determining that an attorney is not absolutely immune from legal malpractice actions when the client consents to settlement, they are also uniform in expressing a desire to foster protection over the negotiation process.

Courses of Action for Attorneys Confronting Post-Settlement Malpractice Claims

A. The Contributory/Comparative Negligence Defense

In a post-settlement malpractice action, an attorney should defend the action by claiming client contributory/comparative negligence. The defense should be presented by introducing evidence of the client's subjective reasons for settling the case.

The client contributory/comparative negligence defense is generally recognized in legal malpractice actions; however, some courts do not permit the issue to reach a jury. This reluctance is supported by the Restatement (Third) of Law Governing Lawyers, which asserts that the client contributory negligence defense is available in jurisdictions that recognize the same defense to general negligence actions. The Restatement cautions, however, that the lawyer/client relationship imposes fiduciary duties by which "clients are entitled to rely on their lawyers to act with competence, diligence, honesty, and loyalty." The lawyer/client relationship imposes numerous duties on the lawyer, while imposing few on the client. Yet, this cannot relieve clients from accepting responsibility for their own acts or omissions which result in unfavorable settlements.

Courts that permit the client comparative negligence defense, however, proceed with caution, premised on the view that attorneys should not be permitted to circumvent responsibility to former clients under the guise that the client should have known how to respond or act. Thus, even when a legal document contains simple English that needs no interpretation by a lawyer, the defense of client contributory negligence has been barred in certain jurisdictions. . . .

Courts should, however, permit the comparative negligence defense to proceed to the fact finder where the client settled a claim and now seeks to hold an attorney liable for malpractice committed in the negotiation of that settlement. In a majority of post-settlement malpractice claims, the former clients do not claim they did not understand the settlement agreement. Instead, this majority group freely admits they voluntarily entered into settlement, conceding they understood the agreement and abandoned their right to a trial. Only after settlement did these former clients contend there was "something else" their former lawyer should have done to secure a better result.

Although there will be cases where the client is genuinely aggrieved by a negligent attorney, the majority of post-settlement malpractice litigation arises from the client's own conduct. In those cases, the comparative fault defense should be considered by the fact finder.

While the comparative fault defense is available in the typical legal malpractice action, its use has been limited in post-settlement malpractice litigation. . . . [Courts] provide minimum guidelines to which an attorney should adhere in advising a client regarding settlement. . . . [T]he lawyer should hold an appreciation of (1) the relevant facts; (2) the present and future potential strengths and weaknesses of his case; (3) the likely costs, both objectively (monetarily) and subjectively (psychological disruption of business and family life) associated with proceeding further in the litigation; and (4) the likely outcome if the case were to proceed further.

Many cases of legal malpractice occur from "perceived" negligence by attorneys who fail to adhere to the [above] criteria. Common practice dictates that attorneys review the four factors in detail with their client prior to settlement. In post-settlement malpractice litigation analysis, courts tend to focus only on the result obtained (the settlement sum) to gauge the lawyer's liability exposure, ignoring the traditional factors preceding settlement. Hence, an attorney wishing to marshal an effective defense must take pre-settlement steps aimed to protect his client's interest. This will safeguard against subsequent malpractice claims within the framework developed by the courts.

B. The "Release and Settlement Agreement": Solidifying the Deal

The "release and settlement agreement" is the final written document ending the litigation and, in many instances, the lawyer-client relationship. An historical review of related lawyer-client concern over apparent complications arising from contingency fee arrangements creates an additional post-settlement malpractice defense. To assure a client's comprehension of contingency fee contracts, many state bar associations require clients and attorneys to review and execute a "statement of client rights" which thoroughly explains the contingency fee agreement. This statement obligates the attorney to adhere to specific reporting and accounting requirements concerning fees throughout the client's case. It also provides the client with a remedy against unscrupulous attorneys.

Similar to the "statement of client rights," an attorney should be required to provide a client with a statement of the case before settlement. This statement would precisely articulate the ramifications of settlement and act as written confirmation of the attorney's work on the case. . . .

Conclusion

Post-settlement malpractice actions are quite unique. While the Pennsylvania Supreme Court effectively banned these lawsuits, providing former counsel immunity rather than engaging in the arduous analysis inherent to malpractice litigation, the better course of action is to permit attorneys to present the client comparative fault defense. This will allow an attorney to present evidence of the client's subjective reasons for settling the litigation. Additionally, through the use of a pre-settlement statement of the case form, attorneys will provide their clients sufficient information to adequately prepare for a successful negotiation and settlement process.

Note — Preventing Negotiation Malpractice

In the *Muhammad* case, Justice Larsen wrote a stinging dissent accusing the majority of creating a "Lawyer's Holiday" by barring malpractice against lawyers for negligence committed in the negotiation of civil settlements. He reasoned by comparison, "If a doctor is negligent in saving a human life, the doctor pays. If a priest is negligent in saving the spirit of a human, the priest pays. But if a lawyer is negligent in advising his client as to settlement, the client pays." Justice Larsen's dissent reflects the general view that most courts have taken in rejecting the Pennsylvania Supreme Court's protection of the negotiation process from claims of malpractice.

When negotiation malpractice cases do proceed to a jury trial, the jury is required to assess the negotiated outcome. The dilemma of evaluation confronted in these cases is "compared to what?" Most often the comparison is to the likely result if the negotiated claim had proceeded to trial. This requires, in effect, a "trial within a trial." Although this approach is thought to apply an objective standard, it does not take into account the give and take of the negotiation process and the subjective, or nonmonetary, interests that may in reality have driven the negotiation. The "trial within a trial" approach reverts to a distributive negotiation model that launders out integrative aspects that favorably distinguish negotiation from trial.

Judging a negotiated outcome by an objective, monetary gauge fails to factor in the interest-based approach to which most of the new negotiation literature is directed. It raises the same concerns as does grading law students at the end of a negotiation course only on the quantitative, monetary results of a final negotiation role-play. As expressed by Epstein, "[E]very aspect of a negotiated settlement, particularly its conclusion, is a subjective evaluation premised on the client's needs and desires, coupled with the various influences that affect that client's ultimate desire to settle". . . . Gauging a lawyer's liability exposure only on the monetary result obtained can have a chilling effect on good integrative bargaining by attorneys.

Professor Epstein proposes that attorneys protect themselves from malpractice claims by regularly using a form entitled, "Pre-Settlement Statement of Client's Case," which the client is to sign before settlement. This form memorializes all the facts, assessments, and advice that were considered to decide upon settlement. The concluding sentence of the form states, "[Y]our attorney may use this document as a defense in a malpractice action if permitted by law." Although not a release per se, it is clearly intended to relieve the attorney of malpractice liability.

This "CYA" approach may or may not be effective protection, but is it the way you want to practice law? Each of us must ask how a precautionary approach with an eye ahead to defending malpractice claims will influence our relations with clients and affect our interaction with other attorneys. Will fear of malpractice hinder our nimbleness and creativity as negotiators? Was the *Muhammad* decision correct in its premise that opening up negotiation to after-the-fact legal scrutiny may impede negotiation and discourage settlement? If so, will judicial resources and client interests be adversely impacted?

As you consider these questions, please be aware that malpractice verdicts against lawyers for their good-faith efforts in negotiating on behalf of clients appear to be rare. Being alert to client concerns, including their emotional needs, and keeping them informed are the best preventions. Reading this book and studying the negotiation process will prepare you to be an effective negotiator, with appreciative clients. Clients who feel their lawyers have done all they can to faithfully attend to their interests do not sue them.

CHAPTER
12

Obstacles to Agreement and Negotiation Assistance

A. Obstacles

Negotiations may stall due to a variety of obstacles. Indeed, some negotiations never get started because talking together is prevented by the history of the relationship or other barriers.

The psychological traps and different perceptions that create conflicts can persist or reappear to serve as obstacles that prevent a negotiated resolution of the conflict. Drawing from your own experience, as well as from the previous readings in this book, you are familiar with some of the obstacles that can get in the way of a negotiated settlement. Many of these arise from the cognitive and emotional factors, as well as interpersonal dynamics, as discussed in Chapter 2. Other barriers are structural or strategic. Common obstacles to negotiated settlements, as well as some negotiated transactions, include the following:

- Over-competitiveness
- Complexity of issues
- Concern about setting precedent
- Demonizing opposition
- Differing perceptions
- Differing case evaluations
- Egos/reputations
- Fear of looking weak
- Fixation on single position/solution
- Greed
- Hidden agendas

- Lawyer incentives not to settle
- Linear thinking
- Optimistic overconfidence
- Over-investment in case
- Past baggage
- Personality clashes
- Poor communication
- Reactive devaluation
- Self-fulfilling prophecies
- Stereotypes
- Strong feelings

When any of these barriers make negotiations difficult, cumbersome, or unlikely to succeed, assistance is available. Using a third-party neutral to facilitate or manage the negotiation, and perhaps to make suggestions, can be helpful in promoting settlement. The third party may be a judge with power to order the parties to participate, a special master or evaluator appointed by the court to provide settlement assistance, or a mediator connected to the court or in private practice.

We examine here processes available through the courts and from private mediators to help reach settlements. First, we learn more about barriers and how neutral third parties can overcome some of the most persistent barriers to negotiated resolution.

❖ **Robert H. Mnookin,** *WHY NEGOTIATIONS FAIL:*
AN EXPLORATION OF BARRIERS TO THE RESOLUTION OF CONFLICT

8 Ohio St. J. Disp. Resol. 235 (1993)

Conflict is inevitable, but efficient and fair resolution is not. Conflicts can persist even though there may be any number of possible resolutions that would better serve the interests of the parties. . . . In our everyday personal and professional lives, we have all witnessed disputes where the absence of a resolution imposes substantial and avoidable costs on all parties. . . .

My first example involves a divorcing family in California who were part of a longitudinal study carried out by Stanford psychologist Eleanor Maccoby and me. Mary and Paul Templeton spent three years fighting over the custody of their seven-year-old daughter Tracy after Mary filed for divorce in 1985. Mary wanted sole custody; Paul wanted joint physical custody. This middle-income family spent over $37,000 [in 1985 dollars] on lawyers and experts. In the process, they traumatized Tracy and inflicted great emotional pain on each other. More to the point, the conflict over who would best care for their daughter damaged each parent's relationship with Tracy, who has suffered terribly by being caught in the middle of her parents' conflict. Ultimately the divorce decree provided that Mary would have primary physical custody of Tracy, and Paul would be entitled to reasonable weekend visitation. The parents' inability to negotiate with one another led to a result in which mother, father, and daughter were all losers. . . .

My last example is an Art Buchwald story—but it isn't a laughing matter, at least, not for Buchwald. He and his partner, Alain Bernheim, submitted Buchwald's two and a half page "treatment" for a story called "King for a Day" to Paramount Pictures pursuant to contracts providing that Bernheim would produce any film based on the story idea and that Buchwald and Bernheim would each share in the profits. In 1989, Buchwald and Bernheim sued Paramount for breach of contract. They claimed that the studio had based Eddie Murphy's film, "Coming to America." on their treatment but had failed to give them their due. After three years of bitter litigation, a trial judge awarded Buchwald $150,000 and Bernheim $750,000. In the initial newspaper accounts, both sides claimed victory, but this is hardly an example of "win-win." Paramount claimed to be the winner because the legal fees of the plaintiffs' lawyers exceeded $2.5 million and the total recovery of only $900,000 was a small fraction of the $6.2 million Buchwald and Bernheim had requested in their final arguments. As it turns out, Buchwald and Bernheim will not have to pay the full legal fees because of a contingency arrangement with their law firm, but Buchwald has acknowledged that his share of out-of-pocket expenses alone exceeds $200,000 and that as a consequence, he will have no net recovery. On the other hand, Buchwald ridiculed Paramount's claim of victory. How, he asked, could it be a victory for a defendant to pay out nearly $1 million in damages, and, in addition, have legal fees of its own in excess of $3 million? Seems like lose-lose to me.

On her death bed, Gertrude Stein was asked by Alice B. Toklas, "What is the answer? What is the answer?" After a long silence, Stein responded: "No, what is the question?" Examples like these, and I am sure you could add many more of your own, suggest a central question for those of us concerned with dispute resolution: Why is it that under circumstances where there are resolutions that better serve disputants, negotiations often fail to achieve efficient resolutions? In other words, what are the barriers to the negotiated resolution of conflict? . . .

Strategic Barriers

The first barrier to the negotiated resolution of conflict is inherent in a central characteristic of negotiation. Negotiation can be metaphorically compared to making a pie and then dividing it up. The process of conflict resolution affects both the size of the pie, and who gets what size slice. . . .

Even when both parties know all the relevant information, and that potential gains may result from a negotiated deal, strategic bargaining over how to divide the pie can still lead to deadlock (with no deal at all) or protracted and expensive bargaining, thus shrinking the pie. For example, suppose Nancy has a house for sale for which she has a reservation price of $245,000. I am willing to pay up to $295,000 for the house. Any deal within a bargaining range from $245,000 to $295,000 would make both of us better off than no sale at all. Suppose we each know the other's reservation price. Will there be a deal? Not necessarily. If we disagree about how the $50,000 "surplus" should be divided (each wanting all or most of it), our negotiation may end in a deadlock. We might engage in hardball negotiation tactics in which each tried to persuade the other that he or she was committed to walking away from a beneficial deal, rather than accept less than $40,000 of the surplus. Nancy might claim that she won't take a nickel less than $285,000, or even $294,999 for that matter. Indeed, she might go so far as to give a power of attorney to an agent to sell only at that price, and then leave town in order to make her commitment credible. Of course, I could play the same type of game and the result would then be that no deal is made and that we are both worse off. In this case, the obvious tension between the distribution of the $50,000 and the value creating possibilities inherent in any sale within the bargaining range may result in no deal.

Strategic behavior—which may be rational for a self-interested party concerned with maximizing the size of his or her own slice—can often lead to inefficient outcomes. Those subjected to claiming tactics often respond in kind, and the net result typically is to push up the cost of the dispute resolution process. (*Buchwald v. Paramount Pictures Corp.* is a good example of a case in which the economic costs of hardball litigation obviously and substantially shrunk the pie.) Parties may be tempted to engage in strategic behavior, hoping to get more. Often all they do is shrink the size of the pie. Those experienced in the civil litigation process see this all the time. One or both sides often attempt to use pre-trial discovery as leverage to force the other side into agreeing to a more favorable settlement. Often the net result, however, is simply that both sides spend unnecessary money on the dispute resolution process.

The Principal-Agent Problem

The second barrier is suggested by recent work relating to transaction cost economics, and is sometimes called the "principal/agent" problem. . . . The basic problem is that the incentives for an agent (whether it be a lawyer, employee, or officer) negotiating on behalf of a party to a dispute may induce behavior that fails to serve the interests of the principal itself. The relevant research suggests that it is no simple matter—whether by contract or custom—to align perfectly the incentives for an agent with the interests of the principal. This divergence may act as a barrier to efficient resolution of conflict.

Litigation is fraught with principal/agent problems. In civil litigation, for example—particularly where the lawyers on both sides are being paid by the hour—there is very little incentive for the opposing lawyers to cooperate, particularly if the clients have the capacity to pay for trench warfare and are angry to boot. Commentators have suggested that this is one reason many cases settle on the courthouse steps, and not before: for the lawyers, a late settlement may avoid the possible embarrassment of an extreme outcome, while at the same time providing substantial fees. . . .

Overcoming . . . Barriers: The Role of Negotiators and Mediators

The study of barriers can do more than simply help us understand why negotiations sometimes fail when they should not. It can also contribute to our understanding of how to overcome these barriers. . . .

First, let us consider the strategic barrier. To the extent that a neutral third party is trusted by both sides, the neutral may be able to induce the parties to reveal information about their underlying interests, needs, priorities, and aspirations that they would not disclose to their adversary. This information may permit a trusted mediator to help the parties enlarge the pie in circumstances where the parties acting alone could not. Moreover, a mediator can foster a problem-solving atmosphere and lessen the temptation on the part of each side to engage in strategic behavior. A skilled mediator can often get parties to move beyond political posturing and recriminations about past wrongs and to instead consider possible gains from a fair resolution of the dispute.

A mediator also can help overcome barriers posed by principal/agent problems. A mediator may bring clients themselves to the table, and help them understand their shared interest in minimizing legal fees and costs in circumstances where the lawyers themselves might not be doing so. In circumstances where a middle manager is acting to prevent a settlement that might benefit the company, but might be harmful to the manager's own career, an astute mediator can sometimes bring another company representative to the table who does not have a personal stake in the outcome.

A mediator can also promote dispute resolution by helping overcome cognitive barriers. Through a variety of processes, a mediator can often help each side understand the power of the case from the other side's perspective. Moreover, by reframing the dispute and suggesting a resolution that avoids blame and stresses the positive aspects of a resolution, a mediator may be able to lessen the effects of loss aversion. My colleague Amos Tversky thinks that cognitive barriers are like optical illusions—knowing that an illusion exists does not necessarily enable us to see things differently. Nevertheless, I believe that astute mediators can dampen loss aversion through reframing, by helping a disputant reconceptualize the resolution. By emphasizing the potential gains to both sides of the resolution and de-emphasizing the losses that the resolution is going to entail, mediators (and lawyers) often facilitate resolution.

With respect to . . . reactive devaluation, mediators can play an important and quite obvious role. Reactive devaluation can often be sidestepped if the source of a proposal is a neutral—not one of the parties. Indeed, one of the trade secrets of mediators is that after talking separately to each side about what might or might not be acceptable, the mediator takes responsibility for making a proposal. This helps both parties avoid reactive devaluation by allowing them to accept as sensible a proposal that they might have rejected if it had come directly from their adversary. . . .

B. The Spectrum of Dispute Resolution

The above article introduces the role of a mediator in overcoming barriers to negotiating an agreement. There are a variety of options available to resolve your clients' disputes. Direct negotiation anchors one end of a spectrum of dispute resolution procedures. At the other end is a trial in court. Negotiation and trial are polar opposites. Parties who opt for trial have relatively little control over either the process or the outcome. Trials are formal and public, conducted under detailed procedural and evidentiary rules, with a judge in control. A judge or jury decides the outcome, and in doing so is bound to follow established legal principles. By contrast, negotiation gives parties maximum control over both the process and its outcome.

In between direct negotiation and trial is a continuum of alternative dispute resolution (ADR) processes. The continuum moves from processes that have characteristics very similar to negotiation to ones that closely resemble a trial. The key characteristic that distinguishes negotiation-like processes from trial-like methods is whether a neutral party has the ability to impose a binding outcome on the participants. Proceedings in which the neutral can decide the result are all forms of adjudication. Processes that authorize the neutral to facilitate, persuade, even pressure parties to reach agreement—but not to impose a result on them—are all forms of assisted negotiation.

Mediators, for example, assist negotiators in reaching a settlement, but do not have the power to require disputants to reach agreement or impose a decision. For that reason, mediation and all of its variants are on the nonbinding, assisted-negotiation side of the spectrum. By contrast, in traditional arbitration the neutral does have the power to decide the outcome, so arbitration falls on the binding, adjudicative side of the spectrum. However, the terminology can be misleading. One example is a process known as advisory or judicial arbitration, which does not necessarily result in a binding decision and can promote a negotiated settlement. We present below dispute resolution processes as a spectrum of procedural shadings, with the central dividing characteristic or line being whether a neutral has authority to impose a binding outcome on the parties. All the procedures to the left of the dividing line are available as a form of third-party assisted negotiation.

Dispute Resolution Spectrum

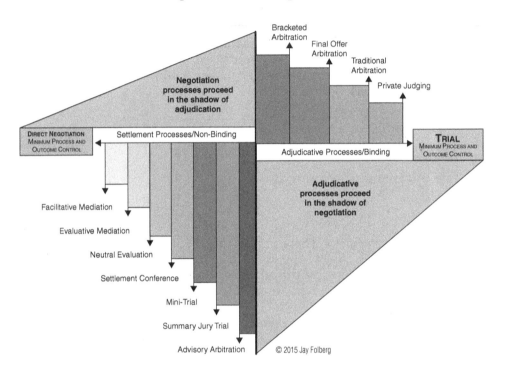

Whenever a dispute involves a legal claim, the plaintiff can, at least in theory, obtain a binding decision from a court. The elephant in the closet of nonbinding settlement efforts is the likely outcome if the dispute proceeds to trial. For this reason a "shadow of adjudication" extends across the nonbinding, negotiation side of the spectrum. Similarly, disputants can halt even a binding procedure by reaching agreement. Settlement negotiations, in effect, lurk in the closet of adjudication: We refer to this on our chart as the "shadow of negotiation."

The process possibilities on the nonbinding, negotiation side of the spectrum are infinite, limited only by what the parties can create, agree upon, and afford. The spectrum displays the settlement processes and methods that are most often discussed in the literature and commonly used, now or in the recent past. The most widely used nonbinding form of assisted dispute resolution is mediation. Mediation is available privately as a service for a fee and through court-connected or court-mandated programs, where there may or may not be a fee. We look first at the process of mediation as an aid to reaching negotiated agreements and then explore the use of other nonbinding forms of assistance to lawyers in settling disputes. In Chapter 13 you will read about how to best represent clients in mediation and how to use mediation to their advantage for purposes of favorably negotiating agreements.

C. Mediation

1. What Is Mediation?

Mediation is a process of assisted negotiation in which a neutral person helps parties reach agreement. The process varies depending on the style of the mediator, the nature of the dispute, and the wishes of the participants. Mediation differs from direct negotiation in that it involves the participation of an impartial third party. The process also differs from adjudication, in that it is consensual, informal, and usually private. The participants need not reach agreement, and the mediator has no power to impose an outcome.

In some contexts you may find that this definition does not fully apply. The process is sometimes not voluntary, as when a court requires litigants to mediate. Occasionally mediation is required to be open to the public, as when a controversy involves governmental entities who are subject to "open meeting" laws. A mediator's goal is not always to settle a dispute; the neutral may focus instead on helping disputants improve their relationship or complete a transaction.

2. What Do Mediators Do?

Mediators apply a wide variety of techniques. Depending on the situation, a settlement-oriented legal mediator may use the following approaches, among others:

- Help litigants design a process that ensures the presence of key participants and provides information and focuses their attention on finding a solution to a dispute.
- Allow the principals and their attorneys to present legal arguments, raise underlying concerns, and express feelings directly to their opponents and the mediator, and hear the other side's perspective firsthand.
- Help participants focus on their interests and identify imaginative settlement options that satisfy them.
- Moderate negotiations, translate communications, act as consultant about bargaining tactics, and reframe disputants' positions and perceptions.
- Assist each side to assess the likely outcome if the case is litigated and consider the full costs if the conflict continues.
- Work with disputants to draft a durable agreement and, if necessary, implement it.

3. What Is the Structure of Mediation?

Because mediation is informal, lawyers and clients have a great deal of freedom to shape the process, and in practice, good neutrals and advocates vary their approach and tactics significantly to respond to the circumstances of particular cases.

"Commercial," sometimes called "civil" or "legal," mediation typically involves contract, tort, property, employment, intellectual property, statutory, and other civil claims. "Marital" and "community" mediation focus respectively on family and neighborhood issues, and other forms of mediation are associated with collective bargaining, public policy, and other kinds of disputes. A typical commercial mediation is likely to proceed through the stages described below.

a. Pre-Mediation

Before the disputants meet to mediate, the neutral often has telephone conversations with the lawyers, usually without the parties, to deal with issues such as who will attend the mediation session and what information will be exchanged and provided to the mediator ahead of time. The mediator and lawyers can use this time to build a relationship and for the mediator to learn about obstacles that have made settlement difficult.

b. The Opening Session

Traditionally, legal mediations begin with the parties, their lawyers, and the mediator meeting together to discuss the dispute—known as the "opening" or "joint" session. The content and structure of the opening session varies considerably, depending on the participants' wishes and goals for the process. When mediation is focused on reaching a monetary settlement, the joint session is likely to be dominated by presentations and arguments of lawyers. If the goal is to find an interest-based solution or to repair a ruptured relationship, the mediator is much more likely to encourage the parties themselves to speak and to attempt to draw out underlying issues and emotions with everyone present.

c. Private Caucusing

After disputants have exchanged perspectives, arguments, and perhaps questions in the opening session, most commercial mediators move the process into private meetings, or "caucuses," in which they talk with each side individually. The purpose of caucusing is to permit disputants, counsel, and the mediator to discuss issues privately. By keeping the parties separated with communications channeled through her, a mediator can also shape the disputants' dialogue in productive ways. In traditional commercial mediation participants usually spend most of their time separated, with the mediator shuttling back and forth between them.

d. Joint Discussions

If parties are interested in exploring an interest-based resolution or, especially, repairing a broken relationship, even mediators who rely on caucusing are likely to encourage disputants to meet together. Mediators sometimes also ask subgroups of disputants to meet for specific purposes, for instance to permit experts to examine tax questions in a business breakup, or an employee and supervisor to talk about an emotional issue. When mediations reach agreement the lawyers, and sometimes also the clients, usually meet to sign a memorandum of agreement.

e. Follow-Up Contacts

Increasingly, the mediation process is not limited to in-person meetings between the mediator and the disputants. If a case is not resolved at a mediation session, the neutral is likely to follow up, facilitating telephone or e-mail negotiations or convening another face-to-face session.

f. Variations in Format

The model described above is the traditional format of legal or "commercial" mediation, but you may encounter significant variations in your practice. In some areas of the country, particularly the West Coast, legal mediators often do not meet jointly with parties and lawyers. If they convene the disputants at all, it is only to exchange opening greetings and discuss ground rules; all substantive discussions occur in a caucus format.

Mediators who handle family disputes, by contrast, have traditionally conducted the entire process in a series of joint meetings with the parties that occur over a period of weeks or months. In this model, disputants talk together without attorneys present but can consult with their counsel between sessions.

Problem — Death of a Student

In late August, Scott Krueger arrived for his freshman year at the Massachusetts Institute of Technology. Five weeks later, he was dead. In an incident that made national headlines, Krueger died of alcohol poisoning following an initiation event at a fraternity. Nearly two years later, Krueger's parents sent MIT a demand letter stating their intent to sue. The letter alleged that MIT had caused their son's death by failing to address what they claimed were two long-standing campus problems: a housing arrangement that they said steered new students to seek rooms in fraternities, and what their lawyer called a culture of alcohol abuse at fraternities.

MIT's lawyers saw the case as one that could be won. An appellate court, they believed, would rule that a college is not legally responsible for an adult student's voluntary drinking. Moreover, under state law the university could not be required to pay more than $20,000 to the Kruegers (although that limit did not apply to claims against individual university administrators). MIT officials felt, however, that a narrowly drawn legal response would not be in keeping with its values. They also recognized that there were aspects of the institution's policies and practices—including those covering student use of alcohol—that could have been better. MIT's president, Charles M. Vest, was prepared to accept responsibility for these shortcomings on behalf of the university, and felt a deep personal desire for his institution to reach a resolution with the Krueger family. MIT also recognized that defending the case in court would exact a tremendous emotional toll on all concerned. The Kruegers would be subjected to a hard-hitting assessment of their son's behavior leading up to his death, whereas MIT would be exposed to equally severe scrutiny of the Institute's culture and the actions of individual administrators. Full-blown litigation in a case of this magnitude was also sure to be expensive, with estimated defense costs well in excess of $1 million.

How might mediation be initiated and used to satisfactorily resolve the Kruegers' claim?

Note: An Example of Mediation in Aid of Negotiation*

The question, as MIT saw the above situation, was not whether to seek to engage the Kruegers in settlement negotiations, but how. The university decided to forego a traditional legal response to initiate negotiations and replied instead with a personal letter from President Vest to the Kruegers, which noted the university's belief that it had strong legal defenses to their claims but offered to mediate.

The Kruegers responded with intense distrust. Tortuous negotiations ensued. The parents eventually agreed to mediate, but only subject to certain conditions: At least one session would have to occur in Buffalo, New York, where the Kruegers lived. MIT would have to offer a sincere apology for its conduct; without that, no sum of money would settle the case. There would be no confidentiality agreement to prevent the parents from talking publicly about the matter, while at the same time any settlement could not be exploited by MIT for public relations purposes. The Kruegers would have the right to select the mediator. And President Vest would have to appear personally at all the mediation sessions. The university agreed to most of the conditions, and the mediation went forward.

MIT's lawyers believed that it was important that the Kruegers' lawyers and the mediator understand the strength of the university's defenses, but plaintiff counsel knew that subjecting the Kruegers to such a presentation would make settlement impossible. To resolve the dilemma, the lawyers bifurcated the process. The first day of the mediation, which the Kruegers would not attend, would focus on presentations by lawyers and would be held in Boston, near where MIT

---

* Confidentiality is one of the most important attributes of mediation. The facts in the following account that have not previously been published have been approved by attorneys for both parties.

is located. One week later, the mediation would resume at a conference center located a 40-minute drive outside Buffalo, this time with the Kruegers present. Their counsel selected that location so that "no one could leave easily." On the second day the Kruegers would personally meet President Vest, and the parties would begin to exchange settlement proposals.

Counsel had agreed that the mediator, Jeffrey Stern, should begin the day by having a private breakfast with Mr. and Mrs. Krueger and their lawyers. The Kruegers vented their anger, first to Stern and later to President Vest. "How could you do this?" they shouted at Vest, "You people killed our son!" They also challenged Vest on a point that bothered them terribly: Why, they asked him, had he come to their son's funeral but not sought them out personally to extend his condolences? Vest responded that he had consulted with people about whether or not to approach the Kruegers and was advised that, in light of their anger at the institution, it would be better not to do so. That advice was wrong, he said, and he regretted following it.

Vest went on to apologize for the university's role in what he described as a "terrible, terrible tragedy." "We failed you," he said, and then asked, "What can we do to make it right?" Mrs. Krueger cried out again at Vest, but at that point her husband turned to her and said, "The man apologized. What more is there to say?" Their counsel, Leo Boyle, later said that he felt that, "There's a moment . . . where the back of the case is broken. You can feel it. . . . And that was the moment this day." The mediator gradually channeled the discussion toward what the Kruegers wanted and what the university could do.

Hard bargaining followed, much of it conducted though shuttle diplomacy by the mediator. In the end the parties reached agreement: MIT paid the Kruegers $4.75 million to settle their claims and contributed an additional $1.25 million to a scholarship fund that the family would administer. Perhaps equally important, President Vest offered the Kruegers a personal, unconditional apology on behalf of MIT that no court could have compelled and that would not have been believed if it were. At the conclusion of the process Vest and Mrs. Krueger hugged each other. For MIT, the settlement, although expensive, made sense: It minimized the harm that contested litigation would have caused to the institution. And, most important, the university felt that it was the right thing to do.

What did the mediator contribute to overcoming obstacles in the negotiation process? During the first day, Stern questioned both lawyers closely about the legal and factual issues, creating a foundation for realistic assessments of case value later in the process. The initial money offers put forth by each party were far apart, but the mediator put them into context so that neither side gave up in frustration. According to plaintiff counsel Brad Henry, Stern's greatest contribution was probably the way he responded to the Kruegers' feelings:

> What he did most masterfully was to allow a lot of the emotion to be directed at him. He allowed it almost to boil over when it was just him with the Kruegers, but later he very deftly let it be redirected at President Vest and the university. . . . He also prepared Charles Vest for the onslaught. . . . Mediation can be like a funeral — especially with the death of a child. He mediated the emotional part of the case, and then let the rest unfold on its own.

Questions

1. What barriers made it difficult for the parties in the Krueger case to negotiate with each other directly? In what ways was mediation likely to be more effective at overcoming those difficulties than would direct negotiation?
2. What goals did the university have in proposing mediation? What did the student's family appear to be seeking from the process?
3. What did the Kruegers obtain in mediation that they could not likely have obtained in direct negotiation or have won at trial?

4. Goals for the Process

When you advise your client about the use of mediation, it is important to clarify the goals. The basic goal may seem obvious: to settle a legal dispute on terms as favorable as possible for your client. But the goals are often more complex. The goals may include the ones listed below.

a. Resolve a Legal Claim on the Best Possible Monetary Terms

Most trial lawyers take a narrow approach to the process, particularly after reaching an impasse in direct negotiations, seeking the best possible monetary result. One plaintiff's personal injury lawyer, for example, described the process as:

> An opportunity — a time for you, as the legal representative of your client, to avoid putting your client through the litigation "mill" . . . and get results. . . . It is a means of essentially "selling" your client's lawsuit to a buyer, who buys off the expense and exposure of an ongoing lawsuit. The client has the money to begin the life restructuring process and has avoided the pressures and uncertainties of litigation. (Kornblum 2004)

Perhaps in response to this view from the lawyers who choose them, commercial mediators often see their primary role as facilitating distributive bargaining over money. One neutral, for example, wrote that "[i]n the typical civil mediation, money is the primary (if not the only) issue" (Contuzzi 2000), and another has said that "[t]he goal of resolution is always the same: allowing the parties to negotiate to a 'reasonable ballpark,' in which they, with the help of the mediator, identify 'home plate' based on what a jury will consider 'a reasonable verdict range'" (Max 1999).

In a tort/insurance dispute litigants and counsel are likely to enter the mediation process assuming that it will focus primarily on legal arguments and positional bargaining over money. Although this kind of negotiation often produces less-than-optimal results, a mediator can do a great deal to assist parties even when money is the only issue over which the disputants are willing to bargain.

Typical Mediator-Assisted Negotiation Over Money

An inexperienced plaintiff's lawyer was representing an automobile accident victim in negotiations with the defendant's insurer. The victim had
suffered broken bones and had out-of-pocket damages totaling $6,000.
Requested by the defendant's adjuster to make a settlement demand, the
plaintiff counsel asked for $1.2 million. The adjuster was incredulous: In
her experience, plaintiff lawyers rarely demanded more than ten times the
"out-of-pockets." She refused to "dignify" the plaintiff's "wild number" with
a response, and the result was a complete breakdown of talks. The case went
to mediation. In a private meeting with the plaintiff and his counsel, the
mediator asked about their goals in the negotiation. The lawyer said that
he was willing to be flexible, and the client indicated that he was seeking a
much more modest amount than their $1.2 million demand might suggest.
The neutral asked the plaintiff lawyer to make a new offer at a much lower
level. She offered to tell the adjuster that the plaintiff had done this only
to accommodate the mediator's request that both sides "cut to the chase,"
and that the plaintiff expected the defendant to respond in a similar vein.
Three hours later the case settled at $27,500.

b. Develop a Broad, Interest-Based Resolution

Some lawyers employ mediation to facilitate interest-based bargaining and
to develop creative resolutions. The barriers to settlement through direct negotiation often impede the consideration of creative, interest-based resolutions
available through mediation.

Typical Mediator-Assisted Negotiation Involving Other Interests

A company that processed hazardous chemical waste and one of its residential abutters had been embroiled in a series of disputes over the company's
applications for licenses to expand its operations. Negotiations between
attorneys reached an impasse and they suggested mediation. During the
mediation, the discussion at first focused exclusively on the meaning of certain state hazardous waste regulations, but the mediator noticed that the
abutter became most angry when he mentioned the company's practice of
parking large trucks filled with waste on the street across from his house.
The company insisted that such situations resulted from unpredictable
traffic jams at the plant, while the abutter maintained that the problem
showed the company's basic callousness about its neighbors' safety. As he
spoke with the parties in caucus, the mediator found that the company also
wanted to end the practice, and could do so if it could widen its driveway to
accommodate two trucks at a time. This was impossible, however, because
the driveway was wedged between a building and the abutter's property

line. That part of the abutter's land was not, however, being used. As part of a settlement, the mediator convinced the abutter to convey a narrow strip of his unused land to the company at a modest price. The company in turn agreed to widen its driveway, solving the truck parking problem and increasing the value of the abutter's remaining land.

c. Repair the Parties' Relationship

Lawyers sometimes suggest mediation to their clients whose interests might be served if the dispute being negotiated could be resolved in a way that preserved the relationship strained by the conflict, or that created a beneficial relationship between rivals. The act of filing suit is usually understood as a decision to sever connections, but an appreciable percentage of the time this does not occur. Getting the parties together with a skilled mediator may facilitate the goal, perhaps unspoken, of allowing a partnership to be continued, a mutually profitable vendor and customer relationship renewed, or a tech license created in a patent dispute.

d. Choices Among Goals

Although a particular mediation can have more than a single purpose, the process can be viewed as falling along a continuum between purely monetary outcomes and broader interest-fulfilling results. How likely is it in practice that if an attorney seeks a goal, he will be able to achieve it—how often, in other words, can parties in commercial mediation expect to leave the process with only a monetary settlement, an interest-based solution, or a repaired relationship?

The answer will be heavily influenced by the nature of the case, the attitudes of clients and counsel, the reason direct negotiations have not resolved the conflict, and the skills of the mediator. Relationship repair in mediation is often not relevant; in most automobile tort cases, for example, the parties enter the dispute as strangers and usually have no incentive to relate with each other in the future. Even when a dispute does arise in a relationship, the parties often litigate bitterly before mediating, and in such situations reviving their relationship is very difficult. Sometimes, however, both sides recognize that it is in their interest to heal their rupture. This is most common in settings in which the parties' past connection has been strong and their alternatives to undertaking a repair are not attractive, for example a quarrel between a divorcing couple over parenting their children.

Relationships can be important in commercial settings as well; partners in small businesses, may have a strong interest repairing their relationship because neither is able to buy the other out—in the words of one lawyer, "it's just too expensive to get divorced"—and continued conflict will destroy the value of the enterprise for everyone. A study of mediations of civil disputes arising from relationships (excluding unionized labor and divorce cases, and focused on cases involving lawyers) found a pattern of outcomes shown in the following table:

Outcomes of Legal Mediation in "Relationship" Cases			
Repair of relationship	Money plus integrative term(s) but no repair	Money terms only	Impasse
17%	30%	27%	27%

When parties mediate a legal dispute arising from a significant prior relationship using a professional mediator, it appears that they are able to repair their relationship about 15 to 20 percent of the time, achieve a settlement that is usually centered on money but has at least one significant integrative term about 30 percent of the time, and achieve a monetary settlement or reach impasse in 25 to 30 percent of cases. Interestingly, focusing only on those cases that settled, agreements that contained a relationship repair or money plus at least one integrative term totaled 47 percent, a substantially higher percentage than pure-money settlements (Golann 2002). Another study found that nonmonetary terms were included in most settlements of contract disputes, but seldom in personal injury (mainly auto accident) cases (Wissler 2006).

As a lawyer you may encounter situations in which a client's only goal is to end a ruptured relationship on the best possible terms. The data suggest that in cases that arise from a prior relationship, it is often feasible to obtain agreements with at least one term of value to the parties apart from money, and that in a small but appreciable percentage of cases parties can repair their relationship.

5. Mediator Styles

One challenge you face when representing clients in mediation is selecting a neutral. Most jurisdictions now offer a large number of potential mediators, and different neutrals use widely varying approaches. Depending on the dispute, the personalities and goals of the participants, and the obstacles blocking settlement, you may want a specific style or set of qualities in a mediator. Information about the general approach of mediators and their expertise is readily available on provider organizations' and mediators' websites, as well as from other attorneys who have had experience with them. Selection of a mediator is more fully covered in Chapter 13.

a. Classifying Styles

It is possible to classify mediators according to the goals they pursue and the methods they use to achieve them, and to show the results graphically, as in the following much-cited reading.

❖ **Leonard L. Riskin,** *Mediator Orientations,*
Strategies and Techniques

12 Alternatives 111 (Summer 1994)

The classification system starts with two principal questions: 1. Does the mediator tend to define problems narrowly or broadly? 2. Does the mediator think she should evaluate—make assessments or predictions or proposals for agreements—or facilitate the parties' negotiation without evaluating? The answers reflect the mediator's beliefs about the nature and scope of mediation and her assumptions about the parties' expectations.

Problem Definition

Mediators with a *narrow* focus assume that the parties have come to them for help in solving a technical problem. The parties have defined this problem in advance through the *positions* they have asserted in negotiations or pleadings. Often it involves a question such as, "Who pays how much to whom?" or "Who can use such-and-such property?" As framed, these questions rest on "win-lose" (or "distributive") assumptions. In other words, the participants must divide a limited resource; whatever one gains, the other must lose.

The likely court outcome—along with uncertainty, delay and expense—drives much of the mediation process. Parties, seeking a compromise, will bargain adversarially, emphasizing positions over interests.

A mediator who starts with a *broad* orientation, on the other hand, assumes that the parties can benefit if the mediation goes beyond the narrow issues that normally define legal disputes. Important interests often lie beneath the positions that the participants assert. Accordingly, the mediator should help the participants understand and fulfill those interests—at least if they wish to do so.

The Mediator's Role

The *evaluative* mediator assumes that the participants want and need the mediator to provide some directions as to the approximate grounds for settlement—based on law, industry practice, or technology. She also assumes that the mediator is qualified to give such direction by virtue of her experience, training, and objectivity.

The *facilitative* mediator assumes the parties are intelligent, able to work with their counterparts, and capable of understanding their situation better than either their lawyers or the mediator. So the parties may develop better solutions than any that the mediator might create. For these reasons, the facilitative mediator assumes that his principal mission is to enhance and clarify communications between the parties in order to help them decide what to do.

The facilitative mediator believes it is inappropriate for the mediator to give his opinion, for at least two reasons. First, such opinions might impair the appearance of impartiality and thereby interfere with the mediator's ability to function. Second, the mediator might not know enough—about the details of the case or the relevant law, practices, or technology—to give an informed opinion.

Each of the two principal questions—Does the mediator tend toward a narrow or broad focus? and Does the mediator favor an evaluative or facilitative role?—yield responses that fall along a continuum. Thus, a mediator's orientation will be more or less broad and more or less evaluative.

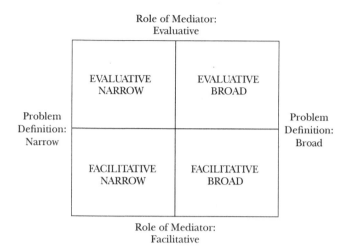

Mediators usually have a predominant orientation, whether they know it or not, based on a combination of their personalities, experiences, education, and training. Thus, many retired judges, when they mediate, tend toward an evaluative-narrow orientation.

Yet mediators do not always behave consistently with the predominant orientations they express. . . . In addition, many mediators will depart from their orientations to respond to the dynamics of the situation. . . . [As an] example: an evaluative-narrow mediator may explore underlying interests (a technique normally associated with the broad orientation) after her accustomed narrow focus results in a deadlock. And a facilitative-broad mediator might use a mildly evaluative tactic as a last resort. For instance, he might toss out a figure that he thinks the parties might be willing to agree upon, while stating that the figure does not represent his prediction of what would happen in court. . . . Many effective mediators are versatile and can move from quadrant to quadrant (and within a quadrant), as the dynamics of the situation dictate, to help parties settle disputes. . . .

Professor Riskin has since modified his grid by replacing the word "evaluative" with "directive" and "facilitative" with "elicitive." (The "broad" versus "narrow" continuum remains the same.) Most writing on mediator styles continues to employ Riskin's original evaluative-facilitative terminology. To avoid inconsistent terms, we use evaluative and facilitive in this book. Students interested in exploring the issue of mediator style more deeply should read Professor Riskin's 2003 article, "Decisionmaking in Mediation: The New Old Grid and the New New Grid System," 79 Notre Dame L. Rev. 1 (2003).

b. Do Mediators Have a Single Style?

Do legal mediators use a single goal-orientation and style throughout their practice, or at least during a single mediation? Investigators filmed several different neutrals mediating the same civil case in role-play format. They found, as Professor Riskin suggests, that good neutrals do not maintain a single orientation; rather they adapt their approach to the conditions they encounter as the process moves forward.

Indeed the filmed mediators often changed their style several times during a single caucus meeting. All began in a broadly facilitative mode, asking about the parties' business and personal interests, but they were usually met with narrowly evaluative comments from the lawyers about the legal case. The mediators adjusted to the attorneys, remaining facilitative but focusing on legal issues rather than other concerns. Periodically during the process, however, most of them returned to "broad" questions, asking about clients' interests and suggesting nonmonetary solutions. Some disputants responded by moving toward a broader focus, though most continued to remain narrowly evaluative.

The experiment confirmed Riskin's observation that successful legal mediators are not consistently either facilitative or evaluative. The neutrals in the study did become increasingly evaluative over the course of each mediation, but their evaluative advice more often concerned the bargaining situation ("If you make that offer, I'm concerned that they will react by . . .") than the legal merits.

Although commentators tend to speak in terms of a mediator's "preferred style," the stylistic changes of the mediators in the experiment also seemed to be driven much more by the bargaining styles and values of the parties and their lawyers than by the mediators' inherent tendencies. Whether a party was open to resuming a broken relationship, for example, had much more impact on what happened than the mediator's orientation.

Question

4. What type of mediator would you select if you were a lawyer representing the following clients?
   a. The family of the deceased MIT student.
   b. The company in the abutter-chemical company case.
   c. The plaintiff in the "$1.2 million demand" personal injury mediation.

6. Mediation Techniques to Overcome Negotiation Obstacles

If mediation is invoked in litigated cases, it is usually because parties and their attorneys are unable to negotiate effectively on their own, due to one or more of the barriers discussed above, or the court has a program encouraging mediation. The goal in using mediation is to stimulate constructive negotiations. A commercial mediator might begin by seeking information that answers two questions:

- What obstacles are preventing the parties from settling this dispute themselves?
- What strategy is most likely to overcome these barriers?

A mediator's understanding of what is keeping the parties apart will deepen over the course of a mediation, and the obstacles themselves may change as the process goes forward. Ideally a mediator's strategy will be attuned uniquely to each case. In practice, however, many commercial mediators use a standard sequence of techniques to deal with the barriers most likely to be present, customizing their approach as they go along. This section describes a six-step strategy suggested by the authors when training commercial mediators (The mediation process in divorce and family cases may differ. See Folberg et al. 2004). By knowing what mediators are trained to do, you will have a better understanding of the process so you can prepare for it and shape the mediation to best meet the needs of your client.

a. Build a Foundation for Settlement

The Challenge: Missing Elements — People, Data, Interactions. Negotiations often fail because some essential element is missing. One side may have the wrong people — a key decision maker may be missing, or one of the bargainers may be so emotional he cannot make good decisions. At other times, parties do not have the data they need to settle: Defense counsel may not, for instance, know how the claimed damages were computed and without this information cannot get authority to settle. Such problems are difficult to fix once mediation begins.

Response: Identify Issues and Address Them in Advance. To identify and resolve such problems, it is best to start before the parties meet to mediate. The first step is to ask the lawyers for mediation statements and set up telephone conversations with each of them. Ask each attorney whom he plans to bring and who needs to attend from the other party. If a decision maker is absent, work to bring her to the table. If key information is missing, suggest that a party provide it. Mediators can elicit information and persuade people to attend in circumstances in which the same request would be rejected if made by a party.

b. Allow Participants to Argue and Express Feelings

The Challenge: Unresolved Process and Emotional Needs. If parties don't settle, it's often because someone wants something more than just particular settlement terms. A litigant might be looking instead for an empathetic hearing: the opportunity to appear before a neutral person, state his grievances or defense, and know he has been heard. Or a party may have a need to express strong feelings directly to an adversary. Until they feel heard, parties are often not ready to settle. The need to express strong feelings to one's adversary is a very human one, felt by executives and mailroom clerks alike

Response: Provide an Opportunity to Speak and Feel Heard. Mediation is not a court session and mediators are not judges, but the process can give parties the satisfaction of receiving a hearing not bound by narrow rules of evidence. They can see their lawyer argue their case, or present it themselves, and listen to an opponent's arguments. The mediator will not decide the dispute and might never express an opinion about the merits, but she can demonstrate she has heard the disputants. The experience of telling one's story and feeling heard by a neutral person can have a surprising impact on a person's willingness to settle. Arguing the merits also focuses participants on the facts and legal principles relevant to the controversy, and knowing that a neutral person will be listening encourages them to think through their arguments and avoid extremes. Beyond the merits, parties can express some of their feelings about the dispute and each other.

c. Moderate the Bargaining and Offer Coaching

The Challenge: Positional Tactics Leading to Impasse.   Negotiators often have trouble reaching settlement because they use a positional approach to bargaining, trading monetary concessions until they reach agreement. We have seen that positional bargaining can be successful but that it often makes negotiators frustrated and angry, for example, when one side makes an offer that the other perceives as "insulting."

Response: Become the Moderator of the Process and Coach.   Earlier mediation training encouraged mediators to prevent adversarial bargaining over money alone by convincing parties to focus on principles and interests. In commercial mediation, however, parties usually arrive suspicious of each other, focused on legal issues, and determined to engage solely in money bargaining. A mediator's only practical option in such cases is often to facilitate the process the parties want while looking for an opportunity to move them toward a more effective approach.

One way to facilitate money negotiations is to act as a coach. You can, for example, in caucus ask a bargainer to support its number with an explanation ("I'll communicate it, but if they ask how you got there what should I tell them?"), or help a disputant assess how a planned tactic will work ("What do you think their response will be if you start at $10,000?"). A mediator can give bargainers advice about how to keep the process moving ("If you want them to get to $100,000 with the next round, I think your offer to them needs to be in the range of $700,000 to $800,000 . . ."). By using these steps in combination with a continuing discussion of the case, a mediator can often orchestrate a "dance" of concessions to move the parties toward settlement.

d. Seek Out and Address Hidden Issues

The Challenge: Disregard of Hidden Issues and Missed Opportunities.   Negotiations in legal cases are often blocked by hidden psychological obstacles. Participants in commercial mediation typically arrive with "game faces on," presenting a businesslike demeanor even as feelings boil beneath the surface. When this occurs, simply giving a disputant the chance to express emotions, as discussed earlier, is often not enough.

Response: Probe for and Deal with Hidden Issues.   Even as you are carrying out other tasks, look for clues to hidden emotions and overly narrow approaches to settlement. Try to broaden the negotiation by identifying unexploited opportunities for gain that may include nonmonetary terms.

e. Test the Parties' Alternatives; If Necessary, Evaluate the Adjudication Option

The Challenge: Lack of Realism About the Outcome in Adjudication. Participants in legal disputes often justify hard-bargaining positions in terms of the merits of the dispute. They are asking for a great deal or offering little, they say, because they have a strong legal case. Both parties usually claim that they will easily win in court. To some degree parties bluff about litigation options to justify their bargaining positions and do not expect to be taken literally. To a surprising degree, however, disputants actually believe their clashing predictions. There are two basic causes for disputants' distorted thinking about legal alternatives. One is lack of information; the other, an inability to accurately interpret available data because of psychological traps and lack of objectivity (as outlined in Chapter 2).

Response: Foster an Information Exchange. Even though discovery rules are meant to require each side to disclose key evidence, discovery may not be completed and it is often surprising how little one party knows about the other's case even after years of litigation. As a mediator, you can be an effective facilitator of information exchange. If, for example, a plaintiff has explained its theory of liability in detail but has given no explanation for its damage claim, you can suggest it flesh out damages to help the defendant get authority to settle. Parties will often respond cooperatively to a mediator's request, although they would have refused the same inquiry coming from their opponent.

Response: Reality Test. Even when parties have the relevant information, we have seen that they often do not interpret it accurately. The least intrusive way to solve merits-based problems is through questions that help parties focus on evidence and issues they have glossed over. It is important both to ask questions pointed enough to prompt someone to confront a problem and to avoid comments so tough the disputant concludes the mediator has taken sides against her. Begin with open-ended questions asked in a spirit of curiosity; in this mode, you are simply trying to understand the dispute and the parties' arguments. ("Tell me what you think are the key facts here," or "Can you give me your take on the defendant's contract argument?") Your questions can progress gradually from open-ended queries ("Have you thought about . . . ?") to more pointed requests ("They are resisting making a higher offer because they believe you won't be able to prove causation. . . . What should I tell them?"). You might also want to take a party through an analysis of each element in the case, using systematic questions to prevent disputants from skipping over weaknesses. This can help counteract disputants' tendency to be overoptimistic. It also assists lawyers who are dealing with an unrealistic client, and can give a disputant a face-saving excuse for a compromise it secretly knows is necessary.

Response: Evaluative Feedback. In some cases questions and analysis are not enough; a disputant might be wedded to an unrealistic viewpoint or require support to justify a settlement to a supervisor. In such situations, a commercial mediator may go further and offer an opinion about how a court is likely to decide a key issue or even the entire case. Evaluations can be structured in a wide variety of ways; for example, "My experience with state court judges is that they usually deny summary judgment in this kind of situation," or "If the plaintiff prevails on liability, what I know of San Francisco juries suggests they would value damages at somewhere between $125,000 and $150,000." You should never say how you *personally* would decide the case, but rather you should frame your opinion as a *prediction* of the attitude of an *outside decision maker*. Expressing one's personal opinion about what is "right" or "fair" in a dispute is almost always a bad idea, because it is likely to leave a listener feeling that the mediator has taken sides against him. Properly performed, a neutral evaluation can be helpful in producing an agreement, but a poorly done or badly timed opinion can be harmful to the process.

f. Break Bargaining Impasses

The Challenge: Closing the Final Gap.   Often barriers to agreement are too high, causing bargaining to stall and provoking an impasse.

Response: Persevere and Project Optimism.   When in doubt, persevere. Parties get stuck at some point during a mediation, often during the late afternoon or early evening, when energy levels decline and each side has made all the compromises it feels it ought to and more. The key thing to remember at this point is that the mediation probably *will* succeed; if you can keep the parties talking, they will find a solution. The disputants will be looking for signals about whether it is worth continuing, and it is important to send positive ones, if possible within the bounds of reality.

Response: Invite Disputants to Take the Initiative.   Another simple tactic is to ask the disputants to take the initiative. You could say, "What do you think we should do?" and then wait quietly. If disputants realize they cannot simply "hang tough" and demand that the mediator produce results, they sometimes offer surprising ideas.

Response: Test Flexibility or Make a Mediator's Proposal.   Another option is to privately test the disputants' flexibility. Parties may refuse to offer anything more to an opponent but be willing to give private hints to you. You could, for example, ask "What if?" questions ("What if I could get them down to $150,000; would that keep the process going?") or propose bracketed bargaining ("If I can get the plaintiffs to come down on their demand to $300,000, would you up your offer to $100,000?"). A mediator's proposal will often break an apparent impasse and produce agreement. Even if it doesn't, the proposal may prompt parties to rethink their positions and restart direct bargaining. (These techniques are explained more in Chapter 13.)

Response: Adjourn and Follow Up.   If the disputants are psychologically spent or have run out of authority, the best response may be to adjourn temporarily. You can follow up with shuttle diplomacy by telephone; propose a second, shorter mediation session; or set a deadline to prompt the parties to make difficult decisions. This is true even if a mediator's proposal has been offered and rejected.

7. *"Deal Mediation"*

You now understand, as many practicing lawyers do, the potentially significant role that a mediator can play in facilitating negotiation, enhancing communication, and even transforming relationships. It should therefore come as no surprise that some have theorized about—and in some cases implemented—intervention strategies that apply these same principles at points "upstream" from active disputes.

The following article asks a simple question: Could third-party mediators be helpful in negotiating deals, just as they are in disputes? It posits a potential role for mediators in helping the parties to overcome psychological, emotional, and relational barriers to reaching an agreement in commercial transactions.

❖ Scott R. Peppet, *CONTRACT FORMATION IN IMPERFECT MARKETS: SHOULD WE USE MEDIATORS IN DEALS?*

38 Ohio St. J. on Disp. Resol. 283 (2004)

[M]any of the same barriers to negotiation that plague litigation settlement exist in commercial transactions, particularly during the closing stage of a deal when lawyers attempt to negotiate terms and conditions. [A] transactional mediator could help lawyers and clients to overcome such barriers. By a "transactional mediator," the author means an impartial person or entity that intervenes in a transactional negotiation pre-closing to facilitate the creation of a durable and efficient contract.

In one experiment, for example, small teams of experienced executives were given detailed information about two simulated companies. They were then assigned to represent one company or the other and asked to evaluate the companies and negotiate a merger. Although agreement was possible, only nine of the twenty-one pairings reached agreement. In addition, the executives disagreed wildly about the relevant valuations—selling prices ranged from $3.3 million to $16.5 million. This suggests that occasionally transacting parties fail to "close the deal" because of strategic posturing. [Moreover], as in litigation, transacting parties may fail to find Pareto-efficient agreements. . . . Information asymmetries and strategic posturing may lead to inefficiencies. . . . Interestingly, the researcher in this corporate acquisitions experiment re-ran the simulation offering each negotiating pair the service of a trained mediator, but not requiring that they use the mediator. Those executives that made use of the mediator reached more efficient contracts than those that did not. . . . [M]ediators should theoretically be able to help merging companies resolve disagreements over "social issues," such as how to name the post-merger corporation, how to resolve status and position questions (e.g., who will be CEO), and where to locate the new company's headquarters.

Howard Raiffa also suggests that a mediator might serve as a "contract embellisher" in transactions. [A]t the start of bargaining a mediator could privately interview each party about its needs, priorities, and perceptions. The mediator would lock away that information and the parties would be left alone to negotiate a deal. At the conclusion of their negotiation, but prior to closing the deal, the intervenor would return [. . .] try to use his private information about the parties' interests to craft a superior deal. He would then show his substitute agreement to each party privately. If both sides agreed that the mediator's suggestion was superior to their own contract, the substitution would be made. There would be no haggling about the terms of the mediator's proposal—it would be a take-it-or-leave-it situation. . . .

In complex transactions, lawyers, accountants, bankers, and other agents are generally brought in to assist in the closing stage. Lawyers in particular are needed to draft legal language for an acquisition agreement or other contract. As the closing stage progresses, due diligence may not eliminate all uncertainties about the company or assets in question [and] [l]awyers will therefore bargain over contract language to shift the risks associated with these remaining uncertainties.

A lawyer-mediator might prevent the parties' lawyers from blowing up the deal unnecessarily, and, perhaps more importantly, from reaching an inefficient set of contract terms. Although the bargaining about a single contract term may be largely distributive contracting attorneys can generally create value by trading between terms. For example, if a contract contains ten legal provisions (A, B, . . . J), parties X and Y will value those terms differently. If X finds term A extremely important and Y term B, they can create joint gains by allocating the risk in term A as X prefers and the risk in term B as Y prefers. And so on.

Empirical analysis of contracts shows that parties often do not trade risk in complex—yet value-creating—ways. Instead, in many domains contracts are simpler than one might expect. Various explanations have been offered for this simplicity, including behavioral explanations and the network effects theory. Another, less-explored, explanation is that the threat of strategic behavior prevents parties from complex contracting. To create a tailored term requires disclosing information about one's interests and preferences. This, again, permits exploitation. In the absence of trust, parties may resort to a standard term to minimize this risk.

A mediator might help the parties to overcome these strategic difficulties, thereby permitting more complex contracting. Again, a mediator can solicit and compare information from each side, potentially finding value-creating trades. The mediator might test the viability of various packages of trades of legal terms, asking each side in confidence which of several sets of terms the party would accept, but not revealing the origin of the various packages. In this way, the mediator can surmount the adverse selection problems that might otherwise prevent tailoring contract language during the deal's closing stage. . . .

[Besides helping the parties to overcome strategic barriers to transactions, mediators can also help them to overcome psychological barriers.] A neutral is in an ideal position to identify self-serving assessments by one or both parties. At a substantive level, if the neutral has sufficient expertise she can check each side's assumptions about "what's fair" and keep the parties from locking in to diverging stories about how a transaction should be priced or closed. Moreover, the mediator may be able to offer a neutral assessment or fair proposal that the parties will adopt. At a procedural or process level, a neutral can also help the parties avoid spinning very biased interpretations of how their bargaining is unfolding.

Negotiating parties must constantly assess information received from the other side. Research has shown, however, that negotiators . . . sometimes overly devalue an opponent's proposal or concession merely because their opponent made it. This phenomenon is known as "reactive devaluation." [A] neutral can help parties to overcome reactive devaluation in transactional bargaining by either adding noise to the parties' communication or proposing solutions of her own. Adding noise may be as simple as raising Party A's proposed solution privately with Party B without telling B that the idea came from Party A. If B assumes that the idea originated with the neutral, B may be more willing to consider it on the merits.

A neutral may be less susceptible to the endowment effect than a partisan agent, and therefore able to help parties to overcome it. For example, a neutral may be able to provide both sides with market information against which they can test their (biased) evaluations. This is particularly plausible vis-à-vis the legal terms and conditions in a contract. A lawyer-neutral might be familiar with the legal norms in a given context and be able to point the parties towards compromise legal language. Rather than start with a standard form or with a first draft, which would typically become the original endowment against which the parties compared, the neutral could manage the negotiation process so that the parties instead would work collaboratively to build a contract draft from framework through to completion.

In addition to managing information exchange and helping parties to overcome these cognitive and social psychological biases, a neutral can help parties to manage emotional and relational difficulties in their negotiations. This may facilitate trust and permit more efficient outcomes.

. . . [N]egotiation breakdowns occur in transactional bargaining, sometimes to the detriment of both parties. To some extent, agents such as investment bankers and lawyers already serve to mediate emotional conflicts during mergers, acquisitions, and other transactions. A neutral sometimes has an advantage over an agent in this regard, however. An agent may naturally take his client's perspective as given and discount the likelihood that the other side has a valid interpretation of events or more benign intentions than the client understands. A neutral positioned between two parties can often help them to gain such perspective. In strategic situations it is easy to assume that when the other bargainer "starts high" or "holds out," they do so because they intend to harm you or to treat you unfairly. Bargainers are less likely to attribute such actions to the exigencies of circumstance. By screening some overly opportunistic offers and at times sending fuzzy rather than clear information between the parties, a mediator can blunt such emotions and thereby keep the negotiations on track. Over time, avoiding emotional disagreements may help the parties to establish trust. This not only leads to more amiable negotiations, but also has serious substantive benefits. If the parties trust each other they may be better positioned to find value-creating solutions to their substantive differences. They may be able to rely more on informal agreements rather than contractual obligations and may be more flexible in the face of unexpected bumps in the road. Perhaps most importantly, they may avoid the destructive cycle of misattributions that can lead parties to "blow up" a deal or reach a Pareto-inefficient agreement.

Question

5. Why do you suppose deal mediation is not as prevalent as mediation of disputes?

D. Judicial Settlement Conferences and Court ADR Programs

1. Judge-Led Settlement Conferences

Judges have an interest in encouraging settlement and have always been available to informally provide settlement assistance to lawyers and their clients. Our court system currently depends on having over 95 percent of all cases filed settled prior to trial. Judges often used Rule 16 of the Federal Rules of Civil Procedure and its state equivalents to discuss settlement possibilities with attorneys in pretrial conferences. In 1983, Rule 16 was amended to specify that judicially hosted pretrial conferences with lawyers included the purpose of facilitating settlement of the case. Fed. R. Civ. P. 16(a)(5). The rule now specifies that judges may "take appropriate action with respect to . . . settlement and the use of special procedures to assist in resolving the dispute when authorized by statute or local rules." Fed. R. Civ. P. 16(c)(2)(1). In addition, judges may "require that a party or its representative be present or reasonably available by telephone in order to consider possible settlement of the dispute." Fed. R. Civ. P. 16(c)(1).

A judge-led settlement conference is similar to an evaluative mediation, usually conducted in an abbreviated fashion and often without the parties present. However, when the mediator wears a judicial robe, the evaluation tends to carry more weight, particularly if the judge will be making rulings in the case or is assigned to conduct the trial. Judicial settlement conferences can be thought of as "muscle mediations." Some mediators bristle at equating judicial settlement conferences with mediation because of the muscle factor, which they see as coercive. In fact, judicial settlement conferences can be as varied as the judges who conduct them and the time available. Some judges take their settlement role very seriously and perfect a mediation style that incorporates their judicial power, which may be welcomed by attorneys for some cases.

So what is it that judges provide to help overcome obstacles and assist in negotiation? Federal Judge Magistrate Wayne Brazil, drawing on his extensive experience and a survey of attorneys, summarized judicial negotiation assistance as follows:

> What judges have to contribute to settlement that lawyers value most is . . . penetrating, analytical exposition and thoughtful, objective, knowledgeable assessment.

They want the perspective of the experienced neutral. Data . . . shows that a judge's opinion that a settlement offer is reasonable is likely to have a great affect on a recalcitrant client, especially if that client is not often involved in litigation.

There also are many ways judges can contribute to the quality of the settlement dialogue itself: they can defuse emotions, set a constructive and analytical tone, help parties focus on the pertinent matters, and ask questions that expose under-developed areas. Judges can help keep litigants talking when they otherwise might retreat into noncommunication. In these and other ways, a judicial officer can improve visibility, efficiency, and efficacy of the negotiation process. (*Settling Civil Cases* 45-46 (1984))

2. Court ADR Programs

Some judges are better than others in moving parties toward settlement. However, many judges question the appropriateness of direct judicial interven-tion in the settlement process. Recognizing the importance of promoting set-tlement to relieve civil caseloads and reduce delay and the limits of settlement conferences, judges convened bench-bar committees in the 1980s to recom-mend alternative methods to resolve cases. Local experimentation led to suc-cesses, which were replicated and refined in other jurisdictions. Traditional settlement conferences conducted by judges were augmented and sometimes replaced by more innovative dispute resolution options to assist negotiation. A rich array of court-connected ADR processes developed. Informal "settlement weeks" and case evaluation panels, both utilizing volunteer lawyers, led to stat-utes and court rules that required litigants to engage in ADR.

Mediation of different types, often conducted for the court by lawyers in their own offices, became the most popular form of court-directed ADR. Some courts hired full-time staff to direct and manage cases in ADR programs. The Alternative Dispute Resolution Act of 1998 requires all federal district courts to establish an ADR program by local rule. Participation in some settlement pro-cesses, including early neutral evaluation and mediation, can be compelled in federal courts, as in many state courts. (We consider the policy arguments about mandatory participation in Chapter 14.)

Although court ADR processes vary greatly, they share some common ele-ments. Court ADR is intended to encourage negotiation and settlement by:

- Relieving each attorney from being the one to initiate settlement discussions.
- Providing a stimulus or requirement for attorneys to explore settlement early.
- Promoting or require involvement of key decision makers.
- Using attorneys as neutrals to augment judicial resources.
- Providing more flexibility than formal adjudication.
- Avoiding involving the judge who will preside at trial.

One perhaps unintended consequence of court-connected ADR programs, particularly mediation, has been to educate attorneys and business executives about the positive potential of nonbinding forms of ADR. Even though most cases entered the early court programs involuntarily, satisfaction rates were high. Occasional complaints about the quality of volunteer neutrals or bureaucratic restrictions could be remedied by having mutually respected neutrals serve privately for a fee, outside the court. Corporate and insurance clients faced with long waits in court and increased litigation expenses pushed for more use of private ADR. Plaintiffs' lawyers, reluctant at first, became more supportive of nonbinding, voluntary forms of ADR when they realized that these could speed settlement and collection of damages for clients in need and payment of their contingent fees. Greater efficiency, lower costs, more control, less risk, and improved outcomes were the driving forces for increased use of both court-based and private ADR. The seeds were planted for what would later become a change in the legal culture regarding how disputes are negotiated and resolved.

Look once again at the Dispute Resolution Spectrum near the beginning of this chapter. On the left side of the chart, under the heading "Settlement Processes/Non-Binding," a number of alternatives are listed. Nearly all of these except evolved in whole or in part through court programs. Mediation is now familiar to you. Others—Neutral Evaluation, Settlement Conference, Mini-Trial, Summary Jury Trial, and Advisory Arbitration—have not yet been discussed.

We briefly explore here some of these latter options. They all are designed to help overcome the most common obstacle to negotiated agreement—different assessments of what will happen if the dispute goes to trial. If all parties had the same estimate of the court outcome in a contested case and how much a trial would cost, each side's BATNA would be similar. Settlement would be much easier. Several ADR mechanisms provide all parties with the same proxy or forecast of what will happen in court if negotiations fail. The principal distinctions between these ADR procedures is the nature of the assessment, at what point in the litigation process it is provided, and based on what degree of case presentation.

Early neutral evaluation (ENE) is a process designed to improve settlement prospects by giving litigants an advisory evaluation of the case well before preparation for litigation is completed. The ENE process lies somewhere between mediation and nonbinding arbitration. Although public funds are used to support ENE and other court-connected settlement assistance programs and parties may be mandated to use them, little empirical research had been done to measure their benefit in federal courts prior to the Civil Justice Reform Act of 1990. One of the first studies to use a control group and combine quantitative data with qualitative surveys and interviews to determine if ENE promoted negotiated settlements reported the following conclusions.

Our most important findings include the following: (1) Approximately two-thirds of those who participated in the mandatory ADR program felt satisfied with the process and believed it worthy of the resources devoted to it (dissatisfaction with the program resulted primarily from dissatisfaction with the particular neutral assigned to the case); (2) while the percentage of parties who reported saving money approximately equaled the percentage who reported that the process resulted in a net financial cost, the net savings were, on average, more than ten times larger than the cost of an ENE session; (3) approximately half the participants in the program reported that participation decreased the pendency time of their cases; (4) the majority of parties and attorneys reported learning information in the ENE session that led to a fairer resolution of their case; and (5) the ENE process varied significantly from case to case and from neutral to neutral, and the most important factor in determining the success of the process in any one case was the individual neutral involved. (Joshua Rosenberg and Jay Folberg, "Alternative Dispute Resolution: An Empirical Analysis," 46 Stan. L. Rev. 1487, 1488-1499 (1994).)

Another important finding of this study was how the ENE participation requirement overcame attorneys' fear of initiating settlement negotiations.

In addition to requiring participants to focus on their case earlier, ENE also eliminated another significant obstacle to serious settlement discussions—the fear that initiating settlement discussion would give the other side a strategic negotiating advantage. In cases that did not go through ENE, 27 percent of the attorneys reported that earlier settlement discussions were impeded because neither side wanted to initiate such discussions out of fear of being perceived as weak. By forcing the parties to discuss their case and possible settlement at an early stage, ENE facilitated useful discussions that might never have commenced otherwise. (Rosenberg and Folberg 1994, 1512-1513.)

Notes and Questions

A subsequent, controversial study of six federal court ADR programs, four involving mediation and two using ENE, was less favorable. Known as the "RAND Study," it concluded that "we have no strong statistical evidence that lawyer work hours [or time to disposition] are significantly affected by mediation or neutral evaluation in any of the six programs studied . . ." (Kakalik et al. 1996). However, another study by the Federal Judicial Center of five different federal courts was more encouraging. (See Stienstra et al. 1997.)

6. Based on what you know about early neutral evaluations and nonbinding arbitration, what cases are most appropriate, or inappropriate, for each process?
7. If your client, a small manufacturer with limited resources, was sued for unlicensed use of the plaintiff's patented manufacturing process, and settlement negotiations have failed, should your client be compelled to participate in a judicial settlement conference? (See G. Heileman Brewing Co. v. Joseph Oat Corp., 871 F.2d 648 (7th Cir. 1989). See also FRCP 16(b).) Summary jury trial? (See Strandell v. Jackson County, Illinois, 838 F.2d 884 (7th Cir. 1988).) An early neutral evaluation? Are your arguments for one or the other of these processes different?
8. May the court compel the defendant's nonparty insurance company to attend a settlement conference if it appears there is coverage? (See In re Novak, 932 F.2d 1397 (11th Cir. 1991).)

9. If a court compels participation in a settlement program, what level of participation is required? Can anyone be compelled to settle? To speak? Can "good faith" participation be required? If so, how might "good faith" be defined? (See John Lande, "Using Dispute System Design Models to Promote Good-Faith Participation in Court-Mandated Mediation Programs," 50 UCLA L. Rev. 69 (2002); Edward F. Sherman, "Court-Mandated Alternative Dispute Resolution: What Form of Participation Should be Required?," 46 SMU L. Rev. 2079 (1993).)

10. In the above situation for the same client, if your client did agree to participate in one of the court's ADR programs, could you insist that it be conducted confidentially, without public or press access? (See Cincinnati Gas & Electric Co. v. General Elec. Co., 854 F.2d 900 (6th Cir.1988).)

11. Assuming it is appropriate for courts to compel participation in their ADR programs, may or should the courts require the parties to pay administrative costs?

The **mini-trial**, which has more accurately been called "maxi-negotiation," evolved primarily as a private process outside the courts but is sometimes offered by courts utilizing court resources and jury panels. In the 1980s, the CPR Institute for Dispute Resolution and other organizations promoting ADR in the business arena touted the benefits of mini-trials. The process is unique in that it brings together key decision makers from each party as members of a panel hearing "best shot" presentations of evidence and arguments by advocates for each party to the controversy, thus potentially laying a foundation for focused negotiations aimed at settlement, which follow immediately upon the conclusion of the "hearing."

In the typical mini-trial proceeding, principals of each party sit on either side of a neutral third-party referee or mini-trial "judge," who supervises the process. As lawyers for the parties present rigorously abbreviated cases, with summaries of best evidence (including, perhaps, videos of key witnesses) and arguments, the principals and the referee act as inquisitors, probing the main elements of each party's case. At the conclusion of the presentations, the principals have the opportunity to negotiate face to face, perhaps with the assistance of the neutral. The latter may at some point be called upon to offer a nonbinding advisory opinion regarding a resolution of the controversy. Then the principals can negotiate more with that opinion in hand. (See ABA, Sub-committee on Alternative Means of Dispute Resolution, *The Effectiveness of the Mini-Trial in Resolving Complex Commercial Disputes: A Survey* (1986).)

Mini-trials are not widely used today, largely because of their expense and the significant lawyer and executive time they require. Moreover, when a mini-trial is not used until the conclusion of discovery, the possibility of deriving significant cost savings is substantially diminished. Today, whether or not they are so described, abbreviated mini-trial formats are sometimes employed in the context of mediation.

A mediator may ask each side to summarize before the other side the testimony to be offered and present a closing argument, after which the principals can further discuss a settlement.

The **summary jury trial** is a non-binding ADR process designed to promote settlement in trial-ready cases. A judge presides over the trial, where attorneys for each party present the case to a jury, generally without calling witnesses but relying instead on the submission of exhibits. After this abbreviated trial, the jury deliberates and then delivers an advisory verdict. After receiving the jury's advisory verdict, the parties may use it as a basis for subsequent settlement negotiations or proceed to trial.

Advisory or non-binding arbitration. Nonbinding arbitration occurs after substantial trial preparation is completed. An experienced trial attorney drawn from a court list hears adversarial presentations, in summary form, presented by the parties' attorneys. Witnesses are sometimes called and exhibits may be submitted. The arbitrator issues a monetary award or decision on the merits. If neither party objects, the award is entered as a court judgment to conclude the litigation. Any party may object to the award and request a trial de novo, usually at the risk of paying the other side's court costs if it does not do better at trial than it fared under the arbitration award. The parties, informed by the arbitration result, may, of course, negotiate a settlement.

Question

12. Can you think of any types of cases in which a mini-trial might be cost effective and worth the effort?

CHAPTER
13

Negotiating in a Mediation

A. Introduction

As we saw in the preceding chapter, when obstacles get in the way of a negotiated agreement, lawyers may turn to mediation. The purpose remains to reach an agreement favorable to your client. This chapter is about how to effectively negotiate in behalf of a client with the assistance of the mediator.

Mediators of legal disputes have significant power, whether or not they use it. Although mediators cannot compel parties to settle, they can greatly influence the process of negotiating, opening opportunities for advocates to mold the process to their clients' needs. Lawyers can use the mediation process to their advantage by approaching it actively and keeping in mind its special characteristics.

Mediation was shaped by the concepts of principled negotiation and problem solving. Advocacy, advantage, and winning are words not usually associated with these concepts. However, lawyers and their clients would not rationally choose to mediate if they did not feel that it would be to their advantage compared to the alternatives. So, attorneys must be proactive throughout the mediation process to help it work to their clients' advantage. Advocacy in mediation may look and feel different than it does in some forms of direct negotiation or trial, but it is nonetheless advocacy to fulfill your client's interests.

The first important issue to decide is what goal your client wants to achieve in mediation. The desired goal will strongly influence the approach you take to the mediation process and how you relate to the mediator. If you see your objective as solving a problem or repairing a relationship, you will be inclined to treat the mediator like a member of your team, revealing your interests and soliciting the neutral's advice about how to achieve them. If the focus is on relationship repair, both lawyer and mediator may gradually withdraw as the process progresses to give the parties an opportunity to relearn how to communicate directly and positively. If, however, your goal is to obtain the best possible monetary settlement, your relationship with the mediator will be different.

You can utilize the mediator's knowledge and neutrality, for example, by getting an objective perspective on the negotiation obstacles, and if you employ principled bargaining techniques you will be able to work together cooperatively to overcome them. However, at the point that you begin to compete with the other side for the best possible terms, your goal and that of the neutral may diverge, because the mediator cannot take sides. Indeed, competitive bargainers talk about "spinning" a mediator to advance their client's objectives. They also see themselves as bargaining not simply with the other side, but also with the mediator, in a three-sided process. Attorneys bargain with neutrals, for example, over what the mediator will say about their offers to their opponent, what she will tell them about the attitudes of persons in the other room, and whether and how the mediator will employ impasse-breaking tactics such as evaluation or a mediator's proposal.

There is another potential advantage of using mediation to assist in negotiating a good outcome. As a lawyer you may recognize that your client's unrealistic evaluation or intractable attitude is part of the problem and a barrier to a reasonable settlement. Not wanting to alienate or lose your client, you may enlist the mediator to help persuade a "difficult" or "unrealistic" client to look at the case from a different perspective. This is not inconsistent with acting in your client's best interests; you, in effect, are recruiting the mediator to become an ally in getting the best for your client. In doing so, you are taking advantage of the mediator's neutrality and allowing the mediator to be an advocate for settlement. Consider the advice below from an experienced commercial mediator.

❖ **Jeffrey G. Kichaven,** *HOW ADVOCACY FITS IN EFFECTIVE MEDIATION*

17 Alternatives 60 (1999)

Clients and attorneys generally have one of two conceptions of what it means to win in mediation. Some define winning as "clobbering the other side." Others see it as "the satisfaction of our own needs," regardless of whether the other side suffers along the way. In the litigation context, and in many others, clients often start out in a "clobbering" mode. They may believe they have been "done wrong," and want revenge. And more revenge. And more.

This is a serious problem for lawyers. Such a client is almost never satisfied with the result, with the process, or with counsel's performance, because the other side, no matter how badly clobbered, rarely has suffered enough. A vengeful client . . . has a hard time planning, in advance, the specific result to be achieved or the goal against which success or failure will be measured. No matter what happens to the other side, it could always have been worse! These clients believe that their attorneys have failed them. Yet the lawyers have done all that they can. Far better is the situation in which the client focuses on the satisfaction of his or her own needs. This client is better able to give clear instructions and if the client's own goals are satisfied, it doesn't matter very much whether the other side suffers a lot, a little, or even at all.

Mediation has an important role in the pursuit of this second concept of the win . . . In the hands of skilled mediators and counsel, the process can be designed to minimize the incentives to clobber and enhance the likelihood that the parties will engage in goal-oriented, client-satisfying negotiation.

In mediation after mediation, clients and lawyers come to change their negotiating tune. The desire for revenge is trumped by a desire for finality: A desire to eliminate the newly perceived enhanced risks of continued litigation; to eliminate the certainty of the mental, emotional and financial drains of conflict; and to get on with one's career and life with a "bird in the hand" settlement. . . . The key to all this, however, is profoundly counterintuitive. In mediation, your effectiveness as an advocate will vary in direct proportion to that of opposing counsel, not the inverse proportion you might expect in the generally "clobbering" mode of traditional litigation.

In this sense, you and opposing counsel have become each other's best friends. You have given each other's clients what you often cannot give your own: The means by which one can achieve a balanced perspective . . . with the craving to clobber taking a back seat. Let's face it: It's tough for a lawyer to break bad news to his or her own client. It's tough on clients, too, to go beyond denial, even when that bad news is broken with candor and compassion. Yet in virtually every unsettled case, bad news needs to be broken and accepted. In some cases, it's the other side that needs it. In others, it's your side. In most cases, there's plenty of bad news to go around.

In mediation, you and opposing counsel have found uniquely qualified messengers to deliver this essential communication—each other. The mediator works along with you to make sure that the bad news is not only delivered to your client, but also received. Effective mediation advocates, therefore, must be able to hold both conceptions of "the win" in mind simultaneously, side by side, each in its appropriate place, each conception taking the forefront when appropriate.

B. When to Mediate

Assuming that mediation is appropriate for your client's needs, when is the right time to undertake it? Sometimes there is no choice: If direct negotiations have stalled or failed to start, parties may be required to mediate by a contract clause or court order, and in such circumstances the issue of timing is academic. If a disputant does have a choice, however, the issue is an important one. To answer the timing question, you and your client must again consider your goals for the process. If your primary objective is to solve a problem or restore a relationship, it is usually best to mediate as soon as possible. If not, the parties' positions are likely to harden and one of them may replace the relationship with a new one, making a repair nearly impossible.

If relationships are not a priority, then the issue of timing is more complex. By delaying mediation an advocate may be able to improve his client's bargaining position—for instance, by winning a round in court. But in doing so the client will incur costs, and its opponent may react in kind. As we know, the American legal system does not ordinarily allow litigants to recover their legal expenses and makes no provision for the non-legal costs of conflict. As a result, parties must "swallow" any expenses that they incur in an effort to improve their bargaining position. The phenomenon of loss aversion then becomes an even greater obstacle to agreement.

Disputants tend to enter legal mediation at particular points along the litigation continuum, in particular when they face either a sharp increase in cost or the risk of a significant loss in adjudication. Natural points for mediation are before a legal case is filed, before the start of costly discovery, before a significant court ruling, and just before trial.

Before a Formal Legal Action Is Filed.   A supplier and customer involved in a dispute over the quality of goods supplied under a contract, for example, may opt to mediate in order to minimize the damage to a profitable relationship and avoid the expense of hiring outside law firms. Or a discharged employee may decide to mediate before filing a charge of discrimination with a state agency, in order to avoid the inflamed feelings that often result from such a step. Whenever disputants decide to enter mediation before filing a lawsuit they accept a trade-off: Each side has less information about the case, but they have also avoided the cost of litigating to obtain that information. Business clients appear to be electing with increasing frequency to enter mediation before filing suit. However, most plaintiff's lawyers believe they will get more serious attention to their client's claim and more leverage if they file a lawsuit first.

After Preliminary Discovery.   Parties may file suit and undertake some discovery—for example, an exchange of documents—but enter mediation at the point when they face more costly and adversarial processes, such as depositions. In essence, the parties' common wish to avoid a higher level of conflict serves as a "settlement event." Thus Jeffrey Senger of the U.S. Justice Department has written that

> [o]ne approach . . . is to follow the 80-20 rule: 80 percent of the relevant information that parties learn from discovery often comes from the first 20 percent of the money they spend. Tracking down the last, difficult-to-obtain data is the most expensive part of discovery. . . . If parties conduct initial core discovery, they may find all they need to know in order to resolve the case appropriately. Following this approach, parties can agree to take abbreviated depositions of the key witnesses and then proceed to ADR. If necessary, they also may serve certain essential interrogatories and requests for production of vital documents. Often this will give them everything they need to determine their negotiation position with reasonable accuracy. . . . (Senger 2004)

"In the Shadow" of a Significant Ruling.   Parties sometimes elect to mediate when they are approaching a significant stage in the court process, such as a motion for summary judgment. In such situations, each side knows that its bargaining position will either improve or deteriorate, depending on the court's decision. One might think that if one side were willing to mediate because it fears a loss, its opponent would refuse in hope of obtaining a gain. As we have seen, however, humans are generally much more sensitive to losing than to winning, and as a result both parties in a case are often motivated to mediate at the point at which they face the risk of a significant loss in adjudication.

Shortly Before Trial.   This has been the traditional point at which to pursue settlement, either through direct bargaining or mediation, for several reasons. First, as trial approaches, attorneys must prepare intensively, imposing higher costs on them or their clients. Second, trial represents the ultimate win-or-lose event, triggering feelings of loss aversion. Finally, there are cultural assumptions about the "right" time to broach settlement: In the legal community, this used to mean that mentioning mediation early in a case was considered a sign of weakness, while raising the issue on the eve of trial was acceptable, an assumption that no longer appears to be true.

C. How to Initiate the Process

In the past, lawyers were often reluctant to propose mediation, out of concern that an adversary would see it as a sign of weakness. That attitude has largely disappeared. In some parts of the United States, many lawyers now find it easier to propose mediation than to suggest direct negotiation. Lawyers have several options for initiating the process.

Point Out That Settlement Discussions Are Inevitable.   Given the phenomenon of the "vanishing" civil trial, settlement discussions are nearly inevitable at some point. You may like to litigate if it's what you do for a living. But given that the parties will be talking settlement sooner or later in any event, why not do it now and save everyone the distraction and expense of litigation?

Rely on a Policy.   If a lawyer represents an organization that has a uniform policy of exploring ADR early in every dispute, she can cite the policy as the reason for suggesting mediation. The most prominent example is the "CPR Pledge," which appears at *www.cpradr.org/PracticeAreas/ADRPledges.aspx*. More than 4,000 companies have signed this pledge, and 1,500 law firms have signed a similar commitment to explore ADR with their clients in appropriate cases.

Cite a Rule.   Some court systems require counsel to discuss ADR or to make a good-faith effort at settlement in every case. Even if no judicial mandate exists, lawyers may consider contacting an ADR administrator or clerk of court, and ask that the judge in the case suggest mediation to both sides.

Invite a Third Party to Do It.   Another way to have a third party play "matchmaker" is to ask a private neutral or provider organization to approach an adversary and advocate mediation. Although the opponent will probably know that opposing counsel initiated the contact, this allows lawyers to avoid the burden of "selling" the process to a reluctant adversary.

So far we have assumed that the issue is to persuade one's opponent to mediate. In some situations, though, the major obstacle is one's own client. In the words of one litigator:

> There are no hard and fast rules as to when that perfect moment has arrived to mediate, [but] one point is clear. Before you begin, recognize that the first obstacle to starting the dialogue early may well be your own client, particularly if you have not represented him in the past. He may wonder if you lack confidence in yourself or the case if you push for settlement too early. On the other hand, if you don't mention settlement to the more sophisticated client, he may well wonder whether you are looking to "milk" a case that will likely never be tried. As such,

begin with the adversary only after you have reached a consensus with your own client.... (Stern 1998.)

D. Preparing to Mediate

As you prepare to mediate, the following list of problems to avoid serves as a good starting place. We will examine some of these points in more detail after this overview.

❖ **Tom Arnold,** *Twenty Common Errors in Mediation Advocacy*

13 Alternatives 69 (1995)

Trial lawyers who are unaccustomed to being mediation advocates often miss important opportunities. Here are twenty common errors, and ways to correct them.

Problem: Wrong Client in the Room

CEOs settle more cases than vice presidents, house counsel, or other agents. Why? For one thing, they don't need to worry about criticism back at the office. Any lesser agent, even with explicit "authority," typically must please a constituency which was not a participant in the give and take of the mediation. That makes it hard to settle cases.

A client's personality also can be a factor. A "Rambo" who is highly self-confident, aggressive, critical, unforgiving, or self-righteous doesn't tend to be conciliatory. The best peace-makers show patience, creativity and sometimes tolerance for the mistakes of others. Of course, it also helps to know the subject.

Problem: Wrong Lawyer in the Room

Many capable trial lawyers are so confident that they can persuade a jury of anything (after all, they've done it before) that they discount the importance of preserving relationships, as well as the common exorbitant costs and emotional drain of litigation. They can smell a "win" in the court room, and so approach mediation with a measure of ambivalence. Transactional lawyers, in contrast, having less confidence in their trial outcome, sometimes are better mediation counsel. At a minimum, parties should look for sensitive, flexible, understanding people who will do their homework, no matter what their job experience. Good preparation makes for more and better settlements. A lawyer who won't prepare is the wrong lawyer. Good mediation lawyers also should be good risk evaluators and not averse to making reasonable risk assumptions.

Problem: Wrong Mediator in the Room

Some mediators are generous about lending their conference rooms, but bring nothing to the table. Some of them determine their view of the case and like an arbitrator urge the parties to accept that view without exploring likely win-win alternatives. The best mediators can work within a range of styles described by Leonard L. Riskin. As Mr. Riskin described them, these styles fall along a continuum from being totally facilitative, to offering an evaluation of the case, to being highly directive and adjudicative. Ideally, mediators should fit the mediation style to the case and the parties before them, often moving from style to style as a mediation progresses, relatively more facilitative at the beginning and more instructive or directive as the end comes into view. Masters of the questioning process can render valuable services whether or not they have relevant substantive expertise. . . .

Problem: Wrong Case

Almost every type of case, from antitrust or patent infringement to unfair competition and employment disputes, is a likely candidate for mediation. Occasionally, cases don't fit the mold, not because of the substance of the dispute, but because one or both parties want to set a precedent. For example, a franchisor that needs a legal precedent construing a key clause that is found in 3,000 franchise agreements might not want to submit the case to mediation. Likewise, an infringement suit early in the life of an uncertain patent might be better resolved in court; getting the Federal Circuit stamp of validity could generate industry respect not obtainable from ADR.

Problem: Omitting Client Preparation

Lawyers should educate their clients about the process and the likely questions the mediator will ask. At the same time, they need to understand that the other party (rather than the mediator) should be the focus of each side's presentation.

Problem: Not Letting a Client Open for Herself

At least as often as not, letting the properly coached client do most or even all of the opening, and tell the story in her own words, works much better than lengthy openings by the lawyer.

Problem: Addressing the Mediator Instead of the Other Side

Most lawyers open the mediation with a statement directed at the mediator, comparable to opening statements to a judge or jury. Highly adversarial in tone, it overlooks the interests of the other side that gave rise to the dispute. Why is this strategy a mistake? The "judge" or "jury" you should be trying to persuade in mediation is not so much the mediator as the adversary. If you want to make the other party sympathetic to your cause, most often at least it is best not to hurt him. For the same reason, plenary sessions should demonstrate your client's humanity, respect, warmth, apologies, and sympathy. Stay away from inflammatory issues, which are better addressed by the mediator in private caucuses with the other side.

Problem: Making the Lawyer the Center of the Process

Unless the client is highly unappealing or inarticulate, the client should be the center of the process. The company representative for the other side may not have attended depositions, so is unaware of the impact your client could have on a judge or jury if the mediation fails. People pay more attention to appealing plaintiffs, so show them off.

Prepare the client to speak and be spoken to by the mediator and the adversary. He should be able to explain why he feels the way he does, why he is or is not responsible, and why any damages he caused are great or only peanuts. But he should also consider extending empathy to the other party.

Problem: Failure to Use Advocacy Tools Effectively

You'll want to prepare your materials for maximum persuasive impact. Exhibits, charts, and copies of relevant cases or contracts with key phrases highlighted can be valuable visual aids. A ninety-second video showing one or more key witnesses in depositions making important admissions, followed by a readable-sized copy of an important document with some relevant language underlined, can pack a punch.

Problem: Timing Mistakes

Get and give critical discovery, but don't spend exorbitant time or sums in discovery and trial prep before seeking mediation. Mediation can identify what's truly necessary discovery and avoid unnecessary discovery. . . .

Problem: Failure to Listen to the Other Side

Many lawyers and clients seem incapable of giving open-minded attention to what the other side is saying. That could cost a settlement.

Problem: Failure to Identify Perceptions and Motivations

Seek first to understand, only then to be understood. [B]rainstorm to determine the other party's motivations and perceptions. Prepare a chart summarizing how your adversary sees the issues: Part of preparing for mediation is to understand your adversary's perceptions and motivations, perhaps even listing them in chart form. . . .

Problem: Hurting, Humiliating, Threatening, or Commanding

Don't poison the well from which you must drink to get a settlement. That means you don't hurt, humiliate, or ridicule the other folks. Avoid pejoratives like "malingerer," "fraud," "cheat," "crook," or "liar." You can be strong on what your evidence will be and still be a decent human being. All settlements are based upon trust to some degree. If you anger the other side, they won't trust you. This inhibits settlement. The same can be said for threats . . . Ultimatums destroy the process and destroy credibility.

Problem: The Backwards Step

A party who offered to pay $300,000 before the mediation, but comes to the mediation table willing to offer only $200,000, injures its own credibility and engenders bad feelings from the other side. Without some clear and dramatic reasons for the reduction in the offer, it can be hard to overcome the damage done. The backwards step is a powerful card to play at the right time—a walk away without yet walking out. But powerful devices are also dangerous. There are few productive occasions to use this one, and they tend to come late in a mediation. A rule of thumb: Unless you're an expert negotiator, don't do it.

Problem: Too Many People

Advisors—people to whom the decision-maker must display respect and courtesy, people who feel that since they are there they must put in their two bits worth—all delay mediation immeasurably. A caucus that with only one lawyer and vice president would take twenty minutes, with five people could take an hour and twenty minutes. What could have been a one-day mediation stretches to two or three.

Problem: Closing Too Fast

A party who opens at $1 million and moves immediately to $500,000 gives the impression of having more to give. Rightly or wrongly, the other side probably will not accept the $500,000 offer because they expect more give. By contrast, moving from $1 million to $750,000, $600,000, $575,000, $560,000, $550,000, sends no message of yield below $500,000, and may induce a $500,000 proposal that can be accepted. The "dance" is part of communication. Skip the dance, lose the communication, and risk losing settlement at your own figure.

Problem: Failure to Truly Close

Unless parties have strong reasons to "sleep on" their agreement, to further evaluate the deal, or to check on possibly forgotten details, it is better to get some sort of enforceable contract written and signed before the parties separate. Too often, when left to think overnight and draft tomorrow, the parties think of new ideas that delay or prevent closing.

Problem: Breaching Confidentiality

Sometimes parties to mediation unthinkingly, or irresponsibly, disclose in open court information revealed confidentially in a mediation. When information is highly sensitive, consider keeping it confidential with the mediator. Or if revealed to the adversary in a mediation where the case did not settle, consider moving before the trial begins for an order in limine to bind both sides to the confidentiality agreement.

Problem: Lack of Patience and Perseverance

The mediation "dance" takes time. Good mediation advocates have patience and perseverance.

Problem: Misunderstanding Conflict

A dispute is a problem to be solved together, not a combat to be won.

Questions

1. Most attorneys using commercial mediation are trial lawyers, who generally view claims and litigation as a competition for dollars. Do you think
   Arnold's list of problems applies to all lawyers, or just to competitive
   advocates in distributional situations?
2. Can you recast Arnold's list of problems as positive statements about how
   to be effective in mediation?

E. Selecting a Mediator

The most important issue in arranging for mediation, apart perhaps from
agreeing on who will attend the process, is to select the right neutral. As was
discussed in Chapter 12, mediators vary in characteristics such as the breadth
or narrowness of their approach, substantive expertise, and willingness to use
facilitative or evaluative techniques. When selecting a legal mediator you will
typically be able to choose among former or practicing litigators, transactional
lawyers, and ex-judges, as well as professionals in fields ranging from psycho-
therapy to civil engineering. Your goal should be to select a neutral with qualities that match the needs of your case.

One approach is to think about what barriers are making it difficult to negotiate directly with the other side. The answer will give you an insight into what
qualities a neutral will need to help you overcome them. If, for example, the
key problem is that your opponent has an abrasive or insulting manner, then
a mediator with strong process skills may be the best choice. If your own client needs "cover" to justify a compromise to an outside constituency or has an
unrealistically high expectation, then an evaluative neutral may be helpful. If
the parties are very angry or need to repair their relationship, then a neutral
with skills in counseling may be what is called for. In many situations more than
one barrier exists, calling for a mediator with a blend of abilities. Experienced
lawyers sometimes look for a mediator whom the other side will endorse, on the
theory that such a neutral is most likely to be able to persuade their opponent
to compromise.

❖ David S. Ross, *STRATEGIC CONSIDERATIONS IN CHOOSING A
MEDIATOR: A MEDIATOR'S PERSPECTIVE*

2 J. Alt. Disp. Resol. in Emp. 7 (Spring 2000)

Because the mediation process is only as effective as the mediator who man-
ages it, choosing the right mediator is critical. The mediator selection process
demands a thoughtful balancing of many criteria, including:

* Mediation experience
* Mediation process skills

- Substantive expertise
- Reputation for neutrality
- Creativity
- Strong interpersonal skills and an ability to connect with people, and
- The ability to help parties reach agreement

Since every case is different, it makes sense to prioritize these criteria based on the needs of the case and parties. . . .

Substantive Expertise.   People often ask whether they should choose a mediator with substantive expertise or one with strong process skills. A short answer is "both." A longer answer is that in most employment disputes, process skills count as much or more than substantive expertise. However, more mediators are specializing in specific substantive areas [such as] employment law, so parties now can more easily choose a mediator with both substantive expertise and process skills.

References.   Participants should take the time to speak directly with individuals—ideally both lawyers and principals—who have worked with a proposed mediator to learn their candid assessment of the mediator's strengths and weaknesses, mediation style, and overall effectiveness. Most mediators provide references upon request. If they do not, then press the mediator to do so.

Opposing Counsel's Recommendations.   What should you do if opposing counsel proposes a mediator? There may be a strong instinct to reject such a proposal. My experience suggests that sophisticated lawyers should seriously consider mediators proposed by opposing counsel, honestly hashing out the advantages and disadvantages of various candidates. . . .

Attorneys should consult with their clients when choosing a mediator. . . . Encouraging client participation in the mediator selection process empowers clients. Finally, and perhaps most importantly, it builds trust in the attorney-client relationship and in the mediation process, promoting a sense of shared responsibility in making mediation work.

Assuming you have identified the skills you want in a mediator, how can you determine whether a particular candidate possesses them? Common sources of information about mediators include recommendations from colleagues, references, and the opposing party's suggestions. In addition, companies and law firms that engage regularly in mediation sometimes create private data banks with information about their experience with various neutrals.

Some organizations and government agencies develop rosters of mediators who are approved to handle their cases. Mediators and ADR provider organizations also provide prospective clients with information and mediator bios. Such documents typically emphasize the neutral's qualifications, but advocates may be able to read between the lines to determine suitability or identify potential bias. In addition, most mediators are willing to talk informally with attorneys who express interest in hiring them or have case managers who can provide more information.

Questions

3. What might be the advantage of selecting a transactional lawyer rather than a litigator as your mediator? What might be the advantage of selecting a litigator rather than a transactional lawyer as your mediator?
4. Generally, when would a retired judge be a good person to have as a mediator?
5. Under what circumstances might it be to your client's advantage to allow the other side to select a mediator who knows the opposing attorney well and may have engaged in a similar type of law practice as the opposing attorney? For example, if you represent a defendant insurance company, when might you allow a personal injury plaintiff's lawyer to choose another experienced plaintiff's lawyer as the mediator?
6. If you wished to propose a mediator with whom you had worked repeatedly, what would be the best way to do so?
7. Assume you have agreed to mediate one of the role-playing cases previously assigned to you to negotiate by your teacher in this course. Further assume you are now in the process of selecting a neutral. What qualities and experience would you look for in a mediator for that particular case? If you can obtain biographies of mediators in your area, review some and prioritize the candidates. (You can find biographies online at *www.jamsadr.com.*)

F. Consideration of Who Should Be Present, the Format, and Court-Connected Mediation

1. Ensuring the Presence of Necessary Participants

We know that mediation is an intensely personal process. Therefore, the presence of the right people is a critical factor in its success. Who these people are in a particular case will depend on your objectives and the disputed issues.

- If the primary goal is to repair a personal relationship, then the presence of the principals themselves, to talk out their problems and regain the ability to relate productively with each other, is usually essential.
- If the parties' relationship is attenuated, as, for example, in the case of a rent dispute between a corporate landlord and a former commercial tenant, the presence of principals may be less important. In an employment case the director of human resources may be the most appropriate company representative.
- If the objective is to work out an imaginative solution, then it is important that the participants be capable of thinking "outside the box" and know enough about the parties' interests to identify and flesh out useful options.
- Working out a novel solution to a business dispute, for instance, may require the presence of executives who know the business.

- If the only goal is to settle a legal claim on the best possible monetary terms, as is true in many negligence cases, then the primary concern is probably that the bargainers arrive at the table with sufficient settlement authority, or that those with such authority are available by phone.

Jerry Spolter, a mediator with JAMS (Judicial Arbitration and Mediation Services) in San Francisco, reports the following experience regarding a lack of authority.

A recent mediation session I conducted highlights what can happen when the attorneys don't address authority issues in advance. Everything went great for about five hours. The joint session was textbook material, with lots of helpful information exchanged; the private caucuses peeled away postured "positions" to reveal the parties' real interests. And then it happened: Although the physician accused of malpractice was in the room, the doc wouldn't make a move until his personal attorney gave the OK.

Unfortunately, the personal attorney was on a chairlift in the Sierra with a dead battery in her cell phone. And since this was a malpractice case requiring the doc's consent, "my" mediation was suddenly in trouble. To make matters worse, the doc's insurance representative had to consult two "invisible-hierarchy" decision-makers at headquarters three time zones away to discuss increasing settlement authority and it was now after business hours there. If only I had received a "heads up" beforehand, we could have resolved the authority problems in advance and taken advantage of the momentum we had generated that day to settle the case. Instead, the parties are now scurrying around trying to acquire the necessary authority to put Humpty Dumpty back together again. (The Recorder 4 (Mar. 8, 2000).)

2. *Influencing the Format*

Mediation can occur in a wide variety of formats. The parties, for example, can choose to meet entirely in joint session or rely heavily on caucusing. They can bargain with each other directly or through attorneys. The best format for a particular case again depends on your overall goal.

- In a case focused on relationship repair, you will probably want the clients to have as much opportunity as possible to communicate directly. It may make sense, for instance, to arrange for the principals, at some point in the mediation, to talk without counsel present, or perhaps to remain in joint session throughout the process.
- In a highly emotional case, it may be important for a party to meet with the mediator ahead of time to begin venting, and for the mediator to carefully structure the party's interactions with the other side. Some relationships are so charged that the parties should never be in the same room together. If there is any history of physical intimidation or violence, scheduling separate mediation meetings at different times may be necessary.
- In factually complex cases, it may be necessary to arrange for enough time for each side to present a lengthy opening statement, perhaps supported by computerized exhibits or comments from an expert.

It is important to bear in mind that experienced advocates often ask for changes in the usual format of commercial mediation. If you see a reason to vary the format, you should alert the mediator to this before the process begins.

3. Planning for Court-Connected Mediation

The discussion to this point has assumed that you have the freedom to design an effective mediation process in conjunction with the mediator and the other party. Sometimes, however, your client may be required by a contract clause to engage in mediation. More often, the court in which your case is pending will require litigants to go through mediation as a precondition to trial. Many state and federal courts have mandatory mediation programs. They are most prevalent in family disputes but have become common in general civil litigation as well. States such as Florida, Texas, and California require most civil cases filed in their courts to go through mediation. Most federal district courts require some form of ADR prior to trial, with mediation most often required.

Courts may order mediation but leave process choices to the parties, with court rules available only as a default mechanism. Many jurisdictions, however, channel cases into court-connected programs, assign mediators, require principals to attend, and impose other significant restrictions on the process. Litigants may have the option to opt out of restrictions by agreement, but in the context of adversarial litigation this can be difficult to accomplish.

If you have a case that is subject to mandatory mediation, whether by contract or court rule, you should consider the following questions, in addition to the general issues that arise in planning for any mediation. The most important are:

- Is the mandated mediation process adequate?
- If not, how should you respond to it?
- Is it in your client's interest to pay for a noncourt process, if permitted?

In considering the adequacy of the process, several issues are likely to arise that are peculiar to mandatory programs.

- Will you have a role in choosing the neutral? Some programs require parties to select a mediator from panels that consist of attorney-mediators with varying levels of experience. Others assign a mediator, sometimes a full-time court employee, to each case. Some programs and clauses give parties the option to select a private mediator. And contract clauses sometimes designate a named individual as the neutral.
- Who will be required to be present at the session? Many courts require each party to send a representative with "full settlement authority." This can create serious problems for organizations that have large numbers of cases pending in different court systems.
- Will you have an opportunity to brief the mediator in advance? Some programs require pre-mediation phone calls with the mediator, while others seek to reduce costs by barring parties from submitting statements or talking with neutrals in advance.

- Will you be required to pay for the process? Some programs are free, relying on volunteer attorney-mediators; others use private neutrals who charge market prices; and still others require parties to pay mediators, but at below-market rates.
- Will you be required to mediate within a specific time frame? Court processes can range from a one-hour process, with the option to extend the time by agreement, to a full-day commitment. If the process is time-limited, the mediator is likely to feel pressure to produce progress quickly, leading him to forego interest-oriented questioning in favor of "cutting to the chase" and soliciting offers.
- What confidentiality guarantees does the program offer?
- Can you change the structure of the process by agreement with the other side? If so, will the other side agree to the changes you seek?

If you do not want to mediate, or you conclude that the mandated process is not adequate, you should consider these questions:

- Is it possible to opt out of the process, for example, by applying for an exemption?
- If not, what is the minimum you have to do to comply with the mandate? Some programs, for example, require parties to participate in "good faith," which can be difficult to define.
- Are there penalties for nonparticipation or noncompliance? For example, if you fail to send a representative with settlement authority, will the court impose costs or attorneys' fees? Will the mediator report to the court about your cooperation? Will the mediator give the court a recommendation as to how the court should rule on unresolved issues, as is true of some divorce mediation programs?

G. Final Preparation and Educating the Mediator

Once you have, with opposing counsel, scheduled the mediation and, chosen the mediator, it is time to prepare for the settlement event. This requires planning not only what you will do, but also the role of the client and any other members of the team. Preparation includes at least four areas: developing a negotiation plan, exchanging information, coaching clients, and educating the mediator.

1. Developing a Negotiating Plan for Use in Mediation

Because mediation is another way to negotiate to meet the needs of your client and achieve its goals, you should plan for mediation in much the same way that you would for a direct negotiation. The points made in Chapter 5 about preparation for negotiation apply here as well. You will want, for example, to consider each side's alternatives to agreement, principles that you can cite and those that your opponent will rely on, the parties' underlying interests, and potential options for settlement. If your primary goal is to obtain the best possible monetary outcome, your plan will be similar to that of a competitive bargainer, complete with a concession strategy. If you see the purpose of the process as solving a common problem, then you are likely to focus on the parties' interests and cooperate in finding ways to address them. Whatever your goal, however, you will need to modify your non-facilitated approach to take advantage of the presence of the mediator, the nature of mediation, including having the parties present, and what develops in the process.

2. Exchanging Information

One of the key aspects of any negotiation is exchanging information, and one of mediation's effects is to enhance the flow of data between the parties. This process often begins well before disputants actually meet to mediate. As an advocate, you will have to think about two types of information:

- What data does your client need to make a good settlement decision?
- What information will help get your adversary to agree to the outcome you are seeking?

If necessary, you should be prepared to enlist the mediator's help in persuading the other side to provide you with data. The neutral may also be able to help you explain to your client why in this context it is a good idea to give an opponent some "free discovery."

What information is relevant depends again on your goals. If the process turns on money, then legal evidence and arguments are likely to be key. If your purpose is to repair a relationship, knowing the "why" behind a disputed action will be important. If the objective is to create a new business arrangement, then financial data may be more useful. As a rule, negotiations that focus on imaginative options require a broader base of information than discussions that revolve solely around money.

Disputants usually need less information to mediate effectively than they would require to try the same case. Still, especially if parties mediate early in a dispute, one side may lack information that is necessary to make an informed decision. The party may not be able to assess the value of its litigation alternative or determine whether an imaginative option is viable. An insurance adjuster, for example, may not be able to obtain the authority needed to settle a claim without documents verifying the plaintiff's medical expenses. In litigation there is ordinarily no reason for a party to show its hand to an adversary, but in mediation disputants know that providing information will increase their chances of reaping a good settlement. Equally important, they know that the mediator is present to help ensure that the exchange will be mutual. As a result, parties in mediation often provide each other with surprising amounts of information.

Questions

8. What types of data gathered before mediation might help an advocate avoid the "twenty common errors" described earlier in the article by Tom Arnold?

9. Assume that you are the lawyer in a negotiation role-play previously assigned by your teacher in this class and that you are now representing the same client in mediation. What additional information, beyond the facts stated in the role-play instructions, would help you mediate well? What data might the other attorney ask you for?

3. Preparing the Client

As we have noted, mediation is in essence a process of negotiation, but one that varies in significant ways from direct bargaining, requiring different preparation of clients. Attorneys usually conduct direct negotiations outside their clients' presence, often without meeting face-to-face. In mediation, by contrast, both clients are ordinarily physically present and the mediator has direct conversations with them. In addition, in the typical caucus-based mediation, disputants spend much of their time isolated from each other, interacting through the neutral rather than directly. Because of these structural differences, lawyers should cover the following topics, in addition to the issues they would address when preparing a client for a direct negotiation:

- How the mediation process will differ from negotiations to which the client is accustomed.
  — The background, personality, and likely approach of the mediator, including the potential for changes in style—for example, from an empathic to an evaluative approach.
  — The likely format of the process and potential variations in it—for instance, the possibility that the client will be invited to meet privately with the other principal.
  — The confidentiality rules that will apply to the process, as well as possible gaps and exceptions in them.
- What role the client should play in the process. In particular,
  — What questions the client should expect from the mediator.
  — What the client should be prepared to say, and when the client should remain silent.
  — What the other side may say and do.
  — How the lawyer and client should coordinate. The client should know, for instance, that it is entirely permissible for the client or the lawyer to ask the mediator to leave the room so that they can talk privately.
- What role the lawyer will play in the process. An advocate should be sure that the client understands that while their overall goal—getting the best

possible outcome—will remain the same, she will adapt her tactics to the special nature of mediation. In particular,

— The attorney will probably take a different tone than she would in a court-room or direct bargaining session. In particular, the presence of the mediator may call for a more conciliatory stance.
— The lawyer may also "pull punches" in order not to antagonize the other side while they explore a possible deal.
— The lawyer may not mention certain key evidence in order to save it for trial.

4. Educating the Mediator

In small cases and court-connected programs, neutrals sometimes arrive at mediation knowing almost nothing about the dispute. In privately conducted mediations, however, lawyers typically make an effort to orient, and begin to persuade, the neutral in advance. Pre-mediation communications can take at least three forms: written statements, joint meetings, and private conversations.

Written Statements

Parties commonly give a mediator written statements, sometimes called mediation "briefs" or "submissions," to read in advance. As they prepare their statements, advocates should consider the following:

• Is it better to prepare a statement, or use an existing document? A customized document has obvious advantages and is preferred, but particularly in smaller cases it may be appropriate to use an existing document or pleading that summarizes the party's views.
• Is it best to submit the statement on an ex parte basis, or exchange it with opposing counsel? Mediators usually prefer that lawyers exchange statements, so that they are free to discuss with the other the points each side makes. In addition, it is the other side that you have to convince. That said, even if you exchange statements, you are ordinarily free to write or call the neutral to discuss sensitive issues privately.

What should be in the mediation statement? A mediator is likely to be interested in knowing the following, among other things:

• How did the dispute arise?
• What are the key factual and legal issues?
• What is the status of any legal proceedings?
• What non-legal concerns are present?
• What barriers have made direct bargaining difficult?
• Have there been prior negotiations and where did they end?
• Are there personal or emotional issues likely to arise?
• Who are the key decision makers in the dispute?

Organizational Discussions

In complex cases, mediators often schedule joint meetings with all counsel to discuss organizational questions and who will be present at the mediation. Such meetings usually occur by conference call, but they are sometimes convened in person. Organizational meetings are typically limited to lawyers, but clients and experts may occasionally participate as well.

Private Conversations

Mediators sometimes take the initiative to talk with lawyers, either separately or together in "pre-mediation" calls. Mediators use these private conversations to ask about obstacles, fill factual gaps, confirm who will be present, and discuss process. Attorneys often want to use these calls to assert legal points made in their written statements. This is usually a mistake. Apart from the fact that the mediator may already have read the briefs, lawyers will have a chance to make their legal arguments during the process itself. At this stage mediators usually want to know about issues that attorneys may be reluctant to include in the briefs, such as non-legal obstacles, what the participants are like, and potential options to resolve the case. Pre-mediation private conversations provide an exceptional opportunity for advocates to shape a mediator's "take" on the back story of a dispute and the parties.

Another alternative used with increasing frequency is for a lawyer and client to meet personally with the neutral immediately before the "formal" process begins. Even if this is not the normal practice of the mediator, an advocate might seek out such a meeting for the following reasons, among others:

- To build a relationship with the neutral.
- To permit a client to begin the process of working through his emotions or to allow the client to get to know the mediator.
- To present sensitive data or proposals.

H. Representing Clients During the Process

We now turn to the point in the mediation process at which the parties and mediator convene together to talk and bargain. This is what many lawyers think of as the "actual" mediation, although by now you know that effective advocacy begins well before the parties meet in person. We have seen that commercial mediation tends to follow a joint-session-plus-caucusing format, while family and problem-solving mediators are much more likely to keep disputants together.

Problem

You represent a company that vacated commercial space because of dissatisfaction with the condition of the building. Your client is being sued by a corporate landlord for rent due under the lease. Both sides have agreed to mediate. Apart from the basic issue of liability, which you see as a 50-50 proposition, you believe that the landlord ignored its responsibility to maintain the building and as a result would not be awarded much even if it did establish a technical violation of the lease.

1. How can you best use the opening session to make the landlord aware of its risk at trial?
2. Can you think of any type of dispute in which an initial joint meeting is likely to be counterproductive?
3. What format would you advocate using instead?

1. Joint Meetings

The Opening Session

Mediators traditionally have begun with a session attended by all disputants. More recently, however, lawyers have pushed back from joint sessions and the all-caucus format is rapidly growing and dominates practice is large parts of the United States (See Folberg, The Shrinking Joint Session: Survey Results, 22 ABA Dip. Res. Mag. Winter 2016.)

Lawyers' most common argument against holding a substantive opening session is that each side already knows the other's arguments—what benefit is there in repeating them? Or, they warn, someone will make inflammatory comments that will destroy the atmosphere for compromise. Moreover, time is limited: Why not get right to the bargaining?

There is often some truth to each of these concerns. No matter how repetitive or uncomfortable an opening session may appear, however, you should be extremely reluctant to ask that it be omitted entirely. An adversary's comments may offend your client (and vice versa), but the experience of speaking directly to an opponent often helps disputants let go of emotions that would otherwise impair their decision making later in the process. Allowing a party to listen directly to an adversary's evidence and arguments can also help bring reality to later discussions, giving each side a better appreciation and assessment of what they will face if the case does not settle. And after a time, even angry listeners usually become more calm. Mediators find that it is almost always useful to hold at least one joint meeting early in the process.

If you do have a reason for avoiding a joint meeting, raise this with your mediator in advance. Before doing so, however, carefully examine the pros and cons. Remember that you have the option of requesting that an opening session be restructured—falling anywhere from cancellation to the "usual format." You might, for example, ask that the session be limited to presentations by experts or comments by executives.

What Role Will You Take in the Session?

You can have a variety of goals for a joint meeting. Even if your objective is solely to get the best possible monetary outcome, you will usually not want to exchange offers during the opening session. Too often, offers made directly by one side to another are reactively devalued. Instead, your strategy should be to create the conditions for successful bargaining later in the process. You can do this in several ways.

Foster a Working Relationship. Advocates and clients can use an opening session, and perhaps also the casual conversation that sometimes occurs as people assemble, to foster a better working relationship with an opponent. This does not necessarily mean repairing a past connection, although that might be desirable. Instead the goal is typically more modest: to create a basis for the parties to bargain effectively later on. Disputants can do this, for example, by demonstrating that they are serious about settlement and are willing to make principled compromises to reach one. Alternatively, a lawyer can use an opening session to help an emotional or angry participant work through difficult feelings.

Gather Information. Lawyers can also use the opening session to gather information. In a joint meeting, unlike discovery or court proceedings, disputants can talk informally with each other. Attorneys and clients also have the opportunity to observe the lawyer and witnesses for the other side, and perhaps also to speak directly with the opposing principal. (The other side, of course, will have the same opportunity to "size up" you and your client.)

Focus the Discussion on Key Issues. Skilled lawyers use the opening session to focus discussion on the issues that are most helpful to their case or that create a platform for effective bargaining. If, for example, an advocate wants to emphasize the evidence (or lack of it) supporting the damage claims in a case, she can alert the mediator beforehand that this issue is significant to her client and then focus attention on it through her comments. If the attorney's primary goal is to explore an interest-based solution, she can use the opening session to send signals about this as well—or to prime the mediator to raise the issue as his own idea. Neither side can control the agenda of an opening session, but attorneys who take the initiative can influence significantly the content of such discussions.

Persuade an Opponent. Finally, lawyers use the opening session to persuade their opponents to compromise. They focus their advocacy on the opposing decision maker, knowing that they will have other chances to talk with the mediator, but the opening session may be their only opportunity to speak directly to the other party. The goal will usually be to convince the other side that it is in its own best interest to compromise. Opponents are more likely to do so if they believe that:

- You are serious about seeking a settlement.
- You are open to options that will advance their interests.
- If discussions fail, you have a good alternative to settlement.
- You are willing to compromise, but will accept impasse sooner than agree to an unfair result.

What Role Will Your Client Take?

Most lawyers are inclined to take the lead in the opening session, treating it as a kind of informal pretrial hearing. As we have already noted, however, clients can play crucial roles in these meetings as well.

Should the Client Speak in the Opening Session?   As a general rule, clients should be active in joint meetings. Opponents tend to "tune out" what an opposing attorney says, but they are usually very interested in hearing from the opposing principal. Mediators also seek a connection with parties and therefore pay especially close attention to what they say. For these reasons, statements from principals are likely to have a greater impact than the same words spoken by an attorney. By participating effectively in a joint session, parties can significantly affect how opponents view them as witnesses, future partners, or negotiators.

- In personal injury and employment cases, in which the plaintiff's pain and suffering or emotional distress is often an important element of the claim, a plaintiff who can persuasively describe how he has suffered increases the settlement value of the claim. In general, whenever a person is likely to be a significant witness in a future adjudication, his presentation in mediation will affect the other side's estimate of the value of the case.
- When parties wish to repair a relationship, as in some business cases, or the principals cannot avoid a continuing relationship, as is true of many family cases involving children, one party's participation in mediation can significantly affect the other side's willingness to settle on terms that maintain a working relationship. Again, statements made by one party directly to another almost always have greater impact than comments made through a lawyer or mediator—for better or worse.
- Parties can often articulate their interests more persuasively if they speak themselves.
- If one side doubts an opponent's commitment to settling, the opponent may be able to dispel those concerns in the opening session.

All this assumes, of course, that a client presents herself positively. If a party is obnoxious, inarticulate, or repulsive, then her participation will lower an opponent's opinion of her case and hurt her bargaining objectives. In such situations the client should remain silent, if possible.

2. Caucusing

Because caucusing is so common in civil mediation outside the family law area, attorneys and mediators you encounter in practice are likely to expect to spend most of the time in caucuses. As a result, you will need either to take action in advance to obtain modifications in the caucus format or plan to reap the greatest advantage from using it.

To make the best use of caucuses, you will have to prepare in two ways. First, you will have to adapt your direct bargaining tactics to the special structure of caucusing, and second, you should deal with the mediator differently from the way you respond to opponents. If, for example, opposing counsel asks your client a question, you would ordinarily feel free to cut him off or step in and answer the question yourself. But if a mediator asks your client the same question in the privacy of a caucus, the considerations are different. You may be more willing to have your client answer a mediator's question because you can insist the mediator treat the answer as confidential, and you may be more reluctant to offend the neutral than opposing counsel. The nature of caucusing typically changes over the course of a mediation, and we therefore discuss early and later caucusing separately.

a. Early Caucuses

Exchanging Information and Arguments

Sophisticated negotiators often spend a good deal of time exchanging information and feeling each other out before making explicit offers. Because legal mediation is at heart a process of negotiation, it is not surprising that good advocates and mediators use caucusing to facilitate the flow of information prior to exchanging demands and offers. A lawyer might, for example, tell a mediator what she wishes the neutral to stress to an opponent as well as questions that she needs answered.

Neutrals, for their part, understand that disputants often come to mediation without data that they need to make settlement decisions, and that good lawyers will work to get points across to an adversary through them. Indeed, to the extent that a party's "questions" are implicit arguments, mediators are often willing to transmit them to encourage the listener to reassess the value of his case.

Also be aware that experienced mediators understand that lawyers usually do not disclose their bargaining strategy completely. Neutrals expect that if an attorney makes a factual representation it will be accurate, but not that lawyers will confide in them about bargaining tactics and true bottom lines.

Initiating Bargaining

Depending on the circumstances, an advocate in mediation may decide to focus either on money bargaining or creative solutions. The format allows lawyers to advance either of these objectives.

Interest-Based Bargaining. Most mediators will urge interest-based bargaining. One practical problem for advocates, however, is that even when they wish to explore nonmonetary terms, they are often reluctant to do so for fear of signaling that their client is not committed to its monetary position. This is particularly true of plaintiffs because they are typically the ones seeking damages. Defense lawyers, by contrast, tend to be receptive to imaginative terms, because they see them as a substitute for paying money.

Mediation can allow a lawyer to have it both ways. He can press "publicly" — in communications sent through the mediator or made in joint session — for the best possible money outcome, while asking the neutral "privately" — through a pre-mediation talk or caucus discussion — to explore nonmonetary options.

A "Hard" Bargaining Strategy. One rarely mentioned aspect of mediation is that it offers protection to parties who opt for a competitive approach, as well as to negotiators pursuing creative solutions. Indeed, the mediation process allows counsel to take tougher stands than would be possible in direct negotiation. Because mediation is more complicated and expensive to arrange than an ordinary bargaining session, participants are more reluctant to walk out in response to an "insulting" proposal. More important, a mediator will work to "scrape the other side off the ceiling" when they erupt at an opponent's stubbornness. Lawyers sometimes take advantage of this dynamic to play "bad cop," knowing that good mediators will instinctively take on a "good cop" role to keep the process alive.

As knowledgeable counsel you can use mediation to enhance both cooperative and competitive bargaining strategies. You can privately encourage the mediator to raise creative options while adhering to a monetary demand, or pursue a genuinely competitive strategy secure in the knowledge that the mediator will work to keep the process from falling apart. As an advocate, you should also keep in mind that the mediator will be interpreting your position and viewpoint to the other side, and you can offer suggestions to the neutral about what you would like him to say in the other room about your current position and thinking.

b. Later Caucuses

As caucusing progresses, the tactics of the disputants and the mediator are likely to evolve. Advocates will continue to probe for information, explore interests, and argue the merits, but as the process continues these aspects usually become less dominant. For one thing, the parties will return to the issues repeatedly, making continued discussion seem repetitive. As a result, during the later stages of a mediation that emphasizes monetary demands, caucuses are likely to become progressively shorter as both sides focus on bargaining. In a creative process, parties often shift their attention gradually from identifying and communicating interests to devising options to satisfy them. In this kind of process caucuses are likely to remain relatively long, but their focus is likely to be on crafting terms to produce the best possible fit of the parties' concerns.

Mediators are also more likely to express opinions as mediation continues. In part this is because as neutrals gather more information, they become increasingly confident about their assessment of the participants and the obstacles to agreement. Parties also typically become more receptive to a mediator's advice; they come to appreciate that the mediator has genuinely listened to their concerns, and from the answers she brings back after each round of caucusing, they know that the mediator has communicated their views clearly to the other side. Competitive bargainers in particular are likely to become more receptive to a mediator's advice when they realize that their positional tactics are likely to lead to an impasse. As mediators become more active in the process, advocates should consider modifying their own tactics in response.

Facilitating Bargaining

One option is to ask the mediator to assess the emotional "temperature" in the other room, or predict how a counterpart is likely to react to a proposal.

Lawyers can also seek to take advantage of the mediator's special status to enhance the effectiveness of their offers.

Obtaining Information.   One of the paradoxes of mediation is how mediators are expected to treat information that they gather during private caucuses. On the one hand, caucus discussions are confidential. On the other hand, one of mediation's key purposes is to foster better communication, and as long as the parties are separated in caucuses, this can only happen if the mediator conveys information between them. How can an advocate take advantage of this seeming contradiction?

In practice most lawyers in mediation designate very few facts as confidential from the other side, and they appear to expect a mediator to reveal at least some of what they say in private caucus. For example, a plaintiff lawyer might tell a mediator, "$500,000 is as low as we'll go at this point. You can tell them 500." The attorney knows that the neutral will interpret this to mean that he can tell the other side that the plaintiff is reducing his demand to $500,000, and also that the plaintiff will probably be willing to go further ("at this point") if the defendant makes an appropriate response.

Experienced lawyers know, in other words, that while mediators will not report sensitive data to the other camp, they will usually feel some license to go beyond simply repeating what a party says, to interpret its general intentions. Unless instructed otherwise, a mediator will convey this information as his own impression, not attributing it to the speaker. The result resembles the way government officials sometimes float trial balloons to the press on a "background" basis. This approach has two advantages. First, the listener may be left a bit unsure what signal has been given, giving the sender leeway to either reinforce or back away from its message in light of the response. Second, the fact that the mediator is the one making the interpretation makes it appear less manipulative, and therefore less subject to reactive devaluation, than if the lawyer had given the signal directly. Advocates should therefore consider what they want a mediator to say about their attitude and offer in the other room, and state their wishes to the neutral. If you want something you or your client say in mediation to truly remain confidential, clearly inform the mediator not to reveal it.

Advocates should also consider whether to ask the mediator about the other side's state of mind. If, for instance, a plaintiff seems agitated during an opening session, defense counsel might later ask the mediator, "Has Smith calmed down?" or "If his lawyer recommends a deal, do you think he'll listen?" Alternatively, a lawyer might ask a mediator to collect specific information, such as whether the other side has retained an expert. These requests for information should be reasonable and in aid of settlement. Lawyers can also ask mediators to explore an adversary's reaction to a potential deal without disclosing their own interest in it.

Questions about what the other side is thinking pose tricky ethical and practical issues for mediators because of the paradox mentioned above. But that does not mean that counsel should not ask them. Lawyers should be aware, however, that if they ask a mediator for information about their opponent, the mediator, as a neutral, may interpret this as permission to provide the other side with the same kind of data about the questioner. As in direct bargaining, in other words, information exchange is a two-way street. That does not mean, however, that asking questions is not helpful, and mediation can amplify the effectiveness of doing so. To take advantage of the mediator's ability to gather and convey information during the caucusing process:

- Ask the mediator questions about the other side's current attitude and intentions.
- Discuss with the mediator what she will say to your opponent about you.
- Use the mediator as a sounding board about how a potential offer will be received.

Using a Mediator's Neutrality. As we have seen, mediators have a key advantage that is not available even to the best advocate: the simple fact that they are seen by disputants as neutral. Although the phenomenon of reactive devaluation makes humans instinctively suspect anything that is proposed by an opponent, mediators can potentially deliver bargainers from its impact. Take, for example, a situation in which a defendant is stubbornly clinging to an offer of $75,000. The mediator could say to the plaintiff, "You know, I think that if we could ever get them up to $100,000, it would be worth serious consideration. . . . What do you think?" By phrasing the issue in this way, the neutral has done two things. First, she has presented the offer as hypothetical—it is not yet "cursed" by the fact that the defendant is actually willing to make it. Second, she has tentatively endorsed its reasonableness. If the plaintiff buys into the potential offer, the mediator will have partially "inoculated" it against being devalued if it materializes. Counsel can take advantage of a mediator's neutrality by:

- Asking a mediator to deliver unwelcome information to the other side.
- Suggesting that a mediator offer a party's proposal or argument as her own.
- Requesting a neutral to certify the fairness of a proposal based on the trade-offs, either to the other side or to an outside constituency, like a board of directors.

Using a Mediator to Carry Out Uncomfortable Tasks. Mediators are freer to use unorthodox tactics to solve bargaining impasses because they needn't worry about maintaining a judge's reserve or showing a litigator's resolve. Attorneys can take advantage of this by asking mediators to take on difficult tasks.

Mediators can take on a wide variety of unusual roles to support the settlement process. They might range from counseling a distraught litigant, to delivering a "hard sell" to a stubborn executive, to acting as the scapegoat for a difficult compromise. If a mediator does not see the need or seems reluctant to take on such a role, however, counsel should take the initiative to ask.

Impasse-Breaking Techniques

Each of the techniques described previously can help you achieve more than might be possible through direct negotiation. Suppose, however, that despite your best efforts the bargaining process hits an impasse. The reasons can be complex. Negotiations may become stalled because of a process issue such as lack of authority, psychological factors such as loss aversion, merits-based problems like misevaluation of the chances of winning in court, or other obstacles.

Impasses occur most frequently when negotiators focus narrowly on monetary solutions, but they are possible even during interest-based bargaining. Two parties may agree, for example, that it would be desirable to restore their business relationship but reach a stalemate trying to decide how to share the costs and rewards of the new arrangement. When an impasse does occur, you can often take advantage of a mediator's assistance to resolve it.

Problem

You are in the late afternoon of a mediation of a commercial contract dispute. You and your client, the plaintiff, have become very frustrated with the slow pace of the bargaining and the defendant's lack of realism. You began with a demand of $5 million, and your most recent proposal was $2.75 million; your client has a final "bottom-line" target of $1.9 million. The defense opened with an offer of $200,000 and has been inching up, their last move being only from $650,000 to $700,000. In a private conversation while the mediator is out of the room, your client tells you that he is willing to drop the demand to $2.5 million, but that unless the defendant's next offer "hits seven figures" (i.e., $1 million) he's inclined to pack up and leave. How might the mediator help you here? What should you and/or your client say to the neutral?

1. Assume that the mediator comes back 30 minutes later with a defense offer of $900,000. What should you do now?
2. Is there any reason that you as an advocate would feel reluctant to ask a mediator to take the kinds of initiatives described above?

Ask the Mediator for Advice.   Mediators are experienced negotiators. More important, they have a unique opportunity to observe and talk candidly with both sides and, at least until the end of the process, are not under pressure to express an opinion themselves. As the process goes on, they often acquire a great deal of information about each party's state of mind, approach to bargaining, and priorities for settlement. A mediator will not help one side obtain an advantage over an opponent, and settlement-oriented neutrals do have an interest in seeing each side compromise as much as possible. But when the negotiation process bogs down, advocates should consider asking the mediator for advice about how to restart it. Lawyers can also use a mediator to educate an unsophisticated or emotional client, or to present difficult truths about what is achievable and what it is not.

Make a Hypothetical Offer.   Counsel who will not make a unilateral concession will sometimes authorize a mediator to make an offer in a hypothetical, or "if . . . then," format. This is also referred to as "bracketing." The motivation can be to test the waters, probe the other side's flexibility, and/or ensure that a potential move will be reciprocated. For instance, a lawyer might say to the mediator, "Given the other side's refusal to go below 250, I cannot see us going beyond

100. However, you could tell them that you think you could get us to 125 if they would respond by breaking 200."

The hypothetical formula gains added impact if it is presented as a final resolution of the case rather than simply as a new move. By proposing an actual settlement, bargainers take advantage of the "certainty effect"—the fact that disputants will often make a special effort if they can achieve complete peace. An advocate wishing to take this approach might say, "You can tell them that if they could only get to 150, you have some optimism that you could convince my client to go there—but only if it would settle the case, once and for all." Such hypotheticals can sometimes short-circuit impasses caused by positional bargaining.

Ask the Mediator to Intervene. If other steps are not effective, lawyers can ask a mediator to intervene directly in the process. Good mediators will delay doing so for as long as possible, knowing that disputants may be alienated by the perception that the neutral is "taking over" the process, or because the mediator wants to avoid asserting control for philosophical reasons. Still, many commercial mediators will intervene actively in a case when the bargaining process appears to be seriously stalled.

If an advocate wants a mediator to adopt a restrained role in the face of impasse, she should make her preference known early in the process. Alternatively, if a lawyer wants the neutral to become more active, she should say that. We discuss below three of the most common interventions used by mediators to resolve impasses—confidential listener, evaluation of the merits, and a mediator's proposal. We also suggest ways in which lawyers can use each tactic to best advantage.

Evaluation. If shuttle diplomacy fails, lawyers often ask mediators to evaluate the legal merits of a case. As we have seen, evaluation is a controversial technique, at least among academics, but can be useful not only with opponents but also with clients. Whenever, for example, an advocate stops a mediator in the hall and suggests that he give the client his "thoughts" about the case, the neutral knows that he is being enlisted in the difficult task of client education and management.

In the large majority of situations, evaluations will be delivered in caucus and will focus on a specific issue, like the strength of a key factual matter, who is likely to prevail on liability, the strength of an affirmative defense, or what the damages are likely to be. It is possible, however, to have a mediator evaluate other issues as well. If, for example, a disputant is suspicious that its adversary will not carry out a proposed settlement, the mediator could assess the risk on the basis of his discussions with the opponent or his experience in other cases.

Before requesting a mediator's evaluation, you should ask yourself two basic questions. First, is the primary obstacle to settling this case really a disagreement about the outcome in court or some other issue that evaluation can address? As we have seen, the real barriers to settlement often lie in issues other than the legal merits. Second, if a mediator does evaluate the merits, are you confident that the result will be helpful—that is, will you get the opinion you want?

Once you have decided to seek an evaluation, the next issue is how to structure it so as to maximize the chances of a helpful result. The first issue is what data the mediator will consider. Bear in mind that a mediator's views about a case are usually based solely on the briefs and documents he sees, augmented by personal observations of the people present at the mediation. This has two implications:

- Like trial, mediation has a "primacy" effect: Evidence and people the mediator actually observes tend to be more vivid, and thus have more impact on her decision making, than data that the neutral merely hears about. Actual documents and face-to-face encounters with potential witnesses are thus likely to have much more impact on a mediator's opinion, and on a judge or jury, than evidence summarized in a brief.
- There is also a "melding" effect: When a mediator cannot personally observe a witness, he must place the person in a category ("nurse," "retired accountant," etc.), then make an assumption about how a fact finder would react to a typical member of that group.

If you want a mediator to give full weight to a witness or a piece of evidence, you should make a special effort to place it directly in front of the neutral. In a construction case, for example, you might ask the mediator to visit the site so that he has a vivid image of the project when he evaluates legal claims arising from it. You may also want to have a mediator meet a key witness. In mediation, unlike a court proceeding, you can arrange for a private meeting without incurring an obligation to expose the witness to your opponent, provided the opponent consents to this arrangement.

A second crucial question is what, exactly, you want evaluated. Don't simply say "the case." In the past, mediators routinely provided global opinions about the likely outcome if a dispute were adjudicated. Increasingly, however, mediators think of evaluation simply as a means to jump-start a stalled negotiation—more like filling a "pothole" in which the "settlement bus" has gotten stuck than building a road to a predetermined destination. Often a prediction limited to a single issue is enough to put the parties back on the path to settlement. The question then is: What specific aspect of the case do you want evaluated?

Finally, you should not expect most evaluations to take the form of an explicit opinion. Good mediators see evaluation as a spectrum of interventions rather than a single event. They rely on pointed questions, raised eyebrows, and other "shadow" techniques, much more than explicit statements, to nudge negotiations back on track. When an advocate hears a mediator make such comments, she should realize that the evaluation process is under way, but in a form less likely to provoke resentment than an explicit conclusion.

Mediator's Proposal. In this method the neutral suggests a set of terms, usually in writing, to all parties under the ground rule that each litigant must tell the mediator privately whether it will agree to the proposal if the other parties do (a variation is that each litigant will respond directly to the mediator within a set deadline). If all say yes, there is a settlement. But if any party rejects the proposal, it never learns whether its opponent was willing to agree. Parties thus know that they can achieve complete peace by saying yes, but that if the effort fails to receive a "yes" from all parties, the mediator will not reveal if there were any "yeses," their bargaining position will not be compromised.

In formulating a proposal, mediators typically try to "balance the pain" that each party will have to bear in order to accept it. In other words, the proposed number is the amount he thinks is most likely to be accepted by all sides, not necessarily his estimate of the likely outcome in court. One concern is that mediator's proposals have a take-it-or-leave-it quality: Once made, a proposal will tend to "set in cement," in the sense that both parties will resist agreeing to terms less favorable than the neutral has recommended. As a result, if a mediator proposes terms that are even minimally acceptable to a party in light of the costs of litigation, it will feel significant pressure to accept it.

A mediator's proposal has some major advantages. For one thing, it allows a party to test a potential settlement without indicating to the other side that it is willing to compromise. The technique often works—parties often stretch to accept a proposal at the end of the mediation, when the alternative is impasse, because it holds out the promise of settling the dispute, while at the same time protecting their bargaining position if it does not. You might first clarify with the mediator about what standard he will use in making a proposal: balancing the pain that each side must suffer to settle, predicting the outcome in court, or something else.

Problem

You represent the plaintiff in an employment dispute. It is five in the afternoon and you have been mediating for nearly eight hours. You began with a demand of $1.5 million, and in response the defendant offered $25,000. After laborious bargaining, you have dropped to $400,000. Your client's bottom line is $350,000 in a cash-only settlement, but would conceivably go to $200,000 if your client were offered a good job back at the company. Unfortunately, the defendant is only at $100,000, having moved there from a prior offer of $85,000. Your client is feeling very frustrated and has told the mediator this. The mediator has gone back to the defense and returned:

1. Should you share with the mediator your client's all cash bottom line and the reemployment alternative? What should you tell the mediator?
2. Assume that the defense suggests a "mediator's proposal." Should you agree? Why or why not?

If the Mediation Session Ends Without Agreement. If a case does not settle at the mediation session, a good mediator will keep working for settlement and will follow up by phone or e-mail until the parties tell her unequivocally to stop, and she sees no plausible way to change anyone's mind. If a neutral does not appear ready to take the initiative, a good advocate can prod her to do so. Neutrals' spirits, like those of other humans, occasionally flag, and some have a narrow conception of their role. A polite reminder that you are counting on a mediator to pull a settlement out of her hat will often encourage the neutral to make further efforts.

If Mediation Negotiations Fail. Sometimes settlement is genuinely unachievable. Even in such situations, a mediator can be of use by helping counsel to design an efficient process of adjudication. A mediator might, for example, facilitate negotiations over a discovery plan. Or the neutral could broker an agreement on an expedited form of arbitration.

How should an advocate leave an unsuccessful mediation process? Litigator David Stern offers the following advice:

> At some point, hours or days after you have started, the mediation process will end. If it ends with an agreement, that is fine. But if you can't reach agreement, accept that as well. Parties and lawyers often get desperate as the mediation nears conclusion, but the dispute remains unsettled. It is possible, but exceedingly unlikely, that the mediation is the last chance to settle the case. More likely, there will be multiple opportunities—at deposition, at court-ordered settlement conferences, before trial, during trial, even after trial and appeal—to settle. As such, do not despair or let your client despair if you walk away without a deal. . . . Search for partial agreements if feasible, or part company respectfully, so that the possibility of future negotiation remains open. In all likelihood, settlement will eventually occur and both you and your client will benefit if you keep that probability in mind. (Stern, 24 Litigation 31 (1998).)

I. Conclusion

Too often attorneys treat the mediation process simply as a safe place in which to conduct positional bargaining, trading arguments and offers until they reach impasse. At that point the mediator may take over the process by making settlement recommendations or offering evaluations. We hope you appreciate that whatever approach you take to bargaining, the mediation process and the mediator can assist you in negotiation. Lawyers who approach mediation actively as advocates for favorable settlement, looking at the mediator as a resource, can use the process to advantage and are able to obtain optimal outcomes for their clients.

CHAPTER
14

Negotiation Limits
and Settlement Policy

Throughout this book we have presented negotiation in a favorable light and suggested that it is worth doing. You know that part of negotiating is carefully considering the alternatives to reaching agreement and deciding when to pursue them rather than negotiating further. There is a more fundamental question: Should you always begin with negotiation, rather than going to court or battle? Even if you generally favor negotiation, are there exceptions? If so, when should you refuse to negotiate?

A. Should You Always Negotiate?

There will be times in your representation of clients and in your personal life when you will face the decision of whether you should bargain with a "devil": A law firm partner betrays you by taking your clients as his and then demands a new, better compensation arrangement; a client's spouse, who instigates a divorce, makes extortionist demands knowing your client values peace over contentious divorce proceedings involving the children; a CEO of a small high-tech company you represent learns that her joint-venture partner, a big foreign corporation, has been secretly using the company's technology under a clandestine license agreement and not reporting or sharing profits. In each instance, emotions run deep and you or your client feel wronged or threatened. You don't want to give in, be perceived as weak, or legitimize your nemeses' conduct by proposing to bargain with them. You want to be vindicated or get revenge.

Robert Mnookin, in the following excerpt from his book, warns that emotional traps can lock us into bad choices unless you and your client carefully examine your thinking process. In addition to the above scenarios, Professor Mnookin also examines decisions to negotiate or not made in infamous conflicts with evil regimes, where lives and liberty were at stake. He analyzes Winston Churchill's fateful choice in May 1940 — Britain's darkest hour — to reject negotiations with Adolf Hitler and to carry on World War II. Nelson Mandela's decision to initiate negotiations with the South Africa apartheid government that had imprisoned him for life is compared with the imprisoned Soviet dissident Natan Sharansky's decision not to negotiate with the KGB for his freedom. He also evaluates the willingness of Rudolf Kasztner, a Hungarian Jew, to negotiate with Adolf Eichmann in the hope of saving Jewish lives.

❖ **Robert Mnookin,** *BARGAINING WITH THE DEVIL:*
WHEN TO NEGOTIATE, WHEN TO FIGHT

1 (Simon & Schuster, 2010)

Should you bargain with the Devil?

In an age of terror, our national leaders face this sort of question every day. Should we negotiate with the Taliban? Iran? North Korea? What about terrorist groups holding hostages?

In private disputes, you may face devils of your own. . . . You are furious. Your gut tells you to fight it out in court. To negotiate with this person would give him something he *wants*. It would reward him for bad behavior. You want your rights vindicated, and the thought of negotiating with your adversary seems wrong. . . .

A disputant must decide: Should I bargain with the Devil, or resist? By "bargain" I mean attempt to make a deal—try to resolve the conflict through negotiation—rather than fighting it out. By "Devil," I mean an enemy who has intentionally harmed you in the past or appears willing to harm you in the future. Someone you don't trust. An adversary whose behavior you may even see as evil.

My question, and this book, have their roots in September 11. In the fall of 2001, less than a month after the attacks, Harvard Law School's Program on Negotiation sponsored a public debate at Harvard on whether President Bush should be prepared to negotiate with the Taliban. This debate led me to begin thinking about a more general question: In any particular conflict, how should you decide whether or not it makes sense to negotiate? . . .

My colleague Roger Fisher and I were invited to discuss how Bush should respond to this offer [to negotiate with the Taliban]. Roger Fisher is probably the best-known negotiation guru in the world. He is the leading proponent of what is called interest-based or "win-win" negotiation. His seminal book, *Getting to Yes*, has sold over three million copies. I am his successor as chair of Harvard's Program on Negotiation. . . .

Essentially, Roger supports the categorical notion—prevalent in the field of dispute resolution—that you should *always* be willing to negotiate.

The core argument behind this notion is straightforward and appealing. Before you resort to coercive measures—such as warfare or litigation—you should try to resolve the problem. To negotiate doesn't mean you must give up all that is important to you. It only requires that you be willing to sit down with your adversary and see whether you can make a deal that serves your interests better than your best alternative does. People and regimes are capable of change. You can't hope to make peace with enemies unless you are willing to negotiate.

You've also heard the categorical answer on the other side. The Faustian parable suggests you must *never* negotiate with the Devil. He's clever and unscrupulous. He will tempt you by promising something that you desperately want. But no matter how seductive the possible benefits, negotiating with evil is simply wrong; it would violate your integrity and pollute your soul.

I must confess a natural aversion to categorical claims of "always" or "never." There are usually examples that can puncture such arguments. In my debate with Roger, I explained that my two greatest political heroes of the twentieth century are Winston Churchill and Nelson Mandela. Each had to decide whether to negotiate with an oppressive and evil enemy. In May 1940, Churchill refused to negotiate with Adolf Hitler, even though Nazi forces had overrun Europe and were about to attach a weakened Britain. In 1985, on the other hand, Nelson Mandela chose to initiate negotiations with a white government that had erected and enforced a racist regime. . . .

"Should you bargain with the Devil?" If I were pressed to provide a one-sentence answer to this question, it would be: "Not always, but more often than you feel like it."

"Not always" because I reject categorical claims that you should always be willing to negotiate. "More often than you feel like it" for two different sorts of reasons. First, the negative traps and strong emotions may make you feel like fighting when clearheaded analysis would demonstrate that you should negotiate. The second relates to morality. You may feel that choosing to negotiate would violate a moral principle you hold dear, or be inconsistent with your sense of self. In the very hardest cases, you may feel deeply torn between the "principled" choice and the "pragmatic" one. When one is forced to choose between the two, I lean heavily in favor of pragmatism, but I want to acknowledge how painful that choice can be.

Why is it painful? Because you may feel that justice requires more than just a pragmatic resolution—it requires condemnation. In your eyes, the enemy has committed an act for which they should be *punished*, not rewarded. Your honor and integrity demand that you resist. This impulse can be just as powerful in business and family disputes as in international conflicts—perhaps even more so.

I have empathy for this desire to punish those who have wronged us. I share it. When we are caught between the demands of principle and pragmatism, what we really need to ask ourselves is, To what extent should we look backward and to what extent should we focus on the future? There's often an inescapable tension between achieving justice for *past* wrongs and the need for resolution. It is another aspect of the Faustian bargain. If you want to resolve the conflict and move forward, you may have to give the devil something you feel *he doesn't deserve*. This is a bitter pill to swallow. . . .

But drawing on my framework and these stories, I can suggest four general guidelines.

1. Systematically Compare the Expected Costs and Benefits.

When we *feel* like fighting, we may jump to the conclusion that negotiating a satisfactory resolution is simply out of the question. The best antidote to that kind of knee-jerk impulse and the negative traps is to go through Spock's five questions carefully. [Spock is a fictional, pragmatic advisor.]

- Who are the parties and what are their interests?
- What are each side's alternatives to negotiation?
- What are the costs of negotiation for each side?

- Are there any potential negotiated agreements that might better serve the interests of both sides than their best alternatives away from the table?
- If such a deal is reached, what is the likelihood that it will be implemented? (In other words, can you trust the other side to live up to it? If not, can it be enforced anyway?)

I am the first to acknowledge that asking these questions will not necessarily lead to a single right answer. This isn't a mechanical exercise, like balancing your checkbook. This is tedious, it's hard, and it requires you to make predictions about future behavior in a context of uncertainty. It isn't value-free. Judgments about values and priorities—what's "good" and "bad," what counts as a benefit and what counts as a cost—will of course be included in your analysis. For example, when evaluating costs, one might ask, "Will a deal here encourage more evil in the future?" Reasonable people assessing the same alternatives may reach different conclusions. . . .

I am not suggesting you ignore your emotions or your intuitions. Instead I'm advising you to probe them. They may be traps, or they may be valuable insights. Ask yourself, What may have triggered this reaction? Is there evidence to support it? Evidence that would point in the opposite direction?

A second criticism of cost-benefit analysis is that it values pragmatic concerns over moral categorical principles. This goes to one of the most profound issues in philosophy: Is it proper to judge the morality of an act only on an assessment of its consequences? Cost-benefit analysis is consequentialist at its core—one makes choices among alternative course of action solely by evaluating and comparing the consequences of those actions. Some philosophers would argue that this is an incomplete and inadequate form of moral reasoning, and many ordinary people would intuitively agree. There are well-known philosophical puzzles that expose its limitations. Consequentialism doesn't explicitly leave room for philosophical and religious traditions that emphasize categorical principles for human conduct. So why do I still insist, at least as a first step, that you assess costs and benefits? To prevent you from relying *solely* on intuition or unarticulated moral claims, and to be suspicious of those who do. Conduct the analysis first. If you are still conflicted, you must make the difficult decision whether your moral principle is so absolute that you cannot negotiate, even under these extenuating circumstances.

2. Get Advice from Others in Evaluating the Alternatives: Don't Do the Analysis Alone.

Like Churchill, you should be willing to expose your reasoning to rigorous questioning by people you respect. When they ask how you reached your decision about whether to negotiate, "I just know it in my gut, I can't explain it" is not an adequate response. . . .

In our own lives, particularly in conflicts that involve demonization, there are times when we all need a War Cabinet. Talk with at least one person who's less emotionally involved. It may be a lawyer. It may be a trusted friend. It may be a group of advisors whose perspectives are different from yours. It may be a mediator who can help all the disputants understand the trade-offs. The point is, let other people help you weed out the traps.

In assessing the costs and benefits of the alternatives, members of your team may disagree. They may be making different trade-offs and predictions, or different value judgments about what counts as a benefit and what counts as a cost. Exposing these differences is helpful, for it will better ensure a considered decision.

3. Have a Presumption in Favor of Negotiation, but Make It Rebuttable.

Suppose your advisors disagree. Suppose that after thinking it through carefully, your mind is in equipoise—you think the costs and benefits of negotiating are roughly equal to those of not negotiating. In case of such a "tie," I would apply a presumption in favor of negotion.

Now the obvious question is: Why tip the scales in *favor* of bargaining with the Devil? Why not be neutral, or even have a presumption *against* negotiation? After all, this is the Devil we're talking about!

The Reason for the presumption is to provide an additional safeguard against the negative traps: Tribalism, Demonization, Dehumanization, Moralism, Zero-Sum Thinking, the Impulse to Fight or Flee, and the Call to Battle. As we've seen, these traps can distort clear thinking. And their effect can be subtle. You may think you're engaging in pure Spockian analysis, but you may be fooling yourself. The traps may already have sprung. You may be starting with your conclusion—having already intuitively decided what to do—and selectively looking for evidence to justify it. My presumption can mitigate this risk. . . .

Note that my presumption is not a flat rule. It is simply a guideline—and it is rebuttable. If you think the situation through and decide you are better off refusing to negotiate, the presumption is overcome. We've seen several examples in this book.

4. When Deciding on Behalf of Others, Don't Allow Your Own Moral Intuitions to Override a Pragmatic Assessment.

When it comes to making decisions that involve a perceived "devil," there is a difference between individuals acting solely on their own behalf and those acting in a representative capacity—deciding on behalf of others. For an individual, a decision to override a pragmatic assessment based on moral intuitions may be virtuous, courageous, and even wise—as long as that individual alone bears the risks of carrying on the fight. This is not true for a business executive deciding on behalf of a corporation, a union representative acting on behalf of a union, or political leader acting on behalf of his nation. Perhaps not even for parent acting on behalf of a child.

A person acting in a representative capacity not only must carefully and rationally assess the expected consequences of alternative courses of action, but also should be guided by that assessment. If cost-benefit assessment favors negotiation, I think it is improper for the representatives to decide nonetheless to go to battle based on his personal moral intuitions.

Questions

1. Does Mnookin trivialize the gravity of Hitler's intentions by analyzing whether or not Winston Churchill should have bargained with Hitler? What purpose is served by focusing on a situation where the folly and consequences of negotiating with Hitler are now so obvious?
2. If you do negotiate with the devil, or your personal nemesis, should your bargaining style or approach be different? If so, how? (See Barbara Gray, "Negotiating with Your Nemisis," 19 Negot. J. 299 (2003).)
3. Some consider trials to represent a failure of attorneys to negotiate a settlement. Do you view trials as a failure? (See Gross and Kent 1991.)

B. Is Settlement of Legal Disputes Desirable?

In this last chapter we come full circle back to where we started. At the beginning of this text we stated, "A law student reading only casebooks might not know that the vast majority of disputes in which lawyers are involved are negotiated to a settlement without trial." Our legal education norms are premised on disputes being resolved by a judgment following a trial. Most people formulating an impression of lawyers based on popular literature and film have an image of lawyers in court, trying cases. This is consistent with our central notion that justice and rights depend on access to courts to resolve disputes according to law.

As you now know, negotiation, whether direct or assisted, is the way most legal disputes are concluded. Negotiation is a consensual process in which the parties may reach an agreement based on any standard or principle they choose, or none at all. Although most lawyer negotiation proceeds in the "shadow of the law," the result may not be law based. Negotiation is informal, lacks the checks and balances of a trial, and does not set legal precedent. Parties may settle because they get what they want by settling, or because one or both lack the resources necessary to litigate. Settlement may also be the result of imbalances of power, risk aversion, or other psychological factors. Rarely is an individually negotiated, civil settlement agreement reviewed by a court for fairness.

The increased interest in negotiation in the early 1980s, either evidenced or led by the popularity of *Getting to Yes*, published in 1981, and the greater use and encouragement of mediation in the 1980s, prompted academic questions about negotiated settlements. Court policies and rules pushing settlements through court ADR programs raised issues about access to justice and fairness. These issues have not been fully addressed, and many of the questions persist. The most influential and often-cited critique of policies encouraging settlement of lawsuits is offered below.

❖ **Owen M. Fiss,** *Against Settlement*

93 Yale L.J. 1073 (1984)

In a recent report to the Harvard Overseers, Derek Bok [then President of Harvard University; former dean of Harvard Law School] called for a new direction in legal education. He decried "the familiar tilt in the law curriculum toward preparing students for legal combat," and asked instead that law schools train their students "for the gentler arts of reconciliation and accommodation." He sought to turn our attention from the courts to "new voluntary mechanisms" for resolving disputes. In doing so, Bok echoed themes that have long been associated with the Chief Justice and that have become a rallying point for the organized bar and the source of a new movement in the law. This movement is the subject of a new professional journal, a newly formed section of the American Association of Law Schools, and several well-funded institutes. It has even received its own acronym—ADR (Alternative Dispute Resolution).

The movement promises to reduce the amount of litigation initiated, and accordingly the bulk of its proposals are devoted to negotiation and mediation prior to suit. But the interest in the so-called "gentler arts" has not been so confined. It extends to ongoing litigation as well, and the advocates of ADR have sought new ways to facilitate and perhaps even pressure parties into settling pending cases. . . .

The advocates of ADR are led to support such measures and to exalt the idea of settlement more generally because they view adjudication as a process to resolve disputes. They act as though courts arose to resolve quarrels between neighbors who had reached an impasse and turned to a stranger for help. Courts are seen as an institutionalization of the stranger and adjudication is viewed as the process by which the stranger exercises power. The very fact that the neighbors have turned to someone else to resolve their dispute signifies a breakdown in their social relations; the advocates of ADR acknowledge this, but nonetheless hope that the neighbors will be able to reach agreement before the stranger renders judgment. Settlement is that agreement. It is a truce more than a true reconciliation, but it seems preferable to judgment because it rests on the consent of both parties and avoids the cost of a lengthy trial.

In my view, however, this account of adjudication and the case for settlement rest on questionable premises. I do not believe that settlement as a generic practice is preferable to judgment or should be institutionalized on a wholesale and indiscriminate basis. It should be treated instead as a highly problematic technique for streamlining dockets. Settlement is for me the civil analogue of plea bargaining: Consent is often coerced; the bargain may be struck by someone without authority; the absence of a trial and judgment renders subsequent judicial involvement troublesome; and although dockets are trimmed, justice may not be done. Like plea bargaining, settlement is a capitulation to the conditions of mass society and should be neither encouraged nor praised.

The Imbalance of Power

By viewing the lawsuit as a quarrel between two neighbors, the dispute-resolution story that underlies ADR implicitly asks us to assume a rough equality between the contending parties. It treats settlement as the anticipation of the outcome of trial and assumes that the terms of settlement are simply a product of the parties' predictions of that outcome. In truth, however, settlement is also a function of the resources available to each party to finance the litigation, and those resources are frequently distributed unequally.

Many lawsuits do not involve a property dispute between two neighbors, or between [a major corporation] and the government . . . , but rather concern a struggle between a member of a racial minority and a municipal police department over alleged brutality, or a claim by a worker against a large corporation over work-related injuries. In these cases, the distribution of financial resources, or the ability of one party to pass along its costs, will invariably infect the bargaining process, and the settlement will be at odds with a conception of justice that seeks to make the wealth of the parties irrelevant.

The disparities in resources between the parties can influence the settlement in three ways. First, the poorer party may be less able to amass and analyze the information needed to predict the outcome of the litigation, and thus be disadvantaged in the bargaining process. Second, he may need the damages he seeks immediately and thus be induced to settle as a way of accelerating payment, even though he realizes he would get less now than he might if he awaited judgment. All plaintiffs want their damages immediately, but an indigent plaintiff may be exploited by a rich defendant because his need is so great that the defendant can force him to accept a sum that is less than the ordinary present value of the judgment. Third, the poorer party might be forced to settle because he does not have the resources to finance the litigation, to cover either his own projected expenses, such as his lawyer's time, or the expenses his opponent can impose through the manipulation of procedural mechanisms such as discovery. It might seem that settlement benefits the plaintiff by allowing him to avoid the costs of litigation, but this is not so. The defendant can anticipate the plaintiff's costs if the case were to be tried fully and decrease his offer by that amount. The indigent plaintiff is a victim of the costs of litigation even if he settles.

There are exceptions. Seemingly rich defendants may sometimes be subject to financial pressures that make them as anxious to settle as indigent plaintiffs. But I doubt that these circumstances occur with any great frequency. I also doubt that institutional arrangements such as contingent fees or the provision of legal services to the poor will in fact equalize resources between contending parties. . . .

Of course, imbalances of power can distort judgment as well: Resources influence the quality of presentation, which in turn has an important bearing on who wins and the terms of victory. We count, however, on the guiding presence of the judge, who can employ a number of measures to lessen the impact of distributional inequalities. He can, for example, supplement the parties' presentations by asking questions, calling his own witnesses, and inviting other persons and institutions to participate as amici. These measures are likely to make only a small contribution toward moderating the influence of distributional inequalities, but should not be ignored for that reason. Not even these small steps are possible with settlement. There is, moreover, a critical difference between a process like settlement, which is based on bargaining and accepts inequalities of wealth as an integral and legitimate component of the process, and a process like judgment, which knowingly struggles against those inequalities. Judgment aspires to an autonomy from distributional inequalities, and it gathers much of its appeal from this aspiration. . . .

The Lack of a Foundation for Continuing Judicial Involvement

The dispute-resolution story trivializes the remedial dimensions of lawsuits and mistakenly assumes judgment to be the end of the process. It supposes that the judge's duty is to declare which neighbor is right and which wrong, and that this declaration will end the judge's involvement. . . . Under these assumptions, settlement appears as an almost perfect substitute for judgment, for it too can declare the parties' rights. Often, however, judgment is not the end of a lawsuit but only the beginning. The involvement of the court may continue almost indefinitely. In these cases, settlement cannot provide an adequate basis for that necessary continuing involvement, and thus is no substitute for judgment.

The parties may sometimes be locked in combat with one another and view the lawsuit as only one phase in a long continuing struggle. The entry of judgment will then not end the struggle, but rather change its terms and the balance of power. One of the parties will invariably return to the court and again ask for its assistance, not so much because conditions have changed, but because the conditions that preceded the lawsuit have unfortunately not changed. This often occurs in domestic-relations cases, where the divorce decree represents only the opening salvo in an endless series of skirmishes over custody and support.

The structural reform cases that play such a prominent role on the federal docket provide another occasion for continuing judicial involvement. In these cases, courts seek to safeguard public values by restructuring large-scale bureaucratic organizations. . . .

The drive for settlement knows no bounds and can result in a consent decree even in the kinds of cases I have just mentioned, that is, even when a court finds itself embroiled in a continuing struggle between the parties or must reform a bureaucratic organization. The parties may be ignorant of the difficulties ahead or optimistic about the future, or they may simply believe that they can get more favorable terms through a bargained-for agreement. Soon, however, the inevitable happens: One party returns to court and asks the judge to modify the decree, either to make it more effective or less stringent. . . .

Justice Rather Than Peace

The dispute-resolution story makes settlement appear as a perfect substitute for judgment, as we just saw, by trivializing the remedial dimensions of a lawsuit, and also by reducing the social function of the lawsuit to one of resolving private disputes. In that story, settlement appears to achieve exactly the same purpose as judgment—peace between the parties—but at considerably less expense to society. The two quarreling neighbors turn to a court in order to resolve their dispute, and society makes courts available because it wants to aid in the achievement of their private ends or to secure the peace.

In my view, however, the purpose of adjudication should be understood in broader terms. Adjudication uses public resources, and employs not strangers chosen by the parties but officials chosen by a process in which the public participates. These officials, like members of the legislative and executive branches, possess a power that has been defined and conferred by public law, not by private agreement. Their job is not to maximize the ends of private parties, nor simply to secure the peace, but to explicate and give force to the values embodied in authoritative texts such as the Constitution and statutes; to interpret those values and to bring reality into accord with them. This duty is not discharged when the parties settle.

In our political system, courts are reactive institutions. They do not search out interpretive occasions, but instead wait for others to bring matters to their attention. They also rely for the most part on others to investigate and present the law and facts. A settlement will thereby deprive a court of the occasion, and perhaps even the ability, to render an interpretation. A court cannot proceed (or not proceed very far) in the face of a settlement. To be against settlement is not to urge that parties be "forced" to litigate, since that would interfere with their autonomy and distort the adjudicative process; the parties will be inclined to make the court believe that their bargain is justice. To be against settlement is only to suggest that when the parties settle, society gets less than what appears, and for a price it does not know it is paying. Parties might settle while leaving justice undone. The settlement of a school suit might secure the peace, but not racial equality. . . .

The Real Divide

To all this, one can readily imagine a simple response by way of confession and avoidance: We are not talking about *those* lawsuits. Advocates of ADR might insist that my account of adjudication, in contrast to the one implied by the dispute-resolution story, focuses on a rather narrow category of lawsuits. They could argue that while settlement may have only the most limited appeal with respect to those cases, I have not spoken to the "typical" case. My response is twofold.

First, even as a purely quantitative matter, I doubt that the number of cases I am referring to is trivial. My universe includes those cases in which there are significant distributional inequalities; those in which it is difficult to generate authoritative consent because organizations or social groups are parties or because the power to settle is vested in autonomous agents; those in which the court must continue to supervise the parties after judgment; and those in which justice needs to be done, or to put it more modestly, where there is a genuine social need for an authoritative interpretation of law. I imagine that the number of cases that satisfy one of these four criteria is considerable; in contrast to the kind of case portrayed in the dispute-resolution story, they probably dominate the docket of a modern court system.

Second, it demands a certain kind of myopia to be concerned only with the number of cases, as though all cases are equal simply because the clerk of the court assigns each a single docket number. All cases are not equal. The Los Angeles desegregation case, to take one example, is not equal to the allegedly more typical suit involving a property dispute or an automobile accident. The desegregation suit consumes more resources, affects more people, and provokes far greater challenges to the judicial power. The settlement movement must introduce a qualitative perspective; it must speak to these more "significant" cases, and demonstrate the propriety of settling them. Otherwise it will soon be seen as an irrelevance, dealing with trivia rather than responding to the very conditions that give the movement its greatest sway and saliency. . . .

[In] fact, most ADR advocates make no effort to distinguish between different types of cases or to suggest that "the gentler arts of reconciliation and accommodation" might be particularly appropriate for one type of case but not for another. They lump all cases together. This suggests that what divides me from the partisans of ADR is not that we are concerned with different universes of cases, that Derek Bok, for example, focuses on boundary quarrels while I see only desegregation suits. I suspect instead that what divides us is much deeper and stems from our understanding of the purpose of the civil lawsuit and its place in society. It is a difference in outlook.

Someone like Bok sees adjudication in essentially private terms: The purpose of lawsuits and the civil courts is to resolve disputes, and the amount of litigation we encounter is evidence of the needlessly combative and quarrelsome character of Americans. Or as Bok put it, using a more diplomatic idiom: "At bottom, ours is a society built on individualism, competition, and success." I, on the other hand, see adjudication in more public terms: Civil litigation is an institutional arrangement for using state power to bring a recalcitrant reality closer to our chosen ideals. We turn to the courts because we need to, not because of some quirk in our personalities. We train our students in the tougher arts so that they may help secure all that the law promises, not because we want them to become gladiators or because we take a special pleasure in combat. To conceive of the civil lawsuit in public terms as America does might be unique. I am willing to assume that no other country—including Japan, Bok's new paradigm—has a case like *Brown v. Board of Education* in which the judicial power is used to eradicate the caste structure. I am willing to assume that no other country conceives of law and uses law in quite the way we do. But this should be a source of pride rather than shame. What is unique is not the problem, that we live short of our ideals, but that we alone among the nations of the world seem willing to do something about it. Adjudication American-style is not a reflection of our combativeness but rather a tribute to our inventiveness and perhaps even more to our commitment.

Questions

4. In what types of cases, other than racial discrimination and other civil rights claims, does it seem most likely that the concerns about settlement set out by Professor Fiss may arise?
5. Are there categories of disputes, other than between neighbors, in which these concerns are unlikely to materialize?
6. Other than the cite to *Brown v. Board of Education*, is there any support for Fiss's arguments?
7. Does Fiss define what he means by justice or a just result? In the context of settlement, how would you define justice?
8. Based on what you have read and learned in this course and in your other studies, do you think Fiss's concerns, as stated in 1984, have been borne out or been proven not to be problematic?
9. Fiss refers to "domestic-relations cases, where the divorce decree represents only the opening salvo in an endless series of skirmishes over custody and support." Does his statement that these cases return again and again to court for adjudication argue for or against negotiation/mediation of parental conflict? Can courts resolve these issues better and with more finality than the divorcing parties? (See Folberg et al. 2004)

Professor Fiss's article provoked considerable debate and a number of responses in defense of settlement. (See, e.g., Lieberman and Henry, "Lessons from the Alternative Dispute Resolution Movement," 53 U. Chi. L. Rev. 424 (1986); Menkel-Meadow, "Whose Dispute Is It Anyway? A Philosophical Defense of Settlement (In Some Cases)," 83 Geo. L.J. 2663 (1995).) Fiss's position also has its defenders who see "why Fiss finds nothing to celebrate in settlements." (See David Luban, "Settlements and the Erosion of the Public Realm," 83 Geo. L.J. 2619 (1995).)

Marc Galanter and Mia Cahill view settlement negotiation versus litigation as a false choice. In a frequently cited article, they refer to negotiation and litigation as one process that they label "litigotiation." They believe that settlements are not intrinsically good or bad and argue that courts and policymakers should approach settlement with a more critical eye, distinguishing "good" settlements from less desirable ones. (See "'Most Cases Settle': Judicial Promotion and Regulation of Settlement," 46 Stan. L. Rev. 1339 (1994).)

Twenty-five years after the publication of *Against Settlement*, a symposium was held in New York City to revisit the theme of Fiss's article in light of new developments and thinking. An entire issue of the *Fordham Law Review* was dedicated to the topic. Professor Michael Moffitt's article, excerpted below, critiques Fiss's view and some of his assumptions, noting that settlement and litigation are co-dependant and exist in one another's shadow.

❖ **Michael Moffitt, THREE THINGS TO BE AGAINST ("SETTLEMENT" NOT INCLUDED)**

78 Fordham L. Rev. 1203 (2009)

Owen Fiss chose a great title for his article, *Against Settlement.*

Without even reading the associated article, most readers are provoked into immediate sympathy or antipathy. I blame (or credit) the word "settlement." "Settlement" has a Rorschach quality, conjuring different images and associations for different viewers. Perhaps we might even be able to derive some understanding of a person's experiences and values based on the meaning he or she makes of the idea of "settlement."

On one end of a definitional spectrum, we might imagine the reactions of some of the people one scholar has labeled "litigation romanticists." For many with this thorough devotion to the ideals of litigation, the word "settlement" has a distinctly negative set of implications. "Settlement" is viewed as synonymous with "compromise," or even "selling out." . . . On the other end of a definitional spectrum, we might imagine the reactions of some of the people who are so thoroughly devoted to the ideals of alternative dispute resolution (ADR) that one could fairly label them "ADR evangelists." For many with this view of the world, settlement" is an almost unquestioned positive. . . .

I. For Settlement and for Litigation

Both litigation and settlement are worthy of celebration, and both are worthy of critical examination. Litigation and settlement do not merely coexist. Instead, litigation and settlement have come to depend on each other in order to function properly.

Treating litigation and settlement as though they were entirely distinct processes is, of course, an oversimplification. In practice, the two are intertwined. The fundamental rules and structure of each clearly acknowledge the importance of the other. Modern civil procedure is structured to facilitate the interaction between litigation and settlement. . . . Similarly, settlement takes place within the confines of the parameters established by the prospect of litigation. . . . [D]isputants compare what they might receive through a settlement with what they expect might happen in litigation. Furthermore, each disputant's settlement behavior is bounded by the prospect of post settlement litigation. In this manner, private law concepts like fraud, unconscionability, and duress affect negotiators' behaviors precisely because litigation exists as a possible adjunct to settlement negotiations. The prospect of litigation shapes settlement behaviors and settlement outcomes.

A. What Litigation Gives to Settlement

. . . Within our common-law system, the court's role in articulating the law has an obvious contribution to settlement dynamics. Put most simply, courts clarify legal rules not only for the disputants in one case, but also for other disputants or prospective disputants who may be similarly situated. . . .

The other feature of litigation that has a profoundly supportive effect on settlement is the fact that courts have the ability to enforce their decisions. . . . This promise of enforcement affects and largely supports settlement in at least two ways. The first, and probably most conspicuous, way is that courts can be called upon to give effect to settlement agreements. In the event disputants decide voluntarily to resolve a matter, and subsequently one disputant reneges on the terms of that agreement, courts are available to give effect to the private settlement. . . .

Enforcement has an even bigger impact on the large-scale cases Fiss might label as "significant." Consider a mass tort, a widespread consumer fraud case, or an institutional reform action. Now consider how unlikely either the plaintiffs or the defendants would be to contemplate voluntary settlement in any of those cases if the court were unable to guarantee that the terms of the settlement would take effect. Without the court's power to enforce contracts, without consent decrees, and without the preclusion doctrines, neither side in any significant case would see an incentive to settle.

The second way the prospect of litigation shapes settlement stems from its effect on the way in which settlement *negotiations* take place. Courts are available, through litigation, to hear post-settlement complaints about any bargaining misbehavior that took place on the road to settlement. If courts were not available to hear such complaints, I strongly suspect that we would encounter more bargaining misbehavior, more expensive bargaining, or both. . . .

Settlement works today, in part, because courts articulate legal rules, establish at least some clarity around legal entitlements, enforce private settlements, and stand ready to audit settlement behavior after an agreement is reached.

B. What Settlement Gives to Litigation

Just as settlement benefits from certain features of modern litigation, litigation benefits from certain features of modern settlement. To illustrate this point, I highlight below two of the things settlement offers to litigation: docket clearance and selective case filtering.

The most conspicuous of settlement's contributions to modern litigation is its capacity to reduce the number of cases demanding judicial resources and attention. Fiss appears to imagine that docket lightening is, in fact, settlement's only contribution to our judicial system. Likening settlement to plea bargaining, he declares both of them to be undeserving of praise. . . . But Fiss's objection is not that all parties would prefer litigation and that many are somehow being prevented from litigating. His argument is that adjudication is superior when viewed from a societal level. The suggestion that the disputants in question might prefer to settle is, apparently, of little interest to Fiss. . . . But there are some kinds of disputes for which litigation is not particularly well suited, and if litigation need not contend with these disputes, it can do a better job of addressing the ones for which it is well designed.

Three different features of settlement make this selective filtering process possible. First, settlement offers the prospect of value creation. Litigation is necessarily backward looking, focused on binary entitlements, and framed in win/lose terms. Courts allocate or reallocate resources in a zero-sum manner. But in at least some disputes, the possible solution set is broader than the litigation model suggests. More than merely splitting the difference between probabilistically adjusted expected values, settlement outcomes can make parties better off, individually and in the aggregate.

Private disputants frequently discover these opportunities. Intellectual property disputes, for example, routinely culminate not in litigation, but rather in licenses or cross-licenses. Companies in disputes over the terms of supply contracts routinely renegotiate and extend contract terms. Divorcing couples routinely allocate child support and alimony in ways that minimize tax implications. Employees routinely return to work for employers with whom they have been in disputes. Private disputants often find ways to convert disputes into deal-making opportunities in which the total benefit for all parties is greater than could be achieved in litigation. . . .

Second, settlement offers the prospect of addressing nonfinancial, and even nonlegal, issues. Being in a dispute is an emotional experience. . . . Litigation operates within an adversarial structure, and whatever else we might say about it, litigation is not well-suited for relationship building. Settlement can help to filter some of these cases in which emotional concerns or relationship interests coexist with—or even overshadow—legally cognizable interests, and, as a result, litigation can reasonably concern itself more exclusively to the narrow purpose for which it is crafted.

Third, settlement offers the prospect of more fluid problem definition than litigation. Many of the most challenging and important cases of the modern world are ones in which litigation's rigid, and often narrow, joinder and standing rules risk excluding people who will be fundamentally affected by the case's outcome. I do not suggest that joinder and standing rules are necessarily too restrictive. Instead, I merely point out that these rules exist in their current form because they focus on the prospect of litigation. They are, to state the obvious, rules of litigation. Not everyone can, or should, be at the litigation table. But we should acknowledge the cost of excluding people from the table. . . .

II. Things to Be Against

. . . The three things I list below are inspired by the central concerns I understand to have motivated Fiss's declaration that he is against settlement. Each describes an aspect of a regrettable present reality. Each also presents a frame through which to observe not only settlement, but also litigation. None of them, however, presents a basis for opposing settlement.

A. Power Imbalances

Disputants do not always have identical "power," however one constructs the concept of power. And in some circumstances, one disputant has vastly more power than the other disputant. At some level, this is inevitable. No mechanism exists for assuring that I will only commit torts against people within my own tax bracket. We want large corporations to enter commercial or employment relationships with individuals. We need the government to engage with individuals, groups of people, and other governments. As long as these kinds of interactions take place, we must assume that disputes will arise. We must assume, therefore, that now and forevermore, power imbalances will mark at least some disputes. . . .

In its idealized form, litigation provides protections aimed against having outcomes determined by the resources of the disputants. A cash register appears nowhere in the traditional image of blind justice, holding the scales aloft, weighing the merits of each circumstance against the relevant law. . . . Litigation, in its perfect form, dispenses justice without reference to disputants' resources. These protections fail often enough, however, that we should not imagine that litigation has "solved" the power imbalance problem. . . . In short, no reasonable observer would suggest that a disputant's resources are actually irrelevant to the outcome that disputant can expect to get in court.

In its idealized form, private settlement occurs without the influence of power imbalances. A significant portion of the law of contracts aims to protect against the injustices that would arise from enforcing agreements struck under inappropriate conditions. . . . Settlement, in its perfect form, is the vehicle through which parties can arrive at mutually preferred outcomes, regardless of their resources. Settlement in practice, like litigation, too often also fails to protect against the possibility that power imbalances will skew the result in ways that deviate from settlement's underlying ideals. . . .

Power imbalances create problems in the real world. The on-the-ground practices of litigation and of settlement present pictures of sloppy, imperfect efforts at overcoming the worst aspects of power imbalances. We might reasonably compare the ideals of each process—ideals that largely assume away the persistence of power imbalances. We might also compare the sloppy reality of litigation with the sloppy reality of settlement.

The one thing we cannot responsibly do is compare the idealized vision of one practice against the sloppy reality of the other. Proponents of litigation must not present the question as, "*Which is better, (a) having a judge protect the powerless litigant through the promotion of public values as articulated by the law, or (b) sending that powerless litigant alone into the hallway to compromise away her rights?*" Proponents of settlement must not present the question as, "*Which is better, (a) employing fully inclusive deliberative discourse to reach an elegant, fair, and creative*

resolution, or (b) sending disputants into a formalistic process navigable only by the rich?"
The idealized visions of both processes are beautiful. The practices of both processes are flawed. If power imbalances skew one process, they skew the other, even if perhaps they do so in different ways. . . .

B. Agency Costs

. . . Agents [lawyers] sometimes negotiate settlements with which their clients are disappointed. In an ideal world, agents would understand and represent fully their principals' views of the relevant interests, parameters, tradeoffs, and opportunities. In practice, agents do not always understand their clients' priorities and underlying interests. In practice, agents sometimes have incentives at least partially at odds with some of their clients' interests. And, as a practical matter, agents cannot always bring every decision back to their clients for a new round of consultation. People do not merely hire agents for the agents' skill sets. Sometimes, a client hires an agent because the client does not have the bandwidth to do everything himself or herself. With the delegation of a task to an agent comes the risk that the agent will behave differently than the client would prefer. . . .

Unfortunately, agency costs are unavoidable in litigation as well. For example, every structure for attorneys' fees is fraught with the prospect of mismatching incentives. Few clients have the capacity to monitor attorneys' behavior in any meaningful way, both because of the cost associated with such monitoring and because of asymmetries in information and expertise. Even if a client were to monitor an attorney's actions, and even if a client were to detect behavior of which the client disapproves, the client's options are limited and unattractive. Firing an attorney is enormously costly, because the client would then need to pay another attorney to get up to speed. Filing a malpractice action against an attorney is possible, but malpractice actions are successful only in the most egregious cases. Courts are hesitant to second-guess an attorney's strategic decisions about how to craft the complaint, how to navigate joinder, whether and how to file a dispositive motion, how to navigate various trial decisions, or whether to file a particular sort of appeal. . . .

Just as attorneys risk settling in ways that clients subsequently dislike, attorneys risk litigating in ways that clients subsequently dislike. In the most egregious cases of each, the attorney's behavior may be the product of malpractice. An attorney may exceed the boundaries of the settlement authority a client has given, or an attorney may make litigation decisions so at odds with industry standards that the attorney risks professional sanction. Most of the time, however, an attorney's behavior—even behavior that may be self-interested—is de facto shielded from review or sanction. In short, the risk of agency problems plague both settlement and litigation.

C. Barriers to Court Access

Because courts are purely reactive, they function properly only if disputants have access to the courthouse. In an idealized vision of litigation, any aggrieved person would not only know his or her rights, but also would understand and have access to the state machinery designed to give effect to those rights. In practice, modern disputants encounter a number of different barriers to court access. The most conspicuous reason disputants might not perceive themselves to have access to the courthouse stems from financial concerns. In short, litigation is expensive, and many accurately perceive litigation's justice as beyond their price range. Litigation can also be costly in terms of time, reputation, and emotion. Even those who can afford its financial costs may perceive other litigation costs to be prohibitively high. In short, litigation's ideal assumes that disputants have unfettered and costless access to the courts—a level of access no disputants currently enjoy in practice. . . .

III. Questions to Keep Asking

. . . Owen Fiss's *Against Settlement* continues to be required reading in law school courses across the country not because it presents the final word on whether we ought to celebrate settlement. . . . *Against Settlement* has an enduring quality because it demands that we wrestle with important questions. In this final Part, I suggest that Fiss presented readers with at least three separate categories of questions: about the practice of settlement, about the ideals of settlement, and about the implications of all of this on legal education. . . . My suggestion is that, while we are exploring these aspects of settlement, we also ask the same questions of litigation. Litigation and settlement are linked in practice. The values they seek to promote are often linked. And they are linked, at least in part, in the challenges they present. Our understanding of each will be richer for understanding the other, and these three lenses provide useful perspectives on each. . . .

Conclusion

Against Settlement deserves robust praise and gratitude from those who care about settlement and about litigation. This essay helpfully suggested at least three perspectives from which to examine each of those processes. It focused attention on power imbalances and their potentially destructive effects. It raised questions about the pitfalls of agency dynamics, particularly in cases involving significant numbers of disputants. It demanded that we wrestle with what it means for people to have access to the court system and to the justice it promises. All three of these perspectives remain at least as vital today as they were in 1984.

Against Settlement deserves robust opposition to the extent it suggests a binary choice between settlement and litigation. If Fiss urges such a choice, the question he poses is not merely a "Which of your children do you love most?" kind of question. Instead, it is one for which neither answer could possibly be adequate: "Which is better, food or water?" Perhaps it is a misreading of Fiss to think that he demands a binary choice. Perhaps he was merely urging us to dampen our enthusiasm for settlement, in the face of what he perceived to be important shortcomings in its implementation at that time and in that context. Certainly, many commentators have re-read Fiss to be suggesting that we ought to be asking more nuanced questions.

Many, for example, have suggested that Fiss merely urges us to think hard before necessarily embracing settlement in all cases. Such a thesis would find many modern supporters, both among those whose primary focus is litigation and among those whose primary focus is settlement. But the title Fiss chose and the language he uses in his article make more nuanced readings like these difficult. If *Against Settlement* means what its language implies—that one could do away with settlement, retain litigation, and be better off for the change—then the article's thesis is flawed both as a theoretical and as a practical matter.

We should celebrate the beauty in each process's internal narrative of justice, of truth, of efficiency, of predictability, and even of morality. Proponents of settlement believe not merely in settlement's efficiency, but also in its ability to bring justice, to discover truth(s), and to provide stability. Proponents of litigation embrace the same values. We might usefully engage the empirical question of whether one process or the other does a better job of promoting each of these values. Both settlement and litigation fail on each of these measures with some reliability, and both processes continue to undergo reforms aimed at improving their performances as measured by these values. But to characterize either as unconcerned with any one of these values is simply false.

If we set out to compare settlement with litigation, we should do so responsibly. We should compare the idealized vision of settlement with the idealized vision of litigation. Or we should compare the sloppy reality of settlement in practice with the sloppy reality of litigation in practice. But more than anything, we should recognize that settlement and litigation are no longer separate—in practice or in theory. Because settlement and litigation are coevolved, symbiotic processes, to stand against one is to stand against the other. I choose, instead, to be for litigation and for settlement.

Questions

10. What does Fiss mean when he refers to the danger of preferring peace over fairness? Is one exclusive of the other? How might Moffitt respond to this question?
11. Other articles in the twenty-fifth anniversary symposium point to the increased cost of litigation, the increased complexity of cases, and the proportionate decrease in court funding as reasons to reexamine Fiss's objections to settlement. How do these changes impact the arguments for and against settlement?

Consider the following situation.

Problem—Family War

An immigrant laborer in the 1950s, Casey, worked at construction sites as a mason's assistant. Mixing cement and mortar on site by hand was slow and labor intensive. Casey improvised various mixing devices driven by small motors, which saved time and labor as well as resulting in a better quality mortar mix. With financial backing from a contractor for whom he worked, Casey eventually obtained several patents for his portable mixers and created a company that manufactured the mixers. The company succeeded and grew. In time, it was a closely held corporation that supported the families of Casey's four adult children, a younger brother, Sean, and sister, Patty, and three adult nephews. Following Casey's death in 2015, the company, which produced sales in excess of $50 million a year, was managed by Sean as CEO, and Patty as CFO. Sean had extensive management experience and had been close to his deceased brother. Patty was a CPA. Each of the nine family members had equal corporate shares and a seat on the corporate board.

The Casey children believed that Sean and Patty received salaries beyond industry norms and incurred excessive expenses. Dividend payments had not increased as sales grew, which the Casey children attributed to high executive salaries and lavish expenses. Outside acquisition offers for the company had been opposed by management, and the rejection decisions were confirmed by one-vote margins on the Board of Directors, with Casey's four children voting as a block in favor of selling the company. They were upset by the rejection of the acquisition offers and felt that Sean's and Patty's resistance was a result of their desire to retain their positions and company perks. Sean and Patty cited Casey's wish that the company remain independent and family-owned. Palpable tension existed between Casey's children on the one side, with Sean and Patty and their three children on the other side. The two sides did not talk together. Casey's oldest son, Marty, was particularly vocal about his objection to management and made statements at corporate meetings and by e-mail accusing Uncle Sean and Aunt Patty of mismanagement, theft, and company exploitation. Marty's brother and sisters chimed in with other accusations and indicated that, under the circumstances, Casey would have sold the company to the highest bidder.

Casey's four children brought a minority shareholders' action to force a sale of the company and for repayment of excess compensation. Sean and Patty cross-claimed for damages based on libel and slander. Each side invoked the wishes and spirit of Casey in support of their positions. Neither side seems interested in reconciling or compromising.

As lawyer for the Casey children, would you recommend negotiation? Why or why not? Might mediation be appropriate?

C. Judicial Encouragement of Settlement

Much of the early impetus for encouraging settlement of cases filed in court came from judges concerned about overloaded dockets. It is not surprising, therefore, that courts throughout the United States established early settlement and ADR programs. Legislators have supported court-sponsored settlement programs; Congress, for example, has required every federal district court in the nation to implement a dispute resolution program (ADR Act of 1998, 28 U.S.C. §651(b)). Settlement programs are most common at the trial level but exist, more and more, in appellate courts as well. Although some court programs offer litigants a choice of settlement processes, mediation has become by far the most popular form of court-connected dispute resolution.

Although the primary motivation is usually to reduce backlogs, courts encourage settlement for other reasons as well. Some cases involve complex technical issues that do not seem well-suited to the limitations of trial presentations. Other cases center on continuing relationships and evoke deep emotions, such as disputes between parents over the custody and visitation rights to their children. Adjudication is often ineffective to resolve such disputes, because it focuses on the past rather than the future and addresses only the presenting problem rather than underlying conflicts. Courts also sometimes promote settlement to divert cases that judges do not want to hear and that court personnel may feel they cannot adequately process. Asbestos-related claims and homeowners' association construction defect cases, for example, can consume vast court resources and can seem unending to court staff.

Judicial efforts to promote settlement and reduce trials raise important policy issues, which involve designing programs not simply to yield the greatest benefit to the system, but also to ensure court access and fairness for participants. Fairness and quality concerns arise most pointedly in the context of court-sponsored settlement programs, especially when courts require litigants to engage in the process.

Many courts, impressed with the value of pretrial settlement programs, have gone beyond encouragement and made participation in the process mandatory. Mandatory settlement conferences, as well as mandated mediation, raise issues of the court's authority to compel participation and the constitutionality of creating procedural barriers to trial.

The First Circuit Court of Appeals, in In re Atlantic Pipe Corp., 304 F.3d 135 (1st Cir. 2002), confronted the issue of whether a federal district court may use its inherent powers to order a party in a civil case to participate in and pay for mediation. The case involved a complex construction dispute with many parties. The court of appeals confirmed the inherent power of a trial judge to order mediation over a party's objection, to require the objector to pay part of the cost of the process, and to name as a mediator a private neutral nominated by one of the parties. The court expressed concern, however, over the lack of any restriction over the extent of the process, particularly in light of the mediator's quoted rate of $9,000 per day, and remanded the case to the trial court for further orders.

Some state appellate courts have upheld judicial settlement conference and mediation mandates against arguments that they violate constitutional rights (See Golann 1989.) Other courts have held that a party cannot be compelled to participate in private mediation or pay the fee of the mediator. (See Jeld-Wen Inc. v. Superior Court, 146 Cal. App. 4th 536, 543, 53 Cal. Rptr. 3d 115 (2007).)

Even though most courts have held that mandating settlement negotiations is constitutional, that does not mean that a particular court has the authority to order participation in any case. Courts ordinarily derive their authority from specific sources, such as constitutional provisions and statutes. Many federal courts, for example, base orders compelling litigants to mediate on court rules adopted pursuant to the Civil Justice Reform Act of 1990, 28 U.S.C. §§471-482, or the ADR Act of 1998, 28 U.S.C. §§651-658. Can a federal court that has not adopted a rule pursuant to these statutes nevertheless order parties to participate in settlement conferences as a matter of "inherent judicial power"? On the one hand, the Seventh Circuit Court of Appeals has ruled that a federal court can use its inherent power to force parties to attend a pretrial settlement conference. (See Heileman Brewing Co. v. Joseph Oat Corp., 871 F.2d 648, 650 (7th Cir. 1989, en banc).) On the other hand, both the Sixth and Seventh Circuits have ruled that federal courts cannot rely on inherent powers to force litigants to engage in "summary jury trials," an ADR process that involves an abbreviated trial to a jury with a nonbinding verdict, usually followed by intensive negotiation. (See In re NLO, Inc., 5 F.3d 154 (6th Cir. 1993); Strandell v. Jackson County, 838 F.2d 884 (7th Cir. 1987).)

Two basic questions regarding mandated settlement processes are who should participate and who should pay for the service. It was a long-standing tradition in many courts that lawyers met with the judge prior to trial to discuss settlement, without clients present. Lawyer "control" of their clients and of the settlement process was a hallmark of the attorney-client relationship in litigation. This tradition has given way to a more client-centered approach, which recognizes the importance of client involvement in the settlement process. However, settlement conferences conducted without clients continue in some jurisdictions, and clients sometimes prefer, for strategic or economic reasons, not to be present.

The *Heileman Brewing* case, cited above, held that federal courts do have inherent power to order the attendance at a settlement conference of a party or corporate representative having full authority to settle. The appellate court found that, in the circumstances of that case, the trial court did not abuse its authority in ordering a represented corporation to send a corporate officer to a pretrial settlement conference and properly imposed sanctions for its failure to do so. Judge Posner, dissenting, expressed concern "that in their zeal to settle cases judges may ignore the value of other people's time." Judge Easterbrook, also dissenting, took issue with the necessity to have a client present when the lawyer could adequately represent the client in settlement negotiations. He argued that lawyers adequately negotiate in collective bargaining and merger talks and are no less suited to negotiate in a settlement conference. (See Riskin 1991.)

Note — Compelled Participation and Good-Faith Bargaining

If a court has the power to order disputants to participate in settlement conferences or mediate, should it require them to satisfy a minimum standard of negotiation conduct? Professor John Lande has examined "good-faith bargaining" requirements for mediation, as imposed on disputants in connection with court ADR programs (Lande 2002). The problem is that virtually none of these rules define what constitutes "good faith" or its absence. According to Professor Lande, the reported cases on good-faith obligations break down as follows:

- Failure to attend mediation at all.
- Failure to send a representative with adequate settlement authority.
- Failure to submit required memoranda or documents.
- Failure to make a suitable offer or otherwise participate in bargaining.
- Failure to sign an agreement.

In practice, courts have found it easiest to sanction objective conduct, such as a party's failure to appear or file a statement. Judges find it much more difficult to determine whether a party has made a "suitable offer" or sent a representative with "adequate settlement authority." There are only a few cases in which sanctions based on subjective conclusions about misconduct in settlement programs have been upheld on appeal.

Attempts to regulate parties' conduct during compelled settlement discussions raise difficult issues. To begin with, a court would have to define what it meant by "good faith." In many cases the court would also have to take evidence about what had been said or done during the mediation process itself, raising serious issues of confidentiality. Assuming that enforcement were feasible, many argue that good-faith bargaining requirements are in conflict with the concept of self-determination, a central value of mediation. Standard I of the Model Standards of Conduct for Mediators (2005) states, "Parties may exercise self-determination at any stage of a mediation, including mediator selection, process design, participation in or withdrawal from the process, and outcomes." If parties have the unfettered right to make their own decisions about mediating, however, how can any specific level of participation in the process be required? At the same time, if parties are ordered to mediation by a court and one party expends substantial resources to comply, should its adversary be permitted to nullify the process by failing to prepare or refusing to bargain?

In response to the difficulty of defining and enforcing "good faith" requirements, some have argued that such rules should be discarded. Professor Lande, for example, proposes that courts limit themselves to enforcing objective standards of conduct, such as a requirement that parties appear at mediation for a minimum period of time (Lande 2002).

The most bizarre story about "good-faith" participation begins in Panama City Beach, Florida, during spring break in 2003, where Joseph Francis filmed an episode in his television series, *Girls Gone Wild*. As alleged in the complaint filed by unidentified minor girls and their parents, Francis enticed, with the help of alcohol, underage girls to engage in various sexual acts, in front of the cameras. A civil action, Doe v. Francis, No. 5:03cv260 (FL ND), was filed about the same time as parallel criminal charges were brought against Francis. A federal judge ordered Francis to participate in mediation of the civil claims, for which he arrived, via his private plane, four hours late.

As recounted in an article by Michael D. Young ("Mediation Gone Wild," 25 Alternatives 103 (June 2007)),

> Francis was wearing sweat shorts, a backwards baseball cap, and was barefoot. He was playing on his electronic device. As [plaintiffs' counsel] began his presentation, Francis put his bare, dirty feet up on the table, facing plaintiffs' counsel. [Plaintiffs' counsel] said four words, "Plaintiffs were minor girls," when Francis barked, "Are the girls minors now?" Continuing, [Plaintiffs' counsel] said, "Plaintiffs are minor girls who were severely harmed by Defendant." Francis then erupted. "Don't expect to get a f*** dime — not one f*** dime!" This was Francis' mantra which he repeated, about fifteen times, during his tantrum that ensued. "I hold the purse strings. I will not settle this case, at all. I am only here because the court is making me be here!" Francis shouted. Seeing there was to be no mediation in "good faith," plaintiffs' attorneys got up to leave the room. Less than three minutes had passed, almost completely taken up by Francis' outburst. As plaintiffs'

attorneys were leaving, Francis' threats escalated. "We will bury you and your clients!" Francis threatened. Francis then got up and faced off with [Plaintiffs' counsel]. Right in [Plaintiffs' counsel's] face, Francis barked, "I'm going to ruin you, your clients, and all of your ambulance chasing partners!" . . . Francis then made the only offer he was to make that day, "suck my d***," Francis shouted repeatedly, as plaintiffs' counsel left the mediation room.

The Judge's contempt order stated, "Coercive incarceration is an appropriate sanction for this situation. Mr. Francis can cure his contempt and have this sanction of incarceration removed upon his proper participation in mediation." The court then ordered the parties to participate in another mediation session, instructing them to arrive the night before. It insisted that Francis "will be dressed and groomed appropriately, i.e., business suit and tie, business shoes and socks." The court further ruled that "This mediation is ordered as an activity of this Court." Finally, the court ruled that Francis would be released from incarceration "when the mediator certifies in person to the court that Mr. Francis has fully complied with this order and has participated in the mediation in good faith."

Questions

12. Assuming mediation communications are considered to be confidential in Florida, how is it that Francis's comments came before the judge and are reported on the court's record and then appear in articles about the mediation?

13. In a first caucus meeting with the mediator, the plaintiff's lawyer says that while its previously communicated $750K demand is "negotiable," it will not make any concessions until the defense puts a "significant offer" on the table. The defense lawyer informs the neutral that she will not make any offer at this point because the plaintiff is "on another planet." She tells the mediator that it's his job first to bring the plaintiff into a zone of reality, and that the $750K demand is not it. The court's ADR rules require the parties to "engage in good-faith bargaining." Is either the plaintiff or the defendant violating its obligation?

14. Assume that in the above mandatory mediation, counsel for the defendant offered $10,000 in response to the plaintiff lowering its demand from $750,000 to $450,000. If applicable rules require that the parties "bargain in good faith," has the defense complied?

15. Consider the situation of defense counsel in the following California case: A court-appointed master ordered the parties to engage in a five-day mediation of a complex construction defect claim. Knowing that such claims necessarily involve expert testimony, the neutral instructed each side to bring its experts to the process. The neutral's charges and the plaintiff's cost for assembling its experts for mediation totaled nearly $25,000. Defense counsel, however, arrived 30 minutes late for the first session and appeared alone. Asked about his failure to bring his client or his experts, he said, "I'm here, you can talk to me." (See Foxgate Homeowner's Association, Inc. v. Bramlea California, Inc., et al., 25 P.3d 1117 (Cal. 2001).) Did the defense counsel's actions in this mediation constitute bad faith?

16. The mediator in *Foxgate* reported to the court that defense counsel took this approach because he believed that his pending motion for partial summary judgment would substantially reduce the value of the plaintiff's claims. Does this justify the lawyer's strategy? The neutral also reported that, in his opinion, the defendant had sufficient time to present the motion before the mediation but had not done so. Does this change your opinion?

17. Can a court require a representative of an insurer, who is not a party, to attend a settlement conference and participate in good faith? (See In re Novak, 932 F.2d 1397 (11th Cir. 1991).)

D. Court Approval of Negotiated Settlements

Earlier in this chapter, it was stated that "[r]arely is an individually negotiated, civil settlement agreement reviewed by a court for fairness." However, when class representatives purport to negotiate a settlement for absent class members, Federal Rule of Civil Procedure 23, and similar state provisions, requires court review and approval for fairness to the class. Although lawyers representing corporate defendants and class plaintiffs may start the case as true opponents, perhaps viewed by one another as "devils" for purposes of negotiation, if a settlement is reached they become united in interest because they each see the bargained-for result as the best outcome to satisfy their needs. The former opponents become united in seeking required court approval for the deal they have negotiated. The role of the court under Rule 23 and its progeny is to determine if the negotiated settlement is fair to absent class members and not just a collusive convenience favorable to those at the table.

This issue was before a federal trial court in a national wage and hour class action against Oracle Corporation seeking a maximum recovery of $52.7 million. The class had not yet been certified or the pleadings finalized when the lawyers for the three named class representatives and Oracle reached a universal settlement agreement. The settlement would have extinguished the potential claims of 1,500 putative class members residing in 35 states by creating an exclusive claims procedure with total payout limited to $9 million.

The court, in denying approval of the settlement, stated,

> By expressly obligating itself only on a "claims-made" approach, Oracle would pay only those who submit claims up to a total of nine million dollars less all fees and expenses. Counsel wants $2.25 million in attorney's fees and $75,000 in expenses. In addition to their own shares of the settlement, $45,000 total would be paid to the three named plaintiffs as "incentive payments." Costs of administration would also be deducted. Because it will be a "claims-made" settlement, there will be no residue. All unclaimed amounts will revert to Oracle. . . . Class actions are ideally suited to the efficient resolution of numerous parallel claims in a single

proceeding and to encourage the pooling of small claims against a common target. They are an engine of justice in our federal courts. But they can also lend themselves to abuse. One form of abuse is collusive settlement. Once the named parties reach a settlement in a purported class action, they are always solidly in favor of their own proposal. . . .

It is also no answer to say that a private mediator helped frame the proposal. Such a mediator is paid to help the immediate parties reach a deal. Mediators do not adjudicate the merits. They are masters in the art of what is negotiable. It matters little to the mediator whether a deal is collusive as long as a deal is reached. Such a mediator has no fiduciary duty to anyone, much less those not at the table. Plaintiffs' counsel has the fiduciary duty. It cannot be delegated to a private mediator. (Judge William Alsup, Madhav Kakani, et al. v. Oracle, No. C 06-06493 WHA, USDCNC (June 19, 2007).)

Note — Class Settlement Fairness and Objectors

In the *Oracle* case, the judge rejected the proposed settlement prior to notice being sent to class members that a settlement was pending. Had Judge Alsup given preliminary approval, the notice then given to the class would have allowed class members to object if any thought the proposed settlement terms were not fair to the class, including the maximum amount available for claims, the amount deducted for attorneys' fees, and the adequacy of notice. Because the defendant and plaintiff class counsel are now on the same side in supporting the settlement they negotiated, objectors can provide the only form of adversarial testing that a proposed settlement will have. The prospect of possible objections plays an important role as a safeguard in protecting the interests of absent class members, tending to sharpen the scrutiny of the court in promoting fairness and preventing collusive negotiations. If an objector raises points that refine the settlement or cause it to be disapproved, the objector can be awarded attorneys' fees and costs.

Plaintiff class lawyers and some corporate defense attorneys have labeled lawyers who file objections "professional objectors — attorneys who make a living by serially objecting to any class action settlement, regardless of merit." Class lawyers accuse repeat objectors of being "hold-up artists" and "extortionists." If objectors are unsuccessful in the approving trial court they have a right to appeal, which can delay the settlement and payment of class counsel fees for years. The potential delay provides objectors with leverage to negotiate with both class counsel and the original defendant for payment (and perhaps refinement of the class settlement) in exchange for dismissal of the objections. This leads class counsel to state, "the delay inherent in appellate review allows professional objectors to hold class counsel's fees hostage by demanding a 'fee' for the release of those fees. . . . Many class counsel have resigned themselves to the reality of professional objectors, simply seeing them as a 'tax' imposed on class action counsel." (Kabateck and Torrijos, "The Rise of Professional Objectors in Class Action Settlements," 5 Daily Journal (July 8, 2010). See also Kullar v. Foot Locker Retail, Inc. and Crystal Echeverria, et al., Objectors, 168 Cal. App. 4th 116 (2008).)

Questions

18. Do you agree with Judge Alsup that a mediator does not care if a settlement deal is collusive and has no duty regarding fairness for class members not at the table?
19. Given the role of objectors in keeping class action settlement negotiations honest, can you suggest any ways that abuse of the objector mechanisim can be prevented?

E. A New Role for Lawyers — Settlement Counsel and Collaborative Law

Experienced trial lawyers totally invest themselves in preparation for a courtroom contest. They are similar to athletes getting ready for a big game or soldiers going into battle. To do well in a competitive situation, they have to focus on winning; they get "psyched up," and they often feel they cannot "back down." Their clients, or they themselves in contingent fee cases, incur "sunk" costs for this preparation. They must get more to recoup their expenses and make the time spent worthwhile. Attorney and client create for themselves an image of victory over an opponent, who, as trial approaches, is seen as the enemy to be defeated. The "demonization" of the enemy becomes a self-fulfilling prophecy based on selected observations of the opponent's behavior, who is also preparing for battle. The trial attorney develops a personal interest in proceeding and justifying the expense of preparation, as well as making good on the advice given and predictions of success at trial. This scenario is mirrored on the other side. The motivation and the interests of the trial attorneys may be in conflict with pursuit of settlement.

Is there a way to insulate the role of the trial attorney, so she can do her job in preparing to win at trial while a settlement is negotiated? In England, solicitors traditionally handle settlement negotiations and "quarterback" the case, calling in a barrister as needed for pleadings, arguments, and trial. This allows the solicitor and the barrister to focus on their separately defined roles of negotiation and trial, much like a secretary of state and a secretary of war. In the United States the same division of roles can be achieved by separately retained settlement counsel and trial counsel. (See Coyne, "The Case for Settlement Counsel," 14 Ohio St. J. Disp. Resol. 367 (1999).) The next and final reading proposes greater use of settlement counsel in business disputes by combining the concept with "collaborative law," which you read about in Chapter 10.

❖ Kathy A. Bryan, *Why Should Businesses Hire Settlement Counsel?*

195 J. Disp. Resol. 195 *(2008)*

I. Introduction

As a former in-house litigation manager, I hired separate settlement counsel in only a few cases and with varying results. With responsibilities for hiring and managing a large portfolio of outside firms, I was loath to increase case-staffing ranks for many reasons—and cost was only one factor. Internal resources must oversee litigation, and having another set of outside lawyer relationships on the same case generally seemed duplicative. Worse, it demanded more of my scarce time to manage both the relationship and the primary litigation firm. In addition, I viewed in-house counsel's role as akin to settlement counsel—coordinating with the litigation team but reaching agreements separately in many cases. In-house attorneys generally tend to share this bias against settlement counsel.

Today, with a greater understanding of the sea change that Collaborative Law has had in family law, I want to reconsider that conclusion and explore whether using separate settlement counsel, and borrowing other techniques from the Collaborative Law movement, enhances and increases the potential to resolve business disputes.

II. Collaborative Law and Collaborative Law Techniques

With humble beginnings in Minnesota family courts in the early 1990s, Collaborative Law (CL) has grown swiftly to include groups in thirty-three states in the United States and in most Canadian provinces, as well as professional associations, law school courses, and even ethical codes. An essential CL element has come to be the disqualification provision, or "Participation Agreement," where the lawyers for both sides agree in writing to work toward a negotiated resolution and, if the case proceeds to court, clients must engage other counsel. Another CL hallmark is the "four-way meeting," in which the parties and counsel participate. Parties also agree to good-faith negotiation, cooperative information exchange, and to consider jointly hiring neutral experts.

This non-adversarial approach promotes resolution that is fundamentally different from the traditional negotiation occurring in the context of a lawsuit. . . . While U.S. businesses and their in-house counsel have come to embrace mediation as a settlement mechanism, relatively few have adopted CL techniques into their day-to-day practices. Instead, most prefer using positional bargaining and court-oriented solutions, most likely resulting in a settlement after a long discovery process, heavy motion practice, and, rarely, trial. CL techniques should be added to the business dispute resolution toolbox. This article examines the types of cases where CL techniques may be appropriate. It also discusses the potential benefits of using settlement counsel in particular.

III. Advantages

A. Preserving Relationships

An often-cited factor for the CL movement's success in family law is the need to preserve relationships in the interests of children, which overrides the parents' openly adversarial mode. Clearly, relationships can be equally critical in business conflict. Companies that create a culture focused on building and enhancing relationships tend to flourish. True, there are competitive situations where all-out legalistic war seems more appropriate, but much of U.S. companies' litigation portfolios concern employees, customers, vendors, suppliers, contractual partners, etc., where continuing relationships are paramount—especially when conflict erupts. In fact, when surveyed, corporate counsel describe the need to preserve relationships as one of the top reasons for using mediation.

Collaborative practices create an environment where relationships can be repaired and healed—as opposed to litigation, arbitration and, sometimes even mediation, with winners and losers often defaulting to a "zero-sum" approach. Claims of personal harm in medical error, employment, and torts all hold promise for benefits from using CL or settlement counsel. Particularly when the dispute involves systemic harm, solutions to a common problem rather than finding fault should be explored at the outset.

B. Reducing Cost and Time to Resolution

Collaborative Law processes can significantly reduce the time to resolution. In family law, the CL process makes it harder for the parties to end the negotiations. It also creates an incentive to keep the parties working to avoid impasse. In particular, the disqualification provision gives the lawyers substantial financial incentive to negotiate a resolution. Many describe this as an "essential feature" of CL. CL is thus an extremely powerful tool to promote early settlement.

For commercial cases where protracted litigation seriously threatens business interests, using a pure form of CL at the outset has real potential. Putting aside for the moment the challenge of convincing the opposing party to use CL, (which is discussed more below) imagine the power of an early four-way meeting with the parties and their lawyers, all taking time out from the oppositional conflict dialogue to engage in structured discussions focused on interests and solutions.

Several other CL techniques hold additional promise for cost savings. Jointly hired neutral experts and truncated information exchange could drastically reduce time and cost. Corporate counsel recognize that the most significant cost savings occurs when the matter is resolved at the earliest possible stage, preferably before expending the costs of discovery and motion practice. When time is critical, and if relationship building overcomes the tendency to maximize adversarial advantage, CL offers an unmatched tool to explore solutions and reach early resolution.

C. Overcoming Adversarial Bias

Adversarial bias—essentially the human tendency to need "to be right" in a dispute—affects everything in litigation. As lawyers, our adversarial training becomes a part of our intellectual DNA. We are so accustomed to positional thinking that we define the dispute in legal terms and forget problem solving in the heat of the conflict. By the time a suit is filed, the parties' relationship has become so strained, and the trust so broken, that both sides are in full riot gear. Worse yet, we don't even recognize it. As Malcolm Gladwell described in his thoughtful book, *Blink*, bias tends to be unconscious.

One reason that CL has grown so quickly in family law probably is that its techniques overcome unconscious adversarial bias and actually create new resolution possibilities. CL acts as a sort of an imposed cooling-off period, allowing parties, and especially their lawyers, to think more clearly and creatively. What does this mean for business disputes? By the time lawyers become involved in the dispute, conflict is usually entrenched and the role of the lawyer is to define the legal position and begin the legal process. The typical question put to the lawyer is, "How strong is our legal claim?" In addition to the answer to that question, the most innovative counsel also concentrates on an interest-based analysis.

In-house counsel generally keep business issues front and center better than outside counsel, who quite naturally view their role as a zealous advocate. Nevertheless, it is difficult for the same lawyer to maintain both mindsets at the same time. Having a set of lawyers solely devoted to overcoming the culture of adversarial negotiation presents the best opportunity to find interest-based solutions.

IV. Overcoming Barriers

A. Opponents' Acceptance

When mediation was in its infancy, it was common to hear the concern that hiring a mediator would be interpreted as weakness by the opposing counsel. Thanks to the broader use and acceptance of mediation, court direction, and in no small measure the International Institute of Conflict Prevention and Resolution's "CPR Pledge©," that refrain is heard less often. CL seems to be in the same nascent stage. As is typical in adversarial situations, the concern is with losing leverage. Several techniques can be employed to lessen this impression. First and foremost, in-house counsel's demand for CL or settlement counsel has the most power to diffuse an unintended signal of weakness. Providing the neutral statement that it is the business policy, or otherwise the standard practice, removes the impression that CL is needed because of factual or legal weakness in the matter at hand. Additionally, the in-house lawyer is uniquely positioned to emphasize the importance of cooperation and good-faith negotiation, which could ring hollow when coming from outside counsel engaged to "defend" the matter. Finally, the in-house counsel can commit to have the right business executives present and can demand the opponent do the same.

Another reasonable approach is to expressly designate in-house lawyers as settlement counsel. While the implicit strength of the disqualification agreement would not apply, in-house lawyers could use the other interest-based negotiating techniques to reduce the effect of ego, open up communication, and broaden the potential resolution options. CL practitioners have found that early focus on interests reduces parties' tendency to become entrenched in their positions. Second, pointing to an established protocol, practice guidance, or pledge helps define the process, provides legitimacy, and, again, takes the focus away from the particular case to a broader company-wide approach. A newly formed CPR Institute committee is developing a business-oriented process to address this need in the commercial context.

Third, when settlement counsel are deployed, it can be done in conjunction with and complementing an aggressive litigation track. For example, settlement counsel need not break off communications just because one side or the other decides to commence litigation. It is difficult for the litigator to say convincingly, "We filed suit this morning, but we still want to talk this afternoon." Settlement counsel can say, "The litigation team started suit this morning, but my job is still to continue to talk settlement this afternoon."

In situations where the potential for good-faith negotiation is low, a dualtrack approach has less risk, although clearly it also is more costly and potentially time consuming.

B. Lack of Sufficient Information

Throughout my career, I have heard litigation lawyers explain that they cannot evaluate a case's strengths and weaknesses, complete a reasonable budget, negotiate a resolution, or recommend mediation, until they have sufficient information about the facts and the law. It is certainly true that information is needed, but today this attitude has become a slippery slope into a rabbit hole of endless discovery.

In the majority of cases, probably more than 80% of the most relevant information is obvious in the first month of a case evaluation, and most of the trial documents already are identified and analyzed. In the business world, significant decisions are routinely made with much less information, and the "80/20 rule" is often invoked. How much more certainty is enough in the legal context? How much "hiding the ball" actually benefits the clients?

In comparison, CL agreements typically provide for "complete and honest" information exchange. In the context of family law disputes, the universe of relevant information may be reasonably defined. The opposite is true in commercial litigation. The mediator's toolbox provides some guidance because mediators sometimes request categories of information after the parties have outlined the issues. These requests are far from the typical discovery request. They are tailored to disclose information helpful to identifying interests and developing mutual gain.

Settlement counsel similarly can define a reasonable information exchange process shielded from disclosure in litigation. Document exchange shrinks significantly when information exchange is designed to identify business interests, rather than strengthen legal claims, and when it is focused on what is needed to evaluate settlement proposals. Therefore, it is possible to exchange documents and engage in the equivalent of the four-way meeting much earlier in the process.

C. Lack of Trust

Today, most commercial litigation is conducted in an atmosphere of mutual distrust, not an atmosphere of trust and good-faith negotiation, to say the least. In many business disputes such as class actions, claims between competitors, failed business ventures, patent infringement actions, etc., there is little likelihood that negotiations can proceed on the basis of mutual trust. In some cases involving longstanding relationships, however, trust can and should be built. How can trust be built in those cases where the potential exists, and how can those cases be identified? Or, alternatively, do we need trust to conduct good-faith negotiation, or just a different mindset?

Since the legal system and legal training is based on the adversarial model, it may be more important to change our mode of thinking than to require trust be present. Just as civil procedure rules were defined in the context of the adversarial system, CL practices are being defined in the context of interest-based negotiation. As these practices evolve and become more refined, it is possible to simply redefine the procedure, without the need to develop trust at the outset. Good-faith negotiation will follow that process.

V. Ideas and Proposals for Future Direction

Reflecting on the development of U.S. mediation practices, there appear to be a number of parallels with the current perspective on CL techniques and the use of settlement counsel in commercial disputes. Both began with understandable skepticism. Both require significant hands-on experience with the tools to shape them to fit the business context. Modifications and adaptations are necessary and should be encouraged.

CL in family law arose as a lawyer-led movement. If CL is to be adopted in commercial matters, it must be client or corporate counsel driven. The economic incentives in law firms simply do not encourage CL or settlement counsel practices. Just as with mediation, it will take demand by general counsel or the judiciary before widespread acceptance by law firms.

A broader dialogue supporting the use of CL techniques in business should include the following:

1. A range of options allowing flexibility in the process, such as borrowing from Leonard Riskin's "grid" concept to refine the range of CL options.
2. Exploring the importance of the disqualification provision in the commercial context, including ethical considerations.
3. More settlement counsel practitioners who are trained in interest-based negotiation and mediation advocacy skills.
4. The use of tiered dispute resolution clauses with an initial step that includes some CL elements, such as the equivalent of a four-way meeting with settlement counsel before the next step, which could be mediation, arbitration, or filing suit.
5. Using different techniques with settlement counsel such as:
   a. For a range of matters within a business. Often settlement counsel can see patterns among classes or types of cases that allow them to maximize settlement opportunities.
   b. Unilaterally. When opposing counsel refuses to engage parallel settlement counsel, even one side's settlement counsel can effectively negotiate directly with litigation counsel.
   c. With and without the disqualification provision. The "pure" form of CL is not always necessary.
   d. With alternative fee arrangements and other economic incentives. Many settlement counsel are adept at using creative fee arrangements with incentives since they are confident that the overall transaction cost will be lower with early and effective settlements.
   e. Designating and developing a modified settlement counsel position, where appropriate, on in-house legal staffs. In-house counsel frequently view themselves as settlement counsel and, when they can be objective about the matter, can be highly effective in that role.
6. More defined information exchange procedures applicable to business settings.
7. Client education on preventive legal counseling and interest-based negotiation.

8. Continuing to increase awareness about educational institutions' tendency to emphasize adversarial training.
9. Promoting graduate legal and business curriculums on problem solving and collaborative methods of dealing with conflict.

VI. Conclusion

There is natural resistance to radical new ideas. Given the rapid growth and stunning impact of CL in family law, it is time to experiment with CL concepts in the business setting. Corporate counsel should take the lead and experiment with using separate settlement counsel and with more pure forms of CL. If successful, CL will begin to take root.

Questions

20. Is there any reason why a law firm or a corporate law department could not have a trial division as well as a settlement or ADR specialist?
21. Is there any distinction between the British legal system and the American one that might undermine the usefulness of the solicitor/barrister role models for purposes of settlement? Is the fact that in England the roles of barrister and solicitor are becoming less rigidly defined likely to increase the use of mediation and other assisted negotiation, which was slower to take hold in England?
22. Is trial experience essential to serve as settlement counsel? What are the best qualifications to be an effective settlement counsel? It is said that, "He who is good with a hammer thinks everything is a nail." Is a lawyer who is skilled at trying cases more likely to think every dispute needs to be tried?

A Final Note and Question

Early in this text we advised that success in negotiation is in large part the result of planning, research and preparation. We now conclude with another key to success—learn from each completed negotiation. Take time to reflect on what happened and, with the benefit of hindsight, what you might have done better. Then make that hindsight a lesson learned for future negotiations. Like with any skill, reflective practice leads to improvement.

Finally, nurture your reputation as a negotiator. Just as your preparation for negotiation will include finding out all you can about your counterpart, so your reputation will precede you in every negotiation. Our last question is: what would you like that reputation to be?

APPENDIX

The appendix to this book is entirely Web based and is shared with Resolving Disputes: Theory, Practice, and Law, Third Edition. This makes it possible for students and teachers to have access to more resources and download and edit materials to meet their individual needs. To access the combined Appendix, enter the following URL:

www.aspenlawschool.com/books/Folberg_ResolvingDisputes_3e

The contents of the Appendix, which will be updated from time to time, include the following:

Negotiation

- Ethical Guidelines for Settlement Negotiations (ABA)
- Federal Rule of Civil Procedure 68
- Model Rules of Professional Conduct (ABA)

Mediation

- Legislation
  o ADR Act of 1998
  o Uniform Mediation Act (NCCUSL)
- Rules
  o Commercial Mediation Procedures (AAA)
  o CPR Mediation Procedure (CPR)
  o Model Standards for Mediators (AAA, ABA, and ACR, 2005)
  o Model Standards of Practice for Family and Divorce Mediators (ACR)
- Reports
  o Final Report of the Task Force on Improving Mediation Quality, Section of Alternative Dispute Resolution, American Bar Association (2008)
  o Report of the Task Force on Mediator Certification, Section of Alternative Dispute Resolution, American Bar Association (2012)
- Directives
  o European Union Directive on Mediation (2008)
- Sample Mediation Agreements

REFERENCES

The titles of books are in italics and the titles of articles are in quotes.

ABA Sub-Committee on Alternative Means of Dispute Resolution (1986). "The Effectiveness of the Mini-Trial," in *Resolving Complex Commercial Disputes: A Survey*. Chicago: American Bar Association.

Adair, Wendy L., & Jeanne M. Brett (2004). "Culture and Negotiation Processes," in M. Gelfand & J. Brett eds., *The Handbook of Negotiation and Culture*. Stanford, CA: Stanford University Press.

Adair, Wendy L., J.M. Brett, A. Lempereur, T. Okumura, P. Shikhirev, C. Tinsley, & A. Lytle (2004). "Culture and Negotiation Strategy," Negotiation Journal.

Adler, Robert S., & Elliot M. Silverstein (2000). "When David Meets Goliath: Dealing with Power Differentials in Negotiations," 5 Harv. Negotiation L. Rev. 1 (Spring).

Alfini, James J. (1999). "Settlement Ethics and Lawyering in ADR Proceedings: A Proposal to Revise Rule 4.1," 19 N. Ill. Univ. L. Rev. 255.

Amanatullah, E.T., & M.W. Morris (2010). "Negotiating Gender Roles: Gender Differences in Assertive Negotiating are Mediated by Women's dear of Backlash and Attenuated When Negotiating on Behalf of Others," 98 Journal of Personality and Social Psychology 256.

Arnold, Tom (1995). "Twenty Common Errors in Mediation Advocacy," 13 Alternatives 69.

Ayres, Ian (1991). "Fair Driving: Gender and Race Discrimination in Retail Car Negotiations," 104 Harv. L. Rev. 817.

Babcock, Linda, & J. Bear (2015). *Gender Relevant Primes and Negotiation*. New York: Bantam Books.

Babcock, Linda, & Sara Laschever (2003). *Women Don't Ask: Negotiation and the Gender Divide*. Princeton, N.J.: Princeton University Press.

Babcock, Linda, & Sara Laschever (2009). *Ask For It: How Women Can Use the Power of Negotiation to Get What They Really Want*. New York: Bantam Books.

Barry, Bruce, Ingrid S. Fulmer & Gerben A. Van Kleef (2004). *I Laughed, I Cried, I Settled: The Role of Emotion in Negotiation*. Stanford, CA: Stanford University Press.

Barry, Bruce & Raymond A. Friedman (1998). "Bargainer Characteristics in Distributive and Integrative Negotiation," 74 J. Personality & Soc. Psychol. 345.

Baumeister, Roy F., W. Scott Simpson, Stephen J. Ware, & Daniel S. Weber (2015). "The Glucose Model of Mediation: Physiological Bases of Willpower as Important Explanations for Mediation Behavior," 15 Pepp. Disp. Resol. L.J. 377.

Birke, Richard, & Craig R. Fox (1999). "Psychological Principles in Negotiating Civil Settlements," 4 Harv. Negotiation L. Rev. 1 (Spring).

Birke, Richard (2010). "Decision Trees—Made Easy," in J. Folberg & Dwight Golann eds., *Lawyer Negotiation 160*. New York: Aspen Publishers.

Birke, Richard (2010). "Neuroscience and Settlement: An Examination of Scientific Innovations and Practical Applications," 25 Ohio St. J. on Disp. Resol. 477.

Birke, Richard (2011). "Neuroscience and Negotiation: What the New Science of Mind May Offer the Practicing Attorney," 17 ABA Disp. Resol. Mag. 4.

Bone, Robert G. (2008). "To Encourage Settlement: Rule 68, Offers of Judgment, and the History of the Federal Rules of Civil Procedure," 102 Nw. U. L. Rev. 1551.

Bowles, H.R., L. Babcock & K.L. McGinn (2005). "Constraints and Triggers: Situational Mechanics of Gender Negotiation," 89 J. of Personality and Soc. Psychol. 951.

Brazil, Wayne (2014). *Don't Apply Risk Analysis to Discounted Settlement Value*. New York: Law360.

Brazil, Wayne D. (1984). "Setting Civil Cases: What Lawyers Want from Judges," 1984 Judges' J. 14 (Summer).

Bryan, Kathy A. (2008). "Why Should Businesses Hire Settlement Counsel?," 195 J. Disp. Resol. 195.

Carter, Jimmy (1982). *Keeping Faith: Memoirs of a President*. New York: Bantam Books.

Chew, Pat K., ed. (2001). *The Conflict & Culture Reader*. New York: New York University Press.

Cialdini, Robert B., (2008). *Influence: Science and Practice*. New York: Pearson Education.

Cialdini, Robert B., Steve J. Martin & Noah Goldstein (2014). *The Small BIG: Small Changes that Spark Big Influence*. New York: Hachette Book Group.

Cohen, Amy (2003). "An (Un) Useful Category of Prescriptive Negotiation Analysis," 13 Tex. J. Women & L. 169.

Cohen, Jonathan R. (1999). "Advising Clients to Apologize," 72 S. Cal. L. Rev. 1009.

Cohen, Jonathan (2001). "When People Are the Means: Negotiating with Respect," 14 Geo. J. Legal Ethics 739.

Condlin, Robert J. (1992). "Bargaining in the Dark: The Normative Incoherence of Lawyer Dispute Bargaining Role," 51 Md. L. Rev. 1.

Contuzzi, Peter (2000). "Should Parties Tell Mediators Their Bottom Line?," 8 Disp. Resol. Mag. 30 (Spring).

Conye, William F. (1999). "The Case for Settlement Counsel," 14 Ohio St. J. Disp. Resol. 367.

Corman, Marjorie A. & Wayne Brazil (2015). "Shaking Decision Trees for Risks and Rewards," 22 ABA Disp. Resol. Mag. 12 (Fall).

Craver, Charles B. (2001). Effective Legal Negotiation and Settlement (5th ed.). Newark: LEXIS.

Craver, Charles B. (2001). "Race and Negotiation Performance: Does Race Predict Success as a Negotiator?," 8 ABA Disp. Resol. Mag. 22.

Craver, Charles B. (2010). "The Inherent Tension Between Value Creation and Value Claiming During Bargaining Interactions," 12 Cardozo J. of Conflict Resol. 1.

Craver, Charles B. (2013). "The Impact of Gender on Negotiation Performance," 14 Cardozo J. of Conflict Resol. 339.

Danzinger, Shai, Jonathan Levav & Liora Avnaim-Pesso (2011). "Extraneous Factors in Judicial Decisions," in Daniel Kahneman ed., Proceedings of the National Acad. of Sciences, www.pnas.org/content/108/17/6889.

Dauer, Edward A. (2005). "Apology in the Aftermath of Injury: Colorado's 'I'm Sorry' Law," 34 COLAW 47.

Dawson, Roger (2001), Secrets of Power Negotiating (2d ed.). Franklin Lakes, NJ: Career Press.

Deutsch, Morton (1973). The Resolution of Conflict. New Haven, CT: Yale University Press.

Dore, Laurie Krath (1999). "Secrecy by Consent: The Use and Limits of Confidentiality in the Pursuit of Settlement," 74 N.D. L. Rev. 283.

Ebner, Noam (2015). "Negotiation via (the New) Email," in M. Benoliel ed., Negotiation Excellence: Successful Deal Making (2nd ed.). Singapore: World Scientific Publishing.

Ebner, Noam, & Jeff Thompson (2014). "Nonverbal Communication and Trust Development in Online Video-Based Mediation," 1 International J. of Online Disp. Resol.

Epstein, Lynn A. (1997). "Post-Settlement Malpractice: Undoing the Done Deal," 43 Cath. U. L. Rev. 459 (Winter).

Fisher, Roger (1991). "Negotiating Power: Getting and Using Influence," in William J. Breslin & Jeffrey Z. Rubin eds., Negotiation Theory and Practice. Cambridge, MA: Program on Negotiation Books.

Fisher, Roger, & William J. Ury, with Bruce Patton (1991). Getting to Yes (2d ed.). New York: Penguin.

Fiss, Owen, (1984). "Against Settlement," 93 Yale L.J. 1073.

Fletcher, Molly (2015). A Winner's Guide to Negotiating. New York: McGraw-Hill.

Folberg, Jay (2008). "Negotiation Lessons from the Pawnshop," 8 Disp. Resol. Alert (Spring).

Folberg, Jay (2016). "The Shrinking Joint Session: Survey Results," 22 ABA Disp. Resol. Mag. (Winter).

Folberg, Jay, Ann L. Milne, & Peter Salem (eds.) (2004). Divorce and Family Mediation – Models, Techniques and Applications. New York: Guilford Press.

Galanter, Marc, & Mia Cahill (1994). "Most Cases Settle: Judicial Promotion and Regulation of Settlements," 46 Stan. L. Rev. 1339.

Geraghty, Peter H. (2008). "Making Threats," YourABA, October 2008 Issue.

Gilligan, Carol (1982). In a Different Voice: Psychological Theory and Women's Development. Cambridge: Harvard University Press.

Gilson, Ronald J., & Robert H. Mnookin (1995). "Disputing Through Agents: Cooperation and Conflict Between Lawyers in Litigation," 94 Colum. L. Rev. 509.

Gladwell, Malcolm (2007). Blink. New York: Little, Brown and Company.

Golann, Dwight (1989). "Making Alternative Dispute Resolution Mandatory: The Constitutional Issues," 68 Or. L. Rev. 487.

Golann, Dwight (2002). "Is Legal Mediation a Process of Reconciliation—Or Separation? An Empirical Study, and Its Implications," 7 Harv. Negotiation L. Rev. 301.

Goleman, Daniel (1995). Emotional Intelligence: Why It Can Matter More Than IQ. New York: Bantam Books.

Goodpaster, Gary (1996). "A Primer on Competitive Bargaining," 1996 J. Disp. Resol. 325.

Gray, Barbara (2003). "Negotiating with Your Nemisis," 19 Negot. J. 299.

Gross, Samuel R., & Kent D. Syverud (1991). "Getting to No: A Study of Settlement Negotiations and the Selection of Cases for Trial," 90 Mich. L. Rev. 319.

Gupta, Shirish (16 Oct. 2015). "Mediations Need a Plan of Action," Daily Journal.

Hawkins, Lee (30 Jan. 2004). "GM's Finance Arm is Close to Settle Racial Bias Lawsuit," The Wall Street Journal.

Hawkins, Paula (2015). *The Girl on the Train*. New York: Penguin Group.

Heen, Sheila, & John Richardshon (2005). "'I see a Pattern Here and the Pattern Is You': Personality and Dispute Resolution," in M.L. Moffitt & R.C. Bordone eds., *The Handbook of Dispute Resolution*. San Francisco: Jossey-Bass.

Hetherington, H. Lee (2001). "The Wizard and Dorothy, Patton and Rommel: Negotiation Parables in Fiction and Fact," 28 Pepp. L. Rev. 289.

Hinshaw, Art, & Jess K. Alberts (2011). "Doing the Right Thing: An Empirical Study of Attorney Negotiation Ethics," 16 Harv. Negotiation L. Rev. 95.

Izumi, Carol (2010). "Implicit Bias and the Illusion of Mediator Neutrality," 34 J. of Law and Policy 71.

Johnston, Jason S., & Joel Waldfogel (2002). "Does Repeat Play Elicit Cooperation? Evidence from Federal Civil Litigation," 31 J. Legal Stud. 39.

Kabateck, Brian S., & Alfredo Torrijos (8 July 2010). "The Rise of Professional Objectors in Class Action Settlements," Daily Journal.

Kahneman, Daniel (2011). *Thinking Fast and Thinking Slow*. New York: Farrar, Straus and Giroux.

Kakalik, James, et al. (1996). *An Evaluation of Mediation and Early Neutral Evaluation Under the Civil Justice Reform Act*. Santa Monica, CA: RAND Corp.

Katsh, Ethan (2005). "Online Dispute Resolution," in Michael L. Moffitt & Robert C. Bordone eds., *The Handbook of Dispute Resolution*. San Francisco: Jossey-Bass.

Kichaven, Jeffrey G. (1999). "How Advocacy Fits in Effective Mediation," 17 Alternatives 60.

Kiser, Randall, et al. (2008). "Let's Not Make A Deal: An Empirical Study of Decision Making in Unsuccessful Settlement Negotiations," 5 J. of Empirical Stud. 451.

Kiser, Randall (2010). *Beyond Right and Wrong: The Power of Effective Decision Making for Attorneys and Clients*. Heidelberg: Springer.

Kiser, Randall (2011). *How Leading Lawyers Think: Expert Insights into Judgment and Advocacy*. Heidelberg: Springer.

Kiser, Randall (2015). "The Emotionally Attentive Lawyer: Balancing the Rule of Law with the Realities of Human Behavior," 15 Nev. L. J. 442.

Kolb, Deborah M., & Judith Williams (2000). *The Shadow Negotiation: How Women Can Master the Hidden Agendas that Determine Bargaining Success*. New York: Simon & Schuster.

Konrath, Sarah H., Edward H. O'Brien & Courtney Hsing (2011). "Changes in Dispositional Empathy in American College Students Over Time: A Meta Analysis," 15 Pers. and Soc. Psychol. Rev. 180.

Korobkin, Russell (2002). "Aspirations and Settlement," 88 Cornell L. Rev. 1.

Korobkin, Russell (2000). "A Positive Theory of Legal Negotiation," 88 Geo. L. J. 1789.

Korobkin, Russell, & Joseph Doherty (2009). "Who Wins in Settlement Negotiations?," 11 Amer. L. & Econ. Rev. 162.

Korobkin, Russell, Michael Moffett & Nancy Welch (2004). "The Law of Bargaining," 87 Marq. L. Rev. 839.

Kritzer, Herbert M., (1987). "Fee Arrangements and Negotiation," 21 L. & Soc. Rev. 341.

Kritzer, Herbert M. (2004). *Risks, Reputation and Rewards: Contingency Fee Legal Practice in the United States*. Stanford: Stanford University Press.

Kubler-Ross, Elizabeth (1969). *On Death and Dying*. New York: Scribner.

Lande, John (2002). "Using Dispute Systems Design Methods to Promote Good-Faith Participation in Court-Connected Mediation Programs," 50 UCLA Law Rev. 69 (October).

Lande, John (2009). "The Movement Toward Early Case Handling in Courts and Private Dispute Resolution," 24 Ohio St. J. on Disp. Resol. 53.

Lande, John, & Forrest S. Mosten (2010). "Collaborative Lawyer's Duties to Screen the Appropriateness of Collaborative Law and Obtain Client's Informed Consent to Use Collaborative Law," 25 Ohio St. J. on Disp. Resol. 347.

Latz, Martin E. (2004). *Gain the Edge*. New York: St. Martin's Press.

Lawrence, James K.L. (2003). "Collaborative Lawyering: A New Development in Conflict Resolution," 17 Ohio St. J. on Disp. Resol. 431.

Lax, David A., & James K. Sebenius (1986). *The Manager as Negotiator: Bargaining for Cooperation and Competitive Gain*. New York: Free Press.

Lax, David A., & James K. Sebenius (2002). "Dealcrafting: The Substance of Three Dimensional Negotiation," 18 Negotiation J. 5.

Lieberman, Jethro K., & James F. Henry (1986), "Lessons from the Alternative Dispute Resolution Movement," 53 U. Chi. L. Rev. 424.

Llamazares, Olegario (2008). *How to Negotiate Successfully in 50 Countries*. Madrid, Spain: Global Marketing Strategies.

Longan, Patrick (2001). "Ethics in Settlement Negotiations: Forward," 52 Mercer L. Rev. 810.

Luban, David (1995). "Settlements and the Erosion of the Public Realm," 83 Geo. L.J. 2619.

Magee, Rhonda V. (2014). "Making the Case for Mindfulness and the Law," 68 NW Lawyer 18 (Apr/May).

Mahoney, Jack (2002). "Editorial Adieu: Cultivating Moral Courage in Business," 7 Business Ethics: A European Review 187.

Malan, Douglas S. (2010). "A Numbers Game," 4 Connecticut Law Tribune 36.

Malhotra, Deepak, & Max H. Bazerman (2007). *Negotiation Genius.* New York: Bantam Books.

Max, Rodney A. (1999). "Multiparty Mediation," 23 Am. J. Trial Advoc. 269.

Mayer, Bernard (2015). *The Conflict Paradox.* San Francisco: Jossey-Bass.

Menkel-Meadow, Carrie (1984). "Toward Another View of Legal Negotiation: The Structure of Problem-Solving," 31 UCLA L. Rev. 754.

Menkel-Meadow, Carrie (1995). "Whose Dispute Is It Anyway? A Philisophical Defense of Settlement (In Some Cases)," 83 Geo L.J. 2663.

Miller, Lee E., & Jessica Miller (2002). *A Woman's Guide to Successful Negotiating: How to Convince, Collaborate, & Create Your Way to Agreement.* New York: McGraw-Hill.

Milton, John (1909). *Paradise Lost.* New York: P.F. Collier & Son.

Mnookin, Robert (2010). *Bargaining with the Devil.* New York: Simon & Schuster.

Mnookin, Robert H. (2003). "Strategic Barriers to Dispute Resolution: A Comparison of Bilateral and Multilateral Negotiations," 8 Harv. Negotiation L. Rev. 1 (Spring).

Mnookin, Robert H. (1993). "Why Negotiations Fail: An Exploration of Barriers to the Resolution of Conflict," 8 Ohio St. J. on Disp. Resol. 235.

Mnookin, Robert H., & Lewis Kornhauser (1979). "Bargaining the in Shadow of the Law: The Case for Divorce," 88 Yale L. J. 950.

Mnookin, Robert H., Scott R. Peppet & Andrew S. Tulumello (2000). *Beyond Winning: Negotiating to Create Value in Deals and Disputes.* Cambridge, MA: Harvard University Press.

Mnookin, Robert H., Scott R. Peppet & Andrew S. Tulumello (1996) "Negotiator's Empathy and Assertiveness," 12 Alternatives 133.

Moffit, Michael (2004). "Contingent Agreements; Agreeing to Disagree About the Future," 87 Marq. L. Rev. 691.

Moffit, Michael (2009). "Three Things to Be Against ("Settlement" Not Included)," 78 Fordham L. Rev. 1203.

Montagu, Ashley (1945). *Man's Most Dangerous Myth: The Fallacy of Race.* Walnut Creek, CA: AltaMira Press.

Nadler, Janice (2004). "Rapport in Legal Negotiation: How Small Talk Can Facilitate E-Mail Dealmaking," 9 Harv. Negot. L. Rev. 233.

Nelken, Melissa L. (2007). *Understanding Negotiation.* Cincinnati: Anderson.

Northcraft, Gregory B., & Margaret A. Neale (1987). "Experts, Amateurs, and Real Estate: An Anchoring-and-Adjustment Perspective on Property Pricing Decisions," in John M. Schaubroeck ed., 39 Organizational Behavior and Human Decision Processes 84.

O'Connor, Kathleen M., & Peter J. Carnevale (1997). "A Nasty but Effective Negotiation Strategy: Misrepresentation of a Common-Value Issue," 23 Pers. & Soc. Psychol. Bull. 504.

O'Hara, Erin Anne, & Douglas Yarn (2002). "On Apology and Consilience," 77 Wash. L. Rev. 1121.

Peppet, Scott R. (2002). "Mindfulness in the Law and ADR: Can Saints Negotiate?," 7 Harv. Negotiation L. Rev. 83 (Spring).

Peppet, Scott R. (2004). "Contract Formation in Imperfect Markets: Should We Use Mediators in Deals?," 38 Ohio St. J. on Disp. Resol. 283.

Peppet, Scott R. (2008). "The (New) Ethics of Collaborative Law," 14 ABA Disp. Resol. Mag. 23.

Peters, Don (1993). "Forever Jung: Psychological Type Theory, The Myers-Briggs Type Indicator and Learning Negotiations," 42 Drake L. Rev. 1.

Poswall, John M. (2003). *The Lawyers: Class of '69.* Sacramento, CA: Jullundur Press.

Prestia, Paul, & Harrie Samaras (2010). "Beyond Decision Trees: Determining Aggregate Probabilities of Time, Cost and Outcomes," 28 Alternatives 89.

Rackman, Neil, & John Carlisle (1978). "The Effective Negotiator—Part I: The Behaviour of Successful Negotiators," 2 Journal of European Industrial Training 6.

Raiffa, Howard (2002). *Negotiation Analysis: The Science and Art of Collaborative Decision Making.* Cambridge, MA: Harvard University Press.

Reilly, Peter (2009). "Was Machiavelli Right? Lying in Negotiation and the Art of Defensive Self-Help," 24 Ohio St. J. on Disp. Resol. 481.

Riskin, Leonard (1991). "The Represented Client in a Settlement Conference; The Lessons of G. Heileman Brewing Co. v. Joseph Oat Corp," 69 Wash. U. L.Q. 1059.

Riskin, Leonard (1994). "Mediator Orientations, Strategies and Techniques," 12 Alternatives 111 (Summer).

Riskin, Leonard (1996). "Understanding Mediator's Orientations, Strategies, and Techniques: A Grid for the Perplexed," 1 Harv. Negotiation L. Rev. 7 (Spring).

Riskin, Leonard (2003). "Decision-Making in Mediation: The New Old Grid and the New New Grid System," 79 Notre Dame L. Rev. 1 (December).

Riskin, Leonard (2003). "Retiring and Replacing the Grid of Mediator Orientations," 21 Alternatives 69.

Riskin, Leonard (2012). "Awareness and the Legal Profession: An Introduction to the Mindful Lawyer Symposium," 61 J. of Legal Educ. 634.

Robbennolt, Jennifer K. (2003). "Apologies and Legal Settlement: An Empirical Examination," 102 Mich. L. Rev. 460.

Robinson, Robert J. (1995). "Defusing the Exploding Offer: The Farpoint Gambit," 11 Negotiation J. 277.

Rosenberg, Joshua D. (2004). "Interpersonal Dynamics: Helping Lawyers Learn the Skills, and the Importance, of Human Relationships in the Practice of Law," 55 U. of Miami L. Rev. 1225.

Rosenberg, Joshua D., & Jay Folberg (1994). "Alternative Dispute Resolution: An Empirical Analysis," 46 Stan. L. Rev. 1487.

Ross, David (2000). "Strategic Considerations in Choosing a Mediator: A Mediator's Perspective," 2 J. Alt. Disp. Resol. in Employment. 7 (Spring).

Rubin, Jeffrey Z. (1993). "Conflict From a Psychological Perspective," in Laviria Hall ed., *Negotiation Strategies for Mutual Gain.* Newbury Parle, CA: Sage.

Rubin, Jeffrey Z. (1991). "Some Wise and Mistaken Assumptions About Conflict and Negotiation," in William J. Breslin & Jeffrey Z. Rubin eds., *Negotiation Theory and Practice.* Cambridge, MA: Program on Negotiation.

Rummel, R.J. (1991). *The Conflict Helix.* New Brunswick, NJ: Transaction.

Salacuse, Jeswald W. (1998). "Ten Ways That Culture Affects Negotiating Style: Some Survey Results," 14 Negot. J. 221.

Saperstein, Guy T. (2003). *Civil Warriors: Memoirs of a Civil Rights Attorney.* Berkeley, CA: Berkeley Hills Books.

Schelling, Thomas C. (1960). *The Strategy of Conflict.* Cambridge, MA: Harvard University Press.

Schneider, Andrea Kupfer (2000). "Perceptions, Reputation and Reality: An Empirical Study of Negotiation Styles," 6 ABA Disp. Resol. Mag. 24 (Summer).

Schneider, Andrea Kupfer (2002). "Shattering Negotiation Myths: Empirical Evidence on the Effectiveness of Negotiation Style," 7 Harv. Negotiation L. Rev. 143 (Spring).

Schneider, Andrea Kupfer, Catherine H. Tinsley, Sandra Cheldelin & Emily T. Amanatullah (2010). "Likeability v. Competence: The Impossible Choice Faced By Female Politicians, Attenuated by Lawyers," 17 Duke J. of Gender L. & Policy 363.

Schroeder, Juliana, Jane Risen, Francesca Gino & Michael I. Norton (2014). "Handshaking Promotes Cooperative Dealmaking," Harvard Business School Working Paper, No. 14-117.

Sebenius, James K. (2002). "Caveats for Cross-Border Negotiations," 18 Negot. J. 122.

Senger, Jeffrey M. (2004). *Federal Dispute Resolution: Using Alternative Dispute Resolution with the United States Government.* San Francisco, CA: Jossey-Bass.

Shea, John J. (2011). "Refuting a Myth About Human Origins," 99 Am. Scientist 99. Quote from Shea response to Letter to the Editor, 99 Am. Scientist 276.

Shell, G. Richard (2006). *Bargaining for Advantage: Negotiation Strategies for Reasonable People.* New York: Penguin.

Sherman, Edward F. (1988). "From 'Loser Pays' to Modified Offer of Judgment Rules: Reconciling Incentives to Settle with Access to Justice," 76 Tex. L. Rev. 1863.

Sherman, Edward F. (1993). "Court-Mandated Alternative Dispute Resolution: What Form of Participation Should Be Required?," 46 SMU L. Rev. 2079.

Sherman, Edward F., & Christopher M. Fairman (2011). "Interplay Between Mediation and Offer of Judgment Rule Sanctions," 26 Ohio St. J. on Disp. Resol. 327.

Shepherd, Andrew (2009). "Uniform Collaborative Law Act Approved by Uniform Law Commission," in Margaret Ryznare ed., *Family Law Prof. Blog.*

Shipley, David, & Will Schwalbe (2007). *Send: The Essential Guide to Email for Office and Home.* New York: Knopf Doubleday Publishing Group.

Spaniel, William (2014). *Game Theory 101: Bargaining.*

Steinberg, Leigh (1998). *Winning with Integrity.* New York: Three Rivers Press.

Stern, David M. (1998). "Mediation: An Old Dog with Some New Tricks," 24 Litig. 31.

Sternlight, Jean R. & Jennifer Robbennolt (2012). *Psychology for Lawyers.* Chicago: American Bar Association.

Stienstra, Donna, Molly Johnson & Patricia Lombard (1997). "Report to the Judicial Conference Committee on Court Administration and Case Management: A Study of the Five Demonstration Programs Established Under the Civil Justice Reform Act of 1990." Washington, DC: Federal Judicial Center.

Sumner, Anna Aven (2003). "Is the Gummy Rule of Today Truly Better Than the Toothy Rule of Tomorrow? How Federal Rule 68 Should be Modified," 52 Duke L. J. 1055.

Sullivan, Jay (2003). "Lawyers and Technology: A Crash Course in Writing Effective E-Mails," 229 N.Y. L.J. 5 (Feb.).

Taft, Lee (2000). "Apology Subverted: The Commodification of Apology," 109 Yale L.J. 1155.

Taleb, Nassim (2007). *The Black Swan.* New York: Random House.

Tesler, Pauline H. (2008). "Collaborative Family Law, the New Layer, and Deep Resolution of Divorce-Related Conflicts," 2008 J. Disp. Resol. 83.

Tierney, John (17 Aug. 2011). "Do You Suffer From Decision Fatigue?" NY Times.

Thomas, K.W., & L.R. Pondy (1977). "Towards an 'Intent' Model of Conflict Management Among Principle Parties," 30 Hum. Rel. 11089.

Ury, William (1991). *Getting Past No: Negotiating with Difficult People.* New York: Bantam Books.

Watson, Joel (2013). *Strategy: An Introduction to Game Theory (3rd ed.).* New York: W. W. Norton & Company.

Welsh, Nancy A. (2004). "Perceptions of Fairness in Negotiation," 87 Marq. L. Rev. 753.

Wetlaufer, Gerald B. (1996). "The Limits of Integrative Bargaining," 85 Geo. L. J. 369.

Wheeler, Michael (2013). *The Art of Negotiation: How to Improvise Agreement in a Chaotic World.* New York: Simon & Schuster.

White, James J. (1984). "Essay Review: The Pros and Cons of 'Getting to Yes;'" in Roger Fisher, "Comments on White's Review," 34 J. of Legal Educ. 115.

Williams, Gerald R. (1983). *Legal Negotiation and Settlement.* St. Paul: West Publishing.

Williams, Gerald R. (1996). "Negotiation as a Healing Process," 1996 J. of Disp. Resol. 33.

Williams, Gerald R., & Charles Craver (2007). *Legal Negotiation.* St. Paul: West Publishing.

Wissler, Roselle L. (2006). "The Role of Antecedent and Procedural Characteristics in Mediation: A Review of the Research," in Margaret S. Harrman ed., *The Blackwell Handbook of Mediation: Bridging Theory, Research, and Practice.* Malden, MA: Blackwell Publishing.

Wood, Robert W. (2007). "Taxing Matters in Settling Cases," 27 Cal. Law. 41.

Young, Michael D. (2007). "Mediation Gone Wild," 25 Alternatives 103.

Zitrin, Richard A. (1999). "The Case Against Secret Settlements" 2 J. Inst. for Study of Legal Ethics 115.

Zitrin, Richard, & Carol M. Langford (1999). *The Moral Compass of the American Lawyer.* New York: Ballantine Books.

WEB SITES

CPR Institute of Dispute Resolution, www.cpradr.org

Cyber Settle, www.cybersettle.com/

Expert Negotiators, www.ExpertNegotiator.com

Fair Outcomes, fairoutcomes.com

Gnarus Advisors LLC, Richard White, Correctly Using Risk Analysis to Calculate Discounted Settlement Value, www.gnarusllc.com/news-law-360

JAMS (The Resolution Experts), www.jamsadr.com

The Litigation Section of the ABA, Ethical guidelines for Settlement Negotiations, www.abanet.org/litigation/ethics/settlementnegotiations.com

Modria, modria.com

Negotiator Pro, www.negotiatorpro.com

Picture It Settled, Negotiation Art Informed By Science, pictureitsettled.com

Project Implicit, https://implicit.harvard.edu/implicit/demo/selectatest.html

TABLE OF CASES

Principal cases are indicated by italics.

INDEX